D1593630

THE LATE ARCHAIC ACROSS THE BORDERLANDS

Texas Archaeology and Ethnohistory Series

Thomas R. Hester, EDITOR

THE LATE ARCHAIC
across the Borderlands

From Foraging to Farming

Edited by Bradley J. Vierra

UNIVERSITY OF TEXAS PRESS ⤙⤚ AUSTIN

Printed in the United States of America
First edition, 2005

Requests for permission to reproduce material
from this work should be sent to:
    Permissions
    University of Texas Press
    P.O. Box 7819
    Austin, TX 78713-7819
    www.utexas.edu/utpress/about/bpermission.html

♾ The paper used in this book meets the minimum
requirements of ANSI/NISO Z39.48-1992 (R1997)
(Permanence of Paper).

Library of Congress Cataloging-in-Publication Data

The Late Archaic across the Borderlands : from foraging to
farming /
edited by Bradley J. Vierra. — 1st ed.
    p.   cm. — (Texas archaeology and ethnohistory series)
    Includes bibliographical references and index.
    ISBN 0-292-70669-3 (cl. : alk. paper)
    1. Indians of Mexico—Mexican-American Border Region—Antiquities.   2. Indians
of North America—Mexican-American Border Region—Antiquities.   3. Indians of
Mexico—Agriculture—Mexican-American Border Region.   4. Indians of North America—
Agriculture—Mexican-American Border Region.   5. Hunting and gathering societies—
Mexican-American Border Region.   6. Excavations (Archaeology)—Mexican-American Border
Region.   7. Mexican-American Border Region—Antiquities.   I. Vierra, Bradley J.   II. Series.
    F1219.1.M63L38   2005
    972'.101

                                                                        2005008323

To
Lewis R. Binford,
Lawrence G. Straus,
and
Cynthia Irwin-Williams

for teaching me about
hunter-gatherer archaeology

CONTENTS

FOREWORD

Richard I. Ford
UNIVERSITY OF MICHIGAN

THE BORDERLANDS HAS a significant place in the study of Archaic lifeways by archaeologists. First, the region was noted for its exceptional preservation of artifacts, plant remains, and painted panoramas found in rockshelters. Then the area was ignored for its seemingly long period of cultural stasis, when nothing appeared to happen. Today the region has reemerged because of its strategic position in the introduction of domesticated plant horticulture into the Southwest. Bradley J. Vierra's important "Borderlands Introduction" becomes our indispensable archaeological guide to the Borderlands and highlights the cultural significance of the region, its variation, and the cultural changes it experienced over time.

At the end of the Pleistocene most of North America witnessed millennia of biotic changes as plants migrated from southern refugia to colonize postglacial landscapes or to replace a slowly dying Pleistocene biota. North of the Red River in Texas the bulk of the edible biomass for the nomadic, post-Paleoindian hunters and foragers consisted of animal products. While increasing in density, most plants were widely scattered and seasonal in edible production. Consequently, human density was low. In the Borderlands, however, the useful energy mass was greater than in the remainder of the continent, human population density was the highest for North America, and cultural expression that was unknown elsewhere blossomed. Most of this is preserved as rock art and museum-quality perishable containers. But this short-lived "cultural florescence," based on deer, rabbits, other desert mammals, cacti fruits, and some nuts, was soon surpassed by the much higher edible biomass found to the north and east, where plant and animal diversity and productivity could support larger and denser populations of animals and humans.

In the Borderlands the human cultures continued the nomadic habits of their immediate ancestors. Through the ensuing centuries the archaeological record confirmed regional cultural variation but not the cultural excitement of the Early Archaic. By the Late Archaic technological, subsistence, and settlement patterns became routine; numerous excavated and surveyed sites presented a database for detailed studies. Vierra's "Late Archaic Stone Tool Technology across the Borderlands" is a first in its detailed discussion of the region's lithic technology and qualitative and quantitative variability. The subsistence resources of the Borderlands in the Late Archaic served as the basis for understanding human settlement and population dispersion. Marsha D. Ogilvie places this archaeological staple into a theoretical perspective in her important chapter, "A Biological Reconstruction of Mobility Patterns in Late Archaic Populations."

Studies in ecologically and geographically distinct areas of the vast Borderlands permit "big picture" comparisons. Robert J. Mallouf's "Late Archaic Foragers of Eastern Trans-Pecos Texas and the Big Bend" establishes a standard for explaining Archaic adaptations in these areas, where few archaeologists visit today. Phil Dering's "Ecological Factors Affecting the Late Archaic Economy of the Lower Pecos River Region" describes a region with neighbors experiencing agricultural harvests while they pursue a forager's marginal meal. South Texas fared equally well by supporting viable populations of dispersed gatherers. "An Overview of the Late Archaic in Southern Texas" by Thomas R. Hester is a critical summary. Like the other chapters, it provides the grist for comparative studies of gatherers and hunters that have not been undertaken for the continent as a whole. R. G. Matson begins this daunting task in his "Many Perspectives But a Consistent Pattern: Comments on Contributions."

Today the Borderlands region garners attention with an archaeological vitality that rivals its political importance. Here archaeologists have found our earliest food-producing societies in the Greater Southwest. Here a human-controlled production economy arose that changed forever the edible biomass of the Borderlands and that permitted the rapid development of socially complex communities unlike any previously experienced in the Borderlands. These themes are developed in one form or another by the remaining chapters in this timely volume.

"The Late Archaic/Early Agricultural Period in Sonora, Mexico" by John P. Carpenter, Guadalupe Sánchez, and María Elisa Villalpando C. sets an important stage for understanding what happens to nonagricultural foragers when cultivation becomes an addition to their subsistence pattern and prepares us for further cultural transformations. "The Transition to Farming on the Río Casas Grandes and in the Southern Jornada Mogollon Region" by Robert J. Hard and John R. Roney provides that perspective as agriculture was introduced into the American Southwest. These chapters are critical for understanding the numerous cultural changes that followed.

Within the United States southeastern Arizona experienced the first significant "agricultural revolution." The practice did not begin here, but it became the driver for numerous cultural practices—village life, permanent architectural features, pottery, status trade, and community rituals—associated with farming communities. Jonathan B. Mabry's "Changing Knowledge and Ideas about the First Farmers in Southeastern Arizona" details the numerous sites that confirm the evolution into a new way of living.

Farming is not inevitable, however, and its acceptance did not produce instant security or cultural advancement. William H. Doleman explains this in his regional overview: "Environmental Constraints on Forager Mobility and the Use of Cultigens in Southeastern Arizona and Southern New Mexico." Bruce D. Smith places the Borderlands' new economics into a global perspective as he presents his unique interpretation of the phenomenon in "Documenting the Transition to Food Production along the Borderlands."

The Borderlands remains underappreciated by American archaeologists, but this is changing with the latest excavated agricultural remains. The importance of the Borderlands to American prehistory will be further advanced by the publication of this book. The region took the cultural lead in the post-Pleistocene adaptation to a new productive environment. It is doing the same again with the spread of anthropogenic ecosystems by the first food producers in the Southwest. The prehistoric people of the Borderlands have always responded creatively to environmental and cultural changes and have left a rich legacy in the archaeological record.

PREFACE

Thomas R. Hester

THE LENGTHY BORDER between the United States and Mexico has been the focus of scholarly research into the evolving nature of frontiers for many years. Studies of the traits of its economies, politics, health care, patterns of human immigration, architecture, history, and archaeology are but a few of the numerous kinds of investigations that deal with "the Borderlands." A major overview of this vast region, *Borderlands Sourcebook: A Guide to the Literature on Northern Mexico and the American Southwest,* was assembled and edited by Ellwyn R. Stoddard and others in the early 1980s (University of Oklahoma Press, 1983).

Most of the border passes through arid to semiarid environments, and this dry, desolate countryside has attracted only the most dedicated fieldworkers from a variety of fields. From the standpoint of its ancient cultures, it has been assumed that not much of importance went on in prehistoric times in the Borderlands context, most especially along the Texas-Mexico frontier. Ethnologists have painted a stark picture of hunters and gatherers always on the edge of famine and with a limited material culture. The farming cultures of the Southwest were studied in isolation, with little consideration of their possible roots in northern Mexico. Archaeological work in the late twentieth and early twenty-first centuries, much of which is reported in this volume, has helped to change this view. Similarly, modern ethnohistorical research of the type done by Maria Wade demonstrates the changing nature of Borderlands societies in light of the relationships, during the sixteenth to eighteenth centuries, among native peoples in the area between the southwestern Edwards Plateau and the deserts of northeastern Mexico. A great amount of insight is provided into the dynamic interactions (involving hunting, trade, and use of the landscape) among Indian groups as well as the mechanisms utilized by some of these groups to manipulate the early Spanish explorers. The view presented by Wade in *The Native Americans of the Texas Edwards Plateau, 1582–1799* (University of Texas Press, 2003) is one that might well be projected back in time, especially in the review of prehistoric settlement patterns and tool assemblages.

With this background, it is clear that the present book, ably pulled together and edited by Bradley J. Vierra, is a significant step in furthering our understanding of Borderlands prehistory. In northern Mexico and the American Southwest, the Borderlands provide a fertile "laboratory" for studying the transition from hunting and gathering to the introduction of agriculture. The Arizona-Sonora area is the subject of chapters by Carpenter, Sánchez, and Villalpando C. and by Mabry. Discoveries of early agriculture in Chihuahua are discussed by Hard and Roney, Doleman, and Ogilvie (the last based on biological research). The persistence of hunting and gathering is notable along the Texas-Mexico border; the chapters by Mallouf, Dering, Vierra, and myself showcase the variability in these groups, although our knowledge still has many shortcomings.

Vierra's book also emphasizes that a lot of additional research will be needed in the Borderlands to define the full range of ancient cultural variation. For example, a unique area not covered in the present book needs to be briefly noted. The lower Rio Grande and its delta constitute a subtropical zone not seen elsewhere along the border. Hunters and gatherers lived on both sides of the Rio Grande, and frontier Mesoamerican cultures were present farther down the Mexican Gulf coast. While we have long known of the special trade relations between the Mexican agriculturalists and the delta hunters and gatherers (involving the trade in ceramics, jade, and obsidian into the delta), we have only recently learned that this process began much earlier than previously thought. For years my own research, and that of other colleagues interested in the delta, has indicated that this pattern of interaction was restricted to Late Prehistoric times (the "Brownsville Complex"), featuring the Late Postclassic Huastecan culture as the source of these exotic artifacts. Recent reanalysis of some of the cemetery sites (where jadeite and nonceramic trade goods have been found), however, places the emergence of the interaction back into the Late Archaic, around 1500 BC. Now we have to wonder if the Olmec and related Preclassic cultures of the Mexican Gulf Coast were the first to establish trade relations with the peoples of the Rio Grande Delta. The reanalysis of the antiquity of trade in the delta is a measure of how fast our views of the Borderlands are changing—changes that will be enhanced by the research avenues outlined in this book.

ACKNOWLEDGMENTS

THE BORDERLANDS IS an expansive and environmentally diverse region. It covers an area from the Gulf of California to the Gulf of Mexico and crosscuts international and state boundaries on both sides of the Mexico/U.S. border. This situation usually makes it difficult for archaeologists to get together and discuss the broad issues affecting their common research interests. Luckily, I had the opportunity to break through this boundary, from the American Southwest into South Texas and then into Chihuahua, Mexico. This opportunity was afforded me by Bob Hard and Britt Bousman at the Center for Archaeological Research, University of Texas at San Antonio. It was my work at a stratified Late Archaic site in South Texas and the invitation to join the Proyecto Arqueológico Cerros con Trincheras del Arcáico Tardío that complemented my research on the Archaic in northwestern New Mexico. Bob supported the idea of a symposium that eventually led to the publication of this book.

As R. G. Matson told me, editing a book is like herding cats. In the case of a book on the Archaic, maybe it is more like a rabbit drive. Nonetheless, it was a long and arduous journey to the completion of this volume. I want to thank all the authors for contributing to such an excellent report on their current research. It reflects the quality of scholarship among the archaeological community conducting research on the Late Archaic. I hope it spurs interest among graduate students to focus their attention on this region of the world. Royalties for this book are being donated to the Society for American Archaeology's Native American Scholarship fund in order to help these students receive their college degrees.

An edited volume cannot be completed without the hard work and help of a team of professionals. I specifically want to thank Kari Schmidt, who did the final read and edit on the volume. Kari was meticulous in checking the final draft. I cannot begin to thank her for all the hard work. Of course the staff at the University of Texas Press took the manuscript to its final completion, and I want to thank all of them for their hard work and support of this project: Theresa May, Allison Faust, Leslie Tingle, and Nancy Lavender Bryan.

This book is dedicated to my mentors: Lewis Binford, Lawrence Straus, and Cynthia Irwin-Williams. It was they who taught me about hunter-gatherer archaeology and gave me the field experience I needed to explore the diverse archaeological record of these ancient foragers. Thank you all.

Finally, the time I spend on my professional activities is time spent away from my family. None of this would have been possible without the love and support of Amy, Andrew, and Phillip.

CHAPTER I

Borderlands Introduction

BRADLEY J. VIERRA

The real wealth of a planet is in its landscape, how we take part
in that basic source of civilization—agriculture.

—*Frank Herbert, Dune*

The transition from foraging to agricultural-based economies was one of
the most significant processes to occur in human history (Harris 1996;
Matson 1991; Smith 1998). Yet it did not occur in all parts of the world. This
was the case across the Borderlands between the United States and Mexico, an
area stretching from the Gulf of California to the Gulf of Mexico. Although
the development of Southwestern culture was based on a foundation of maize
agriculture, nomadic foragers ranged the adjacent Tamaulipas regions of
South Texas and northeastern Mexico. Recent discoveries of Late Archaic villages in southern Arizona and terrace hilltop communities in the deserts of
Chihuahua, Mexico, have radically changed our view of this period. This volume explores these varied archaeological records and current research of the
Borderlands Late Archaic. Understanding why foragers in South Texas failed
to incorporate cultigens into their subsistence base may aid Southwestern
researchers in understanding why agriculture became an important part of this
desert economy.

The Borderlands cover a linear distance of approximately 1,600 km
(1,000 miles) (Figure 1.1). On the west lie the arid creosote-covered lands of
the Sonoran and Chihuahua Deserts, and on the east the brush country of the
Tamaulipas. Separating these two areas is the Trans-Pecos transitional zone,
with the Plateau and Plains to the north and subtropical regions to the south.
The region is characterized by a general increase in effective moisture from
west to east and decreases in seasonal temperatures with increasing seasonality
from south to north. The rainfall regime changes dramatically, with summer
monsoons in the west versus a bimodal pattern with a midsummer low in the
east. The landscape also varies, with the broad river valleys of the Basin and
Range in the west and a gently rolling topography dissected by stream channels
in the east (Blair 1950; Brown 1994; Norwine 1995). The Borderlands therefore
provide a setting within which the Late Archaic (ca. 3000 to 1500 BP) is characterized by a diverse set of agricultural and foraging strategies.

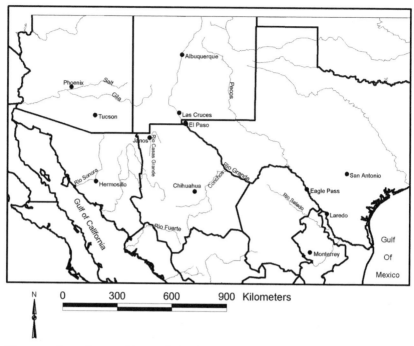

Figure 1.1. General map of the Borderlands region

The concept of the Archaic is generally characterized as a post-Pleistocene mixed hunting and gathering economy, with the possible addition of cultigens during the Late Archaic. It is primarily differentiated from the earlier Paleo-indian period by the presence of distinctly shouldered and notched dart points, more generalized retouched tools, one-hand manos, slab milling stones, and fire-cracked rock features. It is separated from later periods by the initial use of the bow and arrow and ceramics. It is these technological innovations that characterize the Southwestern Ceramic period and the Late Prehistoric in South Texas (Hester 1995; Huckell 1996a; Matson 1991; Vierra 1994c). Figure 1.2 illustrates the various sequences proposed for the Borderlands Archaic, as derived from Bruce Huckell (1996a); Robert Mallouf (1985, 1992, this volume); Solveig Turpin (1995); and Thomas R. Hester (1995, this volume). They all generally begin by about 8500 BP during the Early Holocene, although the Late Archaic appears to terminate later in the eastern Borderlands due to the absence of agriculture (ca. 1100 BP).

Early maize dates in the Borderlands and Greater Southwest cluster about 3000 BP, with several earlier dates mostly from Arizona (Gilpin 1994; Hard and

Roney 1998, this volume; Huckell 1990; Huckell et al. 1999; Mabry 1999, this volume; Simmons 1982; Smiley 1994; Tagg 1996, 1999; Upham et al. 1987; Wills 1985). The earliest date for maize is 3690 BP from McEuen Cave in southeastern Arizona (Huckell et al. 1999; Shackley et al. 2001). Mabry (2002) notes in a recent study that there are twenty Southwestern maize dates older than 3000 BP, indicating the possible arrival of maize by ca. 3700 BP. The current evidence reflects that when maize entered the Southwest its use spread quite rapidly. It is debated, however, as to whether its spread was due to the northern movement of farmers (Berry 1982, 1999; Berry and Berry 1986), the integration of these cultigens into local hunting and gathering economies (Hogan 1994; Irwin-Williams 1973; Minnis 1992; Vierra 1994a, 1994b, 1996; Wills 1985, 1995), or a mixture of the two (Matson 1999, 2001, this volume). So the question is not so much when maize arrived, but rather how long it took for these farmers to move north or for these foragers to become dependent on agriculture. Importantly, the eastern boundary for agriculture appears to lie between the Chihuahuan Desert

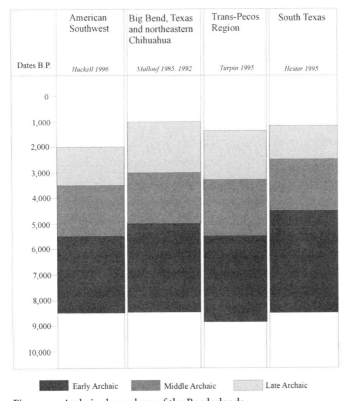

Figure 1.2. Archaic chronology of the Borderlands

and Tamaulipas in the Trans-Pecos region, with no evidence for agriculture in South Texas. Directly dated maize specimens from in situ deposits are lacking for the eastern Borderland areas (Dering, this volume; Mallouf, this volume). The original source for maize agriculture is located to the south in Mexico, where recent studies indicate that maize represents a genetically altered form of a wild grass known as teosinte (Jaenicke-Després et al. 2003). Early maize specimens have been dated to 5420 BP at Guilá Naquitz, Oaxaca (Piperno and Flannery 2001), so it took about 1,500 years before this cultigen finally reached the Borderlands.

Current research has radically changed our perceptions of the Late Archaic across the Borderlands. This includes a diversity of scientific approaches ranging from culture-historical to evolutionary theory. The chapters in this book include both regional syntheses and specific problem orientations. With agriculturalists to the west and foragers to the east, the Borderlands provide a rare laboratory in which to study the question of why people did or did not shift to an agricultural-based economy. Scholars around the world are currently grappling with this problem, and this book provides them with a variety of perspectives and a new series of databases to use in addressing this significant research issue.

Research in the Sonoran Desert and Chihuahuan Desert regions of Sonora and Chihuahua, Mexico, and southern Arizona is illustrated in the chapters by Carpenter, Sánchez, and Villalpando C.; Mabry; and Hard and Roney. Carpenter et al.'s work at the extensive multicomponent site of La Playa, Sonora, has provided new perspectives on the Late Archaic of this region. Here they have identified an archaeological site of over 12 sq km. Much of this includes evidence of the Early Agricultural period, consisting of dense artifact scatters, thousands of roasting pits (some containing maize), possible agricultural features and canals, and cemeteries with several hundred human burials. Large villages have also been discovered in the Tucson Basin of southern Arizona. Mabry summarizes this recent research, including the large-scale excavation of domestic structures, storage pits, roasting pits, middens, cemeteries, large communal-ceremonial structures, and irrigation canals. As he points out, new evidence indicates that maize, squash, and beans may have been used as a suite of early cultigens. Finally, Hard and Roney present their findings of the Late Archaic *trinchera* site of Cerro Juanaqueña, Chihuahua. This site contains approximately five hundred terraces, a hundred rock rings, and midden deposits; however, like La Playa, the site includes only limited evidence for domestic structures. Nonetheless, the surface of the site is littered with chipped stone items and heavily worn basin metates. Not only is domesticated maize present, but domesticated amaranth has also been identified at the site. More importantly, Cerro Juanaqueña is not an isolated occurrence but one of several

Late Archaic *trinchera* hilltop sites situated along the valley of the Río Casas Grandes. This new evidence changes our view of the people of the Late Archaic, from simple desert foragers to early farming communities.

Such large-scale systematic excavations are lacking from southern New Mexico and the Big Bend region of Texas. Current research indicates that although maize was present in southern New Mexico by ca. 3000 BP (Upham et al. 1987), the shift to an economy dependent on agriculture probably did not occur until quite late: that is, ca. AD 1200 during the El Paso phase (Hard et al. 1996). Doleman (this volume) explores the question of why a dependence on maize agriculture appears to have occurred much earlier in the Sonoran Desert of southern Arizona than in the Chihuahuan Desert of southern New Mexico. As he points out, the Sonoran Desert region provides a variety of resources within a more limited area, including broad perennial stream valleys conducive to floodplain agriculture. This environment would have reduced or eliminated seasonal resource scheduling conflicts experienced in other regions of the Southwest (also see Dering, this volume; Hard and Roney, this volume; Huckell 1996b; Stone and Bostwick 1995; Wills and Huckell 1994).

The eastern periphery of the Chihuahua Desert lies in the area of West Texas and northeastern Chihuahua, Mexico. Mallouf reviews the current archaeological evidence from this poorly understood region. This research has documented a marked increase in the presence of Late Archaic vs. Middle Archaic remains in the Big Bend area, something also suggested by Mabry (this volume) for southern Arizona (also see Waters 1986). This could represent the expansion of Archaic populations into the region during a period of more mesic conditions. Late Archaic campsites are distributed across a wide range of environmental settings. Mallouf (this volume) suggests that the limited evidence for maize indicates that it only represents a dietary supplement and that it was probably added to the subsistence base at the end of the Late Archaic during a period of more xeric conditions. The Trans-Pecos region therefore represents the eastern limits of maize agriculture.

Unlike West Texas, extensive excavations have been conducted in the stratified rockshelters of the Lower Pecos River region (Turpin 1991, 1995). This area of the Borderlands is situated along the transition from Chihuahuan Desert to the Tamaulipas brushland. The Late Archaic diet contained a wide variety of plant and animal resources, including lechuguilla and sotol. Dering's study (this volume) indicates that the return rates for these items are similar to those of other low-ranked species like grass seeds and roots. The resource homogeneity, the lack of broad floodplains, and a spring/fall rainfall regime may have contributed to the absence of agriculture in this region (see the discussions of Doleman as well as Hard and Roney in this volume). Bison hunting, rather than agriculture, occurred during a period of more mesic conditions ca. 2500 BP (also see Dillehay 1974; Mallouf, this volume; Turpin 1995:548).

The archaeological record of South Texas also contains no evidence for agriculture. As described by Hester (this volume), the Late Archaic archaeological record is poorly documented in the region but generally reflects short-term campsites that were commonly situated along stream channels. The people exploited a variety of plant and animal resources, including both riverine species and land snails. Nonetheless, cemeteries and middens are present and presumably reflect the repeated reuse of specific resource patches and not sedentism (e.g., Taylor and Highley 1995).

Ogilvie's chapter and my chapter represent specialized research projects along the Borderlands that involve understanding the effects of agriculture on human biology and stone tool technology, respectively. Ogilvie's human biology study of forager, early agricultural, and Pueblo groups is very informative. Specifically, her analysis of the Late Archaic Tucson Basin population indicates that the males resemble foragers but the females resemble agriculturists. This implies that important changes in sexual division of labor were beginning at this time. Ogilvie's study also has implications for my research. My preliminary results from the analysis of chipped stone items from Cerro Juanaqueña indicate a mixed core reduction/biface production assemblage similar to those of other Late Archaic habitation sites. This contrasts with an emphasis on biface production at Late Archaic campsites and core reduction at Ceramic period sites. Barbara Roth (1992, 1998) discusses similar patterns for the Tucson Basin region. The chipped vs. ground stone assemblages at Cerro Juanaqueña appear to indicate conflicting evidence for residential stability and economy at the site (also see Roney and Hard 2002). This could reflect important changes in division of labor related to an increasing dependence on maize agriculture and early village formation.

Finally, Matson and Smith provide reviews of the research presented in this volume. Matson discusses each of the chapters from a Southwestern perspective, whereas Smith offers a global perspective on the Borderlands. As he so aptly points out, many of these chapters describe the Late Archaic as representing that "middle ground" between foragers and agriculturalists, being characterized by "a rich variety of low-level food-producing societies."

In conclusion, if we are going to understand the origins of agriculture and village formation along the western Borderlands, it would help to know why the foragers in the eastern Borderlands failed to incorporate cultigens into their diet. The archaeology of South Texas indicates that cemeteries and middens can occur in a nonagricultural setting. This should be a cautionary note to those in the western Borderlands who suggest that these features are solely characteristic of sedentary agricultural communities. Nonetheless, the chapters in this volume identify several factors that could be contributing to this process, including differences in resource structure (e.g., distance between resource patches), landscape (e.g., broad alluvial valleys), rainfall regime (e.g., summer monsoons), population expansion (e.g., hunter-gatherers or farmers), and seasonality (e.g., the need for storage to solve the over-wintering problem). Finally, the diet-breadth model as derived from optimal foraging theory is discussed by Hard and Roney and by Dering. Various species can be ranked based on a cost-benefit analysis of foraging return rates (Kelly 1995:78–90; MacArthur and Pianka 1966; Stephens and Krebs 1986:17–24). Large game is generally considered to have the greatest return; succulents and grasses, the lowest. Floodplain farming is also seen as a low-investment and high-return strategy (Barlow 1997, 2002; Dering 1999; Simms 1987). It is noteworthy that during more mesic conditions along the Borderlands (ca. 2500 to 3000 BP) floodplain farming was initially used in the west, and a switch to bison hunting occurred in the east. These changing environmental conditions modified the cost-benefit relationship of these resources, thereby allowing for increasing return rates for these regionally divergent Late Archaic subsistence tactics.

REFERENCES CITED

Barlow, K. R.
1997   Foragers That Farm: A Behavioral Ecology Approach to the Economics of Corn Farming for the Fremont Case. Ph.D. dissertation, Department of Anthropology, University of Utah, Salt Lake City.
2002   Predicting Maize Agriculture among the Fremont: An Economic Comparison of Farming and Foraging in the American Southwest. American Antiquity 67:65–88.
Berry, C. F., and M. S. Berry
1986   Chronological and Conceptual Models of the Southwestern Archaic. In Anthropology of the Desert West: Essays in Honor of Jesse D. Jennings, edited by C. J. Condie and D. D. Fowler, pp. 253–327. Anthropological Papers No. 110. University of Utah Press, Salt Lake City.
Berry, M. S.
1982   Time, Space and Transition in Anasazi Prehistory. University of Utah Press, Salt Lake City.
1999   Chronometry and Process: Southwestern Agricultural Beginnings. Paper presented at the 65th Annual Society for American Archaeology Meetings, Chicago.

Blair, W. F.

1950   The Biotic Provinces of Texas. *Texas Journal of Science* 2:93–117.

Brown, D. E.

1994   *Biotic Communities: Southwestern United States and Northwestern Mexico.* University of Utah Press, Salt Lake City.

Dering, P.

1999   Earth-Oven Plant Processing in Archaic Period Economies: An Example from a Semi-Arid Savannah in South-Central North America. *American Antiquity* 64:659–674.

Dillehay, T. D.

1974   Late Quaternary Bison Population Changes on the Southern Plains. *Plains Anthropologist* 19:180–196.

Gilpin, D.

1994   Lukachukai and Salina Springs: Late Archaic/Early Habitation Sites in the Chinle Valley, Northeastern Arizona. *Kiva* 60(2): 203–218.

Hard, R. J., R. P. Mauldin, and G. R. Raymond

1996   Mano Size, Stable Carbon Isotope Ratios, and Macrobotanical Remains as Multiple Lines of Evidence of Maize Dependence in the American Southwest. *Journal of Archaeological Method and Theory* 3:253–318.

Hard, R. J., and J. R. Roney

1998   A Massive Terraced Village Complex in Chihuahua, Mexico, Dated to 3000 Years Before Present. *Science* 279:1661–1664.

Harris, D. R. (editor)

1996   *The Origins and Spread of Agriculture and Pastoralism in Eurasia.* Smithsonian Institution Press, Washington, D.C.

Hester, T. R.

1995   The Prehistory of South Texas. *Bulletin of the Texas Archeological Society* 66:427–459.

Hogan, P.

1994   Forager to Farmer II: A Second Look at the Adoption of Agriculture in the Northern Southwest. In *Archaic Hunter-Gatherer Archaeology in the American Southwest,* edited by B. Vierra, pp. 155–184. Contributions in Anthropology Series, Vol. 13, No. 1. Eastern New Mexico University, Portales.

Huckell, B. B.

1990   Late Preceramic Farmer-Foragers in Southeastern Arizona: A Cultural and Ecological Consideration of the Spread of Agriculture into the Arid Southwestern United States. Ph.D. dissertation,

Department of Arid Lands, University of Arizona. University Microfilms, Ann Arbor.

1996a   The Archaic Prehistory of the North American Southwest. *Journal of World Prehistory* 10(3): 305–373.

1996b   Middle to Late Holocene Stream Behavior and the Transition to Agriculture in Southeastern Arizona. In *Early Formative Adaptations in the Southern Southwest*, edited by B. J. Roth, pp. 27–36. Monographs in World Archaeology No. 25. Prehistory Press, Madison, Wis.

Huckell, B. B., L. W. Huckell, and M. S. Shackley

1999   McEuen Cave. *Archaeology Southwest* 13(1): 12.

Irwin-Williams, C.

1973   *The Oshara Tradition: Origins of Anasazi Culture.* Eastern New Mexico University Contributions in Anthropology 5(1). Paleo-Indian Institute, Eastern New Mexico University, Portales.

Jaenicke-Després, Viviane, E. S. Buckler, B. D. Smith, M. T. Gilbert, A. Cooper, J. Doebley, and Svante Pääbo

2003   Early Allelic Selection in Maize as Revealed by Ancient DNA. *Science* 302:1206–1208.

Kelly, R. L.

1995   *The Foraging Spectrum: Diversity in Hunter-Gatherer Lifeways.* Smithsonian Institution Press, Washington, D.C.

Mabry, J. B.

1999   Las Capas and Early Irrigation Farming. *Archaeology Southwest* 13(1): 14.

2002   Diversity in Early Southwestern Farming Systems and Optimization Models of Transitions to Agriculture. In *Early Agricultural Period Environment and Subsistence*, edited by M. Diehl. Anthropological Papers No. 34. Center for Desert Archaeology, Inc., Tucson. In press.

MacArthur, R. H., and E. R. Pianka

1966   On Optimal Use of a Patchy Environment. *American Naturalist* 100(916): 603–609.

Mallouf, R. J.

1985   A Synthesis of Eastern Trans-Pecos Prehistory. Master's thesis, Department of Anthropology, University of Texas, Austin.

1992   A Commentary of the Prehistory of Far Northeastern Chihuahua, the La Junta District, and the Cielo Complex. In *Historia general de Chihuahua I: Geología, geografía, y arqueología*, edited by A. Márquez-Alameda, pp. 137–162. Universidad Autónoma de Ciudad Juárez y Gobierno del Estado de Chihuahua.

Matson, R. G.

1991   *The Origins of Southwestern Agriculture.* University of Arizona Press, Tucson.

1999   The Spread of Maize to the Colorado Plateau. *Archaeology Southwest* 13(1): 10–11.

2001   The Spread of Maize into the Southwest USA. Paper presented at the Examining the Farming/Language Dispersal Hypothesis Symposium, McDonald Institute for Archaeological Research, University of Cambridge.

Minnis, P. E.

1992   Earliest Plant Cultivation in the Desert Borderlands of North America. In *The Origins of Agriculture: An International Perspective,* edited by C. W. Cowan and P. J. Watson, pp. 121–141. Smithsonian Institution Press, Washington, D.C.

Norwine, J.

1995   The Regional Climate of South Texas: Patterns and Trends. In *The Impact of Global Warming on Texas,* edited by J. Norwine, J. R. Giardino, G. R. North, and J. Valdes, pp. 138–155. Geo Books, Texas A&M University, College Station.

Piperno, D. R., and K. V. Flannery

2001   The Earliest Archaeological Maize (*Zea mays* L.) from Highland Mexico: New Accelerator Mass Spectrometry Dates and Their Implications. *Proceedings of the National Academy of Sciences* 98:2101–2103.

Roney, J. R., and R. J. Hard

2002   Early Agriculture in Northwestern Chihuahua. In *Traditions, Transitions and Technologies,* edited by S. Schlanger, pp. 160–177. University of Colorado Press, Boulder.

Roth, B. J.

1992   Sedentary Agriculturalists or Mobile Hunter-Gatherers?: Recent Evidence of the Late Archaic Occupation of the Northern Tucson Basin. *Kiva* 57(4): 291–314.

1998   Mobility, Technology, and Archaic Lithic Procurement Strategies in the Tucson Basin. *Kiva* 63(3):241–262.

Shackley, M. S., L. W. Huckell, and B. B. Huckell

2001   The 2001 Excavations at McEuen Cave (AZ W:13:6 ASM), Southeastern Arizona. Paper presented at the Pecos Conference, Flagstaff, Arizona.

Simmons, A. H.

1982   Chronology. In *Prehistoric Adaptive Strategies in the Chaco Can-*

yon Region, Northwestern New Mexico, edited by A. H. Simmons, pp. 807–824. Papers in Anthropology, No. 9. Navajo Nation, Window Rock, N.Mex.

Simms, S. R.

1987   *Behavioral Ecology and Hunter-Gatherer Foraging: An Example from the Great Basin.* BAR International Series 381. British Archaeological Reports, Oxford, England.

Smiley, F.

1994   The Agricultural Transition in the Northern Southwest: Patterns in the Current Chronometric Data. *Kiva* 60:165–189.

Smith, B. D.

1998   *The Emergence of Agriculture.* Paperback ed. W. H. Freeman, New York.

Stephens, D. W., and J. R. Krebs

1986   *Foraging Theory.* Princeton University Press, Princeton.

Stone, C., and T. Bostwick

1995   Environmental Contexts and Archaeological Correlates: The Transition to Farming in Three Regions of the Arizona Desert. In *Early Formative Adaptations in the Southern Southwest,* edited by B. J. Roth, pp. 17–26. Monographs in World Archaeology 25. Prehistory Press, Madison, Wis.

Tagg, M. D.

1996   Early Cultigens from Fresnal Shelter, Southeastern New Mexico. *American Antiquity* 61(2):311–324.

1999   Fresnal Shelter. *Archaeology Southwest* 13(1):7.

Taylor, A. J., and C. L. Highley

1995   *Archeological Investigations at the Loma Sandia Site (41LK28): A Prehistoric Cemetery and Campsite in Live Oak County, Texas.* Studies in Archeology 20. Texas Archeological Research Laboratory, University of Texas, Austin.

Turpin, S. A.

1991   *Papers on Lower Pecos Prehistory.* Texas Archeological Research Laboratory Studies in Archeology 8. University of Texas, Austin.

1995   The Lower Pecos River Region of Texas and Northern Mexico. *Bulletin of the Texas Archeological Society* 66:541–560.

Upham, S., R. S. MacNeish, W. C. Galinat, and C. M. Stevenson

1987   Evidence concerning the Origin of Maíz de Ocho. *American Anthropologist* 89:410–419.

Vierra, B. J.

1994a   Aceramic and Archaic Research. In *Across the Colorado Plateau:*

Anthropological Studies for the Transwestern Pipeline Expansion Project, Volume XIV, edited by T. W. Burchett, B. J. Vierra, and K. L. Brown, pp. 375–384. Office of Contract Archaeology and Maxwell Museum of Anthropology, University of New Mexico, Albuquerque.

1994b   Archaic Hunter-Gatherer Mobility Strategies in Northwestern New Mexico. In *Archaic Hunter-Gatherer Archaeology in the American Southwest,* edited by B. J. Vierra, pp. 121–154. Eastern New Mexico University Contributions in Anthropology 13(1). Eastern New Mexico University, Portales.

1994c   Introduction. In *Archaic Hunter-Gatherer Archaeology in the American Southwest,* edited by B. J. Vierra, pp. 5–61. Eastern New Mexico University Contributions in Anthropology 13(1). Eastern New Mexico University, Portales.

1996   Late Archaic Settlement, Subsistence and Technology: An Evaluation of Continuity vs. Replacement Arguments for the Origins of Agriculture in the Northern Southwest. Paper presented at the Conference on the Archaic Prehistory of the North American Southwest, Albuquerque.

Waters, M. R.

1986   *The Geoarchaeology of Whitewater Draw, Arizona.* Anthropological Papers of the University of Arizona No. 45. University of Arizona Press, Tucson.

Wills, W. H.

1985   Early Agriculture in the Mogollon Highlands of New Mexico. Ph.D. dissertation, Department of Anthropology, University of Michigan. University Microfilms, Ann Arbor.

1988   *Early Prehistoric Agriculture in the American Southwest.* School of American Research Press, Santa Fe.

Wills, W. H., and B. B. Huckell

1994   Economic Implications of Changing Land-Use Patterns in the Late Archaic. In *Themes in Southwest Prehistory,* edited by G. J. Gumerman, pp. 33–52. School of American Research Press, Santa Fe.

CHAPTER 2

The Late Archaic/Early Agricultural Period in Sonora, Mexico

JOHN P. CARPENTER

GUADALUPE SÁNCHEZ

MARÍA ELISA VILLALPANDO C.

Introduction

Despite occupying a prominent position between the American Southwest and Mesoamerica, arguably two of the most intensively studied regions in the world, the archaeology of Northwest Mexico remains little investigated and poorly understood. Not unexpectedly, this problem is even more acute with regard to the preceramic occupations. Yet archaeologists have long recognized the arbitrary nature of the international boundary and have identified Archaic components related to traditions in the American Southwest. Moreover, however implicitly, Northwest Mexico figures prominently in virtually all models that seek to explain the diffusion of maize and the origins of the Early Agriculture period.

This chapter outlines the environmental context and the history of investigations within Sonora and establishes the majority of the Sonoran Archaic assemblages firmly within the Cochise Archaic tradition spanning the middle and late Holocene periods. We support a model which suggests that Early Agriculture period populations reflect the northward migration of maize-bearing Uto-Aztecan groups following the end of the middle Holocene (Altithermal). Recent excavations at the La Playa site (SON F:10:3) demonstrate that its occupation is primarily associated with the Early Agriculture period, reaching a maximum size during the late Cienega phase, and reveal close parallels with populations in southern Arizona. Finally, we suggest that the subsequent Ceramic period Trincheras tradition represents a local in situ development from the preceding Early Agriculture period peoples.

Environmental Setting

Sonora encompasses 184,934 square kilometers (or somewhat over 9%) of the Republic of Mexico and includes four distinct physiographic provinces

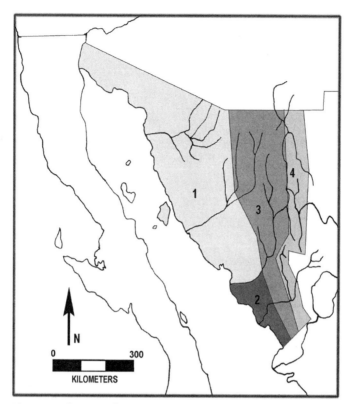

Figure 2.1. Physiographic provinces of Sonora: (1) the Sonoran Desert;
(2) the Southern Coastal Belt; (3) the Basin and Range; and (4) the
Sierra Madre Occidental

(Escarcega 1996:31–32): (1) the Sonoran Desert; (2) the Southern Coastal Belt;
(3) the Basin and Range; and (4) the Sierra Madre Occidental (Figure 2.1).
The Sonoran Desert province extends along the Arizona border from the
Colorado River east to Nogales and south to a point approximately halfway
between Guaymas and the Río Yaqui. This region comprises the coast of the Sea
of Cortés and the broad North Mexican Coastal Plain and is characterized by
typical Sonoran Desert climate and vegetation. The Southern Coastal Belt consists of the southern limits of the coastal plain, which becomes a narrow band
extending south into Sinaloa and is dominated by the broad alluvial deposits
of the Yaqui, Mayo, and Fuerte Rivers. Here the Sonoran Desert vegetation
melds subtly with Sinaloan Thornscrub. These provinces are bordered on the
east by southern extension of the Basin and Range Province, with its north–
south-trending series of mountain ranges and interior valleys. Vegetation is pre-

dominantly Upper Sonoran, with some intermixing of Sinaloan Thornscrub. The easternmost limits of Sonora are defined by the Sierra Madre Occidental, with its towering rhyolitic blocks cloaked in oak and pine.

Previous Investigations

Previous investigations over the last seventy years (although few) have documented Archaic period assemblages throughout much of Sonora (Figure 2.2). In the late 1930s Gordon Ekholm (1940, n.d.) noted slab metates, cobble manos, projectile points, and flaked stone tools at several locations along two tribu-

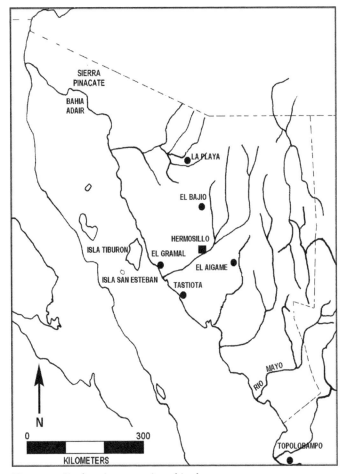

Figure 2.2. Site locations mentioned in the text

taries of the Río Mayo and at a large shell-midden site at Topolobampo on the Sea of Cortés, in northernmost Sinaloa. Ekholm (1940) compared these assemblages to the Cochise tradition that had only recently been defined (and not yet published) by Edward B. Sayles and Ernst Antevs (1941).

Malcolm Rogers believed coastal Sonora to be a likely corridor for "early man" (Hayden 1956:19) and in the early 1940s urged Julian Hayden to explore this region further. Hayden (1956, 1965, 1967, 1969, 1974) recorded a large Archaic shell midden located on an ancient relic estuary at Estero Tastiota and several Archaic period sites in the Sierra Pinacate. In 1949 Donald Lehmer and Bryant Bannister undertook an extensive jeep survey of Sonora with the express purpose of defining the southern extent of Cochise culture (Lehmer 1949:4). They reported finding nonpottery sites in the Río Sonora, Zanjón, Estero Tastiota, and Arroyo Cuchujaqui areas that they compared to the "later Cochise horizons" (Lehmer 1949:5).

In the 1950s George Fay (1955, 1967) defined the "Peralta Complex" on the basis of seventeen Archaic sites to the west of Hermosillo in the vicinity of what is now the airport. Paul Ezell (1954) collected several Archaic projectile points, including Pinto, in his survey of the Papaguería Borderlands, which included extreme northwestern Sonora. He noted that these occurred only in or adjacent to mountains, however, and that virtually all occurred on sites with ceramic components as well, confounding their chronological placement (Ezell 1954:15). Thomas Hinton (1955) reported three San Pedro points as the only Archaic components observed during his survey of the Altar Valley. Frank Holzkamper (1956) collected several projectile points at Estero Tastiota that were subsequently identified by Rogers (Hayden 1956:22) as San Dieguito II through Amargosa I types. The eminent Mexican archaeologist Eduardo Noguera (1958) carried out a brief but extensive reconnaissance and ascribed several sites in the vicinity of Guaymas and Bahía Kino to the Cochise Archaic.

Several lithic sites in northern Sonora were recorded by William Wasley in the late 1950s and early 1960s and are listed in the site card files at the Arizona State Museum. Ronald Ives (1963) observed the association of cultural materials and shell middens associated with a fossil *Chione* shell shoreline in the region extending between Estero Tastiota and Bahía Adair, while noting that an earlier *Turitella* shoreline presumably associated with the late Pleistocene lacked cultural materials.

During the 1970s Tom Bowen (1974, 1976) recorded numerous nonpottery sites along the central coast; but (with the exception of a probable San Dieguito site located near the mouth of the Río Concepción) he concluded that most were likely associated with later Comca'ac (Seri) limited-activity sites. Bowen (1976:90) calls attention to the extensive shell midden at Tecomate on Isla

Tiburón, however, which contains deposits extending at least 2 m below the lowest ceramic horizon, and suggests that a sleeping circle on Isla San Esteban resembles Malpais–San Dieguito I features. Further inland, along the Concepción basin, Bowen (1976) defined his Phase I as essentially the San Pedro stage of the Cochise tradition, which could be considered ancestral to the Trincheras tradition.

In summarizing the Sonoran Archaic, Julio Montané (1996 [1985]) identified the various geoglyphs (intaglios) and trails, as well as at least some petroglyphs, with prepottery traditions. Randall McGuire and Elisa Villalpando (1993) recorded three probable San Pedro phase sites in the Altar Valley. Since 1995 we have documented Archaic components at four widely dispersed localities: at La Playa, along the Río Boquillas to the southwest of Santa Ana; at El Bajío, situated in a large basin between the Río Zanjón and the Río Sonora, approximately 30 km south of Querobabi; at El Gramal, surrounding a small playa near the central coast between San Carlos and Bahía Kino; and at El Aígame, situated on the alluvial floodplain of the Río Mátape, some 60 km southeast of Hermosillo. Notably, these four sites also have Paleoindian components, including Clovis, Folsom, Plainview, and Dalton/Meserve projectile point traditions.

Thus, despite the paucity of work carried out to date, there is ample evidence indicating that Sonora has been the locus of significant human activity since the late Pleistocene. Hayden (1967, 1976, 1987) long argued that the Malpais complex, represented by heavily patinated chopping and scraping tools, reflects a pre–projectile point lithic industry dated to between approximately 37,000 and 7,000 years ago. The antiquity of the Malpais complex, however, like other similar claims for late Pleistocene pre–projectile point traditions in the American Southwest, has yet to be widely accepted.

The Sonoran Archaic components have generally been assigned to two major traditions defined within the American Southwest (Phillips 1989:378–379). Extreme northwestern Sonora, from the Lower Colorado River basin south in a narrow band along the Sea of Cortés to approximately Guaymas, is associated with the San Dieguito/Amargosa tradition, initially defined by Rogers (1929, 1939) in southern California and subsequently extended eastward to the Tucson Basin (Rogers 1958). Although most often considered together, the San Dieguito and Amargosa assemblages reflect two distinct complexes probably separated in time by the Altithermal (ca. 7500 to 4500 BP) (Hayden 1976; Mabry 1998a, 1998b; Mabry and Faught 1998). Hayden (1974, 1976) considered San Dieguito to have evolved from his earlier Malpais complex, whereas the Amargosans were thought to be more recent arrivals ancestral to the Piman-speaking Pinacateños (Hiaced O'odham).

Archaic remains throughout the rest of Sonora have been compared with or directly attributed to the Cochise Archaic tradition. Fay (1955, 1967) described the "Peralta Complex" as a Sonoran variant of the Cochise Culture tradition distinguished only by the presence of a single Pinto-style projectile point, which he interpreted as evidence for Amargosan influence. The Peralta assemblage, however, is consistent with San Pedro phase assemblages elsewhere, including slab and shallow basin metates, cobble manos, San Pedro projectile points, and side and end scrapers. The Pinto point is certainly chronologically intrusive in this assemblage, and the Peralta concept can be discarded.

San Pedro phase assemblages are known in the Southern Coastal Belt, the interior Sonoran Desert, and the Basin and Range Provinces. There also appears to be considerable overlap with San Dieguito/Amargosan assemblages along the central coast between Guaymas and Bahía Kino. As yet, no Archaic components have been recorded in the Sierra Madre province within Sonora, although Robert Lister (1958) reported maize from aceramic contexts at Swallow Cave in the high sierra of adjacent northwestern Chihuahua.

La Playa

La Playa (SON F:10:3) is certainly among the most spectacular and significant archaeological sites within the American Southwest/Northwest Mexico region,

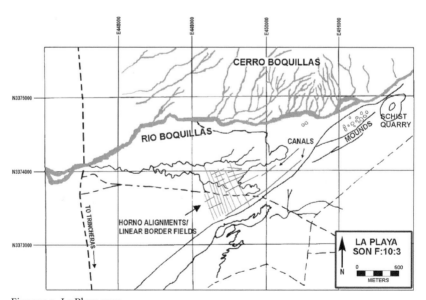

Figure 2.3. La Playa map

Figure 2.4. Photograph showing massive quantities of fire-cracked rock from eroding *hornos* (Photograph by J. Jorge Morales)

extending over approximately 12 sq km along the Río Boquillas, near Trincheras, Sonora, Mexico (Figure 2.3). The Río Boquillas rises in the Sierra Cibuta near Nogales and flows southwest to its eventual confluence with the Río Magdalena a few kilometers to the west of Estación Trincheras. Currently a deeply entrenched arroyo, the Boquillas maintained a perennial flow as recently as the early 1960s.

The La Playa site is situated where the Río Boquillas emerges from a narrow valley constricted by the low hills of the Cerro Boquillas onto a broad, well-developed alluvial floodplain, approximately 515 m (1,700 feet) above sea level. Here several low artificial mounds, several thousand roasting features, several hundred inhumation and cremation burials, along with numerous dog burials, and countless shell, chipped, and ground-stone artifacts are continuously being exposed and eroded by massive sheet and gully erosion (Figure 2.4).

Since 1995 Proyecto La Playa has endeavored to salvage the artifacts and features in most imminent states of destruction and address basic questions of chronology, site structure, subsistence, and regional and interregional interaction. Although Alfred Johnson (1960, 1963) considered La Playa to reflect a Trincheras occupation dated between approximately AD 700 and 1100, our investigations have identified a large number of Pleistocene fauna along with a probable Paleoindian component, a significant Malpais–San Dieguito assemblage, a Middle Archaic (circa 3500 to 1500/1200 BC) component, and evidence for a more-or-less continuous occupation extending from the Late Archaic/ Early Agricultural period (circa 1500/1200 BC to AD 200) through the first half of the twentieth century. Most of the artifacts and features, however, appear to be associated with the Early Agricultural period and include what may well be the largest Early Agricultural period burial population in western North America.

We follow Claudia Berry and Michael Berry (1986) and Mabry (1998c) in summarizing the occupational history of La Playa in terms of major environmental periods. The chronological scheme for these periods is based upon Mabry's (1998d) review of current paleoclimatic data.

Terminal Pleistocene (ca. 14,500 –10,500 BP)
and Early Holocene (10,500 –7500 BP)

The Boquillas Valley offered an oasis-like environment during the late Pleistocene/early Holocene that attracted a large number of animals. Numerous fauna, including the remains of mammoth, bison, camel, horse, deer, peccary, and tortoise, are found within alluvial deposits immediately overlying an extensive paleosol.

Paleoindian artifacts include a previously collected Clovis point (Robles 1974), an unfluted Clovis point (Figure 2.5, top), and two fossilized antler billets. A single tapering stem point is included in the La Playa collection at the Arizona State Museum. Similar types (e.g., Jay, Lake Mojave, Silver Lake, San Dieguito) are widespread throughout the western United States and dated to circa 10,700 and 7000 BP (Lorentzen 1998:142). Malpais/San Dieguito I artifacts are associated with the gravel and cobble deposits of an inverted Pleistocene stream channel that sits immediately atop the paleosol. This assemblage (Figure 2.5, bottom) is characterized by thickly patinated crude cobble choppers and scraper-planes and large flake sidescrapers and knives, manufactured from igneous (basalt, rhyolite, andesite, diorite, latite) stream cobbles derived from the channel deposits. The dating of Malpais/San Dieguito assemblages remains problematic, with age estimates ranging from approximately 37,000 BP (Hayden 1974, 1976) to 4000 BP (Rogers 1939, 1958). The association with the inverted channel deposits indicates an occupation following the abandonment of the channel and thus either is contemporary with or postdates the terminal Pleistocene deposits. Given the absence of patina on probable middle Holocene

Figure 2.5. Probable early Holocene artifacts (Photograph by Natalia Martínez)

artifacts, we can as yet only suggest a possible late Pleistocene/early Holocene context.

Middle Holocene (7500–4500 BP)

The middle Holocene or Altithermal period was initially defined by Antevs (1955) as a shift to higher temperatures and decreased precipitation. The severity of the environmental conditions extant during the Altithermal continues to be debated (Betancourt 1990; Martin 1963; Van Devender 1990), although a marked gap in the radiocarbon record for this period suggests that the Sonoran Desert region was largely abandoned, supporting models that advocate harsher environmental conditions (Berry and Berry 1986; Mabry 1998b, 1998d). Few artifacts at La Playa can be positively assigned to this period. Possible evidence for occupation during this period is limited to a few widely dated projectile point styles, including Pinto and San Jose. These are variably dated to between 9500 and 2800 BP (Lorentzen 1998:145), although Berry and Berry (1986:315) present a reasonable argument for placing the Pinto tradition within the

Figure 2.6. Probable middle Holocene projectile points (Photograph by Natalia Martínez)

middle Holocene period. Of the 254 projectile points collected from La Playa, 7 (2.7 percent) are identified as Pinto/San Jose types (Figure 2.6).

The Late Holocene (4500–2000 BP)

Increased utilization of the Boquillas Valley appears to coincide with a return to more amenable climatic conditions with the onset of the late Holocene after 4500 BP. Thirteen percent of the projectile points may best be associated with the early portion of the late Holocene (that is, prior to the Early Agricultural period) and include four Chiricahua points (4800–2500 BP), twenty-seven Cortaro points (4300–2300 BP), and two Gypsum points (4500–1500 BP) (Lorentzen 1998:144–147).

Twenty-one of twenty-two radiocarbon age determinations fall within the Early Agricultural period. Six of these dates were obtained from bone collagen from burials, and the rest from carbonized material obtained from *hornos* (roasting features) and one from a post mold; the earliest radiocarbon date assigned to this period (3250 ± 40) is from the flexed burial of an adult male

Table 2.1. Early agricultural period radiocarbon age (b.p.) determinations

Sample Number	Feature Type/No.	Radiocarbon Age	Material Dated
A8747	*horno* 6	2000 ± 80	charcoal
A8744	*horno* 9	1960 ± 85	charcoal
A8745	*horno* 7	1960 ± 50	charcoal
A8741	*horno* 18	1940 ± 55	charcoal
A8742	*horno* 18	1885 ± 55	charcoal
AA33185 (AMS)	*horno* 32	1825 ± 50	maize
AA33184 (AMS)	posthole 59	1885 ± 50	maize
AA33182 (AMS)	burial 52	2960 ± 50	mesquite seed
AA53240 (AMS)	burial 12	1919 ± 52	bone collagen
AA53241 (AMS)	burial 113	2587 ± 61	bone collagen
AA53242 (AMS)	burial 291	2572 ± 64	bone collagen
AA53243 (AMS)	burial 323	3720 ± 320	bone collagen
AA53244 (AMS)	burial 324	2556 ± 54	bone collagen
AA53245 (AMS)	burial 360	2254 ± 47	bone collagen
AA53246 (AMS)	burial 364	2975 ± 51	bone collagen
B169394 (AMS)	burial 52	2850 ± 40	bone collagen
B169398 (AMS)	burial 313	1960 ± 40	bone collagen
B169397 (AMS)	burial 111	2010 ± 40	bone collagen
B169396 (AMS)	burial 93	2280 ± 40	bone collagen
B169395 (AMS)	burial 118	3250 ± 40	bone collagen
B169392 (AMS)	burial 11	2490 ± 40	bone collagen

covered with hematite, and the latest radiocarbon date is from maize recovered from within a posthole (1885 ± 50) (Table 2.1).

Of the identified points, 112 projectile points (61%) can be assigned to the Early Agricultural period (San Pedro phase, ca. 1500/1200 to 800 BC, and Cienega phase, 800 BC to ca. AD 200). Michelle Stevens and Jane Sliva (2002) have recently recognized that the San Pedro assemblage actually consists of two point styles; they distinguish the newly recognized Empire point on the basis of technological and chronological differences. The Empire point is similar to the San Pedro points but has a relatively long and narrow triangular body, with a straight stem that is slightly narrower than the body of the blade (Stevens and Sliva 2002:304). The separation of the San Pedro points into two styles has particular chronological significance. At the site of Las Capas, in the Santa Cruz River valley in the Tucson Basin, 40 Empire points were recovered from Stratum 6A, assigned to the Early San Pedro phase (dated at 2897 BP based on the average of seven uncalibrated radiocarbon age determinations), whereas the majority of San Pedro points were recovered from the Late San Pedro contexts (dated at 2692 BP based on the average of eighteen uncalibrated radiocarbon dates) (Hesse and Sliva 2002; Stevens and Sliva 2002).

Figure 2.7. Late Archaic/Early Agricultural period projectile points: Empire (*top row*), San Pedro (*middle row*), and Cienega (*bottom row*)

The La Playa assemblage includes a total of 29 Empire points (16% of the total assemblage) (Figure 2.7, top row) and 38 San Pedro points (21%) (Figure 2.7, middle row). Cienega points represent the most common of the Early Agricultural period projectile points, with 45 examples (24%) (Figure 2.7, bottom row). Cienega points were also found in association with two human burials; one, an extended burial of a male, provided a radiocarbon date of 2280 ± 40 (B-169396 on bone collagen), calibrated to 400–350 BC.

Other Early Agricultural period artifacts include "eared" stone trays, protopalettes, both slab and basin metates, cobble manos, diorite hammerstones and a wide range of flake and core tools, stone cruciforms, and shell ornaments and waste, together with the reamers, rasps, awls, and antler tine punches used in their production. Large (20 cm to 50 cm) pestle-like implements, tabular flaked "hoes," and flaked and/or ground stone disks may also form part of the Early Agricultural period assemblage.

Countless thousands of *hornos,* several hundred human burials, numerous dog burials, shell ornament production and lithic reduction areas, caches of manos and tabular slabs, and a schist quarry are the predominant features associated with the Early Agricultural period. Intriguing evidence for agricultural fields covering some 35 hectares and for canals has also been identified. These features are evident only in aerial photos and remain invisible to surface inspection. Although we initially suspected that these were associated with historic farming, several alignments of contiguous *hornos* (each ranging from 50 m to 150 m in length) are oriented parallel to the canals and at right angles to widely spaced (approximately 10 m) furrows/feeder canals. Radiocarbon dates from adjacent features suggest that these *horno* alignments may be associated with the Cienega phase. Additionally, the highly fractured condition of the fire-cracked rock within the roasting features suggests that water may have been employed in the roasting process, and their linear arrangement may reflect placement along canals.

HORNOS

The forty-eight excavated roasting pits range from 0.45 to 4.02 m in diameter and from 0.50 to 1.18 m in depth, and most have a globular profile. Some roasting features reach monumental mound proportions, however, exceeding 10 m in diameter and rising to 2 m above the surrounding surface; at least some would appear to have been constructed as mounds and probably do not reflect the result of surrounding deflation of previously subterranean features. Their immense proportions are suggestive of community-wide ritual activity.

Analyses of the *horno* contents reveal both abundant plant and animal remains. Maize is present in 9 of the 13 (69%) roasting pits that have been analyzed to date, along with mesquite beans, chenopodium, and amaranth (Sánchez 1998). Maize abundance, as determined by parts per liter (Gasser 1987), is relatively high, with an average of 5.2 ppl per feature. Cheno-ams are also well represented, with an average abundance of 4.08 ppl. By comparison, Robert Gasser (1987:311) indicates that abundance data for Hohokam features average less than 1.0 ppl; features with 5.0 ppl can indicate primary feature function. In contrast, maize ubiquity (measured by presence/absence in excavated features) is rather low, at 63%. This figure is comparable to the Clearwater site (Diehl and Waters 1996) but well below that recorded for other Early Agricultural period sites in the Tucson Basin, which range between 83 and 100% (Sánchez 1998). Initial AMS (Accelerator Mass Spectrometry) radiocarbon dates include a carbonized legume seed (AA33182) at 2960 ± 50, and two maize samples (AA33184 and AA33185) resulted in dates of 1885 ± 50 and 1825 ± 50, respectively.

FAUNAL REMAINS

Preliminary analyses of the La Playa fauna recovered to date indicate that rabbit/hare (*Sylvilagus audubonii* and *Lepus* sp.) and deer (both *Odocoileus hemionus* and *O. virginianus*) represent the majority of the remains. A single *horno* produced the remains of over twenty rabbits, suggesting the use of communal net drives. Desert bighorn (*Ovis canadensis*), antelope (*Antilocapra americana*), and desert tortoise (*Gopherus agassizii*) are also represented within the assemblage. Crab, fish, and sea urchin remains have also been recovered in small amounts and reflect marine resources transported approximately 100 km from the Sea of Cortés (Patricia Martínez, personal communication, 2003).

BURIALS

Based primarily upon burial treatment as well as artifact and feature associations and paleopathological characteristics, we believe that most, if not all, of the several hundred inhumations at La Playa date to the Early Agricultural period. Should absolute dating confirm our suspicions, the 83 burials recovered to date represent the single largest sample for a preceramic population in the U.S. Southwest/Northwest Mexico region. Burials are typically tightly flexed, although semiflexed, seated, and extended inhumations as well as cremation burials also occur. Body position and orientation is highly variable and often suggests that the deceased were bound in textile bundles and placed haphazardly within small burial pits.

Grave offerings are present in approximately 10% of the burials. The paucity of grave goods is somewhat surprising, given the abundant evidence for shell ornament production at the site. The most elaborately furnished burial is that of a middle-aged woman with a desert tortoise carapace containing a basalt tray and pestle nestled in the crook of her left arm. Another female burial contained over 200 shell beads placed in the pelvic area and on her chest. Several individuals of both genders, however, were covered with hematite.

It seems probable that at least some of the cremation burials may be associated with the Cienega phase (Haury 1957; Mabry 1998e). An extremely fine, well-made triangular Cienega point was found with a cremation. Another cremation provided a radiocarbon date of 1675 ± 60 b.p. (AD 262–427), indicating an early Phase I Trincheras association, while yet another was found placed within a partial Santa Cruz Polychrome bowl (circa AD 1200–1400), suggesting that burial practices at La Playa parallel trends observed in southern Arizona.

Preliminary paleopathological analyses indicate that the La Playa population enjoyed relatively good health and show little evidence of developmental disorders or infectious diseases (Barnes 1999; Lincoln-Babb and Minturn 1998). The presence of auditory exostosis in some individuals suggests a possible genetic trait shared with the Matty Canyon populations (Lincoln-Babb 1997; Minturn and Lincoln-Babb 1995). Occipital protuberances, present on at least three individuals, also appear to be a common trait among Early Agricultural period populations at various sites in Arizona (Lincoln-Babb and Minturn 1998). One middle-aged woman who was accorded an uncommon burial position, extended on her back with her arms outspread and legs frogged and covered by a fibrous robe, reveals both an unusual form of cranial deformation and a head shape likely indicative of a distinct biological population (Barnes 1999).

Dental analysis reveals both wear patterns and caries frequencies characteristic of Early Agricultural period populations. The caries frequency for the La Playa population is 9.7%, which is comparable to the Matty Canyon sites (9.9%) and the Wetlands site (7.1%) (Lincoln-Babb and Minturn 1998). According to Christy Turner's (1979) calculations, this percentage falls at the extreme upper limits for hunter-gatherers (0.44–10.3%) and within the lower limits for agriculturists (2.3–26.0%).

DOG BURIALS

Dog burials are among the most abundant feature types at the site. Of the 18 dog burials excavated, 13 lie within the large, dispersed "cemetery" area but do not occur in direct association with their human counterparts. Dogs were generally placed on their left sides in a curled, semiflexed position, without grave offerings. To paraphrase Arthur Saxe (1970), placement within formal cemeteries probably reflects upon the role of canines vis-à-vis group membership.

SHELL ORNAMENT PRODUCTION

Tremendous quantities of marine shell are found throughout the site: 52 genera representing 59 marine shell species have been identified. What percentage reflects the Early Agricultural period assemblage cannot be precisely determined. The greatest variability in shell species is apparently associated with the preceramic components, however, and charred shell is present in the *hornos* dating to the Cienega phase. Comparison with the Cerro Trincheras assemblage (ca. AD 1300–1450) indicates considerable differences between the two assemblages, with few species in common and drastically different percentages. For example, *Conus* sp. dominates the Cerro Trincheras assemblage at 58.35% (Vargas 1995) and represents only 0.13% at La Playa. *Glycymeris gigantea* dominates the La Playa shell assemblage, representing 68.3% of all recovered

Figure 2.8. *Glycymeris* shell bracelet manufacturing process at La Playa

shell. Arthur Woodward (1936), in fact, described La Playa as a "shell bracelet manufactory"; lap stones, rasps, reamers, gravers, split metapodial awls, and antler tine punches are commonly associated with shell-working areas (see Figure 2.8). Other prominent shell species include *Nacarada* sp. (8.4%), *Modiolus subnodosus* (7.6%), *Laevicardium elatum* (1.6%), *Vermetus* sp. (0.9%), *Chione purpurissata* (0.7%), *Olivella dama* (0.3%), and *Arene fricki* (0.3%).

LITHIC INDUSTRY

Quantitative analyses of the flaked and ground stone assemblages are in progress, and we are here necessarily limited to a few preliminary observations. The flaked stone assemblage, in general, is consistent with Early Agricultural period assemblages from the Donaldson and Los Ojitos sites in southeast Arizona (Huckell 1995) and includes a full complement of bifaces, drills, backed knives, scrapers, planes, denticulates, and notched, retouched, and utilized flakes. Tabular agave knives are also present, but whether they can be included within the Early Agricultural period assemblage is questionable.

Approximately 90% of the flaked stone industry utilized locally available raw materials, including quartz, fine- and medium-grained basalt, rhyolite, andesite, diorite, and latite. Fine-grained crypto-crystalline materials constitute approximately 9% of the assemblage, with obsidian representing approximately 0.01%. One knapping station composed of two distinct cherts contained two reconstructible Cienega points that were broken and discarded during manufacture. There does not seem to be a significant difference in raw materials used in the production of San Pedro and Cienega points. At least one San Pedro point was manufactured from a heat-treated chert.

The ground stone assemblage includes a phenomenal number of one- and two-sided cobble manos, slab and basin metates, basalt trays, bowls, proto-palettes, pestles (including the peculiar "horned" type), reamers, rasps, and a large number of hammerstones. Raw materials are predominantly granitics, followed by schist, rhyolite, and basalts. Hammerstones, however, are virtually all manufactured from a dark green diorite.

An arkosic schist quarry is situated atop a low hill where the Boquillas emerges onto the alluvial plain. Here the bedrock was deeply incised, with tabular slabs removed with the aid of quartz cleavers. Although use of the quarry continued through the Trincheras period, characteristic schist implements (particularly the reamers and rasps used in shell ornament production) are common in Early Agricultural period components.

CERAMICS

Several sherds of a previously unidentified pottery type have been found in association with Cienega phase components. This type, named La Playa Plain, is a well-made, coil-and-scraped, polished brown ware with a fine sand temper and is readily distinguished from the Trincheras pottery tradition. One *horno* containing sherds of La Playa Plain produced a radiocarbon date of 1940 $\pm$ 55 (AD 4 to 129). A single sherd was also found within an undated bell-shaped storage pit. La Playa Plain represents approximately 2.5% of the ceramics collected from the site, although this is probably not a true representative sample, because the majority of our efforts have been concentrated in areas perceived to be associated with the Early Agricultural period. Still, it is present in significant numbers and in several contexts that suggest that this type may likely have been manufactured at La Playa, although the possibility that it is intrusive cannot be discounted.

REGIONAL AND INTERREGIONAL INTERACTION

Unquestionably, the vast quantities of marine shell from the Sea of Cortés, 100 km to the west, represent the most significant nonlocal resource encountered at the site. Whether shell was procured directly by the occupants of the site via travel to the coast or, alternatively, was acquired through trade with coastal fisher-foragers (ancestral Comca'ac?) has not been established. Trincheras period sites like Playa Noriega (a Comca'ac site near Bahía Kino with significant quantities of Trincheras Purple-on-Red), however, suggest significant interaction between the Trincheras tradition folk and the prehistoric Comca'ac, and there is presently no reason to believe that this pattern could not have been established during the preceramic period.

Mineral resources were obtained from a variety of far-ranging regions. Virtually all of the obsidian at La Playa comes from the Antelope Wells source on the New Mexico–Chihuahua border, some 350 km to the east. Spectrographic analysis indicates that a high-quality red argillite is derived from the Tonto Basin, approximately 400 km to the north, in central Arizona (James Gundersen, personal communication, 1999). Turquoise from an unidentified source is also present. Hematite, frequently associated with the burials and present as residue on numerous pestles and palettes, may come from known deposits near Magdalena (Fay 1958), approximately 50 km to the northeast. The sources for the crypto-crystalline raw materials, including a wide variety of cherts, chalcedony, and petrified wood, are as yet unknown. Small nodules of chert are only rarely encountered among Río Boquillas cobbles, which are composed almost entirely of igneous parent material from the surrounding mountains.

Discussion

Although we have only begun to scratch the surface, some tentative propositions can nevertheless be put forth. Our efforts lend further support for the consideration of environmental change in constructing models for both Middle Archaic assemblages and the diffusion of maize agriculture. Middle Archaic points account for 15% of the total assemblage. Few, if any, of the Middle Archaic points actually date to the Altithermal period, however, while both earlier Malpais/San Dieguito and later Middle and Late Archaic assemblages are relatively well represented. We believe that La Playa, along with much of the lowland desert Borderlands, was abandoned during at least a portion of the Altithermal, supporting models previously proposed by Berry and Berry (1986), Hayden (1976), Mabry (1998b), and others. Altithermal period projectile points, such as the Pinto and San Jose types, probably reflect incursions by northern groups from the Great Basin and/or Colorado Plateau into the Sonoran Desert during sporadic periods of more ameliorative climatic conditions (Carpenter et al. 2000).

Following the end of the Altithermal, the Sonoran Desert remained as an "empty niche" that was subsequently repopulated by groups associated with new technologies. Gypsum points, along with the various other contracting-stem points, reflect a new technology utilizing adhesives to attach the dart point. As Berry and Berry (1986), Mabry (1998a), and William Marmaduke (1978) have discussed, the contracting-stem point style first appears in central

Mexico, co-occurring with maize in the Tehuacán Valley during the Coxcatlán phase dated by Scotty MacNeish (1967) to 4800–3600 BC and subsequently revised to circa 3600 BC (Long et al. 1989). That the new hafting technology diffused northward along with maize cultivation is a distinct possibility.

Cortaro points, although still poorly dated, can probably be placed in the millennium preceding the Early Agricultural period (Lorentzen 1998:147; Mabry 1998a:79; Roth and Huckell 1992) and apparently reflect a localized development in the Sonoran Desert region. Cortaro points occur most commonly in or adjacent to alluvial settings associated with later San Pedro phase occupations and have also been associated with extremely early maize dates of circa 2000 BC at McEuen Cave (Huckell et al. 1999) and Los Pozos (Gregory 1999; Mabry 1998a:79).

The apparent discontinuity in the archaeological record following the end of Altithermal has been cited by various authors in supporting the introduction of maize as a result of migration from northern Mexico (Berry and Berry 1986; Huckell 1995; Mabry, this volume). Although previous models associate this migration with the San Pedro phase, based on the foregoing discussion we tentatively suggest that the Cortaro assemblage may be associated with the initial arrival of maize-bearing Uto-Aztecan–speaking peoples (Carpenter et al. 2002).

Linguistic evidence places the Proto-Uto-Aztecan (PUA) heartland somewhere between the Mogollon Rim and the northern half of the Sierra Madre Occidental (Fowler 1983; Hill 1996). Glottochronological data suggest that the PUA community diverged into northern (California and Great Basin) and southern (Sonoran) branches around 6000 BP (Miller 1983:118 [note: the figure should read BP and not BC]). Although Jane Hill (1996, 1999, 2000) cites shared cognates for agricultural terms (including maize) in postulating that this divergence occurred following the adoption of maize agriculture, we are tempted by the timing to suggest the Altithermal as a possible impetus for the initial split. That is, with the abandonment of the Sonoran Desert region, some groups sought refuge in the Great Basin, while others withdrew southward into the Sierra Madre Occidental and/or the coastal plains of southern Sonora and Sinaloa. Based upon the great diversity of Uto-Aztecan languages in close proximity, Wick Miller (1983) identifies the *serrana* region between the Río Mayo and the Río Sinaloa as the probable Proto-Sonoran-Uto-Aztecan (PSUA) heartland.

These PSUA groups were likely the first "norteños" to adopt maize agriculture. According to Bruce Benz (1999:32–33), the maize lineage relevant to northern Mexico is postulated to have originated among extremely early populations dispersed from the Río Balsas into the Colima-Jalisco region of West Mexico (where the Reventador race was developed) and then to the coastal plain of Nayarit (where the Jala race emerged), and subsequently to coastal Sinaloa and Sonora (where Chapalote is thought to have emerged). The timing of maize diffusion and the proposed evolutionary developments can presently only be bracketed by the earliest dates for maize in central Mexico and the American Southwest, approximately 3600 to 2000 BC. Thus PSUA groups probably received maize during the late Altithermal or early Holocene and perhaps had a hand in the development of the Chapalote race.

Linguists place the initial divergence of PSUA into the historically observed language groups between approximately 2500 and 1500 BC (Hill 1996, 2000; Miller 1983). Hill (2000) is considerably more confident in demonstrating the widespread dispersal of maize among PSUA speakers. We suspect that the diversification of the Sonoran branch of Uto-Aztecan is linked with the reoccupation of the Sonoran Desert and other regions amenable to maize agriculture. The distribution of known San Pedro or San Pedro–like assemblages very neatly defines the territorial extent of Sonoran Uto-Aztecan speakers in northwestern Mexico (Carpenter et al. 1996; Carpenter et al. 2000).

The subsistence data from La Playa indicate a mixed foraging and farming strategy with intensive maize cultivation combined with an equally extensive utilization of wild plants and animals that we have termed the Sonoran Agricultural Complex (Carpenter et al. 2002). Maize undoubtedly provided a critical storable food source for the winter and early spring months. Yet, even in light of intensification strategies and radically altered settlement patterns, it may have contributed a relatively small percentage of the total calories consumed. Both the low incidence of caries and the ground stone assemblage lend support to this inference.

Maize agriculture, plant species representing year-round seasonality, the numerous inhumation burials, the evidence for multiple activities, the extensive roasting features, the diversity within the lithic assemblage, and the sheer densities of artifacts and features are all indicative of a sedentary population at La Playa during the Early Agricultural period. Anticipating those critics who will call attention to the lack of evidence for domestic structures, we note that we also have no evidence as yet for Trincheras period domestic structures; the lack of identifiable structures can most likely be attributed to the extensive erosion and redeposition of alluvial deposits.

The transition from the Cienega phase to the Trincheras tradition reflects the continuing occupation of Early Agricultural period peoples. The most significant differences are evident in a shift in burial treatment from inhumation to cremation burial and the emergence of the Trincheras pottery tradition. The construction of geoglyphs at La Playa can also be attributed to the Trincheras period.

The Trincheras tradition, in our opinion, does not represent the southern-most component of the Desert Branch of the Hohokam, as has been previously proposed (e.g., Johnson 1960, 1963), but reflects similarities that may be derived from shared linguistic/Early Agricultural period traditions. The emergence of early ceramic horizons characterized by polished brown wares, followed shortly thereafter by red wares and often associated with a predilection for tex-tured surfaces, includes an area extending from the Mogollon Rim south into Durango. The subsequent ceramic period traditions (including the Hohokam, Mogollon, Trincheras, Río Sonora, Huatabampo, and Loma San Gabriel and perhaps even the ancestral western Puebloans) probably may all trace their ori-gins to Early Agricultural period speakers of Sonoran Uto-Aztecan (Carpenter et al. 2000).

Conclusions

Sonora reveals a rich and varied Archaic past. Our research indicates that the Boquillas Valley has been occupied intermittently from the terminal Pleisto-cene through the Middle Holocene and continuously since the end of the Alti-thermal and identifies La Playa as the largest Early Agricultural period commu-nity yet known in the Northwest Mexico/U.S. Southwest region. The material assemblage is consistent with San Pedro and Cienega phase components in southeastern Arizona. The archaeobiological data suggesting a probable shared genetic population further support this relationship. The distribution of simi-lar assemblages throughout much of northwestern Mexico suggests that the Early Agricultural period in the American Southwest reflects just the tip of the proverbial iceberg. Finally, if we are correct, the earliest agricultural evidence in northwestern Mexico should date to the late Altithermal period or earliest years of the late Holocene and be found along well-watered alluvial plains in extreme southern Sonora and Sinaloa.

ACKNOWLEDGMENTS

Our work has been made possible, in part, through funds provided by Consejo de Ciencia y Tecnología (CONACYT), the Instituto Nacional de Antropología (INAH), the Universidad de las Américas–Puebla, and the Arizona Archaeo-logical and Historical Society. Our advances at La Playa, however, can mostly be attributed to the many friends, colleagues, and students who have given so gener-ously of their time and skills. A special debt of gratitude is owed to Ethne Barnes, Jim Holmlund, Bob Jedinak, Austin Lenhart, Lori Lincoln-Babb, Jupiter Marti-nez, Penny Minturn, Mayela Pastrana, Art Rohn, and James Watson.

Antevs, E.

1955   Geologic-Climatic Dating in the West. *American Antiquity* 20:317–355.

Barnes, E.

1999   Lab Analysis, La Playa Burials. Manuscript in possession of the authors.

Benz, B. F.

1999   On the Origin, Evolution, and Dispersal of Maize. In *Pacific Latin America in Prehistory: The Evolution of Archaic and Formative Cultures,* edited by M. M. Blake, pp. 25–38. Washington State University Press, Pullman.

Berry, C. F., and M. S. Berry

1986   Chronological and Conceptual Models of the Southwestern Archaic. In *Anthropology of the Desert West: Essays in Honor of Jesse D. Jennings,* edited by C. J. Condie and D. D. Fowler, pp. 253–327. Anthropological Papers No. 110. University of Utah Press, Salt Lake City.

Betancourt, J. L.

1990   Late Quaternary Biogeography of the Colorado Plateau. In *Packrat Middens: The Last 40,000 Years of Biotic Change,* edited by J. L. Betancourt, T. R. Van Devender, and P. S. Martin, pp. 259–292. University of Arizona Press, Tucson.

Bowen, T.

1974   Esquema de la historia de la cultura Trincheras. In *Sonora: Antropología del desierto,* edited by B. Braniff and R. S. Felger, pp. 347–363. Colección Científica 27. INAH, SEP, Mexico City.

1976   *Seri Prehistory: The Archaeology of the Central Coast of Sonora.* Anthropological Papers of the University of Arizona No. 27. University of Arizona Press, Tucson.

Carpenter, J. P., J. Mabry, and G. Sánchez

2000   Arqueología de los Yuto-Aztecas tempranos. In *Avances y balances de lenguas yutoaztecas: Homenaje a Wick R. Miller,* edited by J. L. Moctezuma Zamarrón and J. H. Hill. Noroeste de México (Special Edition CD-ROM), Centro INAH Sonora, Hermosillo, Sonora/Conaculta-INAH.

Carpenter, J. P., G. Sánchez, and E. Villalpando

1996   Of Language, Lithics and Lunch: New Perspectives on the San Pedro Phase from La Playa, Sonora, Mexico. Paper presented at the Conference on Archaic Prehistory of the Southwest, Albuquerque, New Mexico.

2002   Of Maize and Migration: Mode and Tempo in the Diffusion of *Zea mays* in Northwest Mexico and the American Southwest. In *Traditions, Transitions, and Technologies,* edited by Sarah H. Schlanger, pp. 245–258. University Press of Colorado, Boulder.

Diehl, M. W., and J. A. Waters

1996   Archaeobotanical and Osteofaunal Assessments of Diet Composition and Diversity. In *Archaeological Investigations of the Early Agricultural Period Settlement at the Base of A-Mountain, Tucson, Arizona.* Technical Report No. 96-71. Center for Desert Archaeology, Tucson.

Ekholm, G.

1940   The Archaeology of Northern and Western Mexico. In *The Maya and Their Neighbors,* edited by C. L. Hay, pp. 307–320. D. Appleton-Century Company, Inc., New York.

n.d.   Fieldnotes. Manuscript on file at the American Museum of Natural History, New York.

Escarcega, J. A.

1996 (1985)   Geología de Sonora. In *Historia general de Sonora,* vol. 1: *Periodo prehistórico y prehispánico,* pp. 27–96. 2nd ed. Gobierno del Estado de Sonora, Hermosillo, Sonora.

Ezell, P. H.

1954   An Archaeological Survey of Northwestern Papaguería. *Kiva* 19(2–4):1–26.

Fay, G. E.

1955   Prepottery Lithic Complex from Sonora, Mexico. *Science* 121(3152):777–778.

1958   A Hematite Ore Deposit in Sonora, Mexico. *Southwestern Lore* 24(1):5–6.

1967   *An Archaeological Study of the Peralta Complex.* Occasional Publications in Anthropology, Archaeology Series, No. 1. Colorado State University, Greeley.

Fowler, C. S.

1983   Some Lexical Clues to Uto-Aztecan Prehistory. *International Journal of Linguistics* 49:224–257.

Gasser, R.

1987   Macrofloral Analysis. In *The Archaeology of the San Xavier Bridge Site (AZ BB:13:14) Tucson Basin, Southern Arizona* (Part 3), edited by J. C. Ravesloot, pp. 303–318. Arizona State Museum Archaeological Series 171. University of Arizona, Tucson.

Gregory, D. A.

1999   Data Integration and Synthesis. In *Excavations in the Santa Cruz River Floodplain: The Middle Archaic Component at Los Pozos,* edited by D. A. Gregory, pp. 85–124. Anthropological Papers No. 20. Center for Desert Archaeology, Tucson.

Haury, E. W.

1957   An Alluvial Site on the San Carlos Indian Reservation, Arizona. *American Antiquity* 23:2–27.

Hayden, J. D.

1956   Notes on the Archaeology of the Central Coast of Sonora, Mexico. *Kiva* 21(3–4):19–23.

1965   Fragile-Pattern Areas. *American Antiquity* 31(2):272–276.

1967   A Summary Prehistory and History of the Sierra Pinacate, Sonora. *American Antiquity* 32(3):335–344.

1969   Gyratory Crushers of the Sierra de Pinacate, Sonora. *American Antiquity* 34(2):214–235.

1974   La arqueología en la sierra del Pinacate, Sonora, México. In *Sonora: Antropología del desierto,* edited by B. Braniff and R. S. Felger, pp. 261–265. Colección Científica 27. INAH, SEP, Mexico City.

1976   Pre-Altithermal Archaeology in the Sierra Pinacate, Sonora, Mexico. *American Antiquity* 41:274–289.

1987   Early Man in the Far Southwestern United States and Adjacent Sonora, Mexico. Paper presented at the International Union for Pre- and Proto-Historic Sciences, Commission for the Peopling of the Americas, 11th Congress, Mainz, West Germany.

Hesse, I., and J. Sliva

2002   The Organization of Lithic Technology at an Early Agricultural Village: The View from Las Capas. Paper presented at the 67th Annual Meetings of the Society for American Archaeology, Denver.

Hill, J. H.

1996   The Prehistoric Differentiation of Uto-Aztecan Languages and the Lexicon of Early Southwestern Agriculture. Paper presented at the 61st Annual Meeting of the Society for American Archaeology, New Orleans.

1999   Linguistics. *Archaeology Southwest* 13(1):8.

2000   Dating the Break-up of Southern Uto-Aztecan. In *Avances y balances de lenguas yutoaztecas: Homenaje a Wick R. Miller,* edited by J. L. Moctezuma Zamarrón and J. H. Hill. Noroeste de México (Special Edition CD-ROM). Centro INAH Sonora, Hermosillo, Sonora.

Hinton, T.
1955   A Survey of Archaeological Sites in the Altar Valley, Sonora. *Kiva* 21:1–12.

Holzkamper, F. M.
1956   Artifacts from Estero Tastiota, Sonora, Mexico. *Kiva* 21(3–4):12–19.

Huckell, B. B.
1995   *Of Marshes and Maize: Preceramic Agricultural Settlements in the Cienega Valley, Southeastern Arizona.* Anthropological Papers of the University of Arizona 59. University of Arizona Press, Tucson.

Huckell, B. B., L. W. Huckell, and M. S. Shackley
1999   McEuen Cave. *Archaeology Southwest* 13(1):12.

Ives, R.
1963   The Problem of the Sonoran Littoral Cultures. *Kiva* 28(3–4): 28–32.

Johnson, A.
1960   The Place of the Trincheras Culture of Northern Sonora in Southwestern Archaeology. M.A. thesis, Department of Anthropology, University of Arizona, Tucson.
1963   The Trincheras Culture of Northern Sonora. *American Antiquity* 29(2):174–186.

Lehmer, D. J.
1949   *Archaeological Survey of Sonora, Mexico.* Chicago Natural History Museum Bulletin, December, 4–5.

Lincoln-Babb, L.
1997   Appendix I: Dental Analysis of the La Playa Burials. In *Rescate arqueológico La Playa (SON F:10:3), Municipio de Trincheras, Sonora, México,* edited by J. P. Carpenter, G. Sánchez, and E. Villalpando. INAH, Mexico City.

Lincoln-Babb, L., and P. D. Minturn
1998   Análisis de los restos óseos humanos. In *Salvamento arqueológico La Playa: Informe de la temporada 1997–1998 y análisis de los materiales arqueológicos,* edited by E. Villalpando, J. P. Carpenter, G. Sánchez, and M. Pastrana, pp. 123–129. INAH, Mexico City.

Lister, R.
1958   *Archaeological Excavations in the Northern Sierra Madre Occidental, Chihuahua and Sonora, Mexico.* University of Colorado Stud-

ies, Series in Anthropology, No. 7. University of Colorado Press, Boulder.

Long, A., B. F. Benz, D. J. Donahue, A. J. Jull, and L. J. Toolin

1989   First Direct AMS Dates on Early Maize from Tehuacán, Mexico. *Radiocarbon* 31(3):1035–1040.

Lorentzen, L. H.

1998   Appendix: Common Paleoindian and Archaic Projectile Points in Arizona. In *Paleoindian and Archaic Archaeology of Arizona*, edited by J. B. Mabry, pp. 138–151. Technical Report No. 97-7. Center for Desert Archaeology, Tucson.

Mabry, J. B.

1998a   Archaic Complexes of the Late Holocene. In *Paleoindian and Archaic Sites in Arizona*, edited by J. B. Mabry, pp. 73–88. Technical Report No. 97-7. Center for Desert Archaeology, Tucson.

1998b   Archaic Complexes of the Middle Holocene. In *Paleoindian and Archaic Sites in Arizona*, edited by J. B. Mabry, pp. 65–72. Technical Report No. 97-7. Center for Desert Archaeology, Tucson.

1998c   Frameworks for Arizona's Early Prehistory. In *Paleoindian and Archaic Sites in Arizona*, edited by J. B. Mabry, pp. 1–18. Technical Report No. 97-7. Center for Desert Archaeology, Tucson.

1998d   Late Quaternary Environmental Periods. In *Paleoindian and Archaic Sites in Arizona*, edited by J. B. Mabry, pp. 19–32. Technical Report No. 97-7. Center for Desert Archaeology, Tucson.

1998e   Mortuary Patterns. In *Archaeological Investigations of Early Village Sites in the Middle Santa Cruz Valley: Analyses and Synthesis*, edited by J. B. Mabry, pp. 697–738. Anthropological Papers No. 19. Center for Desert Archaeology, Tucson.

Mabry, J. B., and M. Faught

1998   Archaic Complexes of the Early Holocene. In *Paleoindian and Archaic Sites in Arizona*, edited by J. B. Mabry, pp. 55–64. Technical Report No. 97-7. Center for Desert Archaeology, Tucson.

MacNeish, R. S.

1967   A Summary of the Subsistence. In *The Prehistory of the Tehuacan Valley I: Environment and Subsistence*, edited by D. S. Byers, pp. 290–309. University of Texas Press, Austin.

Marmaduke, W. S.

1978   Prehistoric Culture in Trans-Pecos Texas: An Ecological Explanation. Ph.D. dissertation, Department of Anthropology, University of Texas at Austin. University Microfilms, Ann Arbor.

Martin, P. S.
1963   *The Last 10,000 Years.* University of Arizona Press, Tucson.
McGuire, R., and E. Villalpando
1993   *An Archaeological Survey of the Altar Valley, Sonora, Mexico.*
Arizona State Museum Archaeological Series 184. Arizona State
Museum, University of Arizona, Tucson.
Miller, W. R.
1983   Uto-Aztecan Languages. In *Handbook of North American Indians,*
vol. 10, *Southwest,* edited by A. Ortiz, pp. 113–124. Smithsonian
Institution, Washington, D.C.
Minturn, P., and L. Lincoln-Babb
1995   Bioarchaeology of the Donaldson Site and Los Ojitos. In *Of
Marshes and Maize,* edited by B. Huckell, pp. 106–116. Anthropological Papers of the University of Arizona No. 59. University
of Arizona Press, Tucson.
Montane, J. C.
1996 (1985)   Desde los orígenes hasta 3000 años antes del presente. In *Historia general de Sonora,* vol. 1: *Periodo prehistórico y prehispánico,*
pp. 151–195. 2nd ed. Gobierno del Estado de Sonora, Hermosillo,
Sonora.
Noguera, E.
1958   *Reconocimiento arqueológico en Sonora.* Dirección de Monumen-
tos Prehispánicos, Informe 10. INAH, Mexico City.
Phillips, D. A.
1989   Prehistory of Chihuahua and Sonora, Mexico. *Journal of World
Prehistory* 3(4):373–401.
Robles Ortiz, M.
1974   Distribución de artefactos Clovis en Sonora. *Instituto Nacional de
Antropología e Historia Boletín* 2:25–32.
Rogers, M.
1929   *Report on an Archaeological Reconnaissance in the Mojave Sink
Region.* San Diego Museum of Man Archaeological Papers 1(1).
San Diego Museum of Man, San Diego.
1939   *Early Lithic Industries of the Lower Basin of the Colorado River and
Adjacent Desert Areas.* San Diego Museum of Man Papers 3. San
Diego Museum of Man, San Diego.
1958   San Dieguito Implements from the Terraces on the Rincon, Pan-
tano, and Rillito Drainage System. *Kiva* 24(1):1–23.

Roth, B., and B. B. Huckell

1992 Cortaro Points and the Archaic of Southern Arizona. *Kiva* 57(4):353–370.

Sánchez, G.

1998 Los hornos y sus contenidos arqueobotánicos. In *Salvamento arqueológico La Playa: Informe de la temporada 1997–1998 y análisis de los materiales arqueológicos,* edited by E. Villalpando, J. P. Carpenter, G. Sánchez, and M. Pastrana, pp. 130–157. INAH, Mexico City.

Saxe, A.

1970 Social Dimensions of Mortuary Practices. Ph.D. dissertation, Department of Anthropology, University of Michigan, Ann Arbor. University Microfilms, Ann Arbor.

Sayles, E. B., and E. Antevs

1941 *The Cochise Culture.* Medallion Papers 29. Gila Pueblo, Globe, Ariz.

Stevens, M. N., and R. J. Sliva

2002 Empire Points: An Addition to the San Pedro Phase Lithic Assemblage. *Kiva* 67(3):297–326.

Turner, C. G., II

1979 Dental Anthropological Indications of Agriculture among the Jomon People of Central Japan. *American Journal of Physical Anthropology* 51:619–636.

Van Devender, T. R.

1990 Late Quaternary Vegetation and Climate of the Sonoran Desert, United States and Mexico. In *Packrat Middens: The Last 40,000 Years of Biotic Change,* edited by J. L. Betancourt, T. R. Van Devender, and P. S. Martin, pp. 134–165. University of Arizona Press, Tucson.

Vargas, V.

1995 Concha. In *Excavación arqueológica de Cerro de Trincheras: Informe preliminar de la temporada de campo 1995,* edited by R. H. McGuire and E. Villalpando Canchola, pp. 53–72. Archivo Consejo de Arqueología INAH, Mexico City.

Woodward, A.

1936 A Shell Bracelet Manufactory. *American Antiquity* 2(2):117–125.

CHAPTER 3

Changing Knowledge and Ideas about the First Farmers in Southeastern Arizona

JONATHAN B. MABRY

Archaeological remains of the early farmers of southeastern Arizona (Figure 3.1) have been studied for more than six decades. Over that time-span, knowledge of their site types, subsistence strategies, settlement patterns, material cultures, and chronologies has grown through initial explorations, research expeditions, and cultural resource management projects. An explosion of discoveries in this region since the 1980s has pushed back the earliest dates in the Southwest for agriculture, canals, ceramics, cemeteries, villages, and possibly the bow and arrow. Concurrently, ideas about the circumstances and consequences of the introduction of agriculture to the region, who the first farmers were, and how their societies were different from Archaic hunting and gathering societies have evolved in relation to the sequence of archaeological discoveries, the development of new dating techniques, and the progression of Americanist and Southwesternist research interests and approaches to archaeological interpretation. However, some perennial questions remain unanswered, while many new questions have emerged.

This chapter begins by describing the current landscape and climate of southeastern Arizona, the environmental changes at the beginning of the late Holocene that set the stage for the transition to agriculture in this region, and the environmental variation across the region that led to alternative adaptations in the western and eastern areas. It then reviews the history of research, the conventional wisdoms that held sway for decades, the changing chronological terms and subdivisions, and recent discoveries. It concludes with discussions of current questions about this first agricultural frontier north of Mexico.

A Varied Environment

Southeastern Arizona (Figure 3.1) straddles the edges of the Sonoran Desert and Mexican Highlands sections of the Basin and Range physiographic province (Gehlbach 1981). Here southeastern Arizona is defined as extending from the

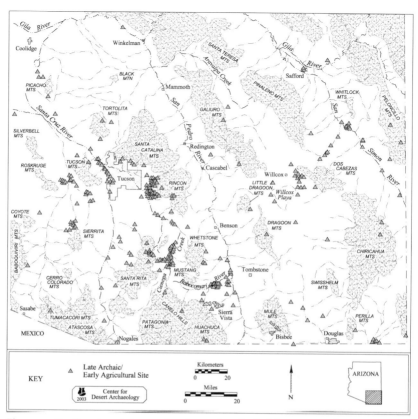

Figure 3.1. Southeastern Arizona, showing major physical features, modern towns and cities, and the locations of almost 200 recorded Late Archaic/Early Agricultural sites (the distribution of sites represents archaeological project locations more than settlement patterns)

Baboquivari Mountains in the west to the New Mexico border in the east and from the Gila River in the north to the Mexico border in the south. Rising steeply between broad valleys, rugged mountain ranges represent about one-third of the surface area of this region. Several of the parallel northwest–southeast-trending ranges rise above 9,000 feet. Valley floor elevations range from about 2,000 feet above sea level at the confluence of the Gila and San Pedro Rivers to about 4,100 feet in the Sulphur Springs and San Bernadino Valleys. Covering most of the remaining two-thirds of the landscape are bajadas—waterless, deeply eroded aprons of downwashed sediments that slope gradually from the bases of bedrock uplands to valley centers. Upper bajadas are erosional surfaces on bedrock or old alluvium, while lower bajadas are composed of coalescing fans of younger alluvium. Large debris fans occur at canyon mouths, and valley floors are drained by arroyos, streams, and rivers. Cycles of cutting and filling of larger channels have formed terraces. Except for the headwaters of the Santa Cruz River in the San Rafael Valley and Whitewater Draw in the southern Sulphur Springs Valley, all major watercourses flow northward. Marshy cienegas occur in places where bedrock formations wedge water tables near the surface. The northern Sulphur Springs Valley has interior drainage, with the Willcox Playa—the remnant of a much larger Pleistocene lake—lying in its center.

In general, the region is a "high desert" covered by a diverse mosaic of desertscrub, grasslands, oak woodlands, and pine forests, with biotic communities varying by altitude zones (Brown 1994a). In the Arizona Uplands zone of the Sonoran Desertscrub biome in the Tucson Basin, Avra Valley, and middle San Pedro Valley, bajadas are densely covered with paloverdes, mesquites, and ironwood trees, particularly along ephemeral washes (Shreve and Wiggins 1964; Turner and Brown 1994). Beneath these leguminous trees, the understory contains chollas, prickly pears, saguaro, and a large variety of other cacti along with ocotillo and bursage, brittlebush, jojoba, and other shrubs. Sonoran Savanna Grasslands formerly covered large portions of the Altar and upper Santa Cruz Valleys (Brown 1994e). To the east, in Chihuahuan Desert Grasslands between 4,000 and 5,000 feet in the upper Santa Cruz, Cienega, San Pedro, and Sulphur Springs Valleys, bajada vegetation is characterized by grasses, shrubs, agaves, yuccas, and sotol (Brown 1994d; McClaran 1995). Chihuahuan Desertscrub has replaced desert grasslands in the lower elevations of the upper San Pedro Valley and San Simon Valley (Hastings and Turner 1965; Brown 1994b).

Throughout the region, along the channel margins and aggrading floodplains of the few remaining permanent watercourses are grassy marshes, gallery forests of deciduous cottonwood, willow, walnut, and hackberry, and extensive mesquite "bosques" (forests) (Hendrickson and Minckley 1984). Dense stands of mesquites and catclaw acacia line the arroyos that incise valley floors. Away from drainages, creosotebush and saltbush dominate the lowest elevations. Above desertscrub and desert grasslands on the granitic western slopes of the Santa Catalina, Rincon, and Santa Rita Mountains are small areas of Interior Chaparral dominated by shrub live oak, manzanita, mountain mahogany, sumacs, and silktassels (Pase and Brown 1994a). Across southeastern Arizona, mountain ranges rising several thousand feet ("sky islands") are covered with evergreen oak, juniper, and piñon ("encinal") woodlands between 4,000 and 6,500 feet (Brown 1994c) and with pine forests (dominated by Ponderosa Pine) above about 6,500 feet (Pase and Brown 1994b). Spruce-fir forests, remnants of the Ice Age, survive at the tops of the highest ranges alongside grassy meadows and aspen stands (Pase and Brown 1994c). Annual and perennial forbs and grasses of many varieties grow in every setting but are densest and most diverse in riparian areas, canyons, and montane meadows.

Rates of evapotranspiration are high because of relatively high temperatures, low humidity, and scarce precipitation; the climate of the region is classified as desert to semidesert (Sellers et al. 1985). Yearly rainfall is biseasonal, with the majority contributed by violent convectional thunderstorms associated with moist tropical air from the Gulf of Mexico during the "monsoon summer" between early July and mid-September. A lesser amount of rain and snow from westerly cyclonic storms falls in the winter, between December and February. The ratio of winter to summer rainfall varies across the region. Winter rainfall represents 45–50% of the total annual precipitation in the western part; it declines to 30–35% in the southeastern corner (Sellers et al. 1985).

Average annual precipitation in the valleys increases from west to east, from about ten inches in the Tucson Basin to fifteen inches near the New Mexico border; it also increases with elevation, with most mountain ranges receiving more than twenty inches and the highest peaks receiving thirty-five inches. Precipitation also varies greatly both annually and seasonally. In most years the total varies 10% from the annual mean, and very dry years may be followed by very wet years (McDonald 1956). There is greater year-to-year variation in winter precipitation than in summer precipitation; at weather stations across the region, coefficients of variation range from 28 to 41% for summer precipitation and from 48 to 58% for winter precipitation (McDonald 1956). Snow is common on mountaintops and at lower elevations for brief periods in the winter. Relative humidity is low throughout the year, reaching its lowest point during the dry "foresummer" of May and June.

Summer high temperatures range from the 100s Fahrenheit on the valley floors to the 70s in the mountains. Winter temperatures vary widely, with an increasing number of freezing nights in the mountains, in higher grasslands, and along major rivers and washes. At 2,400 feet in elevation, Tucson has an average of 250 frost-free days each year, while Willcox, at 4,200 feet, has a frost-free growing season of 200 days. Catastrophic freezes in southern Arizona have an average recurrence interval of about thirteen years with a variance of about five years (Bowers 1980). Daily temperature ranges are large throughout the year, varying by as much as 30–50 degrees Fahrenheit.

Late Holocene Environmental Changes

These climatic characteristics, biotic communities, and landscape processes in southeastern Arizona have not always been the same. Current conditions developed between about 5,000 and 4,000 years ago, when temperatures fell and effective moisture increased after a three- to four-thousand-year period of generally hotter and drier conditions during the middle Holocene. These environmental changes at the beginning of the late Holocene allowed the return of hunting and gathering groups and set the stage for the transition to agriculture in southeastern Arizona and are therefore relevant to review here. The following summary is based on a recent review of geological and biological records of Late Quaternary environmental changes in the Southwest, including alluvial stratigraphies, lake and playa deposits, dune formations, mammal remains, insect fossils, pollen sequences, and packrat midden series (Mabry 1998d). Dates and date ranges in this section are expressed in uncalibrated radiocarbon years before present (b.p.).

Multiple lines of evidence indicate that temperatures declined and rainfall increased throughout the Southwest between about 4500 and 2500 b.p., resulting in higher effective moisture. Lakes rose or refilled, and rivers, streams, and springs flowed again or more heavily. Floodplains began aggrading rapidly. In some areas sand dunes became stabilized, and in other areas sand sheets and parabolic dunes formed on moist ground surfaces. Forests and grasslands expanded, riparian and aquatic plants became more abundant along watercourses and lake margins, and subtropical desertscrub communities reached their modern limits. Piñon pine became more abundant on the Colorado Plateau and expanded to its northern limit in the Great Basin. Bison (in the form of modern *Bison bison*) returned to the Southwest, and modern faunal communities reached their current distributions. Effective moisture reached a late Holocene peak between about 3500 and 3000 b.p., followed by a drought near 2500 b.p. Another moist interval between about 2500 and 1000 b.p. was punctuated by a dry episode near 1500 b.p. Since about 1000 b.p. effective moisture in the Southwest has been relatively low compared to the late Holocene average.

In southeastern Arizona active dunes dammed streams and caused locally high water tables in the Picacho Dune Field starting between 4850 and 4300 b.p. and lasting until 3900 b.p.; a period of surface stability and soil formation was followed by a second interval of dune activity between 2600 and 400 b.p. (Waters 1986a). Along most reaches of the middle Santa Cruz River, channel filling and overbank deposition began sometime between 4000 and 3500 b.p. and terminated with an interval of stability and soil formation near 2500 b.p.; since that time several cut-and-fill cycles have been followed by brief intervals of soil formation near 2000, 1000, and 500 b.p. (Haynes and Huckell 1986; Huckell 1998; Mabry et al. 1999; Waters 1987). In the Cienega Valley an interval of erosion and soil formation prior to 4000 b.p. was followed by rapid alluvial deposition and repeated formation of marshes between about 4000 and 1700 b.p. (Eddy and Cooley 1983; Huckell 1990). In the upper San Pedro Valley a brief period of stability and soil formation near 4200 b.p. has been followed by multiple cut-and-fill cycles until today (Haynes 1987). At the Fairbank site an alluvial fan of a tributary of the upper San Pedro River aggraded continuously between 3000 and 1000 b.p., when a soil formed on the stabilized surface; aggradation then resumed until the late nineteenth century (Huckell 1990). A final highstand of Lake Cochise occurred between 4000 and 3000 b.p. in the northern Sulphur Springs Valley before it returned to a seasonal playa (Waters 1989). The floodplain along Whitewater Draw in the southern Sulphur Springs Valley was characterized by steady aggradation from overbank floods between about 3300 and 1100 b.p., followed by two more cycles of aggradation prior to arroyo incision in the late nineteenth century (Waters 1986b).

Higher percentages of cattail and sedge pollen in a pollen profile at the Murray Springs site in the upper San Pedro Valley indicate the stream began to flow at least seasonally sometime between 5900 and 4300 b.p., lasting until at least 4200 b.p.; these trends were interpreted as indicating moist conditions between 5000 and 4000 b.p. (Mehringer et al. 1967). However, based on a study of modern surface samples in a nearby valley, the high percentages of Chenopodiineae in the same pollen zone represent a dissected land surface, a low water table, and low rainfall during this interval; a shift to dominance of short-spine Compositae that occurred in a zone bracketed between 4230 and 4120 b.p. may mark the beginning of a rise in the water table during a wetter phase that ended by at least 1550 b.p. (Martin 1963). According to pollen samples from the nearby Lehner site, effective moisture briefly decreased near 2500 b.p. and again near 1500 b.p.; beginning sometime between 1100 and 800 b.p., rainfall decreased to the historic average and the water table fell (Mehringer and Haynes 1965).

The plant species represented in radiocarbon-dated packrat middens indicate that by 4000 b.p. the leguminous trees and cacti of the Sonoran Desert had become established throughout their present range, including the Tucson Basin, and grasslands had begun to expand at the expense of Chihuahuan Desertscrub in the higher basins of southeastern Arizona (Van Devender 1990). Pollen from a lake bottom at the northern edge of the Sonoran Desert in central Arizona indicates that grasses became more abundant and oak-juniper woodlands expanded to lower elevations at that time (Davis and Shafer 1992). Between about 4800 and 4000 b.p. bison were hunted by groups based in seasonal camps and using Chiricahua dart points in the southern San Simon Valley (Sayles and Antevs 1941) and in the middle and lower Santa Cruz Valley (Huckell 1996; James 1993).

During historic time (and largely during the last 130 years), marshes ("cienegas") have mostly disappeared from the basins of southeastern Arizona due to falling water tables and arroyo cutting, grasslands in the Avra Valley and the middle Santa Cruz Valley have almost disappeared, Chihuahuan des-ertscrub has encroached on formerly extensive grasslands in the higher basins to the east, and mesquites have become more abundant (Bahre 1991; Cooke and Reeves 1976; Dobyns 1981; Hastings and Turner 1965; Hendrickson and Minckley 1984). All these changes were related at least partly to human impacts, both direct and indirect, although increasing temperatures and droughts have also played important roles.

In summary, various kinds of geological and biological records indicate that climatic and landscape conditions favorable for hunting and gathering and agriculture developed in southeastern Arizona at the beginning of the late Holocene and were present continuously between about 4500 and 2500 b.p. (3200–700 BC). During this relatively moist interval, when agriculture was introduced to the region and became the focus of subsistence, runoff farming and flood farming were possible on regularly flooding alluvial fans and flood-plains, dry farming was possible on active sand dunes that dammed springs and conserved soil moisture, and irrigated farming was possible near permanent springs and along perennial reaches of rivers. The spread of cacti and legumi-nous trees, the formation of extensive grasslands, and the return of bison at the beginning of this time-span also increased wild food resources that became important complements to cultigens and "insurance" against crop failures.

The environmental changes in southeastern Arizona at the beginning of the late Holocene are just beginning to be reconstructed in detail. These envi-ronmental factors were known only in general outline during the first several decades of archaeological investigations and interpretations of early agricul-tural sites in this region, summarized in the next section. In the remainder of this chapter, dates and date ranges are expressed either as numbers of years ago or as uncalibrated radiocarbon years before present (b.p.), followed by approx-imate calibrations to calendar years (BC and AD).

Recognition, Definition, and Development

During the mid- to late 1930s Edward B. Sayles and Ernst Antevs defined the "Cochise Culture" based on their investigation of the stratigraphic relation-ships of buried preceramic sites exposed in arroyo banks in southeastern Ari-zona (Sayles and Antevs 1941). They believed that this hunting and gathering adaptation lasted, without interruption, nearly the entire 10,000 years since the end of the last Ice Age. The "San Pedro Stage" was the third and final stage, and geological correlations suggested that San Pedro stage sites dated between about 5,000 and 2,500 years ago (3000–500 BC). The appearance of projec-tile points in this stage was thought to reflect an increase in the importance of hunting. Resemblances were noted between San Pedro stage artifacts and those from Basketmaker II sites on the Colorado Plateau, previously the oldest known cultural remains in the Southwest.

Over the next two decades the geographic range of the Cochise Culture was expanded by discoveries of similar artifact assemblages at sites in southwestern Arizona (Ezell 1954; Haury 1950), east-central Arizona (Haury 1943, 1957; Wendorf and Thomas 1951), western and central New Mexico (Agogino 1960a, 1960b; Agogino and Hester 1953; Agogino and Hibben 1958; Campbell and Ellis 1952; Dick 1951, 1965; Lehmer 1948; Martin et al. 1949, 1952), and northwestern Mexico (Fay 1956, 1967; Hayden 1956; Johnson 1963, 1966).

In the artifact assemblage recovered from Ventana Cave in southwestern Arizona, Emil Haury and Malcolm Rogers recognized a blending of the Cochise Culture with the Amargosa industry of the lower Colorado River Valley in southwestern Arizona and southeastern California (Haury 1943, 1950; Rogers 1958, 1966). In the San Pedro stage remains that he found at the Cienega Creek site in the Mogollon Highlands of eastern Arizona, Haury (1957) saw the common root of the Hohokam and Mogollon cultures of later prehistory. Local variants of the San Pedro stage were identified in Sonora, Mexico (the "Peralta Complex"; Fay 1956), the middle Rio Grande Valley of central New Mexico (the "Atrisco Focus"; Campbell and Ellis 1952), and the Jornada Basin of southern New Mexico (the "Hueco Phase"; Lehmer 1948).

The presences of maize cobs and squash rinds in deposits radiocarbon dated to about 5,900–5,600 b.p. (4800–4400 BC) in Bat Cave in west-central New Mexico (Dick 1965) and of maize pollen in the lowest cultural stratum at the Cienega Creek site (Martin and Schoenwetter 1960) were widely cited over the next two decades as evidence of the arrival of agriculture in the Mogollon Highlands during the Chiricahua stage, which preceded the San Pedro stage in the Cochise Culture sequence (Haury 1962; Irwin-Williams 1973, 1979; Sayles 1983; Woodbury and Zubrow 1979). The oldest pit structures then known in the Southwest were identified at San Pedro stage sites in the 1950s (Sayles 1983), and by the 1960s maize pollen had been identified in San Pedro stage contexts at the Matty Canyon, Double Adobe IV, and Pantano sites in southeastern Arizona (Hemmings et al. 1968; Martin 1963; Martin and Schoenwetter 1960; Schoenwetter 1962). The first radiocarbon dates obtained from these and other sites indicated a time-span of about 3,500–1,950 years ago (1500 BC–AD 50) for the San Pedro stage (Eddy and Cooley 1983; Sayles 1983). These discoveries led Southwestern archaeologists to associate the San Pedro stage with the spread of agriculture from the Mogollon Highlands to the lowlands of the southern Basin and Range Province and the establishment of the first pit structure settlements in the Southwest.

Old Ideas

The main research goals of these early decades were to define the material culture traits, chronology, and geographic range of the San Pedro stage culture and place it within the regional sequence and within the genealogy of prehistoric Southwestern cultures. Although the primary concern was cultural-historical, the conceptualization of archaeological cultures as adaptations, the interest in stratigraphic and environmental contexts, and the interdisciplinary approach to investigations anticipated the shift in priorities of Americanist archaeology toward reconstructing and explaining cultural adaptations to environments and processes of culture change during the rise of "New Archaeology" in the 1960s and 1970s. However, research designs, sampling strategies, screening of excavated sediments, and systematic collection of subsistence remains were rare practices during this period. Also, a canon of knowledge developed that was steadily added to but seldom reviewed critically. By the 1970s a number of conceptions about the Cochise culture sequence and the transition to agriculture and village life had become explicit or implicit conventional wisdoms among Southwest archaeologists:

1. Beginning during the warm and dry "Altithermal" interval spanning the middle Holocene, the Chiricahua stage represented a movement to the cooler and wetter uplands, where maize first arrived and was gradually incorporated into an economy centered upon wild plants.

2. Intensive collecting of wild plant foods "preadapted" the Cochise culture for the adoption of cultigens from the south, spreading up the mountainous corridor linking the Southwest with Mexico.

3. The maize pollen and cobs found in Chiricahua stage contexts represented experiments with agriculture prior to an increase in its importance during the San Pedro stage.

4. The transition from casual horticulture to agricultural dependence during the San Pedro stage led to the establishment of the earliest settlements in the Southwest and the development of the ancestral culture that eventually diverged into the Mogollon, Hohokam, and Anasazi farming village cultures of later prehistory.

Critiques and Revisions

While most Southwestern archaeologists subscribed to the developing conventional model, a few challenged the reported associations of the radiocarbon-dated materials with maize remains and with Chiricahua and San Pedro stage materials (Berry 1982; Berry and Berry 1986; Eggan 1961; Ford 1981; Jennings 1967; Johnson 1955; Minnis 1985). But, with the exception of a large-scale survey in the San Pedro Valley that documented more sites occupied during the San Pedro stage (Whalen 1971), little work was conducted at San Pedro stage sites in southeastern Arizona during the 1970s. Agriculture was not indisputably confirmed as part of San Pedro stage subsistence until a mix of research projects and cultural resource management projects in the 1980s recovered carbonized maize fragments from sites in the region and directly radiocarbon dated them by the new accelerator mass spectroscopy (AMS) method, which allowed dating of much smaller samples (Bernard-Shaw 1989; Doelle 1985; Elson and Doelle 1987; Fish et al. 1986; Huckell 1984b, 1988, 1990, 1995; Huckell and Huckell 1984; Roth 1989). These maize dates, ranging between about 2800 and 2400 b.p. (1000 – 400 BC), also provided the most reliable and precise dating of the San Pedro stage ever obtained.

During the same decade, the continuity of the Cochise Culture was cast into doubt by Michael Waters' (1986b) reinvestigation of the stratigraphic relationships and ages of some of the type sites; its distinctiveness became increasingly less certain when comparisons were made at the scale of the greater Southwest and western North America (Dean 1987; Huckell 1984a). By this time, following the trend in Americanist and Southwesternist archaeology, cultural histories and relationships had become of less concern to archaeologists working in southeastern Arizona than were cultural adaptations and processes of change. Research designs, sampling strategies, and systematic recovery of subsistence remains were now standard. Huckell (1984a) urged that in the southern Southwest the San Pedro stage be renamed the "Late Archaic Period" and reconceptualized as a subregional variant of the "Southwestern Archaic tradition." These changes were widely accepted, and these terms remain in the vocabulary of many archaeologists working in the region.

A New Temporal Subdivision

Numerous excavations conducted at sites of early farmers in southeastern Arizona during the 1990s were funded by federal and state agencies, and to a lesser extent by private-sector clients, to comply with Cultural Resource Management laws (Clark 2000; Diehl 1997; Ezzo and Deaver 1998; Freeman 1998; Gregory 2001; Huckell et al. 1995; Lascaux and Hesse 2001; Mabry 1990, 1998a, 2003, 2004b; Mabry et al. 1997, 1999; Wellman 2000). Additional fieldwork projects motivated exclusively by research goals and funded by government and private

Table 3.1. Currently known date ranges of Late Archaic/Early Agricultural complexes/phases in southeastern Arizona

Complexes/Phases	Calendar Date Ranges
Cienega (late)	400 BC–AD 50
Cienega (early)	800–400 BC
San Pedro	1200–800 BC
(unnamed)	2100?–1200 BC

grants also focused on early agricultural sites in this region (Huckell et al. 1999; Roth 1995a; Stevens 2000a). By mid-decade the rapidly accumulating discoveries led Huckell (1995) to propose that Southwestern sites with early evidence of agriculture be assigned to the "Early Agricultural Period" and that the term "Late Archaic" be used only to refer to hunter-gatherer sites contemporaneous with the sites of early farmers.

For southeastern Arizona, Huckell (1995) divided the Early Agricultural period into two phases based on differences in age, projectile point styles, architectural forms, and types of ground stone tools and marine shell jewelry. Abundant maize remains, bell-shaped storage pits, and fired-clay human figurines are common to both phases. The earlier "San Pedro Phase" sites typically have large-bladed points with shallow side notches, oval pit structures, and limited varieties of ground stone tools and shell ornaments, while "Cienega Phase" sites have triangular points with deep corner notches, round pit structures, and diverse ground stone and shell assemblages. These distinctions assign most of the sites formerly referred to as San Pedro stage, and many of the material culture traits that defined the stage, to the new Cienega phase.

To date, the term "Early Agricultural Period" has not been universally adopted, but Huckell's phase subdivisions have already been applied by a number of archaeologists working in southeastern Arizona. Currently available radiocarbon dates place the San Pedro phase between about 3000 and 2600 b.p. (1200–800 BC). A few direct dates on maize between about 3700 and 3000 b.p. (2100–1200 BC) have recently been reported from a handful of sites in the region (see below), but it is not known whether one or more material culture complexes are represented in this as-yet-unnamed interval of early agriculture. The available set of dates from Cienega phase sites ranges between about 2600 and 1950 b.p. (800 BC–AD 50). Table 3.1 summarizes the currently known age ranges of late Holocene Archaic and Early Agricultural phases in southeastern Arizona. Figure 3.1 shows the distribution of recorded Late Archaic/Early Agricultural sites in the region. Examples of the projectile point types associated with these sites are shown in Figure 3.2.

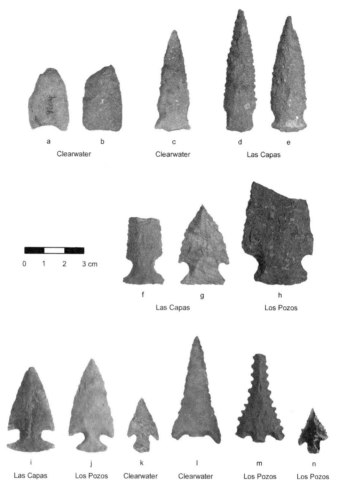

Figure 3.2. Projectile point types from Late Archaic/Early Agricultural sites in southeastern Arizona: (a–b) Cortaro points/bifaces (unnamed interval–Late Cienega); (c) Armijo point (unnamed interval); (d–e) Empire points (San Pedro–Early Cienega); (f–h) San Pedro points (San Pedro–Late Cienega); (i–j) Western Basketmaker points (San Pedro–Late Cienega); (k–n) Cienega points (Early–Late Cienega)

New Knowledge

Although a number of substantial reports and popular articles have already appeared, the rate of publication has not kept up with the explosion of new information since the 1980s about the initial stage of agriculture and settled life in southeastern Arizona. Nonetheless, some important new information about this watershed cultural transition can be summarized briefly.

A Long Interval of Agriculture before the San Pedro Phase

Until recently the San Pedro phase, beginning about 3000 b.p. (1200 BC), was thought to be the first agricultural phase in southeastern Arizona and possibly in the Southwest. However, several direct radiocarbon dates on maize between about 3700 and 3000 b.p. (2100–1200 BC) have now been reported from several sites in the middle Santa Cruz Valley (Lascaux and Hesse 2001; Mabry 2003; Stevens 1999, 2000b; Wellman 2000; Wöcherl and Clark 1997). Also reported from sites in this region are maize dates of 4080 b.p. (Helga Wöcherl, personal communication, 2003) and 4050 b.p. (Freeman 1997), but these dates are problematic because their ^{13}C values were above the typical range for maize or unmeasurable, respectively.

Three sites in the middle Santa Cruz Valley have well-defined agricultural occupations older than the San Pedro phase. A cluster of pits in a deep excavation area at the Las Capas site yielded three dates on maize and other annuals that averaged about 3700 b.p. (2100 BC) (Lascaux and Hesse 2001). Maize dates of 3690 and 3650 b.p. (ca. 2100 BC) were obtained from an occupation with pit structures and storage pits at the Clearwater site (Mabry 2003). The Sweetwater Locus of the Los Pozos site had pit structures, pits, and other features containing maize dating between 3340 and 3230 b.p. (1600–1400 BC) (Stevens 2000b). Elsewhere in the region, several maize dates averaging about 3700 b.p. (2100 BC) have been obtained from McEuen Cave in the Gila Mountains (Huckell et al. 1999; Steve Shackley, personal communication, 2003). The maize dates from these sites have pushed back the beginning of agriculture in this region by almost a millennium.

The possibility remains that even older maize will be found in association with complexes that are currently considered to be Middle Archaic. At the beginning of the late Holocene between 5000 and 4000 b.p., modern climatic conditions were established, stream and river flows increased, alluvial processes created the right conditions for agriculture, and the human population density rose significantly. The earliest radiocarbon dates on maize in southeastern Arizona are now reaching almost back to this time (see above). However, the association of maize remains with the Chiricahua stage (or phase), now dated between about 4800 and 4000 b.p. (3600–2500 BC), is currently only speculative.

The identification of maize pollen in the lowest cultural stratum at the Cienega Creek site (Martin and Schoenwetter 1960) is equivocal, and redating of several charcoal samples with the CO_2 method bracket this deposit between 2650 and 2450 b.p. (850–450 BC) (Wills 1988), largely within the early Cienega phase. Wirt Wills (1988) has also concluded that the earliest maize from Bat Cave dates no earlier than about 3100 b.p. (1300 BC) and has argued that the artifact assemblage from this stratum (originally assigned to the Chiricahua stage) bears little resemblance to the assemblage from the Chiricahua stage type-site. However, maize radiocarbon-dated to about 3700 b.p. (2100 BC) has been found in the same level as a Cortaro point and a Chiricahua point in McEuen Cave, located in the Gila Mountains (Huckell et al. 1999).

Regardless of which material culture complex or complexes are associated with its arrival, it is becoming clear that maize agriculture was practiced in this region for at least a millennium before cultigens became a subsistence focus, before crop productivity was increased through labor investments in canals and terraces, before settlements became larger and more permanent, and before village communities became an important social formation. As in many other parts of the world, the transition to agriculture in this region occurred over a long period and had delayed social and economic consequences.

A Tropical Crop Complex and Possible Native Cultigens

Accumulating evidence indicates that, in addition to maize, several other tropical plants and possibly some native plants were also cultivated by early farmers in southeastern Arizona. A fragment of a probable domesticated common bean (*Phaseolus vulgaris*) was recovered from Las Capas (Michael Diehl, personal communication, 2000); a direct radiocarbon date of 2960 ± b.p. (ca. 1200 BC) was obtained from this specimen (Mabry 2004b). Cotton (*Gossypium* sp.) pollen was identified in several San Pedro phase features at the Valley Farm site in the Santa Cruz River floodplain, but it is not certain whether this represents a cultivated Mexican variety or the wild local variety (Cummings and Moutoux 2000). Carbonized seeds of amaranth (*Amaranthus* sp.), possibly a domesticated variety, have been identified in San Pedro phase contexts at Cerro Juanaqueña, in northwestern Chihuahua, Mexico (Hard and Roney 1999a), and this plant may have been cultivated in neighboring southeastern Arizona as well. Stone pipes with residues of what appears to be tobacco (*Nicotiana* sp.)

were also found at Las Capas, but it may be a native wild species (Michael Diehl, personal communication, 2000).

For decades it has been generally thought that maize arrived first in the Southwest, followed by separate arrivals of squash and beans, centuries apart. However, the carbonized fragment of a domesticated common bean and the cotton pollen recently found at San Pedro phase sites in the middle Santa Cruz Valley (see above) and remains of bean, squash, cotton, and tobacco at sites of the subsequent Cienega phase in southeastern Arizona (Cummings and Moutoux 2000; Fish 1998; L. Huckell 1995a, 1998; Phillips 2000) raise the possibility that groups of cultigens arrived together from Mexico in one or more "waves." Squash may eventually be found in San Pedro phase (and earlier) contexts as more samples are recovered. Early agriculture in this region should be conceptualized as a set of agricultural systems that included diverse technologies and techniques, crop complexes, and cultivation systems (Mabry 2004a).

A Broad-Spectrum Subsistence Strategy

In addition to most settlements being located on alluvial landforms that received runoff and overbank floods, the abundance of maize remains, storage pits and roasting pits containing maize remains, and grinding tools with maize residues reflect the importance of maize production at early agricultural sites in this region. However, the flotation samples and faunal assemblages of San Pedro and Cienega phase sites indicate a wider variety of exploited wild plants and animals than is represented at later Hohokam sites (Diehl 1997, 2001; L. Huckell 1995a, 1995b, 1998, 2000; Phillips 2000; Szuter and Bayham 1995; Thiel 1998; Wöcherl 2001). This diversity of wild food resources indicates that the early agriculturalists of southeastern Arizona were also intensive foragers, hunters, and fishers.

Early Water Control

Archaeologists are beginning to find considerable evidence of water control for agriculture and domestic use by early farmers in this region. At Las Capas, a stratified San Pedro phase site excavated in 1998, a sequence of canals constructed between 3100 and 2400 b.p. (1250–600 BC) conveyed water at least a mile from the then-perennial flow of the Santa Cruz River to irrigate fields near the edge of the floodplain (Mabry 1999, 2004b; Figure 3.3). San Pedro phase ditches found at the nearby Costello-King site in 1995 (Ezzo and Deaver 1998) had gradients toward the river, indicating that they diverted runoff from higher

Figure 3.3. Cross section of an early San Pedro phase canal at Las Capas, ca. 1200 BC (Photograph by Ellen Ruble)

ground to fields, drained overbank river floods from fields, or distributed water to fields from a larger, unidentified primary canal to the east. At Cienega phase sites in the same valley, canals (Mabry 2003; Mabry and Archer 1997) and wells (Freeman 1998; Gregory 2001; Haury 1957; Mabry and Archer 1997) indicate exploitation of both surface flows and water tables. The well-developed canal systems of the later Hohokam culture now have a local precedent, and a long history of indigenous development of irrigation technology and techniques is indicated in the northern Sonoran Desert.

Early Terracing of Hillsides

Maize remains and projectile points dating to the Cienega phase were found in deposits behind stone terrace walls on Tumamoc Hill in the western Tucson Basin (Fish et al. 1986; Paul Fish, personal communication, 2000). At Cerro Juanaqueña in northwestern Chihuahua, Mexico, a hill covered with almost 500 terraces is attributed to the San Pedro phase, based on the dominance of the San Pedro type among the large assemblage of projectile points and radio-carbon dates on maize and other annual plants; several nearby terraced hills are also thought to date to this phase (Hard and Roney 1998, 1999a, 1999b; Hard et al. 1999; Roney and Hard 1999). The investigators at both Cerro Juanaqueña and Tumamoc Hill speculate that the terraces created level surfaces for houses and gardens. These hillside terraces represent large labor investments in long-term infrastructures for settlement and agriculture.

Early Ceramic Technology

Fragments of untempered, fired-clay vessels and figurines in the assemblage of the 2100 BC agricultural occupation at the Clearwater site are now the oldest known fired ceramics in the Southwest, rivaling the ages of the oldest ceramics in Mexico. Prior to this discovery, the oldest fired-clay artifacts in the Southwest were figurine fragments found at Milagro (Huckell and Huckell 1984) and Las Capas (Lascaux and Hesse 2001; Mabry 2004b), in early San Pedro phase contexts dated between about 3100 and 2800 b.p. (1250–950 BC). At Las Capas a few sherds of ceramic vessels were found in late San Pedro contexts dated between about 2800 and 2500 b.p. (950–800 BC) (Mabry 2004b).

Evolution of New Technologies, Traits, and Organizations

Continuity from the San Pedro phase is evident in terms of Cienega phase settlement locations and material culture. However, much larger Cienega phase settlements with hundreds of pit structures (but not occupied at the same time) and evidence of settlement planning have been uncovered in the middle Santa Cruz Valley (Gregory 2001; Mabry 2003; Mabry and Archer 1997; Figure 3.4) and the middle Gila Valley (Clark 2000). At these and other Cienega phase sites in southeastern Arizona are the earliest known examples in the Southwest of large, communal-ceremonial structures ("big houses"), courtyard house groups, cremation burials, new types of ground stone vessels and shell ornaments, and possibly plazas and arrowheads. The big houses represent a level of social organization above the household, while jewelry made from marine shell species native only to the Pacific coast and projectile points made from obsidian from distant sources indicate the development of long-distance trade (Mabry 1998c).

David Gregory (1996) has identified an inherent pattern in the radiocarbon record that causes a clustering of dates near 400 BC, and he argues that Cienega phase architecture can be seriated into early and late subphases before and after that date. R. Jane Sliva (2001) has also identified a general difference between early and late Cienega phase lithic assemblages, with late assemblages possibly indicating less processing of game but a greater diversity of activities.

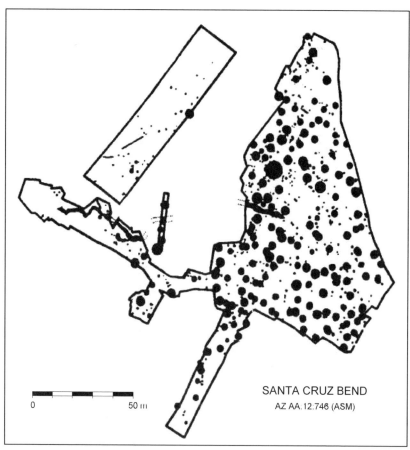

SANTA CRUZ BEND
AZ AA.12.746 (ASM)

0   50 ɪɪɪ

Figure 3.4. Cienega phase pit structures, extramural pits, and other features in the explored areas of the Santa Cruz Bend site (adapted from Mabry and Archer 1997). The relatively large structure has been interpreted as a communal-ceremonial building; the nearby ditch to the south may have drained overflow from a well; a few structures with numerous floor pits were probably specialized storage facilities; some sets of structures have been interpreted as circular house groups sharing central courtyards and storage facilities (Mabry 1998c).

Nonagricultural Sites

Identified outlying basecamps either were used for nonagricultural activities or were used by contemporaneous hunter-gatherer groups that had some material culture traits in common with the agriculturalists living in floodplain settlements. At the Coffee Camp site in the Santa Cruz Flats north of the Tucson Basin, an occupation dating to the interval of the San Pedro phase and having some San Pedro types of material culture did not yield any cultigen remains from numerous flotation samples (Halbirt and Henderson 1993). A few Cienega phase sites in foothill and bajada settings in the Tucson Basin and northern Santa Rita Mountains appear to be seasonal basecamps for hunting deer and procuring and processing upland plant foods (Dart 1986; Huckell 1984a; Roth 1989, 1992, 1995a, 1995b). However, it is also possible that these mid-elevation sites represent the activities of contemporaneous hunter-gatherers (see below).

Discussion

As the pace of discoveries has accelerated, conventional wisdoms have been overturned, and theoretical approaches have changed, many new ideas about the transition to agriculture and settled life in southeastern Arizona have begun to take shape. Their topics reflect how definition of material culture complexes, dating of these complexes and sequences of adaptive changes, and culture histories have become relevant again with the flood of new data and the new requirements of the 1990 Native American Graves Protection and Repatriation Act (NAGPRA) to consult with Native American groups about the cultural affiliations and dispositions of prehistoric human remains. A few ideas that are of particular interest are presented and discussed in this section.

Spatial Variability in Adaptations

Across southeastern Arizona, variation in the resource structures of biotic communities apparently led to local variations in the subsistence-settlement strategies of late Holocene hunter-gatherers and early farmers. In the western part of the region, the Sonoran Desertscrub has relatively low primary productivity of plants but high secondary biomass and high species diversity (Fish and Nabhan 1991). The strongly biseasonal rainfall pattern of the Sonoran Desert also allows for greater structural diversity in plant communities, with more significant arboreal, tall shrub, large cacti, and succulent constituents than in areas of Chihuahuan Desert Grasslands to the east (Turner and Brown 1994). Dominated by low shrubs and grasses, the grasslands have relatively low primary productivity, medium secondary biomass, low species diversity, and more uniform distribution of species across the landscape (Brown 1994d; McClaran 1995). Thus in southeastern Arizona there is a gradient from west to east of decreasing seasonality, species diversity, secondary biomass, and resource "patchiness."

In terms of late Holocene hunting and gathering and early agricultural adaptations, site locations and characteristics suggest that this gradient led to a "collector" (logistical mobility) pattern in the Tucson Basin (Premo and Mabry

2001, 2004), and a forager (residential mobility) pattern in valleys to the east (Mabry and Stevens 2000). Across the region, a dual-zone pattern of settlement was practiced during the Middle Archaic and Late Archaic/Early Agricultural periods, with sites concentrated in riverine/lower bajada settings and on upper bajadas. In the Tucson Basin most multiple-activity, residential sites were located in riverine zones, while upper bajada sites were limited-activity, logistical sites for collecting and processing specific resources. In other basins of southeastern Arizona, some multiple-activity sites were located in riverine/lower bajada zones; but the largest ones were on upper bajadas, and most limited-activity sites were on lower bajadas. The inference that these different patterns represent alternative adaptations to varying resource structures of the environment fits with cross-cultural data on hunter-gatherers. Ethnographic data show that, where resources are patchy and available seasonally, a logistical mobility strategy is most efficient and least risky; where resources are uniformly distributed and available year-round, a residential mobility strategy is optimal (Kelly 1995).

The patterns in southeastern Arizona also fit the predictions of the model presented by Doleman (this volume) to explain the adaptive differences between Archaic groups in southeastern Arizona and south-central New Mexico. In that model, logistical mobility becomes more optimal with increasing temporal, spatial, and stochastic structure of resources; residential mobility becomes more optimal with decreasing structure in these aspects; cyclical residential mobility ("serial foraging") becomes optimal as spatial structure increases but temporal and stochastic structures decrease. With its more even proportions of winter and summer rainfall, greater density of biotic communities, and higher species diversity, southeastern Arizona has better conditions for logistical mobility and serial foraging than does south-central New Mexico (Doleman, this volume). But this model also seems to apply within southeastern Arizona, with its gradient of decreasing seasonality, diversity, secondary biomass, and patchiness of resources from west to east. The model's predictions are met by the contrast between greater logistical mobility of Archaic and Early Agricultural groups in the Tucson Basin and greater cyclical residential mobility of groups in basins to the east.

The early agricultural landscape in southeastern Arizona was also composed of a diverse range of niches. Early cultivation techniques that have been identified or inferred in this region include water-table and flood farming by 3700 b.p. (2100 BC) and irrigated farming by 3100 b.p. (1250 BC); these techniques were significantly different in terms of productivities, risks, labor requirements, and energy efficiencies, and comparisons of these differences allow predictions of the sequences of niche filling and abandonment (Mabry 2004a).

The First Steps toward Sedentism during the Middle Archaic

It has been suggested that in the Tucson Basin and other parts of southern Arizona the high productivity of the Sonoran Desertscrub, the accessibility of other biotic communities, and the storability of wild plant resources may have supported the development of sedentary or semisedentary communities prior to the arrival of maize (Fish and Fish 1991; Fish et al. 1990). In support of this hypothesis are the pit structures, storage pits, and trash middens documented at some Middle Archaic sites in southeastern Arizona. A midden deposit was identified at the Chiricahua stage type-site on the northeastern flank of the Chiricahua Mountains (Sayles and Antevs 1941), and a midden deposit dated between 4840 and 3910 b.p. (3600–2400 BC) contained Chiricahua points and a possible pit structure at the Arroyo site in the Picacho Dune Field (Bayham et al. 1986). An important unresolved question is whether maize remains are present at any of these sites. If maize remains are eventually discovered, as seems increasingly likely, then these sites may instead represent seasonal settlements of incipient agriculturalists that incorporated cultigens into their hunting and gathering subsistence system to create a new subsistence-settlement strategy based on logistical mobility or cyclical residential mobility.

The Origins of Southwestern Villages

Cross-cultural studies indicate that the canal systems and terraces of the San Pedro phase represent reduced residential mobility, increased territoriality, and the development of corporate organization, property ownership, and inheritance rules (Mabry 1996, 2002; Netting 1982). Ethnographic data can also be cited to infer that the large communal-ceremonial structures, courtyard house groups, cemeteries, and possibly plazas present at Cienega phase sites represent the development of social integration above the level of the household (see the references in Mabry 1998c), one of the criteria that have been used to define the threshold of "village" social organization in the prehistoric Southwest (Lightfoot and Feinman 1982; Wills and Windes 1989). These organizational characteristics are more appropriate criteria for defining prehistoric Southwestern "villages" than are specific numbers of inhabitants derived from urban geography models, in which villages are settlements of a certain population size within integrated regional settlement hierarchies.

Old and New Questions

Even with all of this new information and ideas, several old questions remain unanswered, and some important new questions have been raised. What portions of the diets of early farmer-foragers and farmer-collectors were provided by cultigens? What motivated the large labor investments in canals and terraces? How did farmers and hunter-gatherers interact on this agricultural frontier, and were they culturally related? How many people lived together in early settlements? What were the functions of early ceramic figurines and containers? Did all or any of the later village cultures of Southwestern prehistory derive from the early farming culture of southeastern Arizona? This section includes discussions of some similar "big picture" questions.

WAS THERE CONTINUITY BETWEEN THE MIDDLE ARCHAIC
AND LATE ARCHAIC/EARLY AGRICULTURAL PERIODS?

With the possible exceptions of Ventana Cave and Bat Cave (which lie outside of southeastern Arizona), San Pedro phase deposits do not directly overlie Chiricahua phase deposits at any known site, and there is currently a large gap between the latest Chiricahua phase radiocarbon dates and the earliest San Pedro phase dates. However, San Pedro phase deposits may directly overlie deposits containing Chiricahua points and Cortaro bifaces in Ventana Cave and McEuen Cave. At the latter site, those Middle Archaic point types co-occurred with maize. The association of maize with Armijo points and Cortaro bifaces at the Clearwater site also appears to represent the addition of agriculture to a Middle Archaic hunting and gathering base. But the date ranges currently associated with Armijo and Chiricahua points in this region, ca. 3600–2100 BC, still leave a gap of almost a millennium before the appearance of San Pedro material culture. Like the timing of the arrival of agriculture, the transition from the Middle Archaic to the Late Archaic/Early Agricultural period is not well understood at this time.

WAS AN INDIGENOUS CROP COMPLEX DEVELOPED
BY LATE HOLOCENE HUNTER-GATHERERS?

Many researchers have suggested that weedy annuals such as chenopodium and amaranth were cultivated in the Southwest prior to the arrival of tropical cultigens from Mexico (Bohrer 1991; Cordell 1997; Fish et al. 1990; Haury 1962, 1983; Minnis 1992; Toll and Culley 1983; Wills 1995; Winter and Hogan 1986). In this type of transition to agriculture, a new crop or crop complex was introduced into a cultural system that was already partly dependent upon locally domesticated plants, and it displaced or supplemented the older crop complex. Remains of a wide variety of edible weedy annuals are often abundant in flotation samples from the few excavated pre–San Pedro phase sites in southeastern Arizona, but it is not certain whether this variety and abundance represents cultivation, encouragement, or coincidence. The sample sizes from this period are still too small to allow conclusions. The remains of domesticated amaranth and wild or domesticated cotton and tobacco at San Pedro sites, however, may indicate that locally domesticated crops were cultivated alongside tropical cultigens.

DID TROPICAL CULTIGENS ARRIVE IN THIS REGION THROUGH DIFFUSION OR THROUGH MIGRATION?

Some archaeologists have argued that the indigenous hunter-gatherers of the Southwest adopted tropical cultigens from farmers farther south (Ford 1981; Haury 1962; Hunter-Anderson 1986; Irwin-Williams 1973; Kidder 1924; Parry et al. 1994; Wills 1988). In support of this model are the recently identified associations of the earliest directly dated maize in the southern Basin and Range Province with indigenous Southwestern dart-point styles, implying that maize first arrived in the region through diffusion and was adopted by native groups to supplement their hunting and gathering.

Other archaeologists believe that farmers from northern Mexico colonized the southern Basin and Range Province, and then their descendants colonized the Colorado Plateau (Berry 1982; Berry and Berry 1986; Haury 1983; Huckell 1990; Matson 1991, 1999). Bruce Huckell (1990) identifies the north-south–trending river valleys of the southern Basin and Range Province as the paths taken by San Pedro phase farmers spreading floodplain farming techniques northward from Mexico, and Michael Berry (1982) attributes the arrival of agriculture on the Colorado Plateau to the continued northward expansion of that people. R. G. Matson (1991), in a variant of the migration model, argues that the south-to-north migration occurred in stages, as maize varieties and farming techniques were adapted to new climatic and edaphic conditions. Some linguists and archaeologists have linked the spread of agriculture into the Southwest with the northward expansion of Uto-Aztecan–speaking peoples from Mexico during the San Pedro phase (Carpenter et al. 1997, 2000; Hill 1996, 2001).

The recent discoveries of maize as old as 3700 b.p. (2100 BC), and in association with indigenous dart-point styles, challenge the model of the San Pedro people bringing agriculture during a migration northward from Mexico. The San Pedro phase may eventually be reconceptualized as representing a later northward migration or diffusion during the period when a relatively uniform early farming village culture was spreading throughout Mesoamerica. Recognition is growing that, on the northern agricultural frontier of Mexico, maize probably spread through both diffusion and migration—a more plausible scenario than just one of those processes being involved.

Currently there are no known precedents in Mexico for the San Pedro phase canal systems in the middle Santa Cruz Valley; ditches of roughly equal age have been found at a single site in highland Mexico, but in that case they diverted seasonal floods rather than a perennial river flow (Doolittle 1990). Only through systematic subsurface explorations of the floodplains of northern Mexico will we learn whether irrigation technology was also part of the tropical agricultural complex that arrived from Mexico or an indigenous innovation. If the latter, then the early farming culture of the northern Sonoran Desert must be viewed as an important source of cultural change rather than just a secondary agricultural society on the fringe of Mesoamerican civilization.

WERE SOME EARLY AGRICULTURAL GROUPS IN THE REGION TRULY SEDENTARY?

Large numbers of storage pits and thick, extensive, artifact-rich middens are documented at the majority of known San Pedro phase sites and have been interpreted as indicating long-term occupations in riverine zones (Huckell 1990; Mabry 2004b). Formalized uses of space, formal burial areas, communal-ceremonial structures, large numbers of storage pits and specialized storage structures, diverse artifact assemblages representing a wide range of activities, large accumulations of trash, and plant remains representing most seasons of the year have been cited as evidence of year-round occupation of Cienega phase settlements (Huckell 1995; Mabry 1998c). Some of these features may instead represent repeated occupations over long intervals. Relative dating of cultural deposits by measuring the fluoride contents of animal bones demonstrates that "a large number of pit structures, substantial refuse deposits, storage facilities, and burials may have been created by relatively discrete occupations that varied considerably in the number of people present at any given time, the continuity of that presence, and the range of frequency of activities carried out there" (Gregory and Diehl 2000:11). However, canals have been argued to indicate sedentary occupations in at least some well-watered, riverine settings during the San Pedro and Cienega phases (Mabry 2004b).

Whether early agricultural settlements in southeastern Arizona were occupied seasonally or year-round, even for short durations, remains a difficult question to answer. Cross-cultural data on preindustrial agriculturalists show that settlements with canals and other agricultural infrastructures are not ever abandoned completely (Mabry 2002). Other ethnographic data indicate that pit structures and extramural storage pits are associated with seasonal, primarily winter occupations (Gilman 1983). However, botanical remains from early agricultural settlements in southeastern Arizona indicate occupation in every season except winter. Winter occupations are difficult to demonstrate archaeologically (Gregory 2001), but perhaps storage pits filled with maize are the archaeological indicators of winter occupations in this region (L. Huckell 1998). Recent studies comparing the design strategies, technological organizations, and rates of deposition represented by artifact assemblages conclude that the investigated Early Agricultural period sites in southern Arizona represent a wide range of occupation types (Sliva 2004). Other new approaches to addressing this question with archaeological and ethnographic data must also be developed.

HOW DID EARLY FARMERS IN SOUTHEASTERN ARIZONA
USE THE ENTIRE LANDSCAPE?

Current knowledge of San Pedro phase activities is limited to only a few sites located in a single type of landscape setting. To date, limited excavations have been conducted at only ten sites in southeastern Arizona with occupations assignable to the San Pedro phase by a combination of radiocarbon dating, evidence of agriculture, and material culture traits. All of these are buried in alluvial landforms in riparian zones below 3,000 feet in elevation. Some large basecamps in bajada and foothill settings at elevations of up to 5,000 feet have yielded mostly San Pedro points, but none have been excavated. The functions of those sites, and their relationships to the large San Pedro settlements in riparian zones, are unknown. The same observations can be made about the lack of detailed knowledge of landscape use outside of riverine zones during the Cienega phase.

Surveys in the Tucson Basin have identified Late Archaic/Early Agricultural sites in two landscape settings (in riverine zones and in upper bajada zones), and alternative models have been proposed to explain this bimodal pattern. Barbara Roth (1989, 1992, 1995b) suggests that the same groups of farmers exploited both zones. Floodplains were more intensively occupied because of the high labor requirements of agriculture. However, these groups continued to exploit upper bajada resources through either regular expeditions or seasonal occupations. Suzanne Fish et al. (1990, 1992) suggest that the bimodal site pattern represents two independent settlement systems based on agriculture. One system consisted of long-term settlements of sedentary groups practicing floodwater farming on floodplains and adjacent alluvial fans. The other consisted of more frequently shifting settlements of groups focused on dry farming at higher elevations on upper bajadas, with some floodwater farming at the mouths of large mountain canyons.

Lucas Premo and Jonathan Mabry (2001, 2004) used a database with information about sixty-three Late Archaic/Early Agricultural sites in the Tucson

Basin in an attempt to distinguish whether the dual zones of site locations in the Tucson Basin represent a logistical mobility pattern by farming groups (Roth's model), two independent settlement systems based on agriculture (the model of S. Fish et al.), or overlapping logistical and residential mobility patterns by contemporaneous groups of farmers and hunter-gatherers (a third alternative). They concluded that early farmers in the Tucson Basin had a logistical settlement pattern. Sites in riverine zones fit expectations for long-term residential sites (locations near reliable water sources and arable land, high artifact and feature diversities, and large sizes), while upper bajada sites have the expected characteristics of logistical sites (low artifact and feature diversities, small sizes). Models of regional settlement patterns based on survey data are an initial step toward the research goal of understanding how early farmers used the entire landscape, but excavations of sites outside of riverine zones are needed to confirm and expand inferences.

Future Research

Of course, these are only some of the questions now facing archaeologists who are investigating the transition to agriculture and village life in southeastern Arizona. Some answers will likely come from new discoveries in the field, reassessments of old data, new approaches to analysis and interpretation, and comparisons with data coming from other regions. Local details of environmental contexts and changes need to be identified. Sites of early farmers away from floodplains need to be dug, and ways of distinguishing between the logistical sites of farmer task-groups and the residential sites of mobile hunter-gatherers need to be further developed. We need to learn more about late Holocene hunting and gathering groups in the region. Mostly, we need to learn more about the long, unnamed interval of incipient agriculture that preceded the San Pedro phase. It is probable that (based on the answers obtained) some new terms, temporal subdivisions, and explanations will be proposed. What is certain is that archaeologists' knowledge and ideas about the Southwest's "Neolithic" transition will continue to evolve.

REFERENCES CITED

Agogino, George A.
   1960a   The San Jose Sites: A Cochise-like Manifestation in the Middle Rio Grande. *Southwestern Lore* 26:43–48.
   1960b   The Santa Ana Pre-Ceramic Sites: An Archaic Seed-Gathering Culture in Sandoval County, New Mexico. *Southwestern Lore* 25:17–21.

Agogino, George A., and Jim Hester
1953   The Santa Ana Pre-Ceramic Sites. *El Palacio* 60:133–140.
Agogino, George A., and Frank C. Hibben
1958   Central New Mexico Paleo-Indian Cultures. *American Antiquity* 23(4):422–425.
Bahre, Conrad J.
1991   *A Legacy of Change: Historic Human Impact on Vegetation of the Arizona Borderlands.* University of Arizona Press, Tucson.
Bayham, Frank E., Donald H. Morris, and M. Steven Shackley
1986   *Prehistoric Hunter-Gatherers of South Central Arizona: The Picacho Reservoir Archaic Project.* Anthropological Field Studies No. 13. Department of Anthropology, Office of Cultural Resource Management, Arizona State University, Tempe.
Bernard-Shaw, Mary
1989   *Archaeological Investigations at Los Morteros, AZAA:12:57 (ASM), Locus 1, in the Northern Tucson Basin.* Technical Report No. 87-8. Institute for American Research, Tucson.
Berry, Claudia F., and Michael S. Berry
1986   Chronological and Conceptual Models of the Southwestern Archaic. In *Anthropology of the Desert West: Essays in Honor of Jesse D. Jennings,* edited by C. J. Condie and D. D. Fowler, pp. 253–327. Anthropological Papers No. 110. University of Utah Press, Salt Lake City.
Berry, Michael S.
1982   *Time, Space and Transition in Anasazi Prehistory.* University of Utah Press, Salt Lake City.
Bohrer, Vorsila L.
1991   Recently Recognized Cultivated and Encouraged Plants among the Hohokam. *Kiva* 56:227–236.
Bowers, Janice
1980   Catastrophic Freezes in the Sonoran Desert. *Desert Plants* 2(4): 232–236.
Brown, David E.
1994a   *Biotic Communities: Southwestern United States and Northwestern Mexico.* University of Utah Press, Salt Lake City.
1994b   Chihuahuan Desertscrub. In *Biotic Communities: Southwestern United States and Northwestern Mexico,* edited by D. E. Brown, pp. 169–179. University of Utah Press, Salt Lake City.
1994c   Madrean Evergreen Woodland. In *Biotic Communities: South-*

western *United States and Northwestern Mexico,* edited by D. E. Brown, pp. 59–65. University of Utah Press, Salt Lake City.

1994d   Semidesert Grassland. In *Biotic Communities: Southwestern United States and Northwestern Mexico,* edited by D. E. Brown, pp. 123–131. University of Utah Press, Salt Lake City.

1994e   Sonoran Savanna Grassland. In *Biotic Communities: Southwestern United States and Northwestern Mexico,* edited by D. E. Brown, pp. 137–141. University of Utah Press, Salt Lake City.

Campbell, J. M., and F. H. Ellis

1952   The Atrisco Sites: Cochise Manifestations in the Middle Rio Grande Valley. *American Antiquity* 17:211–221.

Carpenter, John P., Guadalupe Sánchez de Carpenter, and Jonathan B. Mabry

1997   The Archaeology of Early Uto-Aztecan Groups. Paper presented at the Friends of Uto-Aztecan Annual Conference, Hermosillo, Mexico, June 19–20.

Carpenter, John P., Guadalupe Sánchez, and María Elisa Villalpando

2000   Of Maize and Migration: Mode and Tempo in the Diffusion of *Zea mays* in Northwest Mexico and the American Southwest. Paper presented at the Seventh Biennial Meeting of the Southwest Symposium, January 13–15, Santa Fe.

Clark, Caven P. (compiler)

2000   *Archaeological Investigations at AZ V:13:201, Town of Kearny, Pinal County, Arizona.* Cultural Resources Report No. 114. Archaeological Consulting Services, Ltd., Tempe, Ariz.

Cooke, Ronald U., and Richard W. Reeves

1976   *Arroyos and Environmental Change in the American Southwest.* Clarendon Press, Oxford.

Cordell, Linda S.

1997   *Archaeology of the Southwest.* Academic Press, San Diego.

Cummings, Linda Scott, and Thomas E. Moutoux

2000   Pollen Analysis. In *Farming through the Ages: 3,400 Years of Agriculture at the Valley Farms Site in the Northern Tucson Basin,* edited by K. D. Wellman, pp. 275–292. SWCA Cultural Resource Report No. 98–226. SWCA, Inc., Tucson.

Dart, Allen

1986   *Archaeological Investigations at La Paloma: Archaic and Hohokam Occupations at Three Sites in the Northeastern Tucson Basin, Arizona.* Anthropological Papers No. 4. Institute for American Research, Tucson.

Davis, O. K., and David S. Shafer

1992   A Holocene Climatic Record for the Sonoran Desert from Pollen Analysis of Montezuma Well, Arizona, USA. *Palaeogeography, Palaeoclimatology, Palaeoecology* 92:107–119.

Dean, Jeffrey S.

1987   The Archaic of Southern Arizona. *Quarterly Review of Archaeology* 8(4):1, 10–14.

Dick, Herbert W.

1951   Evidences of Early Man in Bat Cave and on the Plains of San Augustin, New Mexico. In *Indian Tribes of Aboriginal America*, edited by Sol Tax, pp. 158–163. University of Chicago Press, Chicago.

1965   *Bat Cave.* Monograph 27. School of American Research, Santa Fe.

Diehl, Michael W.

1997   *Archaeological Investigations of an Early Agricultural Period Settlement at the Base of A-Mountain, Tucson, Arizona.* Technical Report No. 96-21. Center for Desert Archaeology, Tucson.

2001   Macrobotanical Remains and Land Use: Subsistence and Strategies for Food Acquisition. In *Excavations in the Santa Cruz River Floodplain: The Early Agricultural Period Component at Los Pozos*, edited by D. A. Gregory, pp. 195–208. Anthropological Papers No. 21. Center for Desert Archaeology, Tucson.

Dobyns, Henry F.

1981   *From Fire to Flood: Historic Human Destruction of Sonoran Desert Riverine Oases.* Anthropological Papers No. 20. Ballena Press, Socorro, N.Mex.

Doelle, William H.

1985   *Excavations at the Valencia Site, a Preclassic Hohokam Village in the Southern Tucson Basin.* Anthropological Papers No. 3. Institute for American Research, Tucson.

Doolittle, William E.

1990   *Canal Irrigation in Prehistoric Mexico: The Sequence of Technological Change.* University of Texas Press, Austin.

Eddy, Frank W., and Maurice E. Cooley

1983   *Cultural and Environmental History of Cienega Valley, Southeastern Arizona.* University of Arizona Anthropological Papers 43. University of Arizona Press, Tucson.

Eggan, Fred

1961   Comment. *Current Anthropology* 2:87.

Elson, Mark D., and William H. Doelle

1987 *Archaeological Assessment of the Mission Road Extension: Testing at AZ BB:13:6 (ASM).* Technical Report No. 87-6. Institute for American Research, Tucson.

Ezell, Paul H.

1954 An Archaeological Survey of Northwestern Papagueria. *Kiva* 19(2–4):1–26.

Ezzo, Joseph A., and William L. Deaver

1998 *Watering the Desert: Late Archaic Farming at the Costello-King Site.* Technical Series 68. Statistical Research, Inc., Tucson.

Fay, George E.

1956 Peralta Complex: A Sonoran Variant of the Cochise Culture. *Science* 124(3230):1029.

1967 *An Archaeological Study of the Peralta Complex in Sonora, Mexico.* Occasional Publications in Anthropology, Archaeology Series 1. Department of Anthropology, Colorado State College, Greeley.

Fish, Paul R., Suzanne K. Fish, Austin Long, and Charles Miksicek

1986 Early Corn Remains from Tumamoc Hill, Southern Arizona. *American Antiquity* 51(3):563–572.

Fish, Suzanne K.

1998 Cultural Pollen. In *Archaeological Investigations of Early Village Sites in the Middle Santa Cruz Valley: Analyses and Synthesis, Part I,* edited by J. B. Mabry, pp. 149–163. Anthropological Papers No. 19. Center for Desert Archaeology, Tucson.

Fish, Suzanne K., and Paul R. Fish

1991 Comparative Aspects of Paradigms for the Neolithic Transition in the Levant and the American Southwest. In *Perspective on the Past: Theoretical Biases in Mediterranean Hunter-Gatherer Research,* edited by G. A. Clark, pp. 396–410. University of Pennsylvania Press, Philadelphia.

Fish, Suzanne K., Paul R. Fish, and John S. Madsen

1990 Sedentism and Settlement Mobility in the Tucson Basin Prior to A.D. 1000. *Perspectives on Southwestern Prehistory,* edited by P. E. Minnis and C. L. Redman, pp. 76–163. Westview Press, Boulder.

1992 Early Sedentism and Agriculture in the Northern Tucson Basin. In *The Marana Community in the Hohokam World,* edited by S. K. Fish, P. R. Fish, and J. H. Madsen, pp. 11–19. Anthropological Papers of the University of Arizona 56. University of Arizona Press, Tucson.

Fish, Suzanne K., and Gary P. Nabhan

1991   Desert as Context: The Hohokam Environment. In *Exploring the Hohokam: Prehistoric Desert Peoples of the American Southwest,* edited by G. J. Gumerman, pp. 29–60. Amerind Foundation, Dragoon, Ariz., and University of New Mexico Press, Albuquerque.

Ford, Richard I.

1981   Gardening and Farming before A.D. 1000: Patterns of Prehistoric Cultivation North of Mexico. *Journal of Ethnobiology* 1(1):6–27.

Freeman, Andrea K. L.

1997   Middle to Late Holocene Stream Dynamics of the Santa Cruz River, Tucson, Arizona: Implications for Human Settlement, the Transition to Agriculture, and Archaeological Site Preservation. Ph.D. dissertation, Department of Anthropology, University of Arizona, Tucson.

1998   *Archaeological Investigations at the Wetlands Site, AZ AA:12:90 (ASM).* Technical Report No. 97-5. Center for Desert Archaeology, Tucson.

Gehlbach, Frederick R.

1981   *Mountain Islands and Desert Seas: A Natural History of the U.S.-Mexican Borderlands.* Texas A&M University Press, College Station.

Gilman, Patricia A.

1983   Changing Architectural Forms in the Prehistoric Southwest. Ph.D. dissertation, Department of Anthropology, University of New Mexico, Albuquerque.

Gregory, David A.

1996   New Issues in the Interpretation of Archaic Period Radiocarbon Dates. Paper presented at the Conference on the Archaic Prehistory of the North American Southwest, University of New Mexico, Albuquerque, October 24–26.

1999   *Excavations in the Santa Cruz River Floodplain: The Middle Archaic Component at Los Pozos.* Anthropological Papers No. 20. Center for Desert Archaeology, Tucson.

2001   *Excavations in the Santa Cruz River Floodplain: The Early Agricultural Period Component at Los Pozos* (editor). Anthropological Papers No. 21. Center for Desert Archaeology, Tucson.

Gregory, David A., and Michael W. Diehl

2000   Duration, Continuity, and Intensity of Occupation at a Late Cienega Phase Settlement in the Santa Cruz River Floodplain. Paper presented at the Southwest Symposium 2000, Santa Fe.

Halbirt, Carl D., and T. Kathleen Henderson (editors)

1993   *Archaic Occupation on the Santa Cruz Flats: The Tator Hills Archaeological Project.* Northland Research, Inc., Flagstaff.

Hard, Robert J., and John R. Roney

1998   A Massive Terraced Village Complex in Chihuahua, Mexico, Dated to 3000 Years Before Present. *Science,* March 13.

1999a   *An Archaeological Investigation of Late Archaic Cerros de Trincheras Sites in Chihuahua, Mexico: Results of the 1998 Investigations.* Report to Consejo de Arqueología, Instituto Nacional de Antropología e Historia. Special Report No. 25. Center for Archaeological Research, University of Texas at San Antonio.

1999b   Cerro Juanaqueña. *Archaeology Southwest* 13(1):4–5.

Hard, Robert J., José E. Zapata, Bruce K. Moses, and John R. Roney

1999   Terrace Construction in Northern Chihuahua, Mexico: 1150 BC and Modern Experiments. *Journal of Field Archaeology* 26(2): 129–146.

Hastings, James R., and Raymond M. Turner

1965   *The Changing Mile: An Ecological Study of Vegetation Change with Time in the Lower Mile of an Arid and Semiarid Region.* University of Arizona Press, Tucson.

Haury, Emil W.

1943   A Possible Cochise-Mogollon-Hohokam Sequence. *Proceedings of the American Philosophical Society* (Philadelphia) 86(2):169–229.

1950   *The Stratigraphy and Archaeology of Ventana Cave.* University of Arizona Press, Tucson.

1957   An Alluvial Site on the San Carlos Indian Reservation, Arizona. *American Antiquity* 23:2–27.

1962   The Greater American Southwest. In *Courses toward Urban Life: Some Archaeological Considerations of Cultural Alternatives,* edited by R. J. Braidwood and G. R. Willey, pp. 106–131. Publications in Anthropology No. 32. Viking Fund, New York.

1983   Concluding Remarks. In *The Cochise Cultural Sequence in Southeastern Arizona,* by E. B. Sayles, pp. 158–166. Anthropological Papers No. 42. University of Arizona Press, Tucson.

Hayden, Julian D.

1956   Notes on the Archaeology of the Central Coast of Sonora, Mexico. *Kiva* 21(3–4):19–23.

Haynes, C. Vance, Jr.

1987   Curry Draw, Cochise County, Arizona: A Late Quaternary Stratigraphic Record of Pleistocene Extinction and Paleo-Indian

Activities. *Geological Society of America Centennial Field Guide– Cordilleran Section,* pp. 23–28. Geological Society of America, n.p.

Haynes, C. Vance, Jr., and Bruce B. Huckell

1986   Sedimentary Successions of the Prehistoric Santa Cruz River, Tucson, Arizona. Open file report. Arizona Bureau of Geology and Mineral Technology, University of Arizona.

Hemmings, E. Thomas, M. D. Robinson, and R. N. Rogers

1968   Field Report on the Pantano Site (AZ EE:2:50). Unpublished MS on file, Arizona State Museum, University of Arizona, Tucson.

Hendrickson, D. A., and W. L. Minckley

1984   Ciénegas: Vanishing Climax Communities of the American Southwest. *Desert Plants* 6:131–175.

Hill, Jane H.

1996   The Prehistoric Differentiation of Uto-Aztecan Languages and the Lexicon of Early Southwestern Agriculture. Paper presented at the 61st Annual Meeting of the Society for American Archaeology, New Orleans.

1997   Dating the Break-up of Southern Uto-Aztecan. Paper presented at the Friends of Uto-Aztecan Annual Conference, INAH Homenaje in Honor of Wick R. Miller, Hermosillo, Sonora, Mexico, June 19–20.

2001   Proto-Uto-Aztecan: A Community of Cultivators in Central Mexico? *American Anthropologist* 103:913–934.

Huckell, Bruce B.

1984a   *The Archaic Occupation of the Rosemont Area, Northern Santa Rita Mountains, Southeastern Arizona.* Archaeological Series No. 147. Vol. 1. Cultural Resource Management Division, Arizona State Museum, University of Arizona, Tucson.

1984b   The Paleo-Indian and Archaic Occupation of the Tucson Basin: An Overview. *Kiva* 49(3–4):133–145.

1988   Late Archaic Archaeology of the Tucson Basin: A Status Report. In *Recent Research of Tucson Basin Prehistory: Proceedings of the Second Tucson Basin Conference,* edited by William H. Doelle and Paul R. Fish, pp. 57–80. Anthropological Papers No. 10. Institute for American Research, Tucson, Ariz.

1990   Late Preceramic Farmer-Foragers in Southeastern Arizona: A Cultural and Ecological Consideration of the Spread of Agriculture into the Arid Southwestern United States. Ph.D. dissertation, University Microfilms, Ann Arbor.

1995 *Of Marshes and Maize: Preceramic Agricultural Settlements in the Cienega Valley, Southeastern Arizona.* Anthropological Papers No. 59. University of Arizona Press, Tucson.

1996 The Archaic Prehistory of the North American Southwest. *Journal of World Prehistory* 10(3):305–373.

1998 Alluvial Stratigraphy of the Santa Cruz Bend Reach. In *Archaeological Investigations of Early Village Sites in the Middle Santa Cruz Valley: Analyses and Synthesis,* edited by Jonathan B. Mabry, pp. 31–56. Anthropological Papers No. 19. Center for Desert Archaeology, Tucson.

Huckell, Bruce B., and Lisa W. Huckell

1984 Excavations at Milagro, a Late Archaic Site in the Eastern Tucson Basin. Unpublished ms. on file, Arizona State Museum, University of Arizona, Tucson.

Huckell, Bruce B., Lisa W. Huckell, and Suzanne K. Fish

1995 *Investigations at Milagro, a Late Preceramic Site in the Eastern Tucson Basin.* Technical Report No. 94-5. Center for Desert Archaeology, Tucson.

Huckell, Bruce B., Lisa W. Huckell, and M. Steven Shackley

1999 McEuen Cave. *Archaeology Southwest* 13(1):12.

Huckell, Lisa W.

1995a Farming and Foraging in the Cienega Valley: Early Agricultural Period Paleoethnobotany. In *Of Marshes and Maize, Preceramic Agricultural Settlements in the Cienega Valley, Southeastern Arizona,* by Bruce B. Huckell, pp. 74–97. Anthropological Papers No. 59. University of Arizona, Tucson.

1995b Paleoethnobotanical Analysis. In *Investigations at Milagro, a Late Preceramic Site in the Eastern Tucson Basin,* by Bruce B. Huckell, Lisa W. Huckell, and Suzanne K. Fish, pp. 33–40. Technical Report No. 94-5. Center for Desert Archaeology, Tucson.

1998 Macrobotanical Remains. In *Archaeological Investigations of Early Village Sites in the Middle Santa Cruz Valley: Analyses and Synthesis,* edited by Jonathan B. Mabry, pp. 57–148. Anthropological Papers No. 19. Center for Desert Archaeology, Inc.

2000 Early Agricultural Period Paleoethnobotany. In *Farming through the Ages: 3,400 Years of Agriculture at the Valley Farms Site in the Northern Tucson Basin,* edited by K. D. Wellman, pp. 227–273. SWCA Cultural Resource Report No. 98-226. SWCA, Inc., Tucson.

Hunter-Anderson, Rosalind L.

1986   *Prehistoric Adaptations in the American Southwest.* Cambridge University Press, Cambridge.

Irwin-Williams, Cynthia

1973   *The Oshara Tradition: Origins of Anasazi Culture.* Eastern New Mexico University Contributions in Anthropology 5(1). Paleo-Indian Institute, Eastern New Mexico University, Portales.

1979   Post-Pleistocene Archeology, 7000–2000 B.C. In *Southwest,* edited by Alfonso Ortiz, pp. 31–43. *Handbook of North American Indians,* vol. 9, edited by William G. Sturtevant. Smithsonian Institution, Washington, D.C.

James, Steven R.

1993   Archaeofaunal Analysis of the Tator Hills Sites, South-Central Arizona. In *Archaic Occupation in the Santa Cruz Flats: The Tator Hills Archaeological Project,* edited by C. D. Halbirt and T. K. Henderson, pp. 345–371. Northland Research, Flagstaff, Ariz.

Jennings, Jesse D.

1967   Review of Bat Cave. *American Antiquity* 32:123.

Johnson, Alfred E.

1963   The Trincheras Culture of Northern Sonora. *American Antiquity* 29:174–186.

1966   Archaeology of Sonora, Mexico. In *Archaeological Frontiers and External Connections,* edited by Gordon F. Eckholm and Gordon R. Willey, pp. 26–37. *Handbook of Middle American Indians,* vol. 4. University of Texas Press, Austin.

Johnson, Frederick

1955   Reflections on the Significance of Radiocarbon Dates. In *Radiocarbon Dating,* by Willard F. Libby, pp. 141–162. University of Chicago Press, Chicago.

Kelly, Robert L.

1995   *The Foraging Spectrum: Diversity in Hunter-Gatherer Lifeways.* Smithsonian Institution Press, Washington, D.C.

Kidder, Alfred V.

1924   *An Introduction to the Study of Southwestern Archaeology, with a Preliminary Account of the Excavations at Pecos.* Papers of the Southwest Expedition 1. Yale University Press, New Haven, Conn.

Lascaux, Annick, and India Hesse

2001   *The Early San Pedro Phase Village: Las Capas, AZ AA:12:111 (ASM).* SWCA Cultural Resource Report No. 01-100. (Draft.)

Lehmer, Donald J.

1948   *The Jornada Branch of the Mogollon.* Social Science Bulletin 17, University of Arizona Bulletin 19(2). University of Arizona, Tucson.

Lightfoot, Kent G., and Gary M. Feinman

1982   Social Differentiation and Leadership Development in Early Pithouse Villages in the Mogollon Region of the American Southwest. *American Antiquity* 47(1):64–86.

Mabry, Jonathan B.

1990   *A Late Archaic Occupation at AZ AA:12:105 (ASM).* Technical Report No. 90-6. Center for Desert Archaeology, Tucson.

1996   The Ethnology of Local Irrigation. In *Canals and Communities: Small-scale Irrigation Systems,* edited by J. B. Mabry, pp. 3–30. University of Arizona Press, Tucson.

1998a   *Archaeological Investigations of Early Village Sites in the Middle Santa Cruz Valley: Analyses and Synthesis* (editor). Anthropological Papers No. 19. Center for Desert Archaeology, Tucson.

1998b   Archaic Complexes of the Middle Holocene. In *Paleoindian and Archaic Sites in Arizona,* by J. B. Mabry, pp. 65–72. Arizona State Parks, State Historic Preservation Office, Phoenix.

1998c   Conclusion. In *Archaeological Investigations of Early Village Sites in the Middle Santa Cruz Valley: Analyses and Synthesis,* edited by J. B. Mabry, pp. 757–792. Anthropological Papers 19. Center for Desert Archaeology, Tucson.

1998d   Late Quaternary Environmental Periods. In *Paleoindian and Archaic Sites in Arizona,* by J. B. Mabry, pp. 19–31. Arizona State Parks, State Historic Preservation Office, Phoenix.

1999   Las Capas and Early Irrigation Farming. *Archaeology Southwest* 13(1):14.

2002   The Role of Irrigation in the Transition to Agriculture and Sedentism in the Southwest: A Risk Management Model. In *Traditions, Transitions, and Technologies: Themes in Southwestern Archaeology,* edited by S. H. Schlanger, pp. 178–199. University Press of Colorado, Boulder.

2003   Rio Nuevo Archaeological Program: Summary of Data Recovery Results from the Clearwater Site. Report to the City of Tucson. On file, Desert Archaeology, Inc., Tucson.

2004a   Diversity in Early Southwestern Farming Systems and Optimization Models of Transitions to Agriculture. In *Early Agricultural Period Environment and Subsistence,* edited by M. W. Diehl.

Anthropological Papers No. 34. Center for Desert Archaeology, Tucson. (Draft.)

2004b   *Las Capas: Early Irrigation and Sedentism in a Southwestern Floodplain* (editor). Anthropological Paper No. 28. Center for Desert Archaeology, Tucson. (Draft.)

Mabry, Jonathan B., and Gavin H. Archer

1997   The Santa Cruz Bend Site, AZ AA:12:746 (ASM). In *Archaeological Investigations of Early Village Sites in the Middle Santa Cruz Valley: Descriptions of the Santa Cruz Bend, Square Hearth, Stone Pipe, and Canal Sites,* by J. B. Mabry, D. L. Swartz, H. Wöcherl, J. J. Clark, G. H. Archer, and M. W. Lindeman, pp. 9–228. Anthropological Papers No. 18. Center for Desert Archaeology, Tucson.

Mabry, Jonathan B., Michael W. Lindeman, and Helga Wöcherl

1999   *Prehistoric Uses of a Developing Floodplain: Archaeological Investigations on the East Bank of the Santa Cruz River at A-Mountain.* Technical Report No. 98-10. Desert Archaeology, Inc., Tucson.

Mabry, Jonathan B., and Michelle N. Stevens

2000   The Archaeology of Archaic Hunter-Gatherers and Early Farmers in Southeastern Arizona. In *The Archaeology of a Land Between: Regional Dynamics in the History and Prehistory of Southeastern Arizona,* edited by Henry D. Wallace and Anne I. Woosley. Amerind Foundation, Dragoon, Ariz., and University of New Mexico Press, Albuquerque. (Draft.)

Mabry, Jonathan B., Deborah L. Swartz, Helga Wöcherl, Jeffrey J. Clark, Gavin H. Archer, and Michael W. Lindeman

1997   *Archaeological Investigations of Early Village Sites in the Middle Santa Cruz Valley: Descriptions of the Santa Cruz Bend, Square Hearth, Stone Pipe, and Canal Sites.* Anthropological Papers No. 18. Center for Desert Archaeology, Tucson.

Martin, Paul S.

1963   *The Last 10,000 Years.* University of Arizona Press, Tucson.

Martin, Paul S., John B. Rinaldo, and Ernst Antevs

1949   *Cochise and Mogollon Sites: Pine Lawn Valley, Western New Mexico.* Fieldiana: Anthropology 38(1). Field Museum of Natural History, Chicago.

1952   *Mogollon Cultural Continuity and Change: The Stratigraphic Analysis of Tularosa and Cordova Caves.* Fieldiana: Anthropology 40. Field Museum of Natural History, Chicago.

Martin, Paul S., and James Schoenwetter
1960   Arizona's Oldest Cornfield. *Science* 132(3418):33–34.
Matson, R. G.
1991   *The Origins of Southwestern Agriculture.* University of Arizona Press, Tucson.
1999   The Spread of Maize to the Colorado Plateau. *Archaeology Southwest* 13(1):10–11.
McClaran, Mitchel P.
1995   Desert Grasslands and Grasses. In *The Desert Grassland,* edited by M. P. McClaran and T. R. Van Devender, pp. 1–30. University of Arizona Press, Tucson.
McDonald, James E.
1956   *Variability of Precipitation in an Arid Region: A Survey of Characteristics for Arizona.* Technical Report 1. University of Arizona Institute of Atmospheric Physics, Tucson.
Mehringer, Peter J., Jr., and C. Vance Haynes, Jr.
1965   The Pollen Evidence for the Environment of Early Man and Extinct Mammals at the Lehner Mammoth Site, Southeastern Arizona. *American Antiquity* 31(1):17–23.
Mehringer, P. J., Jr., P. Martin, and C. V. Haynes
1967   Murray Springs, a Mid-Postglacial Pollen Record from Southern Arizona. *American Journal of Science* 265:786–797.
Miller, Wick R.
1983   Uto-Aztecan Languages. In *Southwest,* edited by A. Ortiz, pp. 113–124. *Handbook of North American Indians,* vol. 10, W. C. Sturtevant, general editor. Smithsonian Institution, Washington, D.C.
Minnis, Paul E.
1985   Domesticating People and Plants in the Greater Southwest. In *Prehistoric Food Production in North America,* edited by R. Ford, pp. 309–340. Anthropological Papers No. 75. Museum of Anthropology, University of Michigan, Ann Arbor.
1992   Earliest Plant Cultivation in the Desert Borderlands of North America. In *The Origins of Agriculture: An International Perspective,* edited by C. W. Cowan and P. J. Watson, pp. 121–141. Smithsonian Institution Press, Washington, D.C.
Netting, Robert McC.
1982   Territory, Property, and Tenure. In *Behavioral and Social Science Research: A National Resource,* ed. R. McC. Adams, N. Smelser, and D. Treiman, pp. 446–502. National Academy Press, Washington, D.C.

Parry, W. J., F. E. Smiley, and G. R. Burgett

1994   The Archaic Occupation of Black Mesa, Arizona. In *Archaic Hunter-Gatherer Archaeology in the American Southwest,* edited by B. J. Vierra, 185–230. Contributions in Anthropology No. 13(1). Eastern New Mexico University, Portales.

Pase, Charles P., and David E. Brown

1994a   Interior Chaparral. In *Biotic Communities: Southwestern United States and Northwestern Mexico,* edited by D. E. Brown, pp. 95–99. University of Utah Press, Salt Lake City.

1994b   Rocky Mountain (Petran) and Madrean Montane Conifer Forests. In *Biotic Communities: Southwestern United States and Northwestern Mexico,* edited by D. E. Brown, pp. 43–48. University of Utah Press, Salt Lake City.

1994c   Rocky Mountain (Petran) Subalpine Conifer Forest. In *Biotic Communities: Southwestern United States and Northwestern Mexico,* edited by D. E. Brown, pp. 37–39. University of Utah Press, Salt Lake City.

Phillips, Bruce G.

2000   Archaeobotany. In *Archaeological Investigations at AZ V:13:201, Town of Kearny, Pinal County, Arizona,* compiled by C. V. Clark, pp. 5-1 to 5-30. Cultural Resources Report No. 114, Archaeological Consulting Services, Tempe, Ariz.

Premo, Lucas S., and Jonathan B. Mabry

2001   Modeling Landscape Use by Early Farmer-Foragers in the Tucson Basin: A GIS Approach. Poster presented at the 66th Annual Meeting of the Society for American Archaeology, April 18–22, New Orleans.

2004   Modeling Landscape Use by Early Farmer-Collectors in the Tucson Basin. In *Las Capas: Early Irrigation and Sedentism in a Southwestern Floodplain,* edited by J. B. Mabry. Anthropological Paper No. 28. Center for Desert Archaeology, Tucson.

Rogers, Malcolm J.

1958   San Dieguito Implements from the Terraces on the Rincon Pantano and Rillito Drainage System. *Kiva* 24(1):1–23.

1966   *Ancient Hunters of the Far West.* San Diego Union-Tribune, San Diego.

Roney, John R., and Robert J. Hard

1999   Northwestern Mexico: New Perspectives on the Late Archaic from Cerro Juanaqueña. Paper presented at the 64th Annual

Meeting of the Society for American Archaeology, March 24–28, Chicago.

Roth, Barbara J.

1989   Late Archaic Settlement and Subsistence in the Tucson Basin. Ph.D. dissertation, Department of Anthropology, University of Arizona, Tucson.

1992   Sedentary Agriculturalists or Mobile Hunter-Gatherers?: Recent Evidence of the Late Archaic Occupation of the Northern Tucson Basin. *Kiva* 57(4):291–314.

1995a   Late Archaic Occupation of the Upper Bajada: Excavations at AZ AA:12:84 (ASM), Tucson Basin. *Kiva* 61(2):189–207.

1995b   Regional Land Use in the Late Archaic of the Tucson Basin: A View from the Upper Bajada. In *Early Formative Adaptations in the Southern Southwest,* edited by B. J. Roth, 37–48. Monographs in World Archaeology No. 5. Prehistory Press, Madison, Wis.

Sayles, Edwin B.

1983   *The Cochise Cultural Sequence in Southeastern Arizona.* Anthropological Papers No. 42. University of Arizona, Tucson.

Sayles, Edwin B., and Ernst V. Antevs

1941   *The Cochise Culture.* Medallion Papers 29. Gila Pueblo, Globe, Ariz.

Schoenwetter, J.

1962   The Pollen Analysis of Eighteen Archaeological Sites in Arizona and New Mexico. In *Chapters in the Prehistory of Eastern New Mexico, I,* by P. S. Martin et al., pp. 168–209. Fieldiana: Anthropology 53. Chicago Natural History Museum, Chicago.

Sellers, William D., Richard H. Hill, and Margaret Sanderson-Rae

1985   *Arizona Climate: The First Hundred Years.* University of Arizona Press, Tucson.

Shreve, Forrest, and Ira L. Wiggins

1964   *Vegetation of the Sonoran Desert.* Stanford University Press, Stanford, Calif.

Sliva, R. Jane

2001   Flaked Stone Artifacts. In *The Early Agricultural Period Component at Los Pozos,* edited by D. A. Gregory. Anthropological Papers No. 21. Desert Archaeology, Inc., Tucson.

2004   *Material Culture of Early Farming Communities in Southern Arizona: Traces of a New Lifeway, 1200 b.c.–a.d. 50* (editor). Anthropological Papers No. 35. Center for Desert Archaeology.

Stevens, Michelle N.
1999   Spectacular Results from Modest Remains. *Archaeology Southwest* 13(1):4–5.
2000a   Cienega Valley Survey Report. Unpublished manuscript on file, Center for Desert Archaeology, Tucson. (Draft.)
2000b   The Sweetwater Locus at AZ AA:12:91 (ASM). In *Further Investigations at Los Pozos,* edited by David Gregory. Anthropological Papers No. 28. Desert Archaeology, Inc., Tucson, Ariz. (Draft.)

Szuter, Christine R., and Frank E. Bayham
1989   Sedentism and Prehistoric Animal Procurement among Desert Horticulturalists of the North American Southwest. In *Farmers as Hunters: The Implications of Sedentism,* edited by S. Kent, pp. 80–95. Cambridge University Press, Cambridge.
1995   Faunal Exploitation during the Late Archaic and Early Ceramic/Pioneer Periods in South-Central Arizona. In *Early Formative Adaptations in the Southern Southwest,* edited by Barbara J. Roth, pp. 65–72. Monographs in World Archaeology No. 5. Prehistory Press, Madison, Wis.

Thiel, J. Homer
1998   Faunal Remains. In *Archaeological Investigations of Early Village Sites in the Middle Santa Cruz Valley: Analyses and Synthesis,* edited by J. B. Mabry, 165–208. Anthropological Papers No. 19, Part 1. Center for Desert Archaeology, Tucson.

Toll, M. S., and A. C. Culley
1983   Archaic Subsistence in the Four Corners Area: Evidence for a Hypothetical Seasonal Round. In *Economy and Interaction along the Lower Chaco River,* edited by P. Hogan and J. C. Winter, pp. 385–392. Office of Contract Archeology, University of New Mexico, Albuquerque.

Turner, Raymond M., and David E. Brown
1994   Sonoran Desertscrub. In *Biotic Communities: Southwestern United States and Northwestern Mexico,* edited by D. E. Brown, pp. 181–221. University of Utah Press, Salt Lake City.

Van Devender, Thomas R.
1990   Late Quaternary Vegetation and Climate of the Sonoran Desert, United States and Mexico. In *Packrat Middens: The Last 40,000 Years of Biotic Change,* edited by J. L. Betancourt, T. R. Van Devender, and P. S. Martin, pp. 134–165. University of Arizona Press, Tucson.

Waters, Michael R.

1986a   Geoarchaeological Investigations of the Picacho Study Area. In *Prehistoric Hunter-Gatherers of South Central Arizona: The Picacho Reservoir Project*, edited by F. E. Bayham, D. H. Morris, and M. S. Shackley, pp. 17–35. Anthropological Field Studies No. 13. Office of Cultural Resource Management, Department of Anthropology, Arizona State University, Tempe.

1986b   *The Geoarchaeology of Whitewater Draw, Arizona.* Anthropological Papers No. 45. University of Arizona Press, Tucson.

1987   Holocene Alluvial Geology and Geo-archaeology of AZ BB:13:14 and the San Xavier Reach of the Santa Cruz River, Arizona. In *The Archaeology of the San Xavier Bridge Site (AZ BB:13:14) Tucson Basin, Southern Arizona*, edited by J. Ravesloot, pp. 39–60. Archaeology Series 171. CRM Division, Arizona State Museum, Tucson.

1989   Late Quaternary Lacustrine History and Paleoclimatic Significance of Pluvial Lake Cochise, Southeastern Arizona. *Quaternary Research* 32:1–11.

Wellman, Kevin D. (editor)

2000   *Farming through the Ages: 3,400 Years of Agriculture at the Valley Farms Site in the Northern Tucson Basin.* Cultural Resource Report No. 98-226. SWCA, Inc., Tucson.

Wendorf, Fred, and Tully H. Thomas

1951   Early Man Sites near Concho, Arizona. *American Antiquity* 17(2):107–114.

Whalen, Norman M.

1971   Cochise Culture Sites in the Central San Pedro Drainage, Arizona. Ph.D. dissertation, University of Arizona, Tucson.

Wills, Wirt H.

1988   *Early Prehistoric Agriculture in the American Southwest.* School of American Research Press, Santa Fe.

1995   Archaic Foraging and the Beginning of Food Production in the American Southwest. In *Last Hunters, First Farmers: New Perspectives on the Prehistoric Transition to Agriculture*, edited by T. D. Price and A. B. Gebauer, pp. 215–242. School of American Research Press, Santa Fe.

Wills, Wirt H., and Thomas C. Windes

1989   Evidence for Population Aggregation and Dispersal during the Basketmaker III Period in Chaco Canyon, New Mexico. *American Antiquity* 54(2):347–369.

Winter, Joseph C., and Patrick F. Hogan

1986 Plant Husbandry in the Great Basin and Adjacent Northern Colorado Plateau. In *Anthropology of the Desert West: Essays in Honor of Jesse D. Jennings,* edited by C. J. Condie and D. D. Fowler, pp. 117–144. Anthropological Papers No. 110. University of Utah Press, Salt Lake City.

Wöcherl, Helga

2001 Faunal Remains. In *Excavations in the Santa Cruz River Floodplain: The Early Agricultural Period Component at Los Pozos,* edited by David A. Gregory, pp. 209–236. Anthropological Papers No. 21. Center for Desert Archaeology, Tucson.

Wöcherl, Helga, and Jeffery J. Clark

1997 The Square Hearth Site, AZ AA:12:745 (ASM). In *Archaeological Investigations of Early Village Sites in the Middle Santa Cruz Valley: Descriptions of the Santa Cruz Bend, Square Hearth, Stone Pipe, and Canal Sites,* by J. B. Mabry, D. L. Swartz, H. Wöcherl, J. J. Clark, G. H. Archer, and M. W. Lindeman, pp. 229–280. Anthropological Papers No. 18. Center for Desert Archaeology, Tucson.

Woodbury, Richard B., and Ezra B. W. Zubrow

1979 Agricultural Beginnings, 2000 BC–AD 500. In *Handbook of North American Indians,* vol. 9, *Southwest,* edited by A. Ortiz, pp. 43–60. W. C. Sturtevant, general editor. Smithsonian Institution, Washington, D.C.

CHAPTER 4

A Biological Reconstruction of Mobility Patterns in Late Archaic Populations

MARSHA D. OGILVIE

Introduction

One of the most important economic, social, and biological transitions in human history is the shift from food-collecting to food-producing systems. As food production required some degree of sedentism, this transition had a major impact on traditional hunter-gatherer lifeways (Binford 1980, 2001; Kelly 1995). The archaeological evidence from the deserts of the American Southwest indicates a major change in the behavioral repertoire of highly mobile Late Archaic populations during the late centuries BC (Huckell 1983, 1990). This first archaeologically detectable evidence of seasonal residential stability saw the incorporation of a new variant, maize (*Zea* sp.), into the hunting and gathering adaptive strategy (B. Huckell 1995; Wills et al. 1996). It has been suggested that agriculture may have enhanced hunter-gatherer productivity in these complex mixed economic systems (Wills and Huckell 1994).

Competing models regarding the interpretation of the archaeologically derived evidence bring the economic organization of incipient Southwestern farmers into question. Were they committed agriculturalists living in settled villages or seasonally mobile groups using agriculture as a buffer to wild resources? This chapter proposes to biologically elucidate the changes in economic structure that facilitated the transition to a more sedentary lifeway.

Background

Traditionally, attempts to reconstruct the economic organization of past human groups have relied on artifactual evidence in conjunction with ethnographic analogy. An accurate reconstruction requires a clear understanding of the behavioral dichotomy in male and female subsistence roles documented in the ethnographic literature (Murdock and Provost 1973). The constraints associated with reproductive biology contribute to behavioral sex differences that shape the division of labor, resulting in limited spatial range for females (Draper and Cashden 1988; Edwards and Whiting 1980; Ember 1983; Ember and Ember 1976; Hilton and Greaves 1995; Hurtado and Hill 1990; Hurtado et al. 1992; Munroe et al. 1984). Subsistence tasks assigned to females are those that are compatible with simultaneous childcare and do not require long-range travel or put children at risk (Brown 1970). Conversely, males tend to perform subsistence tasks that quite often require long-range travel, absence from the home, and increased risk to the individual (see the review in Gaulin and Hoffman 1988; Murdock and Provost 1973).

Generally these traditional approaches have not utilized an important archaeologically derived resource, the human skeletal remains. Bone biology research indicates a clear link between cultural behavior and skeletal morphology (see review in Larsen 1997; Ruff 2000a). The skeleton continually remodels throughout life in response to the forces or loadings imposed by habitual physical activities, such as those associated with repetitive locomotor behavior (Ruff 1992; Ruff et al. 1994; Trinkaus et al. 1994). Bone remodeling results in a skeletal system better adapted to its biomechanical or functional environment, while maintaining an osseous record of its loading history (Chamay and Tschantz 1972). The loading history contained in the geometric structure of the femur is a direct link to past behavior.

Structural geometry research confirms that shifts in subsistence strategies can equate with profound behavioral changes that are accompanied by concomitant size and shape remodeling in the femur (see review in Larsen 1997; Ruff et al. 1994). There is a well-documented trend in increasing gracilization of the lower limb through time (Ruff et al. 1993). It is widely recognized that this trend is associated with the transition from a mobile foraging to a more sedentary farming lifeway (Larsen 1997; Larsen and Kelly 1995). Figure 4.1 illustrates the thick cortical bone from the femur of a highly physically active fossil hominid that clearly contrasts with the relatively thin cortical bone characteristic of sedentary postindustrialized humans (Brock and Ruff 1988; Ruff et al. 1993; Trinkaus et al. 1994). Many researchers document a positive correlation between the amount of maize consumed and the decrease in upper and lower limb strength (see the review in Bridges 1995; Fresia et al. 1990; Ruff et al. 1994; Ruff and Larsen 1990).

The gender-specific dichotomy in mobility roles results in large size and shape differences between the sexes in the femur. Given the tendency for long-range travel and absence from the home, males are characterized by more robust and ovoid-shaped femoral midshafts than those of females (Ruff 1987). Sex differences due to differential "on foot" mobility essentially disappear in modern transportation-dependent people.

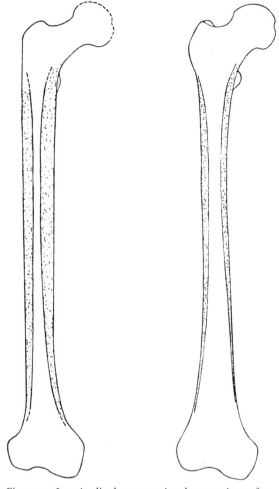

Figure 4.1. Longitudinal cross-sectional comparison of an early *Homo* femur (*left*) and a contemporary postindustrialized human femur (*right*). Note the thickness differences. (Modified from Ruff et al. 1993 with permission of the author)

Archaeological Application

The foraging to farming transition in the American Southwest provides an appropriate setting to test hypotheses regarding the processes by which early agricultural systems developed. Recent archaeological investigations in southeastern Arizona unearthed the oldest skeletal series recovered in association with pre–200 BC maize. The economic context here has been described as "transitional," based on lines of archaeologically derived evidence for mixed foraging and farming strategies (B. Huckell 1995; L. Huckell 1995; Mabry 1998). These rare remains of Late Archaic males and females provide, for the first time, the opportunity to biologically examine the impact of domestication on highly mobile hunter-gatherer lifeways.

Samples

Three skeletal series were selected for comparative study. In the best of all worlds, inclusion of a Hohokam sample would have been ideal; but their practice of cremation did not allow their inclusion. The series represent analogs for three distinct economic stages seen in the American Southwest: foraging, seasonally occupied villages, and permanent agricultural settlements. Figure 4.2 presents an overview of the study area. The mobile foragers and more sedentary late agriculturalists serve as a baseline of comparison for the economically transitional sample.

The small sample sizes involved in this study are a result of the paucity of preserved human remains from the Late Archaic period. Sample sizes were further exacerbated by the need to confine all individuals to similar geographic

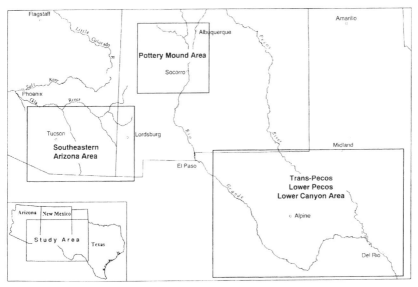

Figure 4.2. Overview map of the study area. Boxes highlight the three study sites. (Courtesy of R. Stauber)

regions to minimize the confounding effects of terrain, genetic variation in local populations, and regional variability in subsistence practices (Bridges 1995; Ruff 2000a). For this reason, the chronological placement of all individuals sampled is not always contemporaneous but is the "universe" for this temporal period.

The appropriateness of comparing the three selected samples was verified using statistical methods. Prior to the use of statistical comparisons, it was necessary to ascertain the effects of both sex and subsistence on bone structure. This was accomplished by standardizing the cross-sectional measurements to account for the expected difference in body size between males and females. The straightforward method of scaling by powers of bone length was chosen for this analysis (Ruff 2000a, 2000b). Such methodology is theoretically sound and appropriate when comparisons are between individuals of similar body shape and size.

As mentioned, similarities in both genetic background and geographical region were important considerations during sample selection to minimize individual shape differences (Ruff 2000a). Descriptive statistical comparisons of length and cross-sectional property values suggest body shape similarity per low coefficients of variation in the pooled sample. Shape similarity was confirmed when a comparison of femoral Anterior/Posterior head diameter versus femoral length found no significant differences among the populations sampled.

Skeletal Series

The Preagriculturalists

The preagriculturalists ($n = 42$) are represented by 19 males and 23 females who traversed the arid landscape of the Trans- and Lower Pecos regions of Southwest Texas, where agriculture was never prehistorically incorporated into the economy. The majority of the burials were recovered from dry rock shelters dating to the Blue Hills Phase of the Late Archaic, ca. 2300 to 1300 BPD (Collins and Labadie 1999; Steele and Olive 1989; Turpin 1986, 1988, 1992, 1995). A drying trend at the end of the Pleistocene established arid grasslands mixed with desert succulent plant communities (Bryant 1986a, 1986b; Shafer 1986a). Hundreds of caves and overhangs in this karstic system provided shelter for the small bands of foragers who first inhabited this area.

As in all arid regions, settlement and subsistence were tempered by the location and availability of water sources (Bayham and Morris 1990; Carmichael 1990; Hard 1990; Speth 1990; Taylor 1964; Vierra 1990). The Rio

Grande, Devil's, and Pecos Rivers provided a reliable supply of water, critical in this otherwise arid setting. Foragers in such desert environments where there is no agriculture must move frequently to take advantage of seasonally available resources (Kelly 1983, 1995). Repeated use sites near critical resource locations, rather than long-term occupations, attest to seasonally fluctuating hunting and gathering forays for small animals and desert plants (Binford 1980; Marmaduke 1978).

Dry conditions in the Pecos preserved perishable artifacts and a wealth of plant and animal remains in the cultural deposits of the dry rock shelters (Ward 1992). Botanical and faunal studies revealed that the basic diet consisted of Carbon 4 (C_4)– and Crassulacean Acid Metabolism (CAM)–rich plants and the animals that consumed them, predominantly rodents, lagomorphs, and fish (Huebner 1991, 1995a, 1995b). Plants with a C_4 photosynthetic pathway include grasses and seeds, while CAM plants are primarily desert succulents. Palynological, paleofecal, and dental microwear studies indicate that sotol (*Dasylirion texanum*), agave (*Agave scabra*), prickly pear (*Opuntia phaecantha*), and lechuguilla (*Agave lechuguilla*) were heavily exploited CAM plants that were a mainstay in the Pecos diet for thousands of years (Bryant 1974, 1986a, 1986b; Danielson and Reinhard 1998; Dering 1979, 1999, this volume; Hartenady and Rose 1991; Riskind 1970; Stock 1984; Storey and Bryant 1966; Williams-Dean 1978). Sotol and lechuguilla were particularly valuable, as they represent one of the few food resources that could be harvested year-round (Huebner 1995a).

The sexual division of labor in the Pecos region is projected from archaeological evidence, coupled with ethnographically documented cases of task specificity in male and female hunter-gatherers (Brown 1970; Murdock and Provost 1973; Shafer 1986b). Observations of desert succulent processing by present-day groups living near the South Texas/Mexican border support the above documented cases (T. Kludt, personal communication, 2000). Procuring and processing fibrous desert succulents is a labor-intensive task requiring the participation of both males and females (Brown 1991; T. Kludt, personal communication, 2002). High group mobility is implied by the necessity of travel to distant plant locations. As the roasting process took several days, all members of the group camped, foraged, and hunted near the earth-oven locations (Dering 1999; Shafer 1986b). Burned rock middens and charred remains of lechuguilla and sotol have been found by the thousands in cultural deposits in Southwest Texas (Vierra 1998).

Strategic site locations in an ecotone provided hunting and foraging opportunities for males and females to exploit riverine, upland, and valley resources. This required frequent travel between these zones. The limited riparian and cienega plant communities, including seeds from a variety of grasses, were either clustered near the rivers or found in locations that necessitated strenuous travel to higher elevations (Dering 1979; Stock 1984).

Male mobility was likely tempered by logistically organized hunting forays (Binford 1980). Excellent chert sources were abundant in the local environment. A portable tool kit geared for foraging and hunting small game was recovered during archaeological investigations at Horseshoe Cave. The kit contained multifunctional tools that could have been used to exploit any of the resources in the canyon (Hester 1983). With the exception of stylistic changes in projectile points, the basic tool kit apparently remained adequate through time for use in a foraging subsistence economy (Dibble and Prewitt 1967). Faunal remains suggest that many of the larger hunted animals, such as white-tailed deer (*Odocoileus virginianus macrourus*), gray fox (*Vulpes* sp.), raccoon (*Procyon lotor mexicanus*), and coyote (*Canis latrans texensis*), were taken during less arid climatic phases. Most of the protein in the diet, however, came from smaller animals such as rodents and lagomorphs that were probably trapped by women and children (Huebner 1995a, 1995b; Murdock and Provost 1973).

Desert succulents, also widely available, provided the raw material for a flourishing fiber industry in the canyon (Shafer 1986a). In addition to being a dietary staple, fiber from succulent plant communities was used for weaving everything from technological items to clothing and children's toys (Shafer 1986b).

Resource abundance in this environment made it unnecessary to carry all burdens on routine excursions. It has been archaeologically noted that artifacts were "stashed and cached" near critical resource locations. The 9,000-year archaeological sequence, with no evidence of abandonment, clearly attests to the successful exploitation strategies employed by the inhabitants of this diverse biotic region (Lundelius 1974; Reinhard et al. 1989; Van Devender and Spaulding 1979; Van Devender et al. 1986).

The Early Agriculturalists

The early agriculturalists ($n = 21$) are represented by 14 males and 7 females from southeastern Arizona, where agriculture was thought to be in the earliest stages (B. Huckell 1988, 1995). They resided in the Tucson Basin during the Late Archaic or Early Agricultural period, approximately 3500–1850 BP (Huckell 1983, 1995). Their subsistence economy was "transitional," based on lines of paleobotanical and archaeological evidence for mixed foraging and farming strategies (L. Huckell 1995; Mabry 1998).

The Tucson Basin is located on the eastern edge of the Sonoran Desert zone and is part of the Santa Cruz River drainage system. This low southern desert is surrounded by the Tucson Mountains on the west, the northern Serrita Mountains on the southwest, and the southern end of the Tortolita and Santa Catalina Mountains on the north. On the east and southeast, the basin is bordered by the Rincon and Santa Rita Mountains.

Around the turn of the nineteenth century, an erosional episode along Cienega Creek and Pantano Wash in the southeastern part of the basin exposed Early Agricultural levels. Subsequently, during a highway expansion project in the vicinity of the Santa Cruz River, additional Early Agricultural sites were encountered. These discoveries caused us to rethink previous assumptions about socioeconomic systems during the late centuries BC (Mabry 1998, this volume; Mabry and Clark 1994). Prior to this time the conventional wisdom was that domesticates had not yet been incorporated into the hunting and gathering adaptive strategy (Matson 1991; Minnis 1985, 1992; Wills 1988a, 1988b, 1992). Archaeological investigations at these recently exposed sites, however, revealed the presence of maize by at least 1000–500 BC (see the references cited in B. Huckell 1995; Mabry 1998).

Cienega residential sites were strategically positioned along the perennial waterways of the Santa Cruz and its tributaries, the most critical resource for the inhabitants of the arid basin. Small special-use sites were located in three surrounding ecological zones: the riverine floodplain, the piedmont (the slopes leading from the major drainages to the mountain fronts), and the uplands bordering the basin (B. Huckell 1995). Positioning themselves in this ecotone provided the inhabitants with both rich soil for agriculture and a variety of microenvironments for hunting and gathering opportunities (L. Huckell 1995, 1996).

Maize fields and agricultural products at the large residential sites provide solid evidence for early agriculture (Eddy 1958; Eddy and Cooley 1983; Hemmings et al. 1967; Huckell 1977; Huckell and Haury 1988; Huckell 1996; Mabry 1998; Mabry et al. 1995). Dentition recovered with the skeletal remains also suggests maize consumption by site inhabitants (Minturn 1999; Minturn and Lincoln-Babb 1995). Excavations revealed large pithouse villages with thick midden deposits, extramural storage, numerous ground-stone artifacts, and food-processing features (Adams 1996; Mabry and Clark 1994; Mabry et al. 1995). Wild plant species recovered from bell-shaped storage pits representing multiple seasons of the year demonstrated that the site inhabitants anticipated being in one location for extended periods (Binford 1982; Eddy 1958; Huckell and Haury 1988; L. Huckell 1995).

Because agriculture requires some degree of sedentism, it is thought that early agricultural populations were relatively more settled than highly mobile Middle Archaic groups (B. Huckell 1995). The shift toward reduced residential mobility would have required a reliance on stored resources and use of logistic strategies to exploit resources most efficiently in different environmental zones (Binford 1980; B. Huckell 1995; Kelly 1983, 1992, 1995). Mobility could decrease because stored resources were reliable and did not require daily long-distance travel. More practical targeting of economically important resources could be accomplished by logistic task groups. This is archaeologically reflected at special-use sites identified in the topographically diverse Tucson Basin. These short-term sites demonstrate that broad-spectrum hunting and gathering of wild plant and animal resources was still an indispensable component of the economy (Eddy 1958; Huckell 1984a, 1984b; L. Huckell 1995, 1996).

Paleoethnobotanical studies indicate that the plant species dominating assemblages were those available in late summer and fall, such as maize (*Zea mays*), amaranth (*Amaranthus* sp.), purslane (*Portulaca* sp.), agave (*Agave* sp.), yucca (*Yucca elata* and *Yucca baccata*), rushes (*Juncus* sp.), acorns (pericarps of *Quercus* sp.), wheelscale saltbush (*Atriplex elegans*), and Arizona walnut (*Juglans major*) (Huckell 1996). The nutritionally important legume family (Chenopodiaceae and Amaranthaceae) thrived in the agriculturally disturbed soils along floodplains at the riverine sites (L. Huckell 1995). The limited presence of spring plants, such as stickleaf (*Mentzelia* sp.), mesquite (*Prosopis* sp.), chenopods (Chenopodiaceae), and saguaro (*Carnegiea gigantea*), suggests partial site abandonment at this time, with people moving back and forth among multiple environmental zones during seasonal rounds.

Obviously, Early Agricultural groups retained some degree of mobility to procure resources at varying distances from home. The rich secondary biomass in the Sonoran biotic region has implications for reduced mobility in females. Some suggest a reduction in long-range mobility during foraging forays, because wild plant resources were widely distributed and easily accessible (Fish et al. 1992). Such clustered resources would equate with a reduction in travel and search time. With foraging costs reduced, the time formerly spent in long-distance travel could be devoted to plant processing, making foraging more efficient. Moreover, this localized abundance of reliable and predictable plant communities was potentially storable, providing food sources during winter and spring months when most wild plants were not yet available (Fish and Fish 1991; Fish et al. 1990; L. Huckell 1995). In addition, many resources, such as acorns and agave, were available within relatively short distances of residences and permanent water sources (Fish et al. 1992). Based on Lewis Binford's (1980) Economic Zonation model, many resources could have been efficiently targeted by simple foraging trips near settlements.

High male mobility was likely conditioned by hunting, a commonly logistically organized activity (Binford 1978, 1980). Reaching the Sonoran desert zone and rugged uplands would have necessitated logistic mobility. Such forays are evidenced by small, extended hunting camps in the surrounding mountains and grasslands (Bayham et al. 1986; B. Huckell 1995). Mule deer (*Odocoileus hemionus canus*), white-tailed deer (*Odocoileus virginianus macrourus*), antelope (*Antilocapra americana*), bighorn sheep (*Ovis canadensis*), elk (*Cervus elaphus*), bobcat (*Lynx rufus*), coyote (*Canis latrans*), and jackrabbit (*Lepus californicus*) represented a significant portion of the diet (Eddy 1958; Thiel 1996). Procuring large game, more commonly targeted than smaller mammals in all biomes, required extensive travel to distant mountain ranges by male hunters, sometimes at distances of 70 km or more (B. Huckell 1995).

The topographic diversity and abundance of resources in the Sonoran Desert zone made for a rich environment for Early Agricultural populations. Our research on these newly investigated sites and related subsistence economies during this critical period is still ongoing.

The Late Agriculturalists

The late agriculturalists ($n = 76$) are represented by 42 males and 34 females who resided at the aggregated community of Pottery Mound, New Mexico. This 500-room pueblo was occupied during the Pueblo IV (PIV) period (700–500 BPD), and abandoned just prior to the Spanish entradas in AD 1540 (Hibben 1955, 1961, 1996). The array of ceramic types littering the site landscape, predominantly Glaze A, reinforces the PIV designation (Brody 1964; Voll 1967).

This massive three-tiered community is located in Valencia County in central New Mexico, at the confluence of the southern edge of the Rio Grande Valley and the northern periphery of the Chihuahuan Desert Zone (Cordell n.d.; Hibben n.d.; Schorsch 1962). The site locality is bordered on the north by Mount Taylor, on the east by the Manzano Mountains, on the west by topographically broken high canyon country, and on the south by the Magdalena and Ladron Mountains. The Rio Grande and its tributary, the Rio Puerco, course along the eastern periphery of the site.

Intensive maize agriculture with specialization of food processing was practiced at Pottery Mound (Cordell 1983, 1997; Wills et al. 1996). Major investment in multistoried adobe architecture and nonportable technology reflects the expectation of permanent residency (Wills 1988a). Ceremonial structures, storage features, flora and fauna indicative of year-round occupation, and a large burial population also demonstrate permanent ties to the land (Schorsch 1962; Wills and Huckell 1994).

This high southern desert is ecologically classified by the U.S. Department of Agriculture as the Upper Sonoran life zone (Bailie n.d.). The predominant plant species on the plain included Russian thistle (*Salosa kali tinfolia*), saltbush (*Atriplex* sp.), sacaton grass (*Aristida* sp.), and juniper (*Juniperus* sp.) (Schorsch 1962). The ecotone within which the site was positioned provided arable soil for agriculture and high-quality wild plant and animal resources. Palynological reconstruction identified three biomes in the vicinity of Pottery Mound during PIV times, including riparian, open grassland, and montane (Emslie 1981; Emslie and Hargrave 1978). The headwaters of the Rio Puerco, approximately 100 km to the north, provided a permanent source of water for the site residents.

Unique insight into the prehistoric lifeways at Pottery Mound comes from the over 800 spectacular kiva murals, the most abundant and well preserved in the Southwest (Brody 1964, 1970; Crotty 1979; Hibben 1960, 1966, 1967, 1975, 1996; Leviness 1959; Vivian 1961). The importance of maize (*Zea* sp.) is reflected in mural depictions of corn plants and subsistence tasks associated with agricultural production. Hundreds of preserved charred cobs have been recovered from the cultural deposits (Hibben 1996). It is likely that other cultigens, beans (*Phaseolus* sp.), squash (*Cucurbita* sp.), and possibly cotton (*Gossypium* sp.), were also grown (W. H. Wills, personal communication, 1997). The grasslands adjacent to the site contained extensive agricultural fields. Additional fields were probably located farther from the main site as insurance against crop disasters (W. H. Wills, personal communication, 1997).

The economic roles of males and females documented in the ethnographic literature are clearly depicted in the kiva paintings (Brown 1970; Murdock and Provost 1973). Males were more heavily engaged in agricultural pursuits at late prehistoric communities than in earlier periods (Ember 1983). Field preparation and crop tending likely reduced the total time males allotted for long-distance mobility in favor of more sedentary agricultural duties.

Strictly in terms of farming tasks, the proportional contribution of females was declining relative to that of males (Ember 1983). Women's total work effort, however, did not decrease. The wide variety of grinding implements at the site supports ethnographic documentation that women were heavily involved in maize processing, often for six to eight hours per day (Adams 1996; Hard 1990; Hard et al. 1996; Lancaster 1986; Murdock and Provost 1973). A broad variety of grinding technologies and various metates, including open troughs, were used with one and two hand manos (Adams 1996). The grinding specificity of such items as graters, grinders, pounders, mortars, and pestles suggests that women were grinding substances other than maize, such as various seeds and pigments. Females in mural tabloids carried burden baskets for wild plant collecting trips, prepared foods, transported fuel and water, and produced pottery (Brown 1970; Hibben 1975; Murdock and Provost 1973).

Mural portrayals of male hunters and over ten thousand recovered faunal remains representing animals brought in from surrounding grasslands and mountains indicate that hunting was practiced at Pottery Mound. As hunting is usually logistically organized, long-distance mobility of some portion of the male population is expected (Binford 1980). Targeting large mammals would require travel to the Manzano Mountains, 20 miles to the east, and the broken high mesa country, approximately 10 miles west of the site. These locations were excellent for mule deer, white-tailed deer, Merriam's elk (*Cervus elaphus merriami*), and bighorn sheep. Pronghorn antelope were locally available, ranging very close to the site in the Puerco Valley. Antelope drives were historically documented in this same prime location.

Ethnobiological research identified over fifty species of birds in the avifauna assemblage, many of which were included in mural depictions (Emslie and Hargrave 1978). Pottery Mound was located on a "fly-way" for migrating birds, implying spring and fall bird hunting. The hundreds of birds and watercourses along the eastern edge of the site, in turn, attracted large numbers of mammals, providing additional hunting opportunities.

Surrounding montane zones with piñon pine (*Pinus edulis*) provided locales for piñon gathering trips in the fall by more mobile members of the community. Piñon nuts are a high-return storable resource and facilitated "overwintering" at a time when other wild resources were not available. Less mobile individuals, including older males and children, could perform tasks closer to home. This reduction in residential mobility with year-round site occupation made it possible for all members of the group to make labor contributions in this highly specialized prehistoric farming community.

The impressive richness of the site, the elaborate murals, and the thousands of decorative potsherds from far-ranging locales cause researchers to speculate that Pottery Mound was a center of trade and ceremonial significance in the American Southwest (W. H. Wills, personal communication, 1990). With only approximately 50% of the site excavated, the extent of our knowledge of Pottery Mound will be improved with future excavations (Hibben 1996).

Methods

A functional approach uses an engineering beam model (Timoshenko and Gere 1971). The model can appropriately be applied to a structure whose length is long relative to its width, making it particularly suitable for structural analysis of the femoral diaphysis (Lovejoy et al. 1976; Ruff 1992; Ruff and Hayes 1983a). When modeled as a beam, structural properties of the diaphysis can be calculated at biologically relevant section locations lying perpendicular to the long axis of the bone (Nagurka and Hayes 1980). Biomechanical analyses of cross sections indicate the strength or rigidity of the beam in resistance to the forces generated during respective physical activities. Biomechanical models predict that the changes in physical activities associated with subsistence shifts will be reflected in behaviorally conditioned skeletal morphology (Ruff 1992, 2000a).

Femora ($n = 199$) from 139 individuals were selected on the basis of completeness, lack of pathological involvement, and availability of associated pelvic remains for secure sex assessment. Standard osteological techniques were employed to evaluate the sex of each individual (see Buikstra and Ubelaker 1994). Preference was always given to the primary sexual characteristics seen in the pelvis.

The loading history of each femoral diaphysis was elucidated through an analysis of structural geometry at biologically relevant locations. It has been determined that the bone structure at the midpoint of femoral length most accurately reflects in vivo locomotor behavior (Ruff and Hayes 1983a, 1983b). Noninvasive computed tomography produced a digitized image of the internal and external contours of bone at the 50% location (Ruff and Leo 1986). The software program SLICE then quantified the amount and distribution of cortical bone in each cross section from the scanned image (Eschman 1992). These data provide the baseline information needed to evaluate relative mobility patterns statistically.

The quantified geometric property values were employed in a cross-sectional shape index. The shape index, known as I_x/I_y, is taken to reflect in vivo locomotor activity most accurately and serves as a proxy for relative mobility (Ruff and Hayes 1983a, 1983b; Ruff et al. 1993). The index is derived by dividing I_x (the amount and distribution of cortical bone in the medial/lateral femoral plane) by I_y (the amount and distribution of cortical bone in the anterior/posterior femoral plane) (Ruff and Hayes 1983a, 1983b). Larger resultant values indicate greater bending strength in the A/P plane that translates to relatively higher levels of mobility.

Results

Two-way Analysis of Variance (ANOVA) was computed within and between sex and subsistence subsets. Results indicate significant sex differences ($p = .0011$) and highly significant differences by subsistence ($p < .0001$). Femoral shape index values, biologically reflected in increasing cross-sectional circularity, suggest decreasing mobility as domesticates increasingly become an inte-

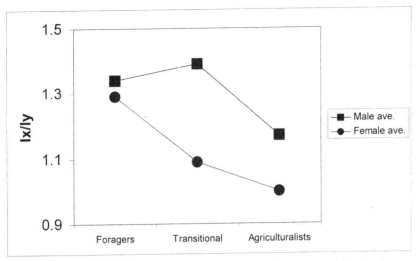

Figure 4.3. Femoral shape index (I_x/I_y) values reflecting decreasing mobility levels as dependence on maize increases. Note the relative differences between the sexes in each subsistence category.

gral component of the economy (see Figure 4.3). An interesting exception is seen in the transitional males (see below).

When grouped by subsistence, the preagricultural foragers, not unexpectedly, have the highest mobility average, the late agriculturalists have the lowest, and the transitional group has an intermediate average (see Figure 4.3). T-tests indicate that the foragers are significantly different from the late agriculturalists, while the "transitional" sample is not significantly different from either the foragers or the late agriculturalists.

Partitioning by sex supports the expected gender-specific differences in mobility roles projected from ethnographic patterning among living peoples. Males, as a group, have significantly larger I_x/I_y values than females, as a group. When values are broken down by both sex and subsistence, however, very interesting patterns are revealed.

Both sexes show a significant reduction in A/P femoral dimensions through time, but they do so at very different rates (see Figure 4.4). Preagricultural male and female foragers display values that are not significantly different from each other. The male mean is only slightly larger than that of their female counterparts, suggesting a residentially mobile strategy.

With incipient farming, femoral resistance to locomotor stress diverges markedly between the sexes (see Figure 4.4). This very dramatic change in relative male and female mobility suggests a perturbation in the sexual division of

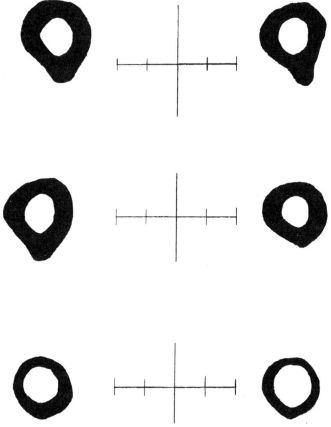

Figure 4.4. Cross sections of right femora at 50% of length, showing size and shape changes in the femur from foraging (*top*) to early agriculture (*center*) to late agriculture (*bottom*). Note structural differences between males (*left*) and females (*right*). Cross sections are oriented with anterior at the top, posterior at the bottom, medial at the right, and lateral at the left. The scale is in centimeters.

labor at this time. It is of interest that shape index values in the economically transitional males basically remain at forager levels. While male mobility does not decline, female mobility values sharply drop to a level not significantly different from that of late agricultural females.

With full-blown late agriculture, I_x/I_y means for the sexes reconverge (see Figure 4.4). This pattern is driven by a rapidly decreasing male I_x/I_y value from the high transitional level. Late agricultural female locomotor behavior continues to decline from transitional levels to the lowest value for both sexes and all subsistence categories.

Summary

The biological evidence from the American Southwest suggests that levels of locomotor behavior during the Late Archaic were intermediate to those of representative samples of foragers and late agriculturalists. These relative mobility patterns suggest that Tucson Basin populations had not yet fully committed to settled agriculture.

An examination of the dichotomy in male and female mobility roles reveals that there was a noticeable impact on the sexual division of labor at this time. The Tucson Basin males maintained behaviors that necessitated high levels of mobility equivalent to those of male Texas foragers. The females, however, showed a dramatic decline in mobility at this time.

Female locomotor behavior was not significantly different from that of the sedentary female agriculturalists from Pottery Mound. The sharp reduction in female mobility with the adoption of agriculture suggests that they were spending more extended periods in proximity to residences, presumably incorporating new sedentary tasks into the domain of women's work. It appears that females from the Tucson Basin were underwriting the costs of the addition of a new, perhaps more predictable, variant into the behavioral repertoire of Late Archaic populations that would eventually lead to more sedentary lifeways.

ACKNOWLEDGMENTS

I want to thank the affiliated Native American tribes for their permission to conduct this research. Thanks are also extended to the University of New Mexico Department of Radiology, Albuquerque; the Maxwell Museum Laboratory of Human Osteology, Albuquerque; Desert Archaeology, Tucson; Arizona State Museum, Tucson; University Hospital, Tucson; Texas Archaeological Research Laboratory, Austin; Austin Radiological Association; and the Witte Museum, San Antonio. Additional support was provided by the Arizona Archaeological and Historical Society, Tucson; the University of New Mexico Department of Anthropology; the Office of Graduate Studies; and the Student Research Allocations Committee at the University of New Mexico. Permission to reproduce Figure 4.1 courtesy of Chris Ruff. Overview map courtesy of R. Stauber. Charles Hilton was responsible for the production of figures.

REFERENCES CITED

Adams, J. L.
    1996   Refocusing the Role of Food Grinding Tools as Correlates for the

Subsistence Strategies of Gatherers and Early Agriculturalists in the American Southwest. Paper presented at the 66th Annual Society for American Archaeology Meetings, New Orleans.

Bailie, B.

n.d.   Life Zones and Crop Zones of New Mexico. *North American Fauna* 35:32–38.

Bayham, F. E., and D. H. Morris

1990   Thermal Maxima and Episodic Occupation of the Picacho Reservoir Dune Field. In *Perspectives on Southwestern Prehistory*, edited by P. E. Minnis and C. L. Redman, pp. 26–37. Westview Press, Boulder.

Bayham, F. E., D. H. Morris, and M. S. Shackley

1986   *Prehistoric Hunter-Gatherers of South-Central Arizona: The Picacho Archaic Project.* Anthropological Field Studies 13. Office of Cultural Resource Management, Department of Anthropology. Arizona State University, Tempe.

Binford, L. R.

1978   *Nunamuit Ethnoarchaeology.* Academic Press, New York.

1980   Willow Smoke and Dogs' Tails: Hunter-Gatherer Settlement Systems and Archaeological Site Formation. *American Antiquity* 45:4–20.

1982   Archaeology of Place. *Journal of Anthropological Archaeology* 1:5–31.

2001   *Constructing Frames of Reference: An Analytical Method for Archaeological Use of Hunter-Gatherer and Environmental Data Sets.* University of California Press, Berkeley.

Bridges, P. S.

1995   Skeletal Biology and Behavior in Ancient Humans. *Evolutionary Anthropology* 4:112–120.

Brock, S. L., and C. B. Ruff

1988   Diachronic Patterns of Change in Structural Properties of the Femur in the Prehistoric American Southwest. *American Journal of Physical Anthropology* 75:113–127.

Brody, J. J.

1964   Design Analysis of the Rio Grande Glaze Pottery of Pottery Mound, New Mexico. Master's thesis, Department of Anthropology, University of New Mexico, Albuquerque.

1970   The Kiva Murals of Pottery Mound. In *Verhandlungen des XXXVIII Internationalen Amerikanistenkongresses*, vol. 2, pp. 101–110. Paper presented at the Internationalen Amerikanistenkongress, Munich, Germany.

Brown, J. K.

1970   A Note on the Division of Labor by Sex. *American Anthropologist* 72:1073–1078.

Brown, K. M.

1991   Prehistoric Economics at Baker Cave: A Plan for Research. In *Papers on Lower Pecos Prehistory*, edited by S. A. Turpin, pp. 87–140. University of Texas Press, Austin.

Bryant, B. M., Jr.

1974   Prehistoric Diet in Southwest Texas. *American Antiquity* 39:407–420.

1986a   Pollen: Nature's Little Capsules of Information. In *Ancient Texans*, edited by G. Zappler, pp. 50–57. Texas Monthly Press, Austin.

1986b   Prehistoric Diet: A Case for Coprolite Analysis. In *Ancient Texans*, edited by G. Zappler, pp. 132–135. Texas Monthly Press, Austin.

Buikstra, J. E., and D. Ubelaker (editors)

1994   *Standards for Data Collection from Human Skeletal Remains.* Research Series, 44. Arkansas Archaeological Survey, Fayetteville.

Carmichael, D. L.

1990   Patterns of Residential Mobility and Sedentism in the Jornada Mogollon. In *Perspectives on Southwestern Prehistory*, edited by P. E. Minnis and C. L. Redman, pp. 122–134. Westview Press, Boulder.

Chamay, A., and P. Tschantz

1972   Mechanical Influences in Bone Remodeling Experimental Research on Wolff's Law. *Journal of Biomechanics* 5:173–180.

Collins, M. B., and J. H. Labadie

1999   Excavation, Rock Art Recordation, Surface Feature Documentation, and Survey at Amistad National Recreation Area. *Texas Archaeology* 43(1)J:3–7.

Cordell, L. S.

1983   *Prehistory of the Southwest.* Academic Press, New York.

1997   *Archaeology of the Southwest.* Academic Press, San Diego.

n.d.   Pottery Mound: Value and Current Status. Unpublished report.

Crotty, H.

1979   The Kiva Murals and the Question of Mesoamerican Influence. Paper presented at the Symposium on New Directions in Native American Art, Albuquerque.

Danielson, R. J., and K. J. Reinhard

1998   Human Dental Microwear Caused by Calcium Oxalate Phytoliths in the Prehistoric Diet of the Lower Pecos Region, Texas. *American Journal of Physical Anthropology* 107:207–307.

Dering, J. P.

1979   Pollen and Plant Macrofossil Record Recovered from Hinds Cave, Val Verde County, Texas. Master's thesis, Department of Anthropology, Texas A&M University, College Station.

1999   Earth-Oven Plant Processing in Archaic Period Economies: An Example from a Semi-Arid Savannah in South-Central North America. *American Antiquity* 64(4):659–671.

Dibble, D. S., and E. R. Prewitt

1967   *Survey and Test Excavations at Amistad Reservoir, 1964–1965.* Survey Report 3, Texas Archaeological Survey, University of Texas, Austin.

Draper, P., and E. Cashden

1988   Technological Change and Child Behavior among the Kung. *Ethnology* 27:339–365.

Eddy, F. W.

1958   A Sequence of Cultural and Alluvial Deposits in the Cienega Creek Basin, Southeastern Arizona. Master's thesis, University of Arizona, Tucson.

Eddy, F. W., and M. E. Cooley

1983   *Cultural and Environmental History of Cienega Valley, Southeastern Arizona.* Anthropological Papers 43. University of Arizona Press, Tucson.

Edwards, C. P., and B. B. Whiting

1980   Differential Socialization of Girls and Boys in Light of Cross-Cultural Research. *New Directions of Child Development* 8:45–57.

Ember, C. R.

1983   The Relative Decline in Women's Contribution to Agricultural Intensification. *American Anthropologist* 85:285–304.

Ember, M., and C. Ember

1976   The Conditions Favoring Matrilocal versus Patrilocal Residence. *American Anthropologist* 73:571–594.

Emslie, S. D.

1981   Prehistoric Agricultural Ecosystems: Avifauna from Pottery Mound. *American Antiquity* 46:853–861.

Emslie, S. D., and L. L. Hargrave

1978   An Ethnobiological Study of the Avifauna from Pottery Mound, New Mexico. Paper presented at the Society for American Archaeology Meetings, Tucson.

Eschman, P.

1992   *SLCOMM*. Eschman Archaeological Services, Albuquerque.

Fish, S. K., and P. R. Fish

1991   Comparative Aspects of Paradigms for the Neolithic Transition in the Levant and American Southwest. In *Perspective on the Past: Theoretical Biases in Mediterranean Hunter-Gatherer Research*, edited by G. A. Clark, pp. 396–410. University of Pennsylvania Press, Philadelphia.

Fish, S. K., P. R. Fish, and J. H. Matson

1990   Sedentism and Settlement Mobility in the Tucson Basin Prior to A.D. 1000. In *Perspectives on Southwestern Prehistory*, edited by P. E. Minnis and C. L. Redman, pp. 76–163. Westview Press, Boulder.

1992   Early Sedentism and Agriculture in the Northern Tucson Basin. In *The Marana Community in the Hohokam World*, edited by S. K. Fish, P. R. Fish, and J. H. Matson, pp. 11–19. Anthropological Papers 56. University of Arizona, Tucson.

Fresia, A. E., C. B. Ruff, and C. S. Larsen

1990   Temporal Decline in Bilateral Asymmetry of the Upper Limb on the Georgia Coast. In *The Archaeology of Mission Santa Catalina de Guale: Two Biocultural Interpretations of a Population in Transition*, edited by C. S. Larsen, pp. 121–132. American Museum of Natural History, New York.

Gaulin, S., and H. Hoffman

1988   Functional Significance of Sex Differences in Spatial Ability. In *Human Reproductive Behavior: A Darwinian Perspective*, edited by L. Betzig, P. Turke, and M. Borgerhoff-Mulder, pp. 129–152. Cambridge University Press, Cambridge.

Hard, R. J.

1990   Agricultural Dependence in the Mountain Mogollon. In *Perspectives on Southwestern Prehistory*, edited by P. E. Minnis and C. L. Redman, pp. 135–149. Westview Press, Boulder.

Hard, R. J., R. P. Mauldin, and G. R. Raymond

1996   Mano Size, Stable Carbon Isotope Ratios, and Macrobotanical Remains as Multiple Lines of Evidence of Maize Dependence in the American Southwest. *Journal of Archaeological Method and Theory* 3:253–318.

Hartenady, P., and J. C. Rose

1991   Abnormal Tooth Loss Patterns among Archaic Period Inhabitants of the Lower Pecos Region, Texas. In *Advances in Dental Anthropology*, edited by M. A. Kelly and C. S. Larsen, pp. 267–278. Wiley-Liss, New York.

Hemmings, E. T., M. D. Robinson, and R. N. Rogers

1967　Field Report on Pantano Site (AZ EE:2:50). Master's thesis, Department of Anthropology, University of Arizona, Tucson.

Hester, T. R.

1983　Late Paleoindian Occupation at Baker Cave, Southwestern Texas. *Bulletin of the Texas Archaeological Society* 53:101–119.

Hibben, F. C.

1955　Excavations at Pottery Mound, New Mexico. *American Antiquity* 21:179–180.

1960　Prehispanic Paintings at Pottery Mound. *Archaeology* 13:267–271.

1961　The Dating of Pottery Mound. In *Illustrated World History*, edited by G. Rainerd. George Rainbird, Ltd., London.

1966　A Possible Pyramidal Structure and Other Mexican Influences at Pottery Mound, New Mexico. *American Antiquity* 31:522–529.

1967　Mexican Features of Mural Paintings at Pottery Mound. *Archaeology* 20:84–87.

1975　*Kiva Art of the Anasazi at Pottery Mound*. KC Publications, Las Vegas.

1996　The Prehistoric Site of Pottery Mound. Lecture presented at the Maxwell Museum Lecture Series, University of New Mexico, Albuquerque.

n.d.　Excavation Procedures Used in the Salvage Project at Pottery Mound. Unpublished field notes.

Hilton, C. E., and R. D. Greaves

1995　Mobility Patterns in Modern Human Foragers. Paper presented at the 64th Annual Meeting of the American Association of Physical Anthropology, Oakland. Abstract published in the *American Journal of Physical Anthropology* Supplement 20:111.

Huckell, B. B.

1977　Excavations at the Hastqin Site: A Multi-Component Preceramic Site near Ganado, Arizona. Report submitted to the Arizona Department of Transportation, Tucson.

1983　Additional Chronometric Data on Cienega Valley, Arizona. In *The Cultural and Environmental History of Cienega Valley, Arizona*, edited by F. W. Eddy and M. E. Cooley, pp. 57–58. Anthropological Papers No. 43. University of Arizona Press, Tucson.

1984a　*The Archaic Occupation of the Rosemont Area, Northern Santa Rita Mountains, Southeastern Arizona*. Arizona State Museum Archaeological Series 147(1). University of Arizona, Tucson.

1984b   The Paleoindian and Archaic Occupation of the Tucson Basin: An Overview. *Kiva* 49(3–4):133–145.

1988   Late Archaeology of the Tucson Basin: A Status Report. In *Recent Research on Tucson Basin Prehistory: Proceedings of the Second Tucson Basin Conference,* edited by W. H. Doelle and P. R. Fish, pp. 57–80. Anthropological Papers No. 10. Institute for American Research, Tucson.

1990   Late Preceramic Farmer-Foragers in Southeastern Arizona: A Cultural and Ecological Consideration of the Spread of Agriculture in the Arid Southwestern United States. Ph.D. dissertation, Department of Arid Lands Resource Sciences, University of Arizona, Tucson. University Microfilms, Ann Arbor.

1995   *Of Marshes and Maize: Preceramic Agricultural Settlements in the Cienega Valley, Southeastern Arizona.* Anthropological Papers No. 59. University of Arizona Press, Tucson.

Huckell, B. B., and E. W. Haury

1988   *Excavations at Two Late Archaic Sites in the Cienega Valley, Southeastern Arizona.* University of Arizona, Tucson.

Huckell, L. W.

1995   Farming and Foraging in the Cienega Valley. In *Of Marshes and Maize: Preceramic Agricultural Settlements in the Cienega Valley, Southeastern Arizona,* edited by B. B. Huckell, pp. 74–97. University of Arizona Press, Tucson.

1996   Paleoethnobotany of Late Preceramic/Early Ceramic Sites along the Santa Cruz River, Tucson, Arizona. Paper presented at the Annual Society for American Archaeology Meetings, New Orleans.

Huebner, J. A.

1991   Cactus for Dinner, Again! An Isotopic Analysis of Late Archaic Diet in the Lower Pecos Region of Texas. In *Papers on Lower Pecos Prehistory,* edited by S. A. Turpin, pp. 175–190. University of Texas Press, Austin.

1995a   The Isotopic Composition and Ecology of Archaic Human Sites in the Eastern Chihuahuan Desert. Ph.D. dissertation, Department of Anthropology, University of Texas, Austin.

1995b   Stable Isotope Analysis of Bone and Soft Tissue from Four Mummies from the Eastern Chihuahuan Desert of Texas. Paper presented at the Second World Congress on Mummy Studies, Cartagena, Colombia.

Hurtado, A. M., and K. R. Hill

1990   Seasonality in a Foraging Society: Variation in Diet, Work Effort, Fertility, and the Sexual Division of Labor Among the Hiwi of Venezuela. *Journal of Anthropological Research* 46(3): 293–345.

Hurtado, A. M., K. Hill, H. Kaplan, and I. Hurtado

1992   Trade-offs between Female Food Acquisition and Child Care among Hiwi and Ache Foragers. *Human Nature* 3(3):185–216.

Kelly, R. L.

1983   Hunter-Gatherer Mobility Strategies. *Journal of Anthropological Research* 39:277–306.

1992   Mobility/Sedentism: Concepts, Archaeological Measure, and Effects. *Annual Review of Anthropology* 21:43–66.

1995   *The Foraging Spectrum: Diversity in Hunter-Gatherer Lifeways.* Smithsonian Institution Press, Washington, D.C.

Lancaster, J.

1986   Groundstone. In *Short-Term Sedentism in the American Southwest: The Mimbres Valley Salado,* edited by B. A. Nelson and S. LeBlanc, pp. 177–190. University of New Mexico Press, Albuquerque.

Larsen, C. S.

1997   *Bioarchaeology: Interpreting Behavior from the Human Skeleton.* Cambridge University Press, Cambridge.

Larsen, C. S., and R. L. Kelly

1995   *Bioarchaeology of the Stillwater Marsh: Prehistoric Human Adaptation in the Western Great Basin.* American Museum of Natural History, New York.

Leviness, W. T.

1959   Pottery Mound Murals. *New Mexico Magazine* 37(3):22–23, 52.

Lovejoy, C. O., A. H. Burstein, and K. G. Heiple

1976   The Biomechanical Analysis of Bone Strength: A Method and Its Application to Platycnemia. *American Journal of Physical Anthropology* 44:489–506.

Lundelius, E. L., Jr.

1974   The Last 15,000 Years of Faunal Change in North America. *Museum Journal* 15:141–160.

Mabry, J. B. (editor)

1998   *Archaeological Investigation of Early Village Life in the Middle Santa Cruz Valley: Analysis and Synthesis.* Anthropological Papers No. 10. Institute for American Research, Tucson.

Mabry, J. B., and J. J. Clark

1994　Early Village Life on the Santa Cruz River. *Archaeology in Tucson* (Center for Desert Archaeology, Tucson) 8(1):1–5.

Mabry, J. B., D. L. Swartz, H. Wocherl, J. J. Clark, G. H. Archer, and M. W. Linderman

1995　*Archaeological Investigations of Early Village Sites in the Middle Santa Cruz Valley: Descriptions of the Santa Cruz Bend, Square Hearth, Stone Pipe, and Canal Sites.* Anthropological Papers 18. Center for Desert Archaeology, Tucson.

Marmaduke, W. S.

1978　Prehistoric Culture in Trans Pecos, Texas: An Ecological Explanation. Ph.D dissertation, Department of Anthropology, University of Texas, Austin.

Matson, R. G.

1991　*The Origins of Southwestern Agriculture.* University of Arizona Press, Tucson.

Minnis, P. E.

1985　Domesticating Plants and People in the Greater American Southwest. In *Prehistoric Food Production in North America,* edited by R. I. Ford, pp. 309–340. Anthropological Papers 75. University of Michigan, Ann Arbor.

1992　Earliest Plant Cultivation in the Desert Borderlands of North America. In *The Origins of Agriculture: An International Perspective,* edited by C. W. Watson and P. J. Watson, pp. 121–141. Smithsonian Institution Press, Washington, D.C.

Minturn, P. D.

1999　Osteology of the Santa Cruz Bend Site: AZ AA:12:746 (ASM). In *Archaeological Investigations of Early Village Sites in the Middle Santa Cruz Valley: Analysis and Synthesis,* edited by J. B. Mabry, pp. 739–755. Anthropological Papers 19. Center for Desert Archaeology, Tucson.

Minturn, P. D., and L. Lincoln-Babb

1995　Bioarchaeology of the Donaldson Site and Los Ojitos: Report on Matty Canyon. In *Of Marshes and Maize: Preceramic Agricultural Settlements in the Cienega Valley, Southeastern Arizona,* edited by B. B. Huckell, pp. 106–116. University of Arizona Press, Tucson.

Munroe, R. L., R. H. Munroe, and H. S. Shimmin

1984　Children's Work in Four Cultures: Determinants and Consequences. *American Anthropologist* 86:369–379.

Murdock, G. P., and C. Provost

1973   Factors in the Division of Labor by Cultural Analysis. *Ethnology* 12:203–225.

Nagurka, M. L., and W. C. Hayes

1980   An Interactive Graphics Package for Calculating Cross-Sectional Properties of Complex Shapes. *Journal of Biomechanics* 13:59–64.

Reinhard, K. J., B. W. Olive, and D. G. Steele

1989   Bioarchaeological Synthesis. Study Unit 3, Southwestern Division Archaeological Overview, U.S. Corps of Engineers. In *From the Gulf to the Rio Grande: Human Adaptation in Central, South, and Lower Pecos, Texas,* edited by T. R. Hester, S. L. Black, D. G. Steele, B. W. Olive, A. A. Fox, K. J. Reinhard, and L. C. Bement, pp. 129–140. Arkansas Archaeological Survey, Fayetteville.

Riskind, D. H.

1970   Pollen Analysis of Human Coprolites of Parida Cave. In *Archaeological Investigations at Parida Cave, Val Verde County, Texas,* edited by R. K. Alexander, pp. 89–101. Papers of the Archaeological Salvage Project No. 19. University of Texas, Austin.

Ruff, C. B.

1987   Sexual Dimorphism in Human Lower Limb Bone Structure: Relationship to Subsistence Strategy and Sexual Division of Labor. *Journal of Human Evolution* 16:391–416.

1992   Biomechanical Analyses of Archaeological Human Skeletal Samples. In *Skeletal Biology of Past Peoples: Research Methods,* edited by S. R. Saunders and M. A. Katzenberg, pp. 37–58. Alan R. Liss, New York.

1993   Biomechanical Analysis of Northern and Southern Plains Femora: Behavioral Implications. In *Skeletal Biology in the Great Plains: Migration, Warfare, Health, and Subsistence,* edited by D. W. Owsley and R. L. Jantz, pp. 35–45. Smithsonian Institution Press, Washington, D.C.

2000a   Biomechanical Analyses of Archaeological Human Skeletal Material. In *Biological Anthropology of the Human Skeleton,* edited by M. A. Katzenberg and S. H. Saunders, pp. 71–102. Alan R. Liss, New York.

2000b   Body Size, Body Shape, and Long Bone Strength in Modern Humans. *Journal of Human Evolution* 38:269–290.

Ruff, C. B., and W. C. Hayes

1982   Subperiosteal Expansion and Cortical Remodeling of the Human Femur and Tibia with Aging. *Science* 217:945–948.

1983a   Cross-Sectional Geometry of Pecos Pueblo Femora and Tib-
         iae—A Biomechanical Investigation I: Method and General Pat-
         terns of Variation. *American Journal of Physical Anthropology* 60:
         359–381.

1983b   Cross-Sectional Geometry of Pecos Pueblo Femora and Tibiae—
         A Biomechanical Investigation II: Sex, Age, and Side Differences.
         American Journal of Physical Anthropology 60:383–400.

Ruff, C. B., and C. S. Larsen

1990   Postcranial Biomechanical Adaptations to Subsistence Strategy
         Changes on the Georgia Coast. In *The Archaeology of Mission
         Santa Catalina de Guale, 2: Bicultural Interpretation of a Popula-
         tion in Transition,* edited by C. S. Larsen, pp. 94–120. American
         Museum of Natural History, New York.

Ruff, C. B., C. S. Larsen, and W. C. Hayes

1983   Structural Changes in the Femur with the Transition to Agricul-
         ture on the Georgia Coast. *American Journal of Physical Anthro-
         pology* 64:125–136.

Ruff, C. B., and F. P. Leo

1986   Use of Computed Tomography in Skeletal Structure Research.
         Yearbook of Physical Anthropology 29:181–196.

Ruff, C. B., A. Walker, and E. Trinkaus

1994   Postcranial Robusticity in *Homo* III: Ontogeny. *American Journal
         of Physical Anthropology* 95:35–54.

Ruff, C. B., A. Walker, E. Trinkaus, and C. S. Larsen

1993   Postcranial Robusticity in *Homo* I: Temporal Trends and Mechan-
         ical I Interpretation. *American Journal of Physical Anthropology*
         91:21–53.

Schorsch, R. L. G.

1962   The Physical Anthropology of Pottery Mound: A Pueblo IV Site
         in West-Central New Mexico. Master's thesis, Department of
         Anthropology, University of New Mexico, Albuquerque.

Shafer, H. J.

1986a   The Lower Pecos Environment: Evolution of the Present Land-
         scape. In *Ancient Texans,* edited by G. Zappler, pp. 34–49. Texas
         Monthly Press, Austin.

1986b   Lower Pecos Lifeways: Housing and Daily Rounds. In *Ancient
         Texans,* edited by G. Zappler, pp. 94–131. Texas Monthly Press,
         Austin.

Speth, J. D.

1990   The Study of Hunter-Gatherers in the American Southwest: New

Insights from Ethnology. In *Perspectives on Southwestern Prehistory*, edited by P. E. Minnis and C. L. Redman, pp. 15–25. Westview Press, Boulder.

Steele, D. G., and B. W. Olive

1989   Bioarchaeology of Region 3 Study Area: Study Unit 3, Southwestern Division Archaeological Overview, US Army Corps of Engineers. In *From the Gulf to the Rio Grande: Human Adaptation in Central, South, and Lower Pecos, Texas,* edited by T. R. Hester, S. L. Black, D. G. Steele, B. W. Olive, A. A. Fox, K. J. Reinhard, and L. C. Bement, pp. 93–114. Arkansas Archaeological Survey, Fayetteville.

Stock, J. A.

1984   The Prehistoric Diet of Hinds Cave (41VV456), Val Verde County, Texas: The Coprolite Evidence. Master's thesis, Department of Anthropology, Texas A&M University, College Station.

Storey, D. A., and B. M. Bryant, Jr.

1966   *A Preliminary Study of the Paleoecology of the Amistad Reservoir Area.* National Science Foundation Research Report G2667. University of Texas, Austin.

Taylor, W. W.

1964   Tethered Nomadism and Water Territoriality, An Hypothesis. In *Actas memorias.* Sobretiro del 35 Congreso Internacional de Americanistas, Mexico City.

Thiel, J. H.

1996   Faunal Exploitation by Early Villagers in the Sonoran Desert. Paper presented at the Annual Society for American Archaeology Meetings, New Orleans.

Timoshenko, S. P., and J. M. Gere

1971   *Mechanics of Materials.* Van Nostrand Reinhold, New York.

Trinkaus, E., S. E. Churchill, and C. B. Ruff

1994   Postcranial Robusticity in *Homo* II: Humeral Bilateral Asymmetry and Bone Plasticity. *American Journal of Physical Anthropology* 93:1–34.

Turpin, S. A.

1986   Bonfire Shelter: An Ancient Slaughterhouse. In *Ancient Texans,* edited by G. Zappler, pp. 88–93. Texas Monthly Press, Austin.

1988   *Seminole Sink: Excavations of a Vertical Shaft Tomb, Val Verde County, Texas.* Plains Anthropologist Memoir 22 (33, part 2).

1992   More about Mortuary Practices in the Lower Pecos River Region of Southwest Texas. *Plains Anthropologist* 37:7–17.

1995   The Lower Pecos River Region of Texas and Northern Mexico. *Bulletin of the Texas Archaeological Society* 66:541–560.

Turpin, S. A., M. Hennberg, and D. W. Riskind

1985   Late Archaic Mortuary Practices in the Lower Pecos River Region, Texas. *Plains Anthropologist* 31:295–315.

Van Devender, T. R., J. Betancourt, and M. Wimberly

1986   Biogeographic Implications of a Pack Rat Midden Sequence from the Sacramento Mountains, South-Central New Mexico. *Quaternary Research* 22:344–360.

Van Devender, T. R., and W. G. Spaulding

1979   Development of Vegetation and Climate in the Southwestern United States. *Science* 222:701–710.

Vierra, B. J.

1990   Archaic Hunter-Gatherer Archaeology in Northwestern New Mexico. In *Perspectives on Southwestern Prehistory,* edited by P. E. Minnis and C. L. Redman, pp. 57–70. Westview Press, Boulder.

1998   *41MV120: A Stratified Late Archaic Site in Maverick County, Texas.* Archaeology Studies Report 7, Archaeological Survey Report 251. Center for Archaeological Research, University of Texas at San Antonio, and Environmental Affairs Division, Texas Department of Transportation, Austin.

Vivian, P. B.

1961   Kachina: The Study of Pueblo Animism and Anthropomorphism within the Ceremonial Wall Paintings of Pottery Mound and Jeddito. Master's thesis, Department of Anthropology, Iowa State University, Ames.

Voll, C.

1967   The Glaze Paint Ceramics of Pottery Mound. Master's thesis, Department of Anthropology, University of New Mexico, Albuquerque.

Ward, C. G.

1992   Shelby Brooks Cave: The Archaeology of a Dry Cave in the Texas Trans Pecos. Master's thesis, Department of Anthropology, University of Texas, Austin.

Williams-Dean, G.

1978   Ethnobotany and Cultural Ecology of Prehistoric Man in Southwest Texas. Ph.D. dissertation, Department of Anthropology, Texas A&M University, College Station.

Wills, W. H.

1988a   Early Agriculture and Sedentism in the American Southwest: Evidence and Interpretations. *Journal of World Prehistory* 2:445–488.

1988b   *Early Prehistoric Agriculture in the American Southwest.* School of American Research Press, Santa Fe.

1992   Plant Cultivation and the Evolution of Risk Prone Economies in the Prehistoric American Southwest. In *Transitions to Agriculture in Prehistory,* edited by A. B. Gebauer and T. D. Price, pp. 153–176. Prehistory Press, Madison.

Wills, W. H., P. Crown, J. Dean, and C. Laudton

1996   Complex Adaptive Systems and Southwest Prehistory. In *Understanding Complexity in the Prehistoric Southwest,* edited by G. J. Gumerman and M. Gell-Mann, pp. 297–339. Addison-Wesley, New York.

Wills, W. H., and B. B. Huckell

1994   Economic Implications of Changing Land-Use Patterns in the Late Archaic. In *Themes in Southwest Prehistory,* edited by G. J. Gumerman, pp. 33–52. School of American Research Press, Santa Fe.

CHAPTER 5

Environmental Constraints on Forager Mobility and the Use of Cultigens in Southeastern Arizona and Southern New Mexico

WILLIAM H. DOLEMAN

Forager or Farmer: The Problem

Every year the New Mexico spring finds me in my backyard, bent over a rototiller, working the clay-rich sediments of an abandoned Rio Grande floodplain. And every year, despite that gas-powered tiller, tons of soil amendments, a nifty drip irrigation system, and cheap city water, I spend most of my free time each summer in that 2,000-square-foot plot, pulling weeds, squashing bugs, and fixing that marvelous drip system—all to produce food that I could buy at the local grocery for a tenth the person-power cost, not to mention the chiropractor bills. But twenty years ago you would have found me in the mountains of northern New Mexico, fly rod in hand, enjoying my attempts to wrest fat trout from one of Mother Nature's bountiful streams. Later in the year, I would be waiting patiently behind a tree for a hundred kilograms of fresh meat to stroll into the range of instant death. But now my rod and my bow gather dust in the garage, and I have to go check the seedlings in my cold frame.

Ever since the now-famous "Man the Hunter" conference in 1966 (Lee and DeVore 1968), archaeologists have wrestled with the question of why anyone would abandon the easygoing life of the hunter-gatherer to become an over-worked agriculturalist. In the Southwestern United States, questions of when, how, and why generally concern the issue of the incorporation of cultigens into the diet (Wills 1988), although some have suggested that early agriculture was imported by immigrating agricultural populations from elsewhere (e.g., Berry 1982; Berry and Berry 1986; Huckell 1990; Matson 1991). A corollary issue is the degree of dependence on agriculture, ranging from use of cultigens to supplement the hunter-gatherer diet to full reliance on cultigens for primary nutrition.

In the American Southwest differences in the timing of these events vary along two dimensions: elevation (i.e., upland versus lowland settings) and region, including, for example, the Colorado Plateau, San Juan Basin, Mogollon

Highlands, and Sonoran and Chihuahuan Deserts. Regional differences are often attributed to differences in demographic or environmental factors. In this chapter I examine differences in environmental characteristics between southeastern Arizona and south-central New Mexico to see if they can account for the radically differential timing of agricultural dependence in the two regions.

Agricultural villages dating to 1200–600 BC are now well documented in southeastern Arizona (see Huckell 1990; Mabry, this volume; Wills and Huckell 1994). With multiple habitation structures, abundant storage features and cultigen remains, and even irrigation canals, these sites indicate reliance on agriculture, not just casual use of domesticated plants.

In southern New Mexico, however, despite evidence for limited use of cultigens as early as ca. 1500 BC (Kirkpatrick et al. 2000:70; MacNeish 1993:319; Tagg 1996; Upham et al. 1987), evidence for significant agricultural dependence does not appear until AD 500–600 in the highlands and even later (AD 1000–1100) in the lowlands (Kirkpatrick et al. 2000:71; see also Hard and Roney, this volume). For example, Hard (1997) used the ubiquity of maize in flotation samples from excavated sites as a measure of agricultural dependence in lowland and upland Jornada Mogollon sites. His analysis revealed that maize is present but in very low quantities (2%) at lowland sites as early as ca. AD 300 and remained low for 800–900 years, until reaching 29% in the Doña Ana phase (AD 1100–1200) and 54% in the ensuing El Paso phase (AD 1200–1450). In upland sites, maize does not appear until ca. AD 500–600 but exhibits high ubiquities throughout the remaining upland Jornada Mogollon sequence. In fact, outside of southeastern Arizona, most reported examples of early maize are from upland rockshelters (see Wills and Huckell 1994), while extensive Late Archaic valley "residential" sites (e.g., the Keystone Dam site; see O'Laughlin 1980) lack the abundant cultigens and rich artifact and storage feature assemblages of the southeastern Arizona sites.

It should be noted that the term "Late Archaic" has different connotations in the two regions, depending on the ways in which the presence/absence of cultigens and ceramics are used as criteria. As Mabry notes (this volume), southeastern Arizona researchers have largely adopted Huckell's (1995) suggestion that the term "Late Archaic" be reserved for purely hunter-gatherer adaptations of the originally conceived San Pedro stage of the region's Cochise culture sequence. Huckell's suggestion that "Early Agricultural" is preferred for sites with evidence of cultigens from the same general period has been less widely accepted, although his subdivision of the period into San Pedro (1200–800 BC) and Cienega (800 BC–AD 150) phases is seeing greater usage. Patricia Gilman et al. (1996:73) argue that the appearance of ceramics by ca. AD 1—used to distinguish the Late Archaic and Early Pit Structure/Ceramic periods—did not represent a major change in subsistence modes.

In south-central New Mexico, with one exception, similar terminological revisions have yet to be offered and accepted. Early researchers generally based discussions of the region's Archaic on data from cave sites and attempted to relate them to Archaic remains in West Texas (e.g., Sayles 1935), West Texas and southwestern New Mexico (Cosgrove 1947), or southeastern Arizona and southwestern New Mexico (Sayles and Antevs 1941; see the discussion in Kirkpatrick et al. 2000:5658). In his initial definition of the Jornada branch of the Mogollon, Donald Lehmer (1948) accommodated the Archaic in his "Hueco" phase, which he applied to the area's numerous aceramic sites and saw as an occupation ancestral to the region's Formative. The latest synthesis of the Archaic period for the region (the "Chihuahua Tradition"; Anderson 1993; MacNeish and Beckett 1987) divides the Archaic into four phases: Gardner Springs (6000–4300 BC), Keystone (4300–2600 BC), Fresnal (2600–900 BC), and Hueco (900 BC–AD 250). This formulation is based upon only a few excavated sites and has yet to be widely accepted, perhaps because (as noted by Kirkpatrick et al. 2000:70) the available survey data for the Archaic of south-central New Mexico are limited and scattered. Other work in the area suggests that south-central New Mexico may mark the intersection of several projectile-point based Archaic "traditions" (Beckett 1983; Doleman 1990; O'Hara 1988). Finally, the terms "early," "middle," and "late" are not consistently applied to the region's Archaic.

Essentially, in south-central New Mexico, the term "Late Archaic" is loosely used to refer to aceramic occupations both with and without cultigens, and its meaning is a function of which cultural rubric the researcher favors. With the appearance of ceramics in the region ca. AD 300–600, the term "Formative," "Ceramic," or "Pithouse" replaces "Archaic." The earliest dates for Jornada Mogollon ceramics remain contested (with Whalen [1981] suggesting AD 300 or earlier and O'Laughlin [1985] arguing for later dates of ca. AD 500–600).

One example of co-occurring early ceramics and cultigens in the Jornada Mogollon region is evident in the Mimbres Mogollon ceramic types recovered from two cultigen-bearing pithouse sites along lower Placitas arroyo near Hatch, New Mexico (Morenon and Hays 1984). Radiocarbon dates from the pithouses exhibit two-sigma calibrated date ranges of AD 134–424 and AD 220–542 (Doleman 1997:130, Table 5.5). Interestingly, these sites lie less than two kilometers from an excavated aceramic Late Archaic site with "classic" characteristics, including domestic hearths with abundant fire-cracked rock and a biface-based lithic technology. Charcoal from this Archaic site yielded two-sigma calibrated dates bracketing the period 370 BC–AD 640, which are statistically indistinguishable from those from the nearby pithouse sites (Doleman 1997:130). This partial contemporaneity suggests that horticultural and hunter-gatherer adaptations coexisted in the "Late Archaic" of south-central New Mexico. Thus the lack of a more detailed cultural sequence for south-central New Mexico might be attributable in part to the very subject of this chapter—the extremely gradual transition from hunter-gatherer to largely agricultural subsistence in south-central New Mexico.

Explanatory Perspectives

Archaeologists' explanations for incorporation of and eventual reliance on cultigens in the prehistoric Southwest have evolved from ones invoking monolithic causes such as population increase, migration, and environmental change (e.g., Irwin-Williams 1973) to ones that more appropriately consider the effect of such causal "pushes" on antecedent hunter-gatherer settlement and subsistence systems. These more sophisticated models commonly focus on one of two major domains in hunter-gatherer adaptive theory: mobility strategies and optimal foraging theory. Both perspectives emphasize a causal relationship between environmental parameters—such as the nature, density, and distribution of food resources—and hunter-gatherer adaptive and behavioral responses to these constraints.

The study of hunter-gatherer mobility strategies focuses on how residential and logistical mobility are used for efficient and effective access to crucial resources throughout the year and began in part with Binford's seminal study (1980; see below; examples of this perspective as it applies to the Late Archaic of the Southwest include Doleman 1995; Huckell 1990; Mauldin 1995; and Wills and Huckell 1994). In addition to theoretical grounds for considering the role of mobility in the adoption of agriculture during the Late Archaic, Ogilvie's study (this volume) provides an empirical basis. Her analysis of skeletal attributes diagnostic of habitual locomotive demands on prehistoric populations before, during, and after the transition to agriculture clearly indicates that the adoption of agriculture had a profound effect on overall mobility. Interestingly, her analysis shows that women's mobility was reduced during the crucial period of initial reliance on cultigens in southeastern Arizona, while that of men remained high (presumably for hunting purposes), suggesting that access to wild food resources remained important.

Optimal foraging theory focuses on hunter-gatherers' choices and risk assessments concerning the inclusion of various food resources in the diet, based largely on cost-return ratios (e.g., Winterhalder and Smith 1992). Hard and Roney (this volume) utilize optimal foraging theory as a framework for discussing differences in the timing of agricultural reliance between the Jornada region of south-central New Mexico and northwestern Chihuahua. They use diet-breadth and risk-reduction models to assess the relative return rates for foraging versus farming in the two regions.

Undoubtedly, both mobility and diet choices played important roles in the processes whereby and the timing with which Late Archaic hunter-gatherers of the Southwest added cultigens to their diet and became increasingly reliant upon them; but the present study focuses solely on mobility strategies.

The most commonly cited "external factor" is demography. In carrying capacity models, this factor is expressed as regional population increase, which yields a Malthusian disparity between available food resources and would-be consumers (Glassow 1980; Irwin-Williams 1973). In such models, maize gradually went from casual supplement to staple in the hunter-gatherer diet as the effective availability of important wild food resources dwindled. More complex models relate regional population packing to reduced hunter-gatherer mobility and competition for access to various important resource zones (e.g., Hunter-Anderson 1986). In fact, Steven Shackley's (1996:11) geochemical source analysis of obsidian from Middle and Late Archaic sites in southeastern Arizona shows just such a change in the late Archaic. In either case, subsistence system adjustments are required, such as some form of resource productivity intensification (i.e., plant cultivation).

Another potentially important external factor is climate change. Huckell (1996), for example, has suggested that a climate-induced change in stream behavior in three southeastern Arizona valleys that occurred ca. 3000 BP created optimal conditions for the region's late Archaic hunter-gatherers to take up agriculture. Huckell's analysis indicates that decreases in summer temperatures and precipitation at this time created more stable vegetation, with the results that streams went from occupying incised channels to meandering across fertile, aggrading floodplains. As such, this climatic change was a contributing factor but not necessarily a primary causal one.

Similarly, Ray Mauldin (1995) has suggested that the changes in settlement and subsistence that occurred after ca. AD 1000 in south-central New Mexico—including the first evidence of true agriculture—were correlated with a documented shift from a warm-dry climatic regime during the period AD 700–1000 to a cool-wet one after ca. AD 1000. Climate-based explanations, however, tend to be regionally idiosyncratic in terms of both climatic specifics and the source of the supporting data. In addition, those climate changes that are most obvious in the paleoclimatic record are also usually represented across broad geographic areas and thus have limited potential for explaining differentially timed cultural changes such as the one that is the focus of the present study.

Regardless of the external factor(s) involved, one of the most important considerations is how specific hunter-gatherer subsistence systems and mobility organization are affected by changes in external factors in different environments. A substantial body of theory—together with supporting ethnographic data—indicates that hunter-gatherer mobility strategies are closely tied to the structure of the environments they occupy. Thus past changes in environmental parameters are likely to have impacted the hunter-gatherer organization-environment equation. This thesis underlies the present study and is discussed further below.

A second—and equally important—issue for understanding hunter-gatherer adoption of cultigens concerns the ways in which transitioning hunter-gatherer systems succeeded in accommodating the labor scheduling demands of agriculture, even in its most incipient forms. The question of how to exploit crucial spring, summer, and fall wild resources—while engaging in the equally crucial tasks of planting and supervising young plants in the spring and harvesting them in the fall—undoubtedly presented a significant challenge to hunter-gatherers experimenting with cultigens (Minnis 1985). Within the system of seasonal residential mobility proposed for the Southwestern preagricultural Archaic (see below), such scheduling conflicts might have been considerable, particularly given the "overwhelming need for careful tending of maize crops" noted by Wills and Huckell (1994:50). Wills and Huckell also argue that cultigen use was never "casual." That is, cultigens—especially maize—were never an insignificant supplement and would only have been used at all if they offered some significant reward for the efforts involved in production. Thus the cultivators had to stay with their cultigens, and scheduling conflicts could only be resolved by occupying residential loci that offered easy access to both agriculturally productive land and favored foraging areas. In other words, resource blooms for all three seasons would be accessible from such loci by short-duration, logistical forays that did not require residential relocation. At the same time, the storable surpluses offered by successful maize cultivation allowed more efficient exploitation of important but limited-availability wild resources (Wills and Huckell 1994:51).

The issue of successful incorporation of cultigens into hunter-gatherer subsistence thus becomes a question of congruence of hunter-gatherer ecology and the organization of mobility, the spatial ecology of natural biotic systems, and the restrictive demands of agriculture. Understanding of the process should thus be properly derived from a theory of hunter-gatherer ecology.

One example of an ecological approach to understanding the adoption of cultigens by Southwestern hunter-gatherers is Hard's (1986) study of the relationship between the timing of agricultural appearance and the suitability of various environments for hunting and gathering as measured by biotic "turnover" (the ratio of annual production to standing biomass). Hard found that cultigens appeared first in low-turnover environments and later in high-turnover ones, where—he argues—the hunter-gatherer lifestyle was able to persist despite demographic and changing environmental challenges. Hard contends that high-turnover environments are more reliable and less susceptible to the effects of exploitation by increasing regional populations. Furthermore, such environments obviate the need for agricultural strategies because foraging is a more reliable strategy. His analysis also offers an explanation for the oft-cited earlier appearance of agriculture in upland locations, because these are characterized by low turnover rates. In many respects, Hard's work inspired the research reported here.

Environmental Structure and Hunter-Gatherer Mobility

Binford and others have suggested that greater environmental structure or "grain"—both temporal and spatial—leads to incongruities in resource distribution and/or availability that must be accommodated by variations in residential and logistical mobility (see Binford 1980 and 2001 for the original and final expositions of this theory; and Kelly 1995: Chapter 4 for an excellent overview of its subsequent development). In essence, Binford used ethnographic data to demonstrate that hunter-gatherer mobility strategies range from being *foragers,* who use frequent residential moves to "move consumers to resources" in homogeneous environments, to being *collectors,* who occupy more permanent residential loci and mount logistical forays to acquire resources in geographically and/or temporally structured ones. In fact, as early as 1977, Henry Harpending and Herbert Davis noted that hunter-gatherer ranges—and hence mobility—vary as an inverse function of not only the abundance and variety of food resources but also the degree to which they are spatially coincident over distances of 10–100 km (Harpending and Davis 1977). At the same time, John Yellen (1977) touched on the role of temporal variation in determining hunter-gatherer mobility by arguing that greater "behavioral plasticity" (including residential mobility) is required in more unpredictable environments such as deserts.

One of the most important factors that conditioned prehistoric hunter-gatherer residential mobility is undoubtedly the relationship between the spatial scale of resource variation and the cutoff distance that separates daily foraging trips and overnight or "logistical" trips. Generally the maximum distance hunter-gatherers are willing to walk round-trip in a single day is 20–30 km, or 10–15 km one way (Kelly 1995:133, 352n6). In order to gain a better understanding of the crucial relationship between environmental spatial scales and hunter-gatherer mobility, R. L. Kelly (1995:131) introduced the concept of "effective foraging radius," which is essentially a function of the return rates for various resources, with game generally offering better returns than plant foods.

Both spatial and temporal environmental structure can, of course, vary at multiple scales, but large-scale variations comparable with scales of hunter-gatherer mobility are the ones of interest here. In the Southwest, and particularly in Basin and Range regions, larger-scale spatial structure and temporal structure are partially correlated, with seasonal resource blooms following an elevational gradient (Huckell 1990; Mauldin 1995; Shackley 1996).

Neither of Binford's mobility extremes—pure logistical or pure residential—was probably pursued by Late Archaic hunter-gatherers in Southwestern Basin and Range regions. The Middle and Late Archaic of much of the Southwest, and in particular the Basin and Range regions of southeastern Arizona and south-central New Mexico, has been commonly modeled as based on the broad-spectrum foraging and seasonally organized mobility between major resource zones that are in turn structured by dichotomous physiography (see Huckell 1990 and Shackley 1990 for southeastern Arizona; Doleman 1995 and Mauldin 1995 for south-central New Mexico). Binford (1980) originally termed this form of hunter-gatherer seasonal residential mobility "seasonal foraging," and it has come to be known as "serial foraging" in the San Juan Basin region to the north (Elyea and Hogan 1983).

Interestingly, the seasonal foraging model proposed for these regions represents a combination of Binford's organizational extremes, involving periodic large-scale seasonal moves and a mixture of mobility forms during particular seasons, depending upon the specific environments involved. Seasonal foraging is correlated with higher degrees and larger scales of both spatial and temporal environmental structure. An important aspect of such systems is that, with large-scale seasonal movements among environmental zones, effective access to these zones changes throughout the year.

Thus it can be argued: if the effective foraging radius of the resources being exploited in a given seasonally exploited environment is less than the spatial extent of that environment, then serial foraging and seasonal residential mobility are in order. Conversely, if different environments are compressed into a space smaller than the average effective foraging radius, greater residential stability and exploitation of multiple environments may be possible. Another consequence of the variable returns of different resources is that gatherers tend to exploit their environments via residential mobility, while hunters can "afford" to use logistical mobility (Kelly 1995:131). This in turn means that gatherers tend to make more efficient use of their environment through the more thorough coverage afforded by greater residential mobility. Kelly's analysis (1995:131) of various hunter-gatherer groups' territorial "coverage" as measured by the ratio of total annual residential distance moved to area exploited revealed that gatherers' coverage ratio (0.54) is 10 times that of hunters (0.05).

Interestingly, this observation is consistent with the common conception that during the long Archaic period Southwestern hunter-gatherers gradually moved down the food chain and from specialist to generalist strategies as they transitioned from hunting large game to gathering a variety of low-return resources such as seeds and small game (e.g., Cordell 1984:166–169; Simms 1984). That is, as Archaic populations increased, more spatially efficient— if less romantic and tasty—plant- and small animal–gathering subsistence modes accommodated ever-shrinking territories (Shackley 1996 offers the more appropriate term "procurement range"). For the Late Archaic of both southeastern Arizona and south-central New Mexico, this means that seasonal residential mobility was probably necessary unless environmental gradients were sufficiently compressed to allow exploitation of multiple environments within an effective foraging radius that was less than the average hunter-gatherer maximum of 10–15 km. Thus both the degree (contrast) and scale of environmental incongruities are important in determining the effects of environmental grain on hunter-gatherer mobility strategies, in terms of the kind of residential mobility used and the complexity of residential mobility strategies (e.g., "pure" foragers and collectors versus serial foragers).

The well-known unpredictability of Southwestern climatic factors— especially precipitation—produces special kinds of both spatial and temporal environmental structures. Following the lead of Yellen (1977), I suggest that, in addition to spatial and temporal variation, a stochastic dimension constitutes another important component of "environmental structure," with greater unpredictability yielding greater temporal grain or contrast. This important aspect of the hunter-gatherer "challenge" has yet to be fully explicated, although Kelly (1995:144–148) discusses the effect of anticipated risk associated with unpredictability on residence-moving decisions. The environmental unpredictability characteristic of deserts is often cited as an important factor conditioning hunter-gatherer subsistence, and Late Archaic foragers probably accommodated stochastic variation by means of residential mobility (see, for example, Mauldin's 1995 discussion of hunter-gatherers' strategic adaptive changes to accommodate long-term variations on environmental parameters versus tactical accommodations for short-term changes). If so, then increasing stochastic structure would have an effect on hunter-gatherer mobility opposite to that of greater spatial and temporal structure—namely, in fostering residential rather than logistical mobility. Stochastic structure undoubtedly also occurs at multiple scales, while rendering the understanding of spatial and temporal structure more difficult. Thus the issue of stochastic structure is a complex one, which undoubtedly requires more sophisticated modeling and measurement than can be offered here.

Finally, variations in overall biotic diversity and productivity are a fourth possible component of environmental structure. In the arid Southwest biotic productivity is linked to precipitation and temperature regimes, reliability, and turnover rates (see the discussion of Hard 1986 above). Species diversity is a function of environmental stability, particularly climatic stability (i.e., lack of seasonality) and predictability (lack of inter- or intra-annual stochastic variation; Pianka 1978:293; see also the discussion of this issue in Yellen 1977). Both of these variables are complex, and a detailed analysis of their variations is beyond the scope of this study. I suggest, however, that they comprise one or more dimensions of environmental structure, with high biotic productivity and high species diversity occurring at smaller spatial scales and effectively reducing large-scale environmental grain. Both serve to increase the number of resource options available to hunter-gatherers, while (possibly) reducing the average travel distance required to acquire adequate nutrition. (In Harpending and Davis's terms [1977] this would be equivalent to increasing the degree to which the resources were "in phase.") Finally, insofar as biotic diversity is a function of environmental stability and predictability, it is also an inverse measure of stochastic variation.

Case Study: Southeastern Arizona and South-Central New Mexico

In the course of pondering the last-minute appearance of true agriculture in south-central New Mexico, I became intrigued by the contrasting situation in southeastern Arizona that has been revealed in the last decade (Mabry, this volume). On the surface, both regions appear to share similar overall environmental attributes; and, as noted above, the Late Archaic subsistence systems of the two areas have been characterized in similar ways. It occurred to me that a comparison between the two areas might shed some light on events in southern New Mexico.

Several researchers have offered "ecological" explanations for the early appearance of sedentism and agricultural dependence in southeastern Arizona (including Huckell 1990, 1995; Roth 1993; and Stone and Bostwick 1996, to name but a few). All have in common two factors necessary for successful floodwater agriculture (Stone and Bostwick 1996:19): the presence of landforms and reliable water sources (see especially Huckell 1996) and compact, high-diversity environments that allowed access to a wide variety of wild resources with minimal travel. Connie Stone and Todd Bostwick (1996), for example, compared three regions in Arizona in terms of geographically constrained environmental structure and found that the timing of agricultural adoption is correlated with environmental structure as well as with archaeological evidence. Furthermore, I am hardly the first researcher to suggest that environmental differences between the Sonoran and Chihuahuan Deserts account for the earlier appearance of village agriculture in the valleys of southeastern Arizona (see Mauldin 1996; Waters and Woosley 1990). My goals here—in a purely exploratory analysis—are to quantify several aspects of environmental structure in the two regions, to determine how great the differences are, and to see if the differences correlate with postulated differences in the timing of agricultural adoption as well as the expectations of hunter-gatherer theory. As such, the analysis serves as a preliminary quantitative evaluation of previous hypotheses, while investigating the analytical utility of a number of environmental measures.

As noted, both regions' environments are dominated by Basin and Range physiography exhibiting a pattern of aligned valleys, flanked by upland and mountain environments and their rich biotic gradients, optimally suited for seasonal or serial foraging by Archaic hunter-gatherers. One important environmental difference between the two areas should be noted, however: larger valleys in southeastern Arizona have perennial streams running through them, while (with the exception of the Rio Grande) those in south-central New Mexico are flat, internally drained basins in which surface water availability is limited largely to ephemeral ponds that appear during the summer monsoon. In south-central New Mexico the main source of reliable water is streams that issue from the uplands onto alluvial fans at the basin-upland interface, and these were the locations where prehistoric agriculture first appeared (Carmichael 1988; Hard 1986; Mauldin 1986; Whalen 1994).

It should also be noted that Shackley (1996:9–11) has argued that upland piñon crops were a crucial seasonal resource during the southwestern Archaic but that the upland woodlands associated with the southeastern Arizona valleys used in the present analysis were too small and unpredictable to form part of a regular seasonal round. Instead, he suggests that the dominant serial moves were between the "lowlands" of southeastern Arizona (including the Basin and Range valley and upland sites studied here) and the Mogollon Highlands to the north—a distance of some 100–200 km. Shackley's model stands in contrast to those of others who have suggested that transhumance between the valleys and uplands of southeastern Arizona constituted a successful seasonal round (see above). I make no attempt here to argue the relative merits of the two models. It is interesting to note, however, that while Shackley's procurement range analysis of Middle and Late Archaic sites in southeastern Arizona showed that fewer distinct resource zones were visited in the Late Archaic, the lowland-upland mix was maintained. This observation suggests that procurement ranges may have become smaller and that the valley-upland model was in effect during the latter period (Shackley 1996:11).

In the following analysis I explore a variety of environmental differences between the two regions in terms of the success that foraging systems might have had incorporating cultigens into their wild resource-based systems. I do not, however, address any of the proposed external causes. Instead, I submit that the various environmental differences discussed below can be viewed as structural variations that fall within the "grain" concept introduced by Binford in his development of a theory of hunter-gatherer ecology, beginning with his elucidation of the forager-collector hunter-gatherer mobility spectrum in 1980. I suggest that Binford's postulated relationship between environmental structure and hunter-gatherer mobility organization is applicable to the "congruence" issue described above.

Measures of Environmental Structure

In order to compare southeastern Arizona and south-central New Mexico, I evaluated several aspects of environmental variation designed to reflect differences in the aspects of environmental structure proposed above (spatial, temporal, and stochastic) as well as biotic diversity/productivity, which is at least partially a function of the first three. The portion of southeastern Arizona included in the study comprises the Santa Cruz, San Pedro, Aravaipa, and Gila River Valleys and lies at the extreme eastern end of the Sonoran Desert biogeographic province in the Arizona Upland subdivision (see Lowe and Brown 1994: Figure 3). In fact, southeastern Arizona includes portions of both Sonoran and Chihuahuan provinces, but expansion of the Chihuahuan Desert biome in the last 100 years has led to invasion of areas that prehistorically belonged to the Sonoran province (Brown 1994:169). The southern New Mexico area lies in the northern end of the Chihuahuan Desert province between the Mogollon Highlands to the west and the Pecos Valley to the east and includes the Rio Grande, Jornada del Muerto, and Tularosa Valleys. Essentials of modern-day climate and vegetation were established in both regions by ca. 4000 BP and prior to the periods of crucial interest in the present research (Van Devender 1990a:126, 1990b:159).

Spatial structure in the two regional environments was measured in a way that reflects distances between biomes and, by inference, their accessibility to

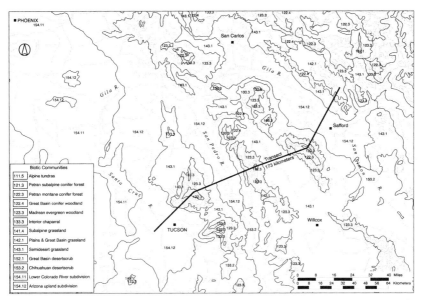

Figure 5.1. Southeast Arizona study area and biome analysis transect (after Brown and Lowe 1994; digital map data courtesy of U.S. Geological Survey Gap Analysis Program [USGS GAP], acquired at ftp://ftp.gap.uidaho.edu/products/arizona/gis/vegcovs/azblp80d.zip).

prehistoric hunter-gatherers. Biomes are "major communities of characteristic plants and animals" that are constrained by large-scale variation in climatic factors, including physiographically controlled ones (Pianka 1978:4142). Biomes are subdivisions of biogeographic provinces and are also equivalent to the biotic communities defined and mapped by Charles Lowe and David Brown (1994:9; Brown and Lowe 1994). From the perspective of modeling hunter-gatherer subsistence, biomes are roughly equivalent to "resource zones," access to which was presumably crucial to prehistoric foragers of the Late Archaic.

Given these considerations, spatial structure was measured along two transects (one in each region), each of which crosses four valley-mountain range systems. Figures 5.1 and 5.2 are derived from Brown and Lowe's map (1994) of Southwestern biotic communities. The transects shown in Figures 5.1 and 5.2 were specifically chosen to cross major valleys and to maximize the number of biomes crossed without producing overly contorted alignments. The linear nature of major valleys in both regions allows this simplistic approach to approximate hunter-gatherer access to various resource zones associated with each valley. For calculation purposes, the transect in each region was divided into "biome gradients," each covering the span from a mountain range "peak"

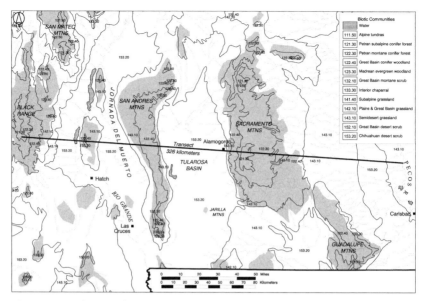

Figure 5.2. South-central New Mexico study area and biome analysis transect (after Brown and Lowe 1994; digital map data courtesy of USGS GAP, acquired at ftp://ftp.gap.uidaho.edu/products/new_mexico/gis/ancillary/Brlowepad.zip).

to the adjacent valley bottom (or the reverse), yielding two biome gradients for most valleys and a total of seven for each region.

For each biome gradient, the following quantitative characteristics were measured as evidence for spatial structure and biome accessibility, with regional averages appearing in Table 5.1: (a) valley-peak distance, (b) both valley and upland width, (c) the ratio of upland to valley width, (d) the number of biomes in each valley-upland gradient, and (e) overall biome density (that is, the number of biomes crossed per 100 km of transect). For the purposes of this study, "valley" biomes include desertscrub and grasslands, while "upland" ones are various forms of woodland and forest. Although not shown on the Brown and Lowe map, riparian habitat was included as a separate biome in valleys with perennial streams, such as the Gila River and the Rio Grande. Valley-peak distance offers a measure of the range required to access all biomes from a given valley location and hence the likelihood that biomes can be accessed via foraging versus logistical trips. Valley and upland widths and the ratio of upland to valley measure the relative contribution of the two major biome types to the overall valley environment. The number of biomes in each gradient is a mea-

Table 5.1. Spatial structure of biome distributions: Averages for seven valley biome gradients in each region

Geographic Zone	Average valley-peak distance (km)	Average valley portion width (km)	Average upland portion width (km)	Average upland-valley ratio	Average number of biomes	Average number of biomes per 100 km
Southeast Arizona	22.0	14.1	7.9	0.60	4.6	16.2
South-Central New Mexico	45.4	31.0	14.4	0.39	4.7	7.8

Table 5.2. Climatic data from selected stations in both regions

Geographic Zone	Precipitation (inches)								Average Difference: July–Jan
	Mean Annual	CV Annual	Mean Winter	CV Winter	Mean Summer	CV Summer	Summer Percent	Rainfall Reliability (Hard 1986)	max temperature (deg F)
Southeast Arizona	13.3	n/a	5.35	53.0	7.9	31.7	59.6	18.8	34.6
South-Central New Mexico	9.2	36.7	3.5	54.7	5.7	39.0	61.7	9.7	38.2

sure of local (valley) biotic diversity, while biome density (calculated across the entire transect) serves as a useful measure of regional biotic diversity.

Seasonality in precipitation and temperature regimes is the principal form of large-scale *temporal structure* in the two regional environments. For the study, seasonality was measured in terms of three variables: (a) warm-season rainfall (April–October) computed as a percentage of total annual precipitation, (b) the length of the frost-free season, and (c) the difference between average July and January high temperatures (Table 5.2). For southeastern Arizona, climatic data were averaged for seven stations located in the four valleys of the region (data were derived from Huckell 1990 and Sellers and Hill 1974). For the Chihuahuan Desert region, data from nine stations in the Rio Grande and Tularosa Valleys were used (Anschuetz and Noyes 1990; Bulloch and Neher 1980; Derr 1981; Noyes and Schmader 1988; United States Department of the Army 1983).

Differences in the long-term aspects of the *stochastic component of environmental structure* should be reflected in year-to-year variability in annual warm- and cool-season precipitation measured as the coefficients of variation (Table 5.2). Given the relationship between biotic diversity and environmental

Table 5.3. Biotic data from selected locations in both regions: Species counts and turnover rates

| | Sonoran Desert | | Chihuahuan Desert | | | |
| Biota | Sonoran Desertscrub Biome | | Chihuahuan Desertscrub | | Semidesert Grassland | |
Data Source	Brown (1994)	Polis (1991)	Brown (1994)	Polis (1991)	Brown (1994)	Polis (1991)
Plants	183*	250	103	n/a	63	n/a
Mammals	25*	64	13	16^P-19^B	18	n/a
Birds	26*	57	9	14^P-15^B	30	n/a
Reptiles & amphibians	37*	70	23	31^P-30^B	6	n/a
Turnover rate (net annual plant production/biomass) (Hard 1986)	$0.12^U-0.25^L$		0.32		0.48	

* Counts include all five subdivisions of the Sonoran Desertscrub biome
[U] Arizona Uplands subdivision
[L] Lower Colorado subdivision
[P] Jornada playa site
[B] Jornada bajada site

stability and predictability, differences in biotic diversity (Table 5.3) may reflect stochastic variation as well.

Biotic productivity is a somewhat loose term and may be conceptually linked to biotic diversity to the extent that a greater *variety* of organisms is more "productive." In desert environments, productivity should be at least partially a function of overall water availability, which is reflected in both average annual precipitation and 95 percent rainfall reliability (defined as the guaranteed minimum precipitation that will fall 95 years out of 100; Hard 1986). These data appear in Table 5.2.

In addition to the spatial measures of biotic diversity presented in Table 5.1, biotic diversity can also be measured in terms of *species density* (defined as the absolute number of different species present in a given ecosystem; Pianka 1978:286). As noted earlier, species density tends to be higher in more stable and predictable environments (Pianka 1978:293), which in turn present the forager with less temporal and spatial stochastic structure and hence less spatial structure. Thus biotic diversity measures aspects of both temporal and spatial structure. The species counts in Table 5.3 are offered as proxies for species density and were derived for one Sonoran Desert biome and two Chihuahuan Desert biomes for plants, mammals, birds, and reptiles and amphibians. Species count data are derived from two sources (Appendix II in Brown 1994 and Polis 1991). Hard's (1986) calculated turnover rates (production/biomass ratios) are included in Table 5.3 as another measure of differences in biotic "productivity" (data are from one station in each region: San Simon in the Gila Valley of southeastern Arizona and El Paso in the northern Chihuahuan Desert).

Results of the Comparisons

My analysis (Tables 5.1–5.3) indicates that southeastern Arizona exhibits a less structured, more fine-grained environment than does southern New Mexico. This is particularly true in the case of spatial structure (Table 5.1). Although the average number of biomes per valley-upland gradient is roughly the same for both areas, the Sonoran Desert averages for peak-to-valley distance and both valley and upland widths are half or less those for the Chihuahuan Desert. That is, there are about twice as many valley-upland gradients packed into a given area in southeastern Arizona as there are in southern New Mexico. This is reflected in the fact that the Sonoran transect averages 16.2 biomes per 100 km versus only 7.8 for the Chihuahuan one. The variety of available resources is also more evenly distributed and is reflected in a markedly higher upland-valley width ratio for the Sonoran case (0.60) and a lower one in southern New Mexico (0.39). In other words, the average areal extent of upland resources in southeastern Arizona is much greater compared with the northern Chihuahuan Desert. In essence, everything a seasonal forager could ask for was much closer to hand in southeastern Arizona. Most importantly, on average, all but the highest-elevation resource zones were within the daily walk limit of 10–15 km for most hunter-gatherers (see above).

Differences in seasonality between the two regions are less marked but nonetheless exist (Table 5.2). In southeastern Arizona, warm-season rainfall accounts for 59.6% of annual rainfall versus 61.7% for southern New Mexico. The length of the frost-free season in southeastern Arizona lowlands is 276 days (versus 212), and the difference between average July and January high temperatures is 34.6, slightly less than the 38.2 degrees F of the Chihuahuan Desert stations. Thus the southeastern Arizona climate appears somewhat less seasonal than that of southern New Mexico. In fact, the classic Sonoran biseasonal rainfall pattern grades into a summer-dominant one somewhere in southeastern Arizona. Jeff Dean (1996: Figure 5) shows the present-day boundary between the Sonoran biseasonal rainfall pattern and the Chihuahuan summer-dominant one as lying just west of the present study's southeastern Arizona region. Given the historical invasion of Chihuahuan Desert plant communities into southeastern Arizona, however, it is possible that this boundary lay farther east in the prehistoric past.

The difference between the two regions in the seasonal distribution of precipitation is actually more marked when the year is divided into three "seasons":

winter (October–March), spring (April–June), and summer (July–August). On average, southeastern Arizona receives ca. 40–50% of annual rainfall in both the winter and the summer seasons and 6–12% in the spring, while south-central New Mexico gets 20–40% in winter, 30–50% in summer, and 12–24% in spring (source: Desert Research Institute Western Regional Climate Center's website regional precipitation maps [http://www.wrcc.dri.edu/precip.html]). These data indicate the greater spring and summer rainfall in south-central New Mexico, a pattern that contrasts with a more bimodal winter-summer pattern in southeastern Arizona.

Evidence for stochastic variation in precipitation shows even greater similarities between the two regions (Table 5.2). In both regions, coefficients of variation for annual cool-season rainfall are greater than for the warm-season, with both warm- and cool-season coefficients of variation being slightly higher in southern New Mexico. As I note below, however, some of the biotic data suggest that stochastic variation may actually be notably higher in the Chihuahuan Desert than in the Sonoran. In any event, both regions exhibit a substantial degree of stochastic variation.

The limited data on biotic diversity presented in Table 5.3 suggest that diversity is greater in the Sonoran Desert than in the Chihuahuan. For the most part, Sonoran Desert species density is greater than that of both Chihuahuan Desert biomes. It should be noted, however, that the Semidesert Grassland is common to both regions and that the counts for the Sonoran Desertscrub reported by Brown (1994: Appendix II) include all subdivisions and not just the Arizona Uplands in southeastern Arizona. Insofar as productivity is related to diversity, these data also suggest greater productivity in southeastern Arizona.

Average annual precipitation (Table 5.2) from seven lowland sites in southeastern Arizona is 13.3 inches, while that for eight lowland locations in the northern Chihuahuan Desert is 9.2 inches, clearly indicating greater overall water availability—and presumably greater overall productivity—in southeastern Arizona. This is reflected in a higher amount of reliable rainfall as well, with San Simon getting at least 18.8 inches in 95 of 100 years, and El Paso getting roughly half that amount (9.7 inches). This difference is also reflected in differences in production/biomass ratios (i.e., turnover rates), which are higher in the two most common Chihuahuan Desert biomes, ranging from 0.32 (Chihuahuan Desertscrub) to 0.48 (Semidesert Grassland), than in the Arizona Upland division of the Sonoran Desert (0.12).

Hard (1986) noted this inverse relationship between turnover rates and overall precipitation, which may be related to differences in biotic diversity in deserts. As noted above, data on species diversity from two sources clearly indicate greater biotic diversity in the Sonoran Desert, particularly when the

Sonoran and Chihuahuan Desertscrub biomes are compared. Although the lower turnover rate for southeastern Arizona is consistent with Hard's model for agricultural adoption, it is not correlated with measures of biotic diversity, as I suggested earlier. Thus the relationship among these environmental characteristics is more complex than originally conceived.

Given that biotic diversity is often correlated with greater degrees of climatic equability, the Sonoran Desert and southeastern Arizona may have been more reliable in biotic productivity, despite having a lower turnover rate. I suggest that the observed differences in biotic diversity and rainfall reliability reflect differences in stochastic variation between the two regions that are not evident in the limited climatic data in Table 5.2. In other words, greater biotic diversity and more reliable productivity in the Sonoran Desert, including its easternmost portions, is an indicator of less overall stochastic variation and hence reduced stochastic environmental structure.

In this light, it is interesting to note that year-to-year variation in productivity may also differ markedly between the two regions. Richard Inouye (1991) gives figures for year-to-year variation in the biomass of desert annual plants (kg/ha) for Cave Creek (true Sonoran Desert in south-central Arizona) and the Jornada Experimental Station north of Las Cruces, New Mexico. At Cave Creek mid-season biomass rose from 26.0 to 76.0 in one year, varying by a factor of 3, while seasonal productivity dropped by a factor of 10 in another. In contrast, October biomass at the Jornada station dropped by a whopping factor of 25.4 from 43.2 to only 1.7 in a single year. If these data are at all representative of their respective regional environments, then stochastic variability in productivity may be considerably larger in the Chihuahuan Desert region.

This does not mean that the Chihuahuan Desert resources were necessarily less interesting to the area's foraging peoples, just less predictable. In fact, it is possible that the higher turnover rates of the more arid Chihuahuan biomes reflect a species-poor "bloom-or-bust" ecology, one whose "blooms" would be well worth exploiting when—and where—they happened.

Discussion

What are the implications of these data for explaining differences in the timing and degree of agricultural dependence between southeastern Arizona and southern New Mexico? The present analysis indicates that expected differences in several aspects of environmental structure—particularly spatial structure—played a role. The results also offer quantitative support for explanations proposed by previous researchers for both southeastern Arizona (e.g., Huckell 1990, 1995; Roth 1993; Stone and Bostwick 1996) and southern New Mexico

(Mauldin 1996; Waters and Woosley 1990). Spatially, the southeastern Arizona environment is twice as fine-grained as that of southern New Mexico, with the various economically important biomes being more closely packed and more evenly represented areally. In contrast, southern New Mexico valleys are much wider, and the less predictable lowland biomes are areally dominant. In southeastern Arizona peak-to-valley distances average 22 km, meaning that a full and more evenly balanced range of regional biotic resources is available within one to two days' walk of most valley locations—which, by the way, are usually coincident with reliable water sources.

In contrast, the upland biotic resources of southern New Mexico are located far from valley floors, albeit less far from the better-watered alluvial fans, where the "true" agriculture of later ceramic periods was pursued. While it might seem that foragers of southern New Mexico could sit on these fans between the valleys and the uplands and exploit the best of both worlds, the region's greater stochastic environmental structure may have made such a strategy risky at best (see Mauldin 1995 for a discussion of regional stochastic patterning in south-central New Mexico precipitation). First, most of the region's upland streams are not perennial, and water availability at any particular fan location is as much a function of the region's patchy summer rains as it is of the more spatially consistent winter precipitation. Second, both a greater stochastic component to rainfall distribution and the region's greater geographic scale mean that the average distance between precipitation-induced resource "blooms" (particularly basin-floor ones) as well as distances between resource zones themselves are greater than for southeastern Arizona. Thus mobility strategies had to accommodate greater distances and incorporate a greater degree of flexibility. In other words, a "boom-or-bust" ecology required a higher overall degree of residential mobility, including a greater degree of seasonal relocation.

I am not arguing that the differences in environmental structure between southeastern Arizona and southern New Mexico produced radical differences in residential mobility. Rather, I am suggesting that substantial differences in spatial structure, together with at least small differences in temporal structure, stochastic variability, and overall reliability of water availability and biotic resource productivity, meant that the Late Archaic hunter-gatherers of southeastern Arizona had more resource options available to them and were less reliant on large-scale residential mobility for success.

Both the scale and frequency of residential movements may have been less in southeastern Arizona. Coupled with greater water availability along perennial valley streams—for agriculture, among other purposes—this difference may have reduced or eliminated scheduling conflicts for burgeoning agriculturalists (as suggested by Wills and Huckell 1994), making it much easier to take up cultivation, whatever the "external driving force." In addition, tighter geo-graphic packing of biomes meant that—even in years of low agricultural pro-ductivity—agriculturalists did not have to go as far to acquire wild resources. In contrast, intensive agriculture was much more of an "either/or" proposition for the seriously "seasonal" Late Archaic foragers of southern New Mexico, who waited until all high-mobility options were exhausted before trading their atl-atls in for digging sticks.

Finally, Dering's analysis of the lower Pecos region in southwest Texas and Mexico (this volume) indicates an even less spatially structured environment than that of south-central New Mexico, and—interestingly—one in which agriculture never took hold at all.

ACKNOWLEDGMENTS

Portions of the research presented in this chapter were supported by the New Mex-ico State Highway Department (NMSHTD Project Nos. TPA-026–1[5], C.N. 2082 and BR-0–TPM-0117[2]) and the University of New Mexico Maxwell Museum of Anthropology. Ron Stauber of the Office of Contract Archeology prepared the graphics. Special thanks go to Brad Vierra for inviting me to contribute and to Bruce Huckell for his comments and insight.

REFERENCES CITED

Anderson, S.
1993   Archaic Period Land Use in the Southern Tularosa Basin, New Mexico. In *Preliminary Investigations of the Archaic in the Region of Las Cruces, New Mexico,* edited by R. S. MacNeish, pp. 48–67. Historic and Natural Resources Report No. 9, Cultural Resources Management Branch, Directorate of Environment. U.S. Army Air Defense Artillery Center, Fort Bliss, Tex.

Anschuetz, K. F., and P. T. Noyes
1990   Environmental Setting. In *Landscape Archeology in the Southern Tularosa Basin, Volume 1: Small Site Distributions and Geomor-phology,* edited by K. F. Anschuetz, W. H. Doleman, and R. C. Chapman, pp. 5–15. OCA/UNM Report No. 185-324D. Office of Contract Archeology, University of New Mexico, Albuquerque.

Beckett, P. H.
1983   The Paleoindian Prehistory of the Tularosa Basin. In *The Prehis-tory of Rhodes Canyon, New Mexico,* edited by P. L. Eidenbach. Human Systems Research, Inc., Tularosa, N.Mex.

Berry, C. F., and M. S. Berry

1986   Chronological and Conceptual Models of the Southwestern Archaic. In *Anthropology of the Desert West: Essays in Honor of Jesse D. Jennings,* edited by C. J. Condie and D. D. Fowler, pp. 253–327. Anthropological Papers No. 110. University of Utah Press, Salt Lake City.

Berry, M. S.

1982   *Time, Space, and Transition in Anasazi Prehistory.* University of Utah Press, Salt Lake City.

Binford, L. R.

1980   Willow Smoke and Dogs' Tails: Hunter-Gatherer Settlement Systems and Archaeological Site Formation. *American Antiquity* 45:4–20.

1982   The Archaeology of Place. *Journal of Anthropological Archaeology* 1:5–31.

2001   *Constructing Frames of Reference: An Analytical Method for Archaeological Theory Building Using Hunter-Gatherer and Environmental Data Sets.* University of California Press, Berkeley.

Brown, D. E. (editor)

1994   *Biotic Communities: Southwestern United States and Northwestern Mexico.* University of Utah Press, Salt Lake City.

Brown, D. E., and C. H. Lowe

1994   *Biotic Communities of the Southwest.* Map published by University of Utah Press, Salt Lake City.

Bulloch, H. E., and R. E. Neher

1980   *Soil Survey of Doña Ana County Area, New Mexico.* United States Department of Agriculture, Soil Conservation Service, in cooperation with the United States Department of the Army, White Sands Missile Range, and the New Mexico Agricultural Experiment Station, New Mexico State University, Las Cruces. United States Government Printing Office, Washington, D.C.

Carmichael, D. L.

1988   Patterns of Residential Mobility and Sedentism in the Jornada-Mogollon Area. Paper presented at the 1st Biannual Southwest Symposium, Arizona State University, Tempe.

Cordell, Linda S.

1984   *Prehistory of the Southwest.* Academic Press, New York.

Cosgrove, C. B.

1947   *Caves of the Upper Gila and Hueco Areas in New Mexico and*

Texas. Peabody Museum Papers 24(2). Harvard University, Cambridge, Mass.

Dean, J. S.

1996   Demography, Environment, and Subsistence Stress. In *Evolving Complexity and Environmental Risk in the Prehistoric Southwest,* edited by J. A. Tainter and B. B. Tainter, pp. 25–56. Proceedings Volume 24, Santa Fe Institute Studies in the Sciences of Complexity. Addison-Wesley Publishing Company, Reading, Mass.

Derr, P. S.

1981   *Soil Survey of Otero Area, New Mexico: Parts of Otero, Eddy, Chavez, and Socorro Counties.* United States Department of Agriculture, Soil Conservation Service, in cooperation with the United States Department of the Army, White Sands Missile Range, and the New Mexico Agricultural Experiment Station, New Mexico State University, Las Cruces. United States Government Printing Office, Washington, D.C.

Doleman, W. H.

1990   Research Goals. In *Archeological Testing of Two Prehistoric Sites at Holloman Air Force Base, New Mexico,* by W. H. Doleman, J. Elyea, and R. Dello-Russo, pp. 8–29. OCA/UNM Report No. 185-424. Office of Contract Archeology, University of New Mexico, Albuquerque.

1995   Human and Natural Landscapes: Archeological Distributions in the Southern Tularosa Basin. Ph.D. dissertation, Department of Anthropology, University of New Mexico, Albuquerque.

1997   *Prehistoric Occupations near the Lower Placitas Arroyo: Excavations along State Road 26 West of Hatch, New Mexico.* OCA/UNM Report No. 185-511. Office of Contract Archeology, University of New Mexico, Albuquerque.

Elyea, J., and P. Hogan

1983   Regional Interaction: The Archaic Adaptation. In *Economy and Interaction along the Lower Chaco River,* edited by P. Hogan and J. C. Winter, pp. 393–402. OCA/UNM Report No. 185-94. Office of Contract Archeology and Maxwell Museum of Anthropology, University of New Mexico, Albuquerque.

Gilman, Patricia A., Valli S. Powell, and Don L. Dycus

1996   The Role of Agriculture and Residential Movement in the Late Archaic and Early Pit Structure Periods of Southeastern Arizona. In *Early Formative Adaptations in the Southern Southwest,* edited by B. J. Roth, pp. 73–84. Monographs in World Archaeology No. 25. Prehistory Press, Madison, Wis.

Glassow, M. A.

1980 *Prehistoric Agricultural Development in the Northern Southwest.* Anthropology Papers No. 16. Ballena Press, Socorro, N.Mex.

Hard, R. J.

1986 Ecological Relationships Affecting the Rise of Farming Economies: A Test from the American Southwest. Ph.D. dissertation, Department of Anthropology, University of New Mexico, Albuquerque.

1997 A Comparative Analysis of Agricultural Dependence in the Northern and Southern Jornada Mogollon Regions. In *Proceedings of the Ninth Jornada-Mogollon Conference,* edited by R. P. Mauldin, J. D. Leach, and S. Ruth, pp. 93–98. Publications in Archaeology No. 12. Centro de Investigaciones Arqueologicas, El Paso, Tex.

Harpending, Henry, and Herbert Davis

1977 Some Implications for Hunter-Gatherer Ecology Derived from the Spatial Structure of Resources. *World Archaeology* 8(3): 275–286.

Huckell, B. B.

1990 Late Preceramic Farmer-Foragers in Southeastern Arizona: A Cultural and Ecological Consideration of the Spread of Agriculture into the Arid Southwestern United States. Ph.D. dissertation, University of Arizona, Tucson. University Microfilms, Ann Arbor.

1995 *Of Marshes and Maize: Preceramic Agricultural Settlements in the Cienega Valley, Southeastern Arizona.* Anthropological Papers No. 59. University of Arizona Press, Tucson.

1996 Middle to Late Holocene Stream Behavior and the Transition to Agriculture in Southeastern Arizona. In *Early Formative Adaptations in the Southern Southwest,* edited by B. J. Roth, pp. 27–36. Monographs in World Archaeology No. 25. Prehistory Press, Madison, Wis.

Hunter-Anderson, R. L.

1986 *Prehistoric Adaptation in the American Southwest.* Cambridge University Press, Cambridge.

Inouye, R. S.

1991 Population Biology of Desert Annual Plants. In *The Ecology of Desert Communities,* edited by Gary A. Polis, pp. 27–54. University of Arizona Press, Tucson.

Irwin-Williams, C.

    1973   *The Oshara Tradition: Origins of Anasazi Culture.* Eastern New Mexico University Contributions in Anthropology 5(1). Eastern New Mexico University, Portales.

Kelly, R. L.

    1995   *The Foraging Spectrum: Diversity in Hunter-Gatherer Lifeways.* Smithsonian Institution Press, Washington, D.C.

Kirkpatrick, David T., Peter Eidenbach, Karl W. Laumbach, and Meliha S. Duran

    2000   *Basin and Range Archaeology: An Overview of Prehistory in South-Central New Mexico.* Human Systems Research, Inc. MS on file at the New Mexico Department of Cultural Affairs Historic Preservation Division, Santa Fe.

Lee, R. B., and I. DeVore

    1968   *Man the Hunter.* Aldine Publishing Co., Chicago.

Lehmer, Donald J.

    1948   *The Jornada Branch of the Mogollon.* Social Science Bulletin 17. University of Arizona, Tucson.

Lowe, C. H., and D. E. Brown

    1994   Introduction. In *Biotic Communities: Southwestern United States and Northwestern Mexico,* edited by D. E. Brown, pp. 8–16. University of Utah Press, Salt Lake City.

MacNeish, Richard S. (editor)

    1993   *Preliminary Investigations of the Archaic in the Region of Las Cruces, New Mexico.* Historic and Natural Resources Report No. 9. United States Army Air Defense Artillery Center, Fort Bliss, Tex.

MacNeish, Richard S., and Patrick H. Beckett

    1987   *The Archaic Chihuahua Tradition of South-Central New Mexico and Chihuahua, Mexico.* COAS Monograph 7. COAS Publishing and Research, Las Cruces, N.Mex.

Matson, R. G.

    1991   *The Origins of Southwest Agriculture.* University of Arizona Press, Tucson.

Mauldin, R.

    1986   Settlement and Subsistence Patterns during the Pueblo Period on Fort Bliss, Texas: A Model. In *Mogollon Variability,* edited by C. Benson and S. Upham, pp. 255–269. Occasional Papers No. 15. New Mexico State University, University Museum, Las Cruces.

    1995   Groping for the Past: Investigating Archaeological Patterns across Time and Space in the Southern Southwestern United States.

Ph.D. dissertation, Department of Anthropology, University of New Mexico.

1996   Exploring Patterns in Late Archaic and Early Ceramic Residential Occupation in the Northern Chihuahuan Desert. In *Early Formative Adaptations in the Southern Southwest,* edited by B. J. Roth, pp. 85–97. Monographs in World Archaeology No. 25. Prehistory Press, Madison, Wis.

Minnis, P. E.

1985   Domesticating Plants and People in the Greater Southwest. In *Prehistoric Food Production in North America,* edited by R. I. Ford, pp. 309–340. Anthropological Papers No. 75. Museum of Anthropology, University of Michigan, Ann Arbor.

Morenon, E. P., and T. R. Hays

1984   *Archaeological Investigations in the Placitas Arroyo, New Mexico.* Final report to Interagency Archeological Services, National Park Service, Denver, Colo. Archaeology Program, Institute of Applied Sciences, North Texas State University, Denton.

Noyes, P. T., and M. F. Schmader

1988   Environmental Overview. In *The Border Star 85 Survey: Toward an Archeology of Landscapes,* edited by T. J. Seaman, W. H. Doleman, and R. C. Chapman, pp. 19–26. Office of Contract Archeology, University of New Mexico, Albuquerque.

O'Hara, J.

1988   Projectile Point Analysis. In *The Border Star 85 Survey: Toward an Archeology of Landscapes,* edited by T. J. Seaman, W. H. Doleman, and R. C. Chapman, pp. 191–208. OCA/UNM Report No. 185-227. Office of Contract Archeology, University of New Mexico, Albuquerque.

O'Laughlin, T. C.

1980   *The Keystone Dam Site and Other Archaic and Formative Sites in Northwest El Paso, Texas.* Publications in Anthropology No. 8. El Paso Centennial Museum, University of Texas at El Paso.

1985   Early Formative Ceramic Assemblages in the Mesilla Valley of Southern New Mexico. In *Views of the Jornada Mogollon,* edited by C. M. Beck, pp. 54–67. Eastern New Mexico University Contributions in Anthropology Volume 12. Eastern New Mexico University, Portales.

Pianka, E. R.

1978   *Evolutionary Ecology.* 2nd ed. Harper and Row, New York.

Polis, G. A.

    1991   Desert Communities: An Overview of Patterns and Processes. In *The Ecology of Desert Communities,* edited by G. A. Polis, pp. 1–26. University of Arizona Press, Tucson.

Roth, B. J.

    1993   Changing Perceptions of the Late Archaic: An Example from the Southern Southwest. *North American Archaeologist* 14:123–137.

Sayles, E. B.

    1935   *An Archaeological Survey of Texas.* Medallion Papers No. 17. Gila Pueblo, Globe, Ariz.

Sayles, E. B., and Ernest Antevs

    1941   *The Cochise Culture.* Medallion Papers No. 24. Gila Pueblo, Globe, Ariz.

Sellers, W. D., and R. H. Hill

    1974   *Arizona Climate.* University of Arizona Press, Tucson.

Shackley, M. Steven

    1990   Early Hunter-Gatherer Procurement Ranges in the Southwest: Evidence for Obsidian Geochemistry and Lithic Technology. Ph.D. dissertation, Arizona State University. University Microfilms, Ann Arbor.

    1996   Range and Mobility in the Early Hunter-Gatherer Southwest. In *Early Formative Adaptations in the Southern Southwest,* edited by B. J. Roth, pp. 5–16. Monographs in World Archaeology No. 25. Prehistory Press, Madison, Wis.

Simms, S. R.

    1984   Aboriginal Great Basin Foraging Strategies. Ph.D. dissertation, University of Utah. University Microfilms, Ann Arbor.

Stone, C., and T. Bostwick

    1996   Environmental Contexts and Archaeological Correlates: The Transition to Farming in Three Regions of the Arizona Desert. In *Early Formative Adaptations in the Southern Southwest,* edited by B. J. Roth, pp. 17–26. Monographs in World Archaeology No. 25. Prehistory Press, Madison, Wis.

Tagg, Martyn D.

    1996   Early Cultigens from Fresnal Shelter, Southeastern New Mexico. *American Antiquity* 61:311–324.

United States Department of the Army

    1983   *Natural Resources Management Plan, White Sands Missile Range.* White Sands Missile Range, N.Mex.

Upham, S., R. S. MacNeish, W. C. Galinat, and C. M. Stevenson

1987   Evidence concerning the Origin of Maíz de Ocho. *American Anthropologist* 89(2):410–418.

Van Devender, T. R.

1990a   Late Quaternary Vegetation and Climate of the Chihuahuan Desert, United States and Mexico. In *Packrat Middens: The Last 40,000 Years of Biotic Change,* edited by J. L. Betancourt, T. R. Van Devender, and P. S. Martin, pp. 104–133. University of Arizona Press, Tucson.

1990b   Late Quaternary Vegetation and Climate of the Sonoran Desert, United States and Mexico. In *Packrat Middens: the Last 40,000 Years of Biotic Change,* edited by J. L. Betancourt, T. R. Van Devender, and P. S. Martin, pp. 134–165. University of Arizona Press, Tucson.

Waters, M. R., and A. I. Woosley

1990   The Geoarchaeology and Preceramic Prehistory of the Willcox Basin, Southeastern Arizona. *Journal of Field Archaeology* 17:163–175.

Whalen, M. E.

1981   Origin and Evolution of Ceramics in Western Texas. *Bulletin of the Texas Archeological Society* 52:215–229.

1994   Moving Out of the Archaic on the Edge of the Southwest. *American Antiquity* 59:622–638.

Wills, W. H.

1988   *Early Prehistoric Agriculture in the American Southwest.* School of American Research Press, Santa Fe.

Wills, W. H., and B. B. Huckell

1994   Economic Implications of Changing Land-Use Patterns in the Late Archaic. In *Themes in Southwest Prehistory,* edited by George J. Gumerman, pp. 33–52. School of American Research Press, Santa Fe.

Winterhalder, B., and E. A. Smith (editors)

1992   *Evolutionary Ecology and Human Behavior.* Aldine de Gruyter, New York.

Yellen, John

1977   Long-term Hunter-Gatherer Adaptation to Desert Environments: A Biogeographical Perspective. *World Archaeology* 8(3):262–274.

CHAPTER 6

The Transition to Farming on the Río Casas Grandes and in the Southern Jornada Mogollon Region

ROBERT J. HARD AND JOHN R. RONEY

P oorly understood variability characterizes the rate at which hunting and gathering economies evolve into farming ones at global and regional scales. In Southwestern North America farming economies were typically established with the formation of early pithouse settlements in the Hohokam, Anasazi, and Mogollon regions between ca. A D 200 and 700. Recent investigations have shown that significant use of maize was underway by ca. 1200 B C in southern Arizona (Huckell 1995; Huckell et al. 1995; Mabry 1998, 2002, 2003; Mabry et al. 1997). The extremes of this variability are particularly evident in the vicinity of the New Mexico–Chihuahua international border. Along the Río Casas Grandes in Chihuahua, Native Americans living at the site of Cerro Juanaqueña had made significant investment in farming by 1200 B C. Yet only 30–200 km to the northeast, the people of the Jornada Mogollon region, living along the Rio Grande, did not markedly invest in farming until ca. A D 1000–1100 (Figure 6.1).

Recent advances in optimal foraging theory combined with new data from Cerro Juanaqueña may offer utility in understanding this variability. A description of the results of four years of excavation at the site provides background for the comparison between the formation of farming communities in the Jornada region versus the Río Casas Grandes region.

Cerro Juanaqueña

Cerro Juanaqueña, dating to 1250 B C, not only represents an early aggregated settlement; it also predates most other *cerros de trincheras* (literally hill with trenches or walls) by about 2,000 years. *Cerros de trincheras* are complexes of hilltop terraces, rock rings, and stone walls that typically date to after A D 1200 and are associated with the large populations of agriculturalists in the Hohokam and Trincheras culture areas of southern Arizona and northern Sonora, Mexico (e.g., Johnson 1960; McGuire et al. 1999; McGuire and McNiff

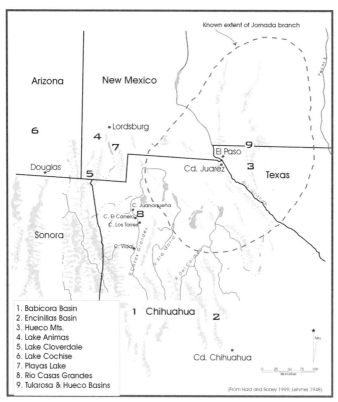

Figure 6.1. Jornada Branch of the Mogollon region (indicated by the dashed line), including both northern and southern areas (Lehmer 1948). Most of the Jornada data used in this paper are from the vicinity of El Paso. Cerro Juanaqueña and three other Late Archaic period *cerros de trincheras* sites are located along the Río Casas Grandes. The numbers 1 to 9 represent locales with paleoecological information.

1990; McGuire and Villalpando 1993; O'Donovan 2002; Sauer and Brand 1931; Stacy 1974; Wilcox 1979; Zavala 1998). Cerro Juanaqueña is a large, aggregated, intensively occupied *cerro de trincheras* with 550 terraces and 99 rock rings. Two-thirds of the features are on a 6-ha area of the summit and upper slopes, and the balance are on a 4-ha area on the western side of the hill just above the floodplain (Figure 6.2).

Native Americans constructed the terraces by first piling the local basalt cobbles to form berms that bow out in the center and pinch in at the ends against 5–40% slopes (Figure 6.3). Occasionally rocks were stacked. The pocket between the apex of the berm wall and the natural slope behind was then filled in with smaller rocks (Figure 6.4). Finally sediment capped the construction to form a level to slightly sloping surface. The mean area of these terraces is 52 m^2 (Hard et al. 1999). The constructed terraces cover a total area of 8 ha and include almost 8 linear km of terrace wall. In order to evaluate construction effort we built a terrace that was similar to the ancient ones (Hard et al. 1999). Volumetric estimates of all features suggest that 40,000 tons of rock and sediment were moved during their construction. This effort would have required thirty person-years of labor, an effort equivalent to the construction of a 550-room pueblo (Hard et al. 1999).

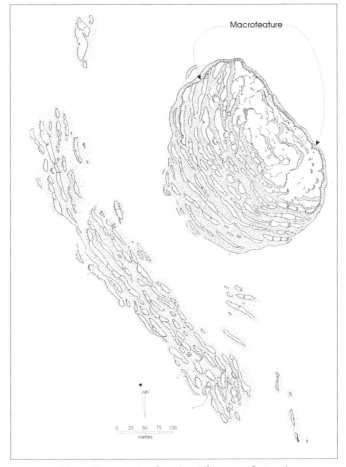

Figure 6.2. Cerro Juanaqueña plan view. The macrofeature is a continuous terrace/berm wall that forms the site perimeter on the north, east, and south sides.

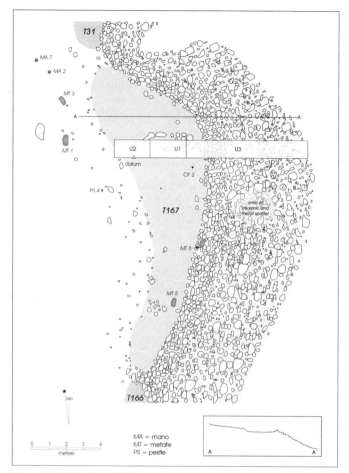

MA = mano
MT = metate
PS = pestle

0 1 2 3 4
meters

Figure 6.3. Plan view of Terrace 167

The site layout shows elements of planning (Hard et al. 1999). About twenty-two adjoined terraces and two walls form a 400-m continuous berm wall or macrofeature (Figure 6.2) that bounds the northern, eastern, and southern sides of the site. About 40% of the terraces form articulated linear groups of about two to five terraces each built on a single contour. Individual terraces within the groups are demarcated by constricted points along the berm walls or by small cross walls lying perpendicular to the berm wall. Typically, multiple terraces or terrace groups are built along the same contour, so one can walk significant distances around the hill with little change in elevation. There is roughly even spacing among bands of terraces up and down slope. No doubt some of these organizational aspects are the result of using the natural topography of the hill to best advantage, but the overall pattern and symmetry to the site indicates that internal site planning was under the direction of a recognized leader (Hard et al. 1999).

The terraces were primarily constructed to serve as living surfaces and house platforms. Household debris, including numerous basin and slab metates, manos, burned and unburned bone, lithic manufacturing debris, projectile points, cores, hammerstones, charred and uncharred bone, ashy sediment, and trash midden deposits, is common on the surface and within the exc... ated terrace construction fill.

While archaeologists have argued that many terrace features on *trincheras* sites in southwestern and northwestern Mexico were constructed as agricultural features, the Cerro Juanaqueña terraces appear to have been too energetically costly to be constructed for this purpose. The approximately 2.5 ha of potential planting area is too small and costly to construct for effective agriculture. If all the terraces were planted in maize the harvest would only support about four adults a year (Hard et al. 1999). The high labor cost per hectare of potential planting area exceeds that of other agricultural terracing systems and would even exceed the costs of constructing Maya raised fields (Hard et al. 1999). In addition, the thin soil and absence of water control features on the terraces

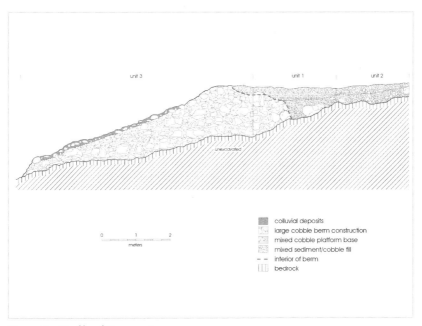

Figure 6.4. Profile of Terrace 167

suggest that farming would have been far more successful in the floodplain of the Río Casas Grandes immediately below the site.

Associated with the terraces are rock rings, which tend to cluster on the hilltop and upper one-third of the slopes. This distribution tends to correlate with the greatest surface concentrations of ground stone. The diameters of the 99 rings are normally distributed, and the mean is 2.63 m (std. dev. = 0.86 m). Most rings were constructed on terrace surfaces or on slight platforms built on the terraces. Some are semicircles with openings in various directions, but most are complete circles or ovals. Excavations revealed little in the way of floor features or in situ assemblages, perhaps in part due to the poorly preserved living floors. One ring (R239) contained a small, shallow, basin-shaped hearth with small burned rocks. Another ring contained a basin metate on the floor. At least some of these rock rings served as foundations for small circular structures.

We excavated two adjacent large storage pits that were constructed into one of the lower terraces. Both were roughly cylindrical, about 90 cm in diameter and 1.8 m–2 m deep. The first was clearly rock-lined. Both contained substantial amounts of charred and uncharred animal bone as well as more charred plant remains than found in other site contexts. An AMS date on maize from one of the pits identified them as contemporaneous with the primary site occupation. These pits offer the first direct evidence of food storage at Cerro Juanaqueña.

The terrace features are associated with a dense and varied assemblage of artifacts, including projectile points, basin metates, slab metates, manos, chipped stone drills or awls, small cruciform-shaped objects, cores, hammerstones, tubular stone pipes, stone and bone pendants, bone awls, and large quantities of debitage (see Vierra, this volume, for an analysis). We recovered over 300 dart points and another 200 bifaces and preforms most likely related to projectile point manufacture. Point styles from both surface and excavated contexts are characteristic of the Late Archaic period. They include forms similar to San Pedro, Hatch, Hueco, En Medio, Shumla, and Diagonal Notched types (Hard and Roney 1998a:1662; MacNeish 1993; Martin et al. 1952; Turner and Hester 1995; Turpin 1991). All of these types were used between 1500 BC and AD 1000 but were most common during the earlier portion of this period (MacNeish 1993; Roth and Huckell 1992; Turner and Hester 1995; Turpin 1991). The other artifacts which corroborate a Late Archaic age include over 500 whole and fragmentary slab and basin metates, small oval to round manos, tubular stone pipes, shallow stone mortars or bowls, small mushroom-shaped pestles, and stone cruciforms (Hard and Roney 1998a:1662, 1999, 2004; Roney and Hard 2002).

The large numbers of manos and metates found on the surface and in excavations offer insight into processing activities at Cerro Juanaqueña. Based on a sample of 80 whole manos from surface contexts, 80% were manufactured

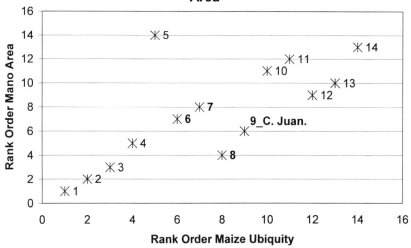

Figure 6.5. Scattergram showing rank order of mano area and maize ubiquity from Cerro Juanaqueña and other Southwestern components. 1 = Southern Jornada Late Archaic; 2 = Cedar Mesa Archaic; 3 = Southern Jornada Mesilla phase (early pithouse); 4 = Antelope Creek phase, Texas; 5 = Black Mesa Late Pueblo; 6 = Southern Jornada Doña Ana phase (late pithouse); 7 = Black Mesa Early Pueblo; 8 = Black Mesa BM II; 9 = Cerro Juanaqueña; 10 = Southern Jornada El Paso phase (pueblo); 11 = Mesa Verde BMIII; 12 = Northern Jornada Lincoln phase (pueblo); 13 = Cedar Mesa BMII; 14 = Mesa Verde PII–PIII (see Hard et al. 1996). Other mixed economies similar to Cerro Juanaqueña are in boldface.

from local basalt, with the balance made from rhyolite and unknown materials. The manos tend to be circular to oval in plan and flat to spheroid in cross section. Most of these shapes were likely used with the heavily worn, large basin metates. The mean area of all manos is 115.3 cm² (std. dev. = 51.6 cm², n = 48), and the mean length is 11.6 cm (std. dev. = 2.7 cm, n = 48). These are small compared to those found in later pueblo sites, yet they are somewhat larger than typical Archaic manos.

Recent research (Hard 1990; Hard et al. 1996; Mauldin 1993; although see Adams 1999) suggests that mano size is related to agricultural dependence. Figure 6.5 is a rank-order scattergram representing maize ubiquity and mano area for fifteen Southwestern components.

Cerro Juanaqueña clusters with the Dona Aña (Late Pithouse) phase of the Jornada Mogollon, Black Mesa Basketmaker II, and Black Mesa Early Pueblo occupations. These exhibit a middle level of agricultural use, falling between most puebloan occupations and dominantly hunter-gatherer adaptations (Hard et al. 1996).

Metates and metate fragments are more common than manos, with as many as 20 metate pieces occurring on one terrace. There are 961 mano and metate pieces on the surface of the site. The basin metates are large and heavily worn, with steeply angled sides that form almost a V-shaped basin. The mean depth of basin wear is 8.06 cm (std. dev. = 3.95 cm, n = 44). This degree of wear represents intensive food-grinding activity over many generations. Estimates of wear rates suggest that the sum of the wear on all of the Cerro Juanaqueña basin metates is the result of 20,000 person-years of food processing (Roney and Hard 2002).

In addition to our work on Cerro Juanaqueña we have documented twelve other *cerros de trincheras* in the Río Casas Grandes drainage and the adjacent Río Santa María drainage (Roney and Hard 2004). Three are radiocarbon-dated to the Late Archaic period and are briefly discussed below (for their locations, see Figure 6.1). The rest are undated, but other evidence suggests that most of them belong to the Late Archaic period as well (Roney and Hard 2004).

Cerro el Canelo is only about half the size of Cerro Juanaqueña, but it is comparable in terms of setting, construction, overall layout, and range of activities represented. The site is constructed on a 160–m high hill along the Río Casas Grandes. It contains about 250 terraces that form 3.9 linear km of construction and 50 rock rings. Like Cerro Juanaqueña, Cerro el Canelo contains linked terraces that form macrofeatures up to 350 m long. Two radiocarbon dates are from the main part of the site. One AMS date on ocotillo is 2990 ± 45 b.p. and places the site as exactly contemporaneous with Cerro Juanaqueña. A second AMS date of 330 ± 60 b.p. on a charred monocot fragment from the same feature is probably the result of a historic fire. In a low saddle near the base of the hill is a stone circle 70 m in diameter, defined by a rubble berm. A fragment of a large mammal bone recovered from the berm yielded a conventional radiocarbon date of 630 ± 50 b.p. Despite this result, we still suspect that the feature is contemporaneous with the other terraces at Cerro el Canelo. The mode of construction, patination on the rocks, and vegetation on the berm are identical to those on the main terrace complex. There is comparatively little evidence of Ceramic period occupation and no ceramic or other artifact associations that suggest Ceramic period use of the feature itself (Roney and Hard 2004). Basin and slab metates, small manos, chipped stone, stone bowls, and a number of Late Archaic projectile points are similar to those at Cerro Juanaqueña, although the density is somewhat lower.

Cerro los Torres is an isolated 80-m high basaltic hill located near the eastern margin of the Río Casas Grandes floodplain, almost a kilometer from the river (Figure 6.1). A majority of the terraces on this site are arc-shaped with rubble berm construction, comparable to those at Cerro Juanaqueña and Cerro el Canelo. A 500-m long continuous rubble berm defines the western and southern edge of the site, and eight well-defined rock rings occur among the 2.3 linear km of terrace and berm walls. The range of artifacts is similar to other Late Archaic *trincheras* sites in the region. A single AMS radiocarbon date from a maize cupule of 2920 ± 55 b.p. places the site occupation as contemporaneous with Cerro Juanaqueña and Cerro el Canelo (Roney and Hard 2004).

Near Haciendas San Diego the Río Palanganas and the Río Piedras Verdes unite to form the Río Casas Grandes. Cerro Vidal is a 120-m-high hill that overlooks this confluence. Terrace construction at this site resembles that documented at other *cerros de trincheras* in northwestern Chihuahua. At Cerro Vidal, however, individual arcs are often difficult to define. Instead the terraces form macrofeatures which describe two concentric rings around the summit, a large lobe appended to these, and an outer berm/terrace which circles the entire complex. There are about 37 rock rings and 2.2 linear km of berm/terrace construction. The density and range of artifacts are similar to those at Cerro el Canelo and Cerro Los Torres. Two AMS radiocarbon dates on maize cupules from the same feature yielded dates of 2100 ± 40 b.p. and 2340 ± 55 b.p. (Figure 6.6). As discussed below, this date is similar to evidence of a late occupation on the lower terraces of Cerro Juanaqueña.

Radiocarbon Dating

Seventeen AMS radiocarbon dates on maize or other short-lived charred plant materials are presented in Figure 6.6 (for additional details, see Roney and Hard 2002: Table 2). Of the twenty-four features excavated, thirteen yielded short-lived plant material suitable for dating which minimized the "old wood" problem. All samples were taken from within cultural terrace fill or terrace walls. During feature excavation we frequently observed downward vertical movement of fill through the voids among the rocks. Botanical preservation was better at lower depths. If dates from a particular feature were anomalous, we submitted additional samples for better evaluation of the results. Figure 6.6 presents the calibrated frequency distribution for these radiocarbon ages, based on the radiocarbon calibration program OxCal (Bronk Ramsey 1999).

The 17 dates fall into three distinct clusters. The earliest is a single date, NSRL 3985, at 3310 BP from Terrace T222. This date is statistically different from 2 other dates from the same feature, as well as the other 13 dates from the site, and should be rejected (Hard and Roney 1998a; Roney and Hard 2002). The next 14 dates cluster around 3000 BP. A T'test statistical procedure (Ward and

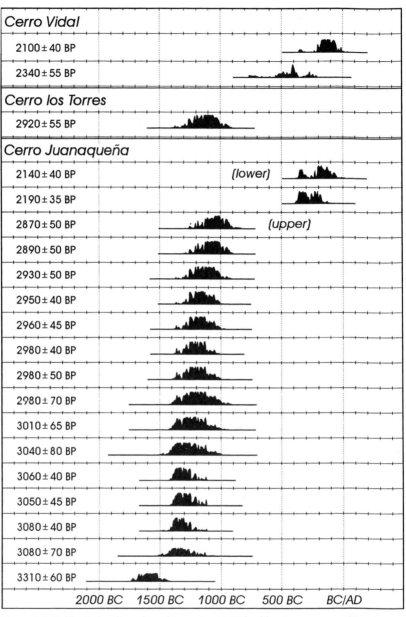

Figure 6.6. Calibrated radiocarbon dates using OxCal calibration program (Bronk Ramsey 1999). "Lower" indicates two dates from a terrace on the lower slope of Cerro Juanaqueña; "upper" refers to the remaining fifteen dates from the upper slope and top of the site.

Wilson 1978) shows that these 14 dates are compatible with a single population, implying that they are statistically contemporaneous. It is then appropriate to average the 14 dates and calibrate the results. This procedure yields a two-sigma result of BC 1270–1140, a calendrical date that approximates the principal occupation at Cerro Juanaqueña. This is contemporaneous with the dates from Cerro el Canelo and Cerro los Torres. We have also used the calibration program OxCal (Bronk Ramsey 1999) to estimate the probable span of this occupation. We found that at the two-sigma level (95.5% confidence interval) the span of the principal occupation is more than 100 years and less than 550 years, with a midrange of about 200–300 calendar years (Hard and Roney 2004; Roney and Hard 2002).

The final cluster consists of the two most recent dates listed in Figure 6.6, which are also statistically contemporaneous. They come from a single terrace in the lower terrace complex at Cerro Juanaqueña. Their two-sigma calibrated average is 360–160 BC. These two dates probably reflect a limited reoccupation of the lower portion of the site. They are contemporaneous with the occupation of Cerro Vidal (Figure 6.6).

Subsistence

Bone is well preserved in the terraces, and faunal analysis by Kari Schmidt and Jennifer Nisengard (1999, 2000) shows that 90% of the 1,794 Number of Identified Specimens (NISP) are lagomorphs; 80% of these are jackrabbits (*Lepus* sp.), with the balance being cottontail rabbits (*Sylvilagus* sp.). Artiodactyls, including deer (*Odocoileus* sp.), pronghorn antelope (*Antilocapra americana*), and a few big horn sheep (*Ovis canadensis*), account for an additional 5% of the NISP, and the other 5% consists of a variety of fish, reptiles, amphibians, birds, rodents, and carnivores. The heavy fractions of our flotation samples yielded 261 identifiable specimens. Fish and rodents dominate this assemblage, accounting for 29% and 53% respectively of the identifiable heavy fraction bone (see Hard and Roney 2004 for further discussion of fish remains).

Charred plant remains were recovered primarily from flotation samples as well as from our screens during excavation. Karen Adams found charred maize parts to be the most common plant present (Table 6.1). Maize was found in 60% of all excavated features (*n* = 20) and 40% of all analyzed light fractions (*n* = 117), suggesting that it was a dietary staple (Adams 1998, 1999a, 1999b; Hanselka 2000; Hard and Roney 1998a, 1999; Roney and Hard 2002). Cheno-am was the next most frequently recovered charred taxon, including both non-domesticated chenopodium and probable domesticated amaranth (see below). Other taxa recovered include unidentified grasses, Plains lovegrass, bulrush,

Table 6.1. Charred plant remains at Cerro Juanaqueña

	Percentage of Features
Taxa	$n = 20$
Corn (*Zea mays*)	60
Cheno-am	45
Unidentified grasses (Gramineae)	20
Bulrush (*Scirpus* sp.)	15
Chia (*Salvia* sp.)	10
Unidentified monocot (Monocotyledon)	10
Plains lovegrass (*Eragrostis intermedia*)	5
Milkvetch (*Astragalus nuttalliana*)	5
Horsepurslane (*Trianthema* sp.)	5
Barrel cactus (*Ferocactus* sp.)	5
Globemallow (*Sphaeralcea* sp.)	5
Wild gourd (*Cucurbita digitata* or *C. foetidissima*)	5

chia, milkvetch, horsepurslane, barrel cactus, an unidentified monocot, globe-mallow, and wild gourd. Many of these taxa are available during late summer and early fall. Astragalus fruits in spring (February to May), and some taxa are available for extended periods from spring through late fall or early winter, including globemallow, barrel cactus, and chia. Thus the ethnobotanical data suggest that farmers relying on a mixed diet of maize and a variety of wild taxa occupied the site at least during the spring, summer, and fall (Hanselka 2000).

Gayle Fritz identified the only other possible cultigen, potentially domesticated amaranth (Fritz et al. 1999), based on scanning electron microscope (SEM) analysis of seed coat thickness. She notes that all of the charred amaranth seeds examined under the SEM have the thin seed coats that are characteristic of domesticated grain amaranth. This finding suggests that future researchers should strive to document the presence of domesticated amaranth during the Archaic period. It is most likely that domesticated amaranth diffused northward from Mesoamerica along with maize and other cultigens.

Wood charcoal taxa found both during excavation and in the flotation samples were mostly mesquite (*Prosopis* sp.), but also included such woody taxa as walnut (*Juglans* sp.), cottonwood/willow (*Populus/Salix*), saltbush (*Atriplex* sp.), and juniper (*Juniperus* sp.). The occasional presence of ocotillo (*Fouquieria* sp.) charcoal suggests it may have been used as construction material. Grass (Gramineae) stems may represent construction material or remains from food processing. The charcoal record suggests that in prehistoric times the environment surrounding Cerro Juanaqueña supported an assemblage of plants similar to those found in the area today. The prevalence of *Prosopis* charcoal in the archaeological record suggests the common use of mesquite wood as fuel.

The evidence suggests that the occupation of Cerro Juanaqueña was at least relatively sedentary and that maize was a dietary staple. Many of the standard indicators of sedentary occupations are present, including substantial household trash accumulations, significant labor investment, site planning, and storage pits. The ground stone assemblage indicates intensive food processing, and the large metates represent nonportable site furniture. About ten isolated human bone fragments have been found, suggesting the presence of as-yet-undiscovered burials. The ethnobotanical spectra represent plants that are harvested from spring until fall. The quantities of maize and amaranth we have recovered indicate that crops were grown at this location, implying occupation through the growing season, from late June through mid-October. (With irrigation, maize could have been planted as early as April and harvested by mid-August.) Substantial use of maize and evidence of food storage is often interpreted as an indicator of winter and early spring occupation. Cerro Juanaqueña represents an occupation size and duration greater than the nondomesticated resources of the region could support. Clearly maize and amaranth were significant in the diet, and tending these crops limited mobility. It is likely that the occupants of Cerro Juanaqueña resided there most of the year, perhaps on the order of nine months annually. However, both limited seasonal abandonment and year-round occupation are compatible with the evidence.

The combined estimated total of 20,000 person-years of site use, the occupation span of 100–500 years, and nine months/year residence result in a series of alternative occupation models. The one we favor suggests that Cerro Juanaqueña was occupied for about 200 years by about 200 people who engaged in intensive food-processing activities (and thus generated metate wear) for about six months of the year (see Roney and Hard 2002).

Optimal Foraging Theory and the Transition to Farming

Cerro Juanaqueña and the other Late Archaic *cerros de trincheras* sites are interesting in their own right, but they are especially important because of their bearing on the initial diffusion of agriculture into North America. The questions posed by chapters in this volume concern the processes of diffusion and adaptation. Why was farming integrated into the economy rapidly in some places and far more slowly in others? The answer to this question depends upon how we model the initial spread of agriculture. Two fundamentally different processes have been proposed to describe the diffusion of agriculture into the Southwestern United States. A long-standing model holds that between 3000 and 4000 BP there was a more or less continuous distribution of low-level preagricultural foraging groups between Mesoamerica and the Southwest. It is thought that seeds and knowledge of agriculture were transmitted from one band to another, eventually reaching the Southwestern United States. Currently there are a number of different processual models suggesting why increased reliance on maize occurred and implicating various push and pull factors. Another approach (most recently articulated by Berry 1982; Hill 2001; Huckell 1995; and Matson 1991) envisions agriculture, at least in part, spreading by actual migration of agriculturalists. These differing points of view parallel discussions surrounding the diffusion of agriculture in other parts of the world. In this context Southwestern North America (Northwest Mexico and the U.S. Southwest) is important as a case study with potential relevance to wider issues.

The two different models have very different implications for our understanding of early agriculture in Southwestern North America. Unfortunately it is very difficult to distinguish between these two alternatives on the basis of archaeological evidence alone; at this point we advocate development of explanatory frameworks that do not, a priori, eliminate either alternative. In northwestern Chihuahua we are exploring this approach by attempting trial formulations that integrate a variety of ecological approaches. Optimal foraging models in particular have utility in this context, as these models suggest that people selected an optimal adaptation to a region whether they were newly arrived immigrants or an indigenous population. An optimality approach also assumes that neither push nor pull factors have preeminence but suggests that the dietary mix that yields the highest return rate will be selected.

Optimal Foraging Theory

Optimal foraging theory's diet-breadth model has utility, because it specifies when an item may be included in the diet. It relies on two independent variables: search costs and processing costs. Search costs are considered to be a function of resource density, as the model assumes random searching. As the density of higher-return-rate items declines, their search costs increase. Processing costs involve the pursuit and handling costs related to the difficulty of obtaining a resource and converting it to an edible form relative to its caloric return. Typically foods are ranked according to their postencounter return rates. The overall foraging efficiency of the diet, however, includes search costs as well as pursuit and handling costs for all items in the diet. An additional, lower-ranked item may then be added to the diet upon encounter if its addition results in an increase in overall foraging efficiency. The model assumes that an item in the optimal diet will always be taken whenever it is encountered (e.g., Barlow 1997, 2002; Winterhalder and Goland 1997). Although the diet-breadth model does not directly address the issue of importance of an item in the diet, the degree to which that item is utilized is related to the *density of higher-ranked items* as well as that item. An additional factor to consider with the diet-breadth model is risk reduction.

One approach to consideration of risk models foragers' contingency decisions as related to potential risks and payoffs is the Z-score model. The Z-score model suggests that foragers will choose a set of resources based on three variables: average return rate, variability, and minimal requirements. The goal is not to fall below the minimal requirements (Winterhalder and Goland 1997:136). If the potential mean yield of resource options is greater than the minimal needs then survival may be enhanced by choosing the resource option that is more predictable (with lower variance). Alternatively, if the minimal needs exceed the average yield of resource options then the higher variance resource would be selected, betting on the potential of riskier yet greater returns that may meet minimal requirements (Winterhalder and Goland 1997). In the effort to reduce risk, there is frequently a reduction in average foraging efficiency.

The Z-score model is only modeling the choices of a single individual or a group of individuals engaging in the same behaviors. Foragers, however, overcome this constraint through four other risk reduction strategies: intraband sharing, sexual division of labor, reciprocal access, and storage. Intraband sharing allows members to pursue alternative resources and then pool the products, thereby offsetting short-term variable returns (Kaplan and Hill 1985; Winterhalder 1986; Winterhalder and Goland 1997). Sexual division of labor may allow men vs. women to pursue prey with differing levels of risk. If resources fail throughout a band's territory, then movement to another territory, perhaps through systems of reciprocal access, can offset regional variability (Winterhalder and Goland 1997). Storage also offsets regular periods of scarcity and abundance that are common in temperate environments. Farmers utilize analogous risk reduction strategies through systems of dispersed fields that offset local stochastic fluctuations in yields (Winterhalder and Goland 1997).

Do the diet-breadth model and associated risk-reduction models, with their focus on resource ranking, density, and variability, have utility in understanding the initial adoption of maize and increasing use of maize? In the American Southwest and Northwest Mexico widespread use of maize was underway shortly after its introduction. Throughout most of Arizona and New Mexico maize played only a minor role in the diet from ca. 1300 BC to ca. AD 100–750 and even later when more sedentary, agrarian communities became widely established (Hard et al. 1996). In the Tucson Basin, southeastern Arizona, and northwestern Chihuahua, however, maize farming quickly became a major part of the diet, and farming communities, including Cerro Juanaqueña, were established by 1200 BC. In contrast, only 30–200 km to the northeast, in the Southern Jornada Mogollon region, farming economies were not established until ca. AD 1000–1200 (Hard 1997; Hard et al. 1996; O'Laughlin 1980; Whalen 1994). Behavioral ecology can provide explanatory models, testable predictions, and relevant variables and define the kinds of evidence needed to explore the variability in the degree and timing of greater levels of maize dependence. As an exploratory use of optimal foraging models, we offer the initial component of a comparison between the Río Casas Grandes and Southern Jornada regions. These two regions represent the extremes of the timing of the formation of farming economies in the Southwest. Yet they both have major streams and are both in the Chihuahuan biotic province, a few days' walk from one another (see Doleman, this volume, for another approach to consideration of the Jornada region).

The diet-breadth model indicates that when a resource is in the optimal diet the frequency with which it is used will be related to the density of higher-ranked resources. If resources with greater return rates than maize are plentiful in the landscape, they should be taken upon encounter, and therefore greater use of lower ranked maize is unnecessary even if maize farming is rather productive.

Ranking Agriculture

Renee Barlow (1997, 2002) has examined the costs and return rates of subsistence maize-based agriculture, utilizing detailed ethnographic accounts from Chiapas and Guatemala to derive return rates that are inversely related to increasing maize field investment. The Mesoamerican yield data appear roughly applicable to the North American Southwest. Barlow's (1997:101) data suggest that the mean yield for all the Chiapas and Guatemala production is 1,390 kg/ha (n = 112, std. dev. = 553 kg/ha). Risa Arbolino's (2001:72) data indicates the average irrigated field corn yield for 22 northern U.S. Southwest Native American groups is 1,151 kg/ha (n = 46, std. dev. = 402 kg/ha). Southwestern yields of other varieties of maize, including ancient ones, may have been less, however, and maize was grown under more variable circumstances than these data suggest (Arbolino 2001). For example, runoff fields below 5,500 ft in elevation produce an average of only 688 kg/ha, and those above 5,500 ft produce 981 kg/ha. Nonetheless, as a starting point to model maize return rates Barlow's study is one of the best currently available.

Barlow models four levels of labor investment in maize farming. The first is the plant and harvest strategy that may produce relatively low yields of 2–5 bu/acre (125–314 kg/ha) with a labor investment of approximately 50 hr/acre, yielding a relatively high return rate of 1,300–1,700 kcal/hour (Figure 6.7).

Return Rates Wild & Maize

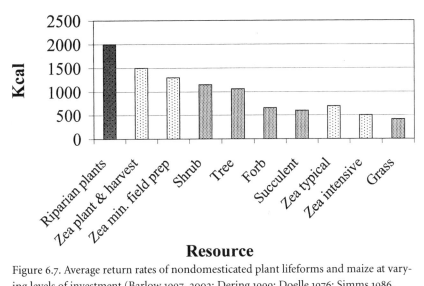

Figure 6.7. Average return rates of nondomesticated plant lifeforms and maize at varying levels of investment (Barlow 1997, 2002; Dering 1999; Doelle 1976; Simms 1986, 1987). Sample sizes: riparian, $n = 1$; trees, $n = 2$; shrubs, $n = 2$; succulents, $n = 2$; forbs, $n = 5$; and grasses, $n = 2$.

Minor investment in maize utilizing a plant and harvest strategy should occur when taxa ranked higher than 1,300–1,700 kcal/hr, such as cattail pollen and roots and most mammals, become limited in availability during parts of the year. If resources with similar or lower return rates (such as pine nuts or bulrush seeds) are included in the diet, then minor use of maize is expected as well.

The next greater level of investment is characterized as slash and burn farming: it involves greater land clearing and field preparation activities before planting but no substantial work during the growing season. In productive, well-watered settings energetic return rates of approximately 1,100–1,500 kcal/hour with yields of 5–15 bu/acre (314–941 kg/ha) and field investments of 150–250 hr/acre may be achieved (Barlow 1997, 2002). Although slash and burn farming was probably not a widely used strategy in the North American Southwest, it is representative of an intermediate investment in fields, involving initial field preparation but little investment after planting. Other strategies such as floodplain farming may also yield these returns.

If conditions are present for such a low-investment productive strategy, it should be pursued with the decline of higher-ranked resources such as pine nuts and bulrush. Accompanying this strategy would be the inclusion of resources such as mesquite, saltbush, and tanseymustard that have return rates of 1,000–1,300 kcal/hr.

Greater investment in agriculture would also be contingent on the local ecological conditions that would allow increased yield relative to time invested (Barlow 1997, 2002). The shift from a plant and harvest strategy to an intermediate (slash and burn–like) level of investment represents perhaps the most critical shift in the evolution of Southwestern farming economies. Barlow (2002) suggests that the Late Archaic farming settlements in the Tucson Basin may represent this level of investment, as well as such early pithouse settlements as the SU site and Basketmaker II sites on Cedar Mesa.

Greater field investment than that of an intermediate strategy is expected to yield declining marginal returns, as represented by the third strategy, which is known as "typical" maize farming. If the better local conditions needed to support an intermediate strategy are not available, a typical maize farming economy could emerge directly from a plant and harvest strategy. Typical maize farming was commonly conducted in the Greater Southwest among most full-time agriculturalists. In Guatemala and Chiapas these maize fields yielded widely varying return rates of 300–1,100 kcal/hr, suggesting that local farming conditions play a significant role in return rates. Analogous prehistoric return rates for well-watered southwestern Colorado are estimated to be 700–900 kcal/hr with yields of 2–20 bu/acre (125–1,254 kg/ha), with field investments of 400 hr/acre (Burns 1983, as cited by Barlow 1997). In the Fremont region return rates were probably even lower (Barlow 1997, 2002). Greater investment in typical farming fields should increase as the availability of such higher-return items such as mesquite and saltbush declines. Nondomesticated taxa that should be added with this farming strategy include acorns, bluegrass, wild sunflower, Indian rice-grass, agave, and sotol. Other small-seeded resources such as amaranth and goosefoot may be included with this group as well, although data are lacking (Barlow 2002).

The final and most intensive farming strategy in Barlow's scheme yielded 850 kcal/hr in Guatemala and is considered to be rare in the Fremont region and the Southwest. Yields under 500 kcal/hr are expected in the West, with field investments on the order of 800 hr/acre and yields on the order of 12 bu/acre (752 kg/ha). Such strategies should only be adopted under stress conditions with the depletion of higher-ranked wild resources. The use of the lowest-ranked nondomesticated resources should be included as part of this strategy, including dropseed, pickleweed, squirrel-tail grass, and some species of wild barley that have return rates of ca. 100–300 kcal/hr (Barlow 1997, 2002).

Are these expectations useful for understanding the variability in the adoption of agriculture in the Southwest? The rapid integration of the plant and harvest strategy across the Southwest at ca. 1000 BC (e.g., Hard and Roney 1998a; Haury 1962; Huckell 1995, 1997; Matson 1991; Minnis 1992; Smiley 1994; Wills 1988) is compatible with the expectations of the model. This level of investment offers higher return rates than many arid land seed resources. Ethnobotanical studies show that many intermediate- to low-return rate resources were a common part of the diet during the Late Archaic period. For example, grama grass (*Bouteloua*), dropseed grass (*Sporobolus*), and New Mexico feather grass (*Stipa neomexicana*) were commonly recovered from the Late Archaic levels at Fresnal Shelter (Bohrer 1981). A plant and harvest maize strategy yields a return rate higher than these resources, so the diet-breadth model suggests that maize should have been added to the diet as soon as it was available, particularly since maize and wild grasses have a similar seasonality. Thus the rapid integration of a plant and harvest farming strategy across the Southwest as soon as maize was available is compatible with the model (Barlow 2002).

Are the different investments in farming in the Río Casas Grandes region and the Southern Jornada region also understandable in terms of this model? We would expect that the Río Casas Grandes region's rapid shift to substantial farming would correlate with lower availability of high-return resources relative to the potential returns obtained by further investment in farming. In contrast, the Southern Jornada Mogollon region's delayed shift to farming should correlate with greater availability of dense, high-return resources relative to the potential return rates from farming. Risk-reduction strategies and relative return rates of farming are likely to have played a role in these options as well. In order to evaluate these hypotheses we will consider elements of the resource structure of each region. The two regions both have a water-controlled environment, Basin and Range topography, a major stream, similar Lower Chihuahuan Life Zone ecology, variable, summer-dominant rainfall, and a similar paleoenvironmental sequence and presumably had access to similar maize-farming technologies.

The differences are that the Jornada area receives only 23.3 cm (std. dev. = 6.9 cm, $n = 34$ years) of annual rainfall and is situated in the Chihuahuan Desertscrub biotic community, with some areas of Semidesert Grassland (Brown 1982b, 1982c; Brown and Lowe 1983). In contrast, the Río Casas Grandes region receives 50% more summer rainfall, for an annual average of 33.4 cm (std. dev. = 9.1 cm; $n = 32$), with two-thirds falling between July and October. It is situated at the base of the Sierra Madre Occidental in grasslands, with Semidesert Grasslands to the east and Plains Grasslands to the west (Brown and Lowe 1983). The paleoecological sequence incorporating both regions is reviewed first.

Paleoecology

In recent years a series of paleoecological studies from within a surrounding radius of 250 km from Cerro Juanaqueña (Figure 6.1) has been completed (Buck and Monger 1999; Castiglia 2002; Fleischauer and Stone 1982; Krider 1998; Metcalfe et al. 1997; Ortega-Ramírez 1995a, 1995b; Urrutia-Fucugauchi et al. 1997; Van Devender 1990, 1995; Van Devender and Worthington 1977; Waters 1989). In addition Lee Nordt (2003) developed an alluvial and isotopic sequence for the Río Casas Grandes below Cerro Juanaqueña as an element of our project. These studies consist of an array of stratigraphic, sedimentological, geomorphic, rock-magnetic, isotopic, and pack-rat midden studies. Combined, these studies offer a consistent picture of the paleoenvironment. The following paleoenvironmental summary uses radiocarbon years BP for all dates except where otherwise noted.

The Late Wisconsin pluvial period was cool and wet, with greater winter rainfall maintaining water in playas including Lake Cochise, Babícora Lake, Encinillas Basin, Cloverdale Lake, Playas Lake, and Lake Palomas. Warm, wet, pluvial conditions existed during the early Holocene, although the drying and refilling of Lake Cochise suggests variability (Waters 1989).

By the early Holocene a brief period of lake shallowing occurred in the Babícora Basin between 11,060 and 9470 BP, correlating with the Younger Dryas (Metcalfe et al. 1997). Grasslands dominated the Tularosa Basin (Buck and Monger 1999), and oak juniper woodlands were present on the Hueco Mountain slopes near El Paso (Van Devender 1995). Grasslands in the highlands of Lake Babícora slowly replaced woodlands during the early Holocene.

After 9000 BP, during the middle Holocene, a widespread period of somewhat drier conditions prevailed, as winter rains lost their dominance to summer. Lake Cochise was dry (Waters 1989); the lowland Tularosa Basin vegetation shifted from grassland to shrublands (Buck and Monger 1999); and the Hueco Mountain slopes vegetation shifted from an oak-juniper woodland to grassland (Van Devender 1990). Grasslands also replaced woodlands in the highlands of the Babícora Basin as a result of warmer, drier conditions. These generally drier conditions were not uniform.

Pluvial Lake Palomas filled again around 8500 BP (Castiglia 2002). The Babícora and Encinillas Lakes are thought to have held water until ca. 7000 BP (Metcalfe et al. 1997). The Laguna El Fresnal portion of Lake Palomas Basin filled again about 6000 BP (Castiglia 2002). Lake Cochise also filled and dried again at ca. 5400 BP (Waters 1989). Possibly two other lake stands took place during the middle Holocene in the Animas Valley (Fleischauer and Stone 1982). Summer monsoons supported grasslands in the Playas Valley, and that lake contained perennial water until 4000 BP (Van Devender 1995; Van Devender and Worthington 1977). Evidence from the Babícora Basin indicates a mid-Holocene period of generally decreased rainfall, although marshes were extant (Metcalfe et al. 1997; Ortega-Ramírez 1995b). In the Río Casas Grandes a plant community consisting of about 60% C_4 grasses formed (Nordt 2003). Perhaps decreased winter moisture and warmer summer temperatures can account for vegetation shifts that suggest increased aridity (including woodland to grassland vegetation shifts at higher elevations and increasing shrublands in the Tularosa Basin), although a regime of high-magnitude floods was underway by ca. 5000 BP.

In the late Holocene another widespread shift occurred over much of the Southwest, bringing moister conditions, continuation of notable high stands, and high-magnitude floods between 5000 and 4000 BP (Ely 1997). In the Río Casas Grandes an erosional event at 5000 BP and deeply entrenched channels are consistent with high-magnitude floods (Nordt 2003). A 4000 BP late Holocene beach ridge at Laguna El Fresnal marks another filling event, on par with the middle Holocene one (Castiglia 2002). Sometime between ca. 4000 and 3000 BP Lake Cochise also filled again (Waters 1989). A deep-water lake refilled in the Babícora Basin and for a brief period resembled Late Pleistocene conditions (Metcalfe et al. 1997:169). Cloverdale Lake also filled. The dating of the Lake Cochise, Babícora Basin, and Cloverdale Lake high stands is imprecise, so correlations with the Southwest-wide high-magnitude floods are unknown. Grasslands continued to dominate in the Río Casas Grandes region and returned to the Tularosa Basin after 4000 BP. Paleosol formation and floodplain building in Río Casas Grandes by 3100 BP correlates with the pronounced absence of high-magnitude floods across the Southwest between 3600 and 2200 BP (Ely 1997; Nordt 2003). The earliest ^{14}C date from the site of Cerro Juanaqueña is 3130 ± 55 b.p., indicating that people began inhabiting the site contemporaneously with the formation of the Trincheras paleosol with a date of 3140 ± 100 b.p. This time appears to mark a pivotal shift in paleoclimate following the cessation of high-magnitude floods after 3400 BP (Ely 1997).

Although high-magnitude floods were absent, moisture levels at ca. 3000 BP may have been relatively high. Southeastern Arizona alluvial stratigraphic studies suggest mesic late Holocene conditions (Mehringer et al. 1967). Data from the San Juan Basin of New Mexico and the Mogollon Highlands of Arizona also suggest that ca. 3000 BP was a moist period (Smith and McFaul 1997; Waters and Haynes 2001). Stalagmite records from the Guadalupe Mountains in southern

New Mexico indicate slightly greater effective moisture between 4000 and 3000 BP and significantly greater moisture in 3000–1700 BP (Polyak and Asmerom 2001). D. E. Wilkens and D. R. Currey (1999) also report a moist interval in the Guadalupe Mountains dated to 3400 BP. Although T. R. Van Devender (1990) does not report a more mesic interval during the late Holocene, a close examination of packrat-midden spectra from the El Paso region's Hueco Mountain slopes suggests a brief return to more mesic species and a decline in desert shrubs and succulents between 3000 and 1700 BP (Mauldin 1995). Moisture at Playa Lake was sufficient to support chub-type fish and salamanders found in raptor deposits and constrained by ^{14}C dates of 3300 and 2400 BP (Van Devender and Worthington 1977). In the Babícora Basin high effective humidity is suggested by marsh deposits and paleosols dating between 3800 and 2800 BP (Ortega-Ramírez et al. 1998:1177).

After 3000 BP an overall drying trend occurs, although pronounced floodplain building in the Río Casas Grandes resumed, consistent with the absence of high-magnitude and erosive flooding until ca. 2200 BP (Nordt 2003). The vegetation in the Río Casas Grandes continued to be dominated by grasslands, but Lake Cochise remained dry (Waters 1989). In the Babícora Basin modern semiarid conditions became established after 3000 BP (Ortega-Ramírez 1995b). S. E. Metcalfe et al's. (1997) Babícora study indicates that a shallowing of the lake occurred before 2470 BP. One Babícora sequence tentatively suggests that drying conditions were underway as early as 3070 BP (Metcalfe et al. 1997). In the Tularosa Basin vegetation shifted to a modern C_3-dominated shrublands, and desert shrublands were established on the Hueco Mountain slopes (Buck and Monger 1999; Van Devender 1990).

A return to cooler, wetter conditions occurred in the highlands of Lake Babícora after 2000 BP. Cerro Juanaqueña was reoccupied at ca. 2200 BP, which correlates with the formation of the Janos paleosol, also dated to 2200–2000 BP. A continued absence of high-magnitude flooding, landscape stability, and C_4-grassland dominance on the Río Casas Grandes are similar to the conditions during the original occupation of Cerro Juanaqueña. Cerro Juanaqueña was abandoned again about the same time that high-magnitude flooding resumed at ca. 2000 BP that is marked by an erosional event (Nordt 2003). The high-magnitude flooding regime persisted until ca. 1100 BP. This may correlate with the expansion of cienega aquatic vegetation at 1400–1800 BP and the refilling of Playa Lake at 1000 BP (Krider 1998). This period of high-magnitude flooding came to an end after ca. 1100 BP, correlating with a warmer and drier interlude at Lake Babícora (Nordt 2003). Grasslands continued to dominate in the Río Casas Grandes Valley (Nordt 2003). A cooler and wetter shift is recorded at Lake

Babícora at ca. 500 BP during a resumption of high-magnitude flooding. This correlates with another refilling of Playa Lake at ca. 300–500 BP (Krider 1998).

In summary, these studies suggest that elements of a cool, wet Late Wisconsin continued into the early Holocene, although localized periods of drying occurred. Drying conditions were widespread by the middle Holocene, albeit with some periods of increased moisture. A period of high-magnitude floods dominated the Southwest between ca. 5000 and 3600 BP, resulting in filling and deposition in the playas in the Río Casas Grandes. Southwestern high-magnitude flooding decreased markedly between 3600 and 2200 BP. Although overall moisture regimes at ca. 3000 BP remained high, the following millennium witnessed a slow drying trend. Cerro Juanaqueña was first occupied at an apparently ideal time, following a long period of floodplain building. Moisture levels were generally high, but there was an absence of high-magnitude floods. Cerro Juanaqueña was abandoned after about two centuries of occupation but reoccupied and abandoned before the high-magnitude flood regime returned at ca. 2000 BP in the Río Casas Grandes Valley. The remaining late Holocene was generally similar to today, but with some isolated periods of increased summer rainfall.

Modern Ecology

According to late nineteenth century reports grama grasslands were highly productive in the southern desert basins. Shrub invasion and desertification was underway by the end of the nineteenth century, a process that appears to be continuing today (e.g. Dick-Peddie 1993; Van Auken 2000; York and Dick-Peddie 1969). Overgrazing is given as the primary cause, but a number of studies suggest that historic declines in rainfall may also have played a role.

The dynamic paleoecology of southern New Mexico and northwestern Chihuahua reflects marked fluctuations between grassland and shrubland throughout the Holocene as moisture regimes vacillated. The geographic settings of the two study regions, however, ensured that because of its higher altitude and closer proximity to the Sierra Madre Occidental the Río Casas Grandes region always received higher levels of summer precipitation than the Southern Jornada region. The modern vegetation map for the Southwest (Brown and Lowe 1983) indicates that Chihuahuan Desertscrub dominates the Southern Jornada region, with a lesser proportion of Semiarid Grassland in the higher elevations.

Semiarid Grassland to the east and Plains Grassland to the west dominate the Rio Casas Grandes region. The Semidesert Grassland is a transitional community lying between the Plains Grassland and the Chihuahuan Desertscrub (Brown 1982c:127). Semidesert Grasslands are best viewed as a fluctuating continuum from desert grasslands to shrublands, related to shifts in precipitation patterns and historic overgrazing. Higher levels of rainfall and deep soils tend to enhance the density of grasses in relationship to shrubs (Brown 1982c). Under climax conditions perennial bunch grasses are interspersed with bare ground. Adequate rainfall, minimal erosion, and deep soils allow perennial grasses to cover vast expanses. Under low summer rainfall conditions, annuals increase at the expense of perennial grasses (Brown 1982c:124; Burgess 1995).

To the west, between 1,400 to 1,500 m, is the Plains variant of the Plains and Great Basin Grassland biotic community (Brown and Lowe 1983). Plains Grasslands border woodland vegetation above ca. 1,500 m and Semidesert Grassland below ca. 1,400 m. Grazing has resulted in shrub invasion; areas that were Plains Grassland have become Semidesert Grassland, and transitions between the two are subtle. In climax conditions this biotic community is composed almost entirely of grasses, with forbs and shrubs constituting less than 10% (Heerwagen 1956, as cited by Dick-Peddie 1993).

A complete evaluation of the utility of the diet-breadth model requires assessment of the density, spatial and temporal distribution of plant and animal resources, and return rates, as exemplified by David Zeanah and his colleagues (1995). Such an ambitious undertaking is far beyond the scope of this study. An initial assessment of nondomesticated food availability is attempted here by simply examining the relative quantity of nondomesticated food plants in each biotic community. Rough consideration of return rates is based on plant lifeform (shrubs, forbs, etc.). We consider farming return rates, based on the work by Barlow and considering local geographic and ecological factors.

Nondomesticated Resources

Optimal foraging theory ranks food resources by their postencounter return rates. Mammals have the highest return rates, and they decline with body size. Artiodactyls and lagomorphs were the major species utilized in both regions, with return rates on the order of 10,000 kcal/hour or more (e.g., Barlow 1997). The similarity of the two environments, the taxa present, and the faunal assemblages found in each region suggests that differential plant availability may be playing a more critical role in the formation of farming economies than animals do. Consideration of plant return rates is our initial concern.

Only a small number of Southwestern plants have been analyzed for return rates, but return rates are somewhat related to lifeform (Zeanah et al. 1995). Return rate data for taxa that are found in these regions were accumulated from

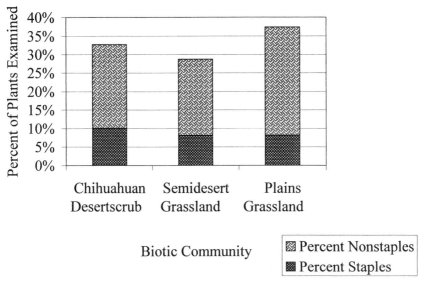

Figure 6.8. Percent staples and nonstaples of nondomesticated plants by biotic community. Percentages are remarkably consistent across communities. Total species examined: Chihuahuan Desertscrub, $n = 119$; Semidesert Grassland, $n = 247$; Plains Grassland, $n = 123$.

studies from the Great Basin plus additional data on mesquite and succulents (Barlow 1997; Dering 1999; Doelle 1976; Simms 1986, 1987). Figure 6.7 shows average return rates by major plant lifeform. Return rates decline in the following order: riparian plants, shrubs, nuts, forbs, succulents, and grasses. Note that these are based on small sample sizes.

Under optimal foraging theory the availability of wild plant foods is a factor in the formation of farming economies. In the absence of more detailed plant density and distribution data, we evaluated the relative number of consumable plants in the Chihuahuan Desert Shrubland, Plains Grassland, and Semidesert Grassland biotic communities (Brown and Lowe 1983). The scientific names of 429 plant species from plant inventories for each biotic community (Brown 1982a; Dick-Peddie 1993) were entered into David Moerman's (2001) massive web-based North American Ethnobotany Database. Compiling these data produced a list of food plants, their lifeform, and if they were used as staples. Virtually all identifications were at the species level, with a few matches at the genus level.

The results presented in Figure 6.8 suggest there is little difference in the frequency of staples or total edible plants among the Southern Jornada Mogol-

Life Forms & Biotic Communities

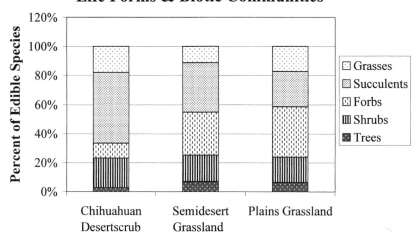

Figure 6.9. Proportion of lifeforms of edible plants by biotic community. Trees are negligible, and shrubs and grasses are similar across communities. The sum of succulents and forbs is similar across communities, and both lifeforms have similar return rates. This chart suggests that in considering only edible species inventories in the three communities there is little difference in overall proportions of lifeforms. Therefore the return rates of the edible plant assemblages from each community are similar. This, however, does not consider plant density or distribution.

lon Chihuahuan Desertscrub and the two grassland communities that characterize the Río Casas Grandes region. In all three, 8 to 10% of all taxa evaluated were staples. Between 29 and 37% of all plants in each of the three communities are food sources. Since lifeforms are related to return rates, are there major differences in the frequency of the lifeforms of edible taxa among the biotic communities?

The stacked bars in Figure 6.9 represent the lifeform proportions of the 156 edible species from the three biotic communities. Trees are negligible in all three. The frequency of edible shrub species is similar across the shrublands and grasslands. Forbs and succulents, which have similar return rates, constitute a large group of alternate resources; and these two lifeforms can be summed for analytical purposes. The sum of the edible succulent and forb frequencies for all three communities is similar across the three communities.

In summary, this vegetation analysis shows that the frequency of edible species, lifeforms, and staples among the Chihuahuan Desertscrub, Plains Grassland, and Semidesert Grassland is similar. We cannot fully consider differential plant density, seasonality, and habitat variability here, additional factors that could significantly affect wild plant resource availability. The descriptions of these biotic communities and the absence of quantifiable information for the Río Casas Grandes region do not allow us to address relative densities of forbs and succulents in the two regions. It is likely the densities of edible shrubs such as mesquite and saltbush were indeed greater in the Chihuahuan Desertscrub biotic community than in the Semidesert Grassland and Plains Grassland (e.g., Brown 1982b, 1982c; Burgess 1995; Dick-Peddie 1993) throughout the Holocene. Riparian habitats as well as bajadas, in both the grasslands and the desertscrub communities, would support significant stands of mesquite and other shrubs.

Farming Potential

Low-investment plant and harvest farming strategies appear to have been ubiquitous across the Southwest during the Late Archaic period. In most places, however, these small fields were not very productive and yielded only a minor part of the diet. In contrast, did the Río Casas Grandes floodplain support high-return, intermediate-investment maize farming that generated sufficient yields, allowing maize to play a larger role in the diet? If so, maize fields would have become a high-density, high-return resource. Under those conditions lower-return foods such as forbs, succulents, and grasses should have played a relatively minor role in the diet and should have been used only when maize was limited in availability.

Alternatively maize farming at Cerro Juanaqueña may have been of the more typical variety, with return rates roughly on a par with forbs and succulents. At this point it is difficult to distinguish between the intermediate and typical alternatives, and both are briefly considered here. The range of farming technologies available to the occupants of Cerro Juanaqueña included dry-farming (rain-fed) fields, floodplain fields, water-table fields, seepage fields, irrigated fields, and *ak chin* (a method of placing fields to take advantage of runoff) fields (Glassow 1980). Next we review these options and their potential return rates.

Dry-farming or rain-fed fields are dependent upon direct moisture falling on the fields (Doolittle 2000). Maize requires about 50 cm of moisture for optimal growth, but a minimal crop can be produced with as little as 15 cm of summer rainfall (Rhode 1995; Shaw 1988). Modern growing season rainfall at Janos is 21.9 cm (std. dev. = 7.7 cm, n = 33 years), which suggests that in most years growing season (July–October) rainfall would exceed the minimum.

Dry farming should routinely produce a minimal crop but would rarely produce an optimal crop. In fact, local farmers now living in the vicinity of Cerro Juanaqueña report that rain-fed farming, combined with only occasional irrigation in dry years, was the primary agricultural strategy until recently. They planted maize in May, relying on winter moisture for germination and summer rains for plant growth and cob formation. The onset of an extended drought in the early 1990s reduced reliance on rainfall and forced greater use of spring-fed irrigation and pumping from the river. By the late 1990s these surface water sources had dried, and underground pumping of irrigation water became the only viable approach. Higher moisture levels 3,000 years ago likely would have enhanced the success of dry farming significantly, reducing its risk.

Floodplain fields along the Río Casas Grandes could potentially be watered by over-bank sheet floods that spread over the floodplain, an approach known as flood-recession agriculture. Modern farmers indicate that this is not a principal source of moisture today, apparently because it is unreliable. Rainfall must be sufficient for over-bank floods, the maize plants must be tall enough to withstand the drenching, and water velocity and sediment loads must be minimal to avoid damaging the crop. In 1999, after several days of strong July thunderstorms, we witnessed the Río Casas Grandes leave its banks and spread over the first alluvial terrace, leaving only a thin veneer of sediment.

The valley bottom below Cerro Juanaqueña appears to be suited for this type of farming: the wide floodplain allows floodwaters to decelerate rapidly, particularly since just downstream the Río Casas Grandes constriction slows steam velocity and forms a flood basin. The Trincheras paleosol probably was the floodplain used for farming ca. 3,000 years ago. Its fine sediment and the absence of gravels suggest that flooding was not flashy, yet its water-holding capacity was good (Nordt 2003). Prior to ca. 3100 BP and the occupation of Cerro Juanaqueña, the floodplain was aggrading under a regime of high-magnitude floods. The formation of the Trincheras paleosol also suggests landscape stability and absence of high-magnitude flooding (Nordt 2003). Across the Southwest high-magnitude floods ceased between 3600 and 2200 BP (Ely 1997), although regional paleoenvironmental reconstructions indicate that moisture levels were higher than today.

Farming based on high water tables or seeps is one of the most dependable strategies. In parts of the floodplain the water table would have been accessible at times by maize taproots. Some maize varieties such as Hopi Blue Corn can penetrate 3 or 4 m, and a 2-m reach is not uncommon. However, the plant must grow sufficiently before the roots reach that length. In addition maize is susceptible to anaeorobiosis if water levels are within the root zone for extended periods. Water levels should be below 1 m to provide adequate moisture without interfering with the flow of oxygen (Nordt 2003).

The redoximorphic features of Trincheras floodplain soil indicate that it experienced a high water table, but one that fluctuated and was not permanently elevated. Between 1997 and 2000 backhoe trenches found the modern water table between 0.5 and 3 m deep, varying with terrace surface (Nordt 2003). The spring at the base of Cerro Juanaqueña is indicative of a high water table, and Donald Brand (1937) noted that in the 1930s springs were common along the Río Casas Grandes. The constriction of the valley may also act to force groundwater closer to the surface. Today farmers do not include water-table farming as a strategy, although in principle it could potentially be successful, given some water table depths. Local inhabitants indicate that the water table fluctuates substantially and can be unpredictable; presumably drought and groundwater pumping affect it. For example, a 4 m deep well in the floodplain recently dried, as did the spring. The individuals we spoke with did not appear to be aware of the correlation between modern alluvial terrace location and water table depth.

Finally, while we have no direct evidence, the existence of irrigation canals by the occupants of Cerro Juanaqueña cannot be eliminated. Irrigation canals would certainly be within the scope of building projects that the occupants of Cerro Juanaqueña could design and build, and 3,000-year-old canals have been found in the Tucson Basin (Mabry 2002). *Ak chin* fields could have been planted, particularly where arroyos empty onto alluvial fans to take advantage of spreading rainfall runoff. Settings suitable for *ak chin* farming exist along the margins of the floodplain.

What farming strategies did the Native Americans of Cerro Juanaqueña pursue, and what were the relative return rates of these strategies? One possibility is that the primary maize-farming strategy was focused on intermediate-cost, high-return floodplain farming, with little investment in higher cost *ak chin* farming and other strategies.

Maize return rates are also included in Figure 6.7 (Barlow 1997, 2002). Casual plant and harvest strategies have the highest return rates. Maize farming that requires minimum to intermediate field investment such as floodplain farming is the next highest. Third is typical maize farming. This was the most common in the Southwest and requires a significant level of field preparation, including water control devices. Fourth, intensive maize farming, which may have been rare in the prehistoric Southwest, has the lowest return rate. Note that plant and harvest maize farming has greater return rates than most non-domesticated lifeforms, except riparian taxa. The return rate of minimal field investment farming (that is, slash and burn or floodplain farming) is similar to that of shrubs and nut resources, while the return rate of typical maize farming is similar to that of forbs and succulents. Only grasses fall below maize farming in return rates.

If intermediate-cost, high-return farming was the principal strategy we would expect future research to show that subsequent occupations indicate a pattern of switching back and forth between emphasis on hunting and gathering and high-return, low-investment farming. Alternating strategies would be affected by the availability of other wild resources with similar returns, particularly shrub and nut resources, as well as mammals. The role of farming in the economy would not be expected to increase appreciably as long as this strategy was being pursued; succulents and forbs would play an increasing role as the return rates of farming declined. Other contemporaneous sites should represent a range of foraging activities, and farming would be limited to floodplain and plant and harvest strategies.

The alternative is that Native Americans at Cerro Juanaqueña were engaged in typical farming strategies. If this is the case, further research should show a range in kinds of farming settlements, technologies, and locations being utilized. These may include *ak chin* farming, dry farming, and the use of water control devices, including irrigation. Increasing population density may have restricted access to shrubs, forbs, and succulents and encouraged typical maize farming. Because the return rates of typical maize farming are roughly similar to those of forbs and succulents, these lifeforms would be extensively utilized if typical maize farming was the strategy of the day. In fact virtually all of the charred seeds found in our botanical samples are forbs, which is more consistent with a typical farming strategy. The defensive character of Cerro Juanaqueña is suggestive of population packing as well.

In contrast to the Río Casas Grandes region, why did the Native Americans living in the Southern Jornada region not invest more in farming during the Late Archaic period? Although only located a few days' walk away, these populations elected to pursue a dominantly mobile, hunting and gathering system for another two millennia before adopting a mixed farming strategy at ca. AD 1000. Our preliminary vegetation comparison suggests that the simple frequency of wild edible species between the two regions is similar.

Unfortunately, the density of forbs and succulents on the landscape is difficult to know. It is almost a certainty, however, that shrub density was higher in the Southern Jornada region than in the Río Casas Grandes region. This is significant, because shrubs generally offer higher return rates than forbs, succulents, and grasses. Succulents probably existed at higher density in the Jornada region as well.

The farming potential in the Southern Jornada region was less favorable than in the Río Casas Grandes region. In the Southern Jornada region two-thirds of the mean annual rainfall of 23 cm falls between July and October, and droughts are common. Although the frost-free season is long, the limited fall, winter, and spring moisture inhibits plant growth until the July onset of the variable summer rains. A histogram of July–October rainfall at Las Cruces from 1959 to 1996 indicates that growing-season rainfall approximates a normal distribution about a mean of 14.9 cm (std. dev. = 5.4 cm, n = 38). This suggests that in about 50% of years the growing season rainfall will be well below the minimal 15 cm of direct moisture that needs to fall on maize fields in the absence of irrigation or water control (Shaw 1988) to produce a scant crop. Even assuming an increase in precipitation during the Late Archaic period, adequate moisture for predictable rain-fed farming is unlikely. In the absence of sufficient precipitation to support dry farming, agricultural fields must be located to take advantage of runoff or other moisture sources.

Based on the distribution of late prehistoric settlements (ca. AD 1100–1400) in the Southern Jornada region, the toes of the alluvial fans in the Hueco Bolson and Tularosa Valley and the Rio Grande were the favored agricultural locations. Runoff from the mountain slopes and alluvial fans spreads and effectively enhances soil moisture. The Rio Grande Valley offered higher soil moisture, with receding spring and early summer floodwaters and a high water table (Bradley 1983). The Rio Grande, however, frequently experienced devastating spring floods, summer droughts, and periods of no flow (Ackerly 1995; Bradley 1983; Mauldin 1997). Prior to the 1915–1916 construction of Elephant Butte dam, historic farmers regularly had to rebuild irrigation systems as a result of dramatic floods (Ackerly 1994, 1995). Raymond Mauldin (1995, 1997) examined tree-ring and historic rainfall data for AD 1600–1900 and concluded that one-third of the years the Rio Grande would experience disastrous floods or droughts. While farming in the Rio Grande Valley may have been productive in some years, the risk was that at least one-third of the time crops would not produce adequately, if at all. In order to offset this risk prehistoric farmers perhaps planted in multiple locations, a strategy that would increase security but decrease return rates, due to the greater work involved (Hard and Merrill 1990; Huckell et al. 2002).

The archaeological record of the Southern Jornada region suggests that high levels of mobility were a key component of the adaptation and that maize played a minor economic role until ca. AD 1000–1100 (e.g., Hard et al. 1996; O'Laughlin 1980; Whalen 1994). The high return rates of shrubs should have made them a key resource, because they have higher rates than succulents, forbs, and typical farming strategies. There is some evidence that mesquite was a significant prehistoric resource, as it was a common taxon in the Late Archaic deposits at Fresnal Shelter (Bohrer 1981). It is not commonly recovered from flotation samples in the region, however, perhaps due to preservation factors. Low-investment farming using a plant and harvest strategy may have been effective on a small scale. Risk-reduction strategies including intraband sharing, regional mobility, and storage were likely to have been utilized in the Southern Jornada region as well.

The late integration of significant levels of farming into the Southern Jornada economy may be related to both the high density of shrubs, succulents, and forbs and the absence of potential farming habitats that produced low-cost, high-yield maize, as found in the Río Casas Grandes. In fact, it is likely that the return rates on typical maize farming in the Southern Jornada area were lower than in many other places in the Southwest. Under these conditions, only a plant and harvest maize strategy was energetically practical. Thus farming was not a significant element in the economy for a full two millennia after the Río Casas Grandes was being farmed.

The Río Casas Grandes floodplain offered greater productivity and lower risk than the Rio Grande Valley. This floodplain offered a local environment in which intermediate-investment farming may have yielded higher returns than many grasses, forbs, and succulents did. Only shrubs yield return rates on a par with intermediate-investment farming (Figure 6.7). Shrubs, although certainly not scarce in the Río Casas Grandes, would have been less dense across the landscape than in the Jornada region. The agricultural potential of the valley was particularly high, because it experienced a climatic regime of high moisture yet an absence of high-magnitude floods, and the water table was high. In addition the river originates at higher elevations where rainfall is significantly greater. A range of farming strategies including rain-fed farming, water-table farming, *ak chin* farming, and perhaps flood-recession farming would be possible. This diversity of potential farming strategies should reduce risk. High-return, high-yield maize farming conditions, combined with the use of available wild resources, provided a stable economic base that supported the aggregated semisedentary population of Cerro Juanaqueña for perhaps two centuries.

The presence of such a productive floodplain in an arid grassland may also have been an important consideration. This landscape did not offer the density of higher-return shrubs found in the vicinity of the Rio Grande. The diet-breadth model suggests that, if shrub resources were sufficiently dense, additional investment in low-investment maize farming would not have been necessary for a given population level. However, grasses and forbs dominated the landscape in the vicinity of Cerro Juanaqueña. Grasses have return rates lower than both floodplain farming and typical farming. Forb return rates are about equivalent to those of typical farming. In other words, farming in the Río Casas Grandes Valley probably offered higher return rates than the landscape's grasses and forbs. In addition the defensive character of the *cerros de trincheras* sites is indicative of population packing. Higher population density may have restricted access to higher-return resources, and perhaps the raiding environment made foraging risky.

Conclusions

In conclusion, we suggest that the high-density, high-return shrubs as well as the succulent and forb resources in the Southern Jornada region were juxtaposed with farming conditions that both were risky and yielded low-return maize harvests. As a result the optimal dietary mix emphasized nondomesticated resources and frequent mobility. Improvement in farming conditions due to increased rainfall during the late Holocene did not produce the low-cost maize yields needed to warrant abandonment of high levels of reliance on shrubs, forbs, and succulents that continued for another two millennia. The relatively high return of shrub resources and the mobility required to exploit them were favored relative to the lower return and higher risk of farming. Minimal investment in plant and harvest farming that was compatible with residential mobility allowed pursuit of the shrub, forb, and succulent resources that dominated the diet until ca. A D 1000.

In contrast, along the Río Casas Grandes we can point to the superior farming conditions that would have offered return rates on a par with typical farming strategies or perhaps as great as those of slash and burn or floodplain farming return rates. A diversity of potential farming strategies served to reduce risk. Under these conditions, increased investment in farming relative to hunting and gathering was an attractive option for two reasons. First, higher densities of lower-return grasses and forbs rather than shrubs characterized the landscape. Recall that grasses have return rates lower than those of most farming strategies and that forbs have return rates similar to those of typical farming strategies. Therefore farming in the Río Casas Grandes tended to have higher return rates than many of the wild plant resources that dominated the landscape. In addition the defensive nature of Cerro Juanaqueña and other *cerros de trincheras* sites suggests that the population was relatively high relative to resources. High populations may have limited access to wild plants due to population density and perhaps because freely foraging on the landscape was dangerous.

Finally, an optimal foraging framework suggests that whether the population is local or recently arrived it should make a similar sequence of decisions based on alternatives available. Neither pushes nor pulls to farming have a necessary priority; they are weighed within the contexts of available alternatives at the local level. The calculation to farm or not to farm and to what degree is related to the relative costs and benefits of available options. The long-term course of cultural evolution is a product of these options and their selection. Although this framework is somewhat different from previous approaches to early farming in the Southwest and derives from the work of Barlow (1997, 2002), it does lend support to the floodplain priority models advocated by others (Huckell 1995; Mabry 1998; Mabry et al. 1997; Smith 1998) and predicted by Matson (1991). This work, however, places floodplain farming in the context of optimal foraging theory and therefore considers the options offered by nondomesticated along with domesticated resources in particular contexts.

ACKNOWLEDGMENTS

The National Science Foundation (BCS-0219185, SBR-9809839, SBR-9708610) and the National Geographic Society Committee for Research and Exploration (Grant #6749-00) provided funding for this work. The Consejo de Arqueología of the Instituto Nacional de Antropología e Historia (INAH) in Mexico City and the Centro INAH Chihuahua in Cd. Chihuahua provided permits, encouragement, and support of the project. The staff at the Center for Archaeological Research at the University of Texas at San Antonio provided equipment as well as administrative and laboratory support. Our wonderful field team made the difficult, hot fieldwork from 1997 to 2000 most enjoyable. We greatly appreciate the support of all these agencies and individuals and are especially grateful to Brad Vierra for the opportunity to participate in an outstanding symposium and for his efforts to produce this volume.

REFERENCES CITED

Ackerly, N. W. (editor)
    1994   Historic and Modern Irrigation Systems. In *El Valle Bajo: The Culture History of the Lower Rio Grande Valley of El Paso*, vol. 1, *Culture and Environment in the Lower Valley*, edited by J. Peterson and D. O. Brown, pp. 130–141. Archeological Research, Inc., El Paso, and Hicks and Co., Austin, Tex.
    1995   Important Variables for Prehistoric Irrigation Studies. In *Soil, Water, Biology, and Belief in Prehistoric and Traditional Southwestern Agriculture*, edited by H. W. Toll, pp. 279–288. Special Publication No. 2. New Mexico Archaeological Council, Albuquerque.

Adams, J.
1999   Refocusing the Role of Food-Grinding Tools as Correlates for Subsistence Strategies in the U.S. Southwest. *American Antiquity* 64:475–498.

Adams, K. R.
1998   Plant Remains Recovered from Juanaqueña, a Late Archaic (3000 BP) Trincheras Site in Northern Chihuahua. Unpublished manuscript on file at the Center for Archaeological Research, San Antonio.

1999a   Plant Remains Recovered in 1998 from Cerro Juanaqueña, Cerro Vidal, and Cerros los Torres, Trincheras Sites in Northern Chihuahua. Unpublished manuscript on file at the Center for Archaeological Research, San Antonio.

1999b   Plant Remains Recovered in 1999 from Cerro Juanaqueña, Cerro Vidal, and Cerros los Torres, Trincheras Sites in Northern Chihuahua. Unpublished manuscript on file at the Center for Archaeological Research, San Antonio.

Arbolino, R. D.
2001   Agricultural Strategies and Labor Organization: An Ethnohistoric Approach to the Study of Prehistoric Farming Systems in the Taos Area of Northern New Mexico. Ph.D. dissertation, Department of Southern Methodist University, Dallas.

Barlow, K. R.
1997   Foragers That Farm: A Behavioral Ecology Approach to the Economics of Corn Farming for the Fremont Case. Ph.D. dissertation, Department of Anthropology, University of Utah.

2002   Predicting Maize Agriculture among the Fremont: An Economic Comparison of Farming and Foraging in the American Southwest. *American Antiquity* 67:65–88.

Berry, M. S.
1982   *Time, Space, and Transition in Anasazi Prehistory.* University of Utah Press, Salt Lake City.

Bohrer, Vorsila L.
1981   Former Dietary Patterns of People as Determined from Archaic-Age Plant Remains from Fresnal Shelter, South-Central New Mexico. *Artifact* 19:41–50.

Bradley, R. J. E.
1983   La Cabrana: A Study of Fourteenth-Century Resource Utilization in Southern New Mexico. Master's thesis, Department of Anthropology, University of Texas at El Paso.

Brand, D. D.

1937   *The Natural Landscape of Northwestern Chihuahua.* University of New Mexico Press, Albuquerque.

Bronk Ramsey, R. C.

1999   OxCal Program v3.3. Radiocarbon Accelerator Unit, University of Oxford. http://www.rlaha.ox.ac.uk/oxcal/oxcal.htm.

Brown, David E.

1982a   Appendix II: Scientific and Equivalent Common Names of Plants and Animals Used as Examples in the Text, Arranged by Biomes. In *Biotic Communities of the American Southwest—United States and Mexico, Desert Plants,* vol. 4, nos. 1–4, edited by D. E. Brown, pp. 316–341. University of Arizona Press, Tucson.

1982b   Chihuahuan Desertscrub. In *Biotic Communities of the American Southwest—United States and Mexico, Desert Plants,* vol. 4, nos. 1–4, edited by D. E. Brown, pp. 169–179. University of Arizona Press, Tucson.

1982c   Semidesert Grassland. In *Biotic Communities of the American Southwest—United States and Mexico, Desert Plants,* vol. 4. nos. 1–4, edited by D. E. Brown, pp. 123–131. University of Arizona Press, Tucson.

Brown, D. E., and C. H. Lowe

1983   *Biotic Communities of the Southwest* (map). General Technical Report RM-78, Rocky Mountain Forest and Range Experiment Station, Forest Service, U.S. Department of Agriculture, Fort Collins.

Buck, B. J., and H. C. Monger

1999   Stable Isotopes and Soil-Geomorphology as Indicators of Holocene Climate Change, Northern Chihuahuan Desert. *Journal of Arid Environments* 43:357–373.

Burgess, T. L.

1995   Desert Grassland, Mixed Shrub Savanna, Shrub Steppe, or Semidesert Scrub? In *The Desert Grassland,* edited by M. P. McClaran and T. R. Van Devender, pp. 31–67. University of Arizona Press, Tucson.

Burns, B. T.

1983   Simulated Anasazi Storage Behavior Using Crop Yields Reconstructed from Tree Rings: AD 652–1968. Ph.D. dissertation, Department of Anthropology, University of Arizona, Tucson.

Castiglia, P. J.

2002   Late Quaternary Climate History of the Pluvial Lake Palomas System, Northern Chihuahua, Mexico. Master's thesis, University of New Mexico, Albuquerque.

Dering, P.

1999   Earth-Oven Plant Processing in Archaic Period Economies: An Example from a Semi-Arid Savannah in South-Central North America. *American Antiquity* 64:659–674.

Dick-Peddie, W. A.

1993   *New Mexico Vegetation: Past, Present, and Future.* University of New Mexico Press, Albuquerque.

Doelle, W. H.

1976   *Desert Resources and Hohokam Subsistence: The Conoco Florence Project.* Archaeological Series No. 103. Cultural Resources Management Section, Arizona State Museum, University of Arizona, Tucson.

Doolittle, W. E.

2000   *Cultivated Landscapes of Native North America.* Oxford University Press, New York.

Ely, L. L.

1997   Response of Extreme Floods in the Southwestern United States to Climatic Variations in the Late Holocene. *Geomorphology* 19:175–202.

Fleischauer, H. L., Jr., and W. J. Stone

1982   *Quaternary Geology of Lake Animas, Hidalgo County, New Mexico.* Circular 174. New Mexico Bureau of Mines and Mineral Resources, Socorro.

Fritz, G.

1994   Are the First American Farmers Getting Younger? *Current Anthropology* 35:305–309.

Fritz, G., K. Adams, R. J. Hard, and J. R. Roney

1999   Evidence for Cultivation of *Amaranthus* sp. (Amaranthaceae) 3,000 Years Ago at Cerro Juanaqueña, Chihuahua. Paper presented at the 22nd Annual Conference of the Society of Ethnobiology, Oaxaca, Mexico.

Glassow, Michael A.

1980   *Prehistoric Agricultural Development in the Northern Southwest: A Study in Changing Patterns of Land Use.* Ballena Press, Socorro, N.Mex.

Hanselka, J. K.

2000   Late Archaic Plant Use and Early Agriculture in Northwestern Chihuahua, Mexico: Insights from Cerros de Trincheras Sites.

Master's thesis, Department of Anthropology, University of Texas at San Antonio.

Hard, R. J.

1990   Agricultural Dependence in the Mountain Mogollon. In *Perspectives on Southwestern Prehistory,* edited by P. E. Minnis and C. L. Redman, pp. 135–149. Westview Press, Boulder, Colo.

1997   A Comparative Analysis of Agricultural Dependence in the Northern and Southern Jornada Mogollon Regions. In *Proceedings of the Ninth Jornada-Mogollon Conference,* edited by R. Mauldin, J. Leach, and S. Ruth, pp. 93–98. Publications in Archaeology No. 12. Centro de Investigaciones Arqueologicas, El Paso, Tex.

Hard, R. J., R. P. Mauldin, and G. R. Raymond

1996   Mano Size, Stable Carbon Isotope Ratios, and Macrobotanical Remains as Multiple Lines of Evidence of Maize Dependence in the American Southwest. *Journal of Archaeological Method and Theory* 3:253–318.

Hard, R. J., and W. L. Merrill

1990   Mobile Agriculturalists and the Emergence of Sedentism: Perspectives from Northern Mexico. *American Anthropologist* 94: 601–620.

Hard, R. J., and J. R. Roney

1998a   A Massive Terraced Village Complex in Chihuahua, Mexico, 3000 Years Before Present. *Science* 279:1661–1664.

1998b   *Una investigación arqueológica de los sitios Cerros con Trincheras del Arcáico Tardío en Chihuahua, México: Las investigaciones de campo de 1997.* Informe al Consejo de Arqueología, Instituto Nacional de Antropología e Historia. Center for Archaeological Research, University of Texas at San Antonio.

1999   *An Archaeological Investigation of Late Archaic Cerros de Trincheras Sites in Chihuahua, Mexico: Results of the 1998 Investigations.* Special Report No. 25. Center for Archaeological Research, University of Texas at San Antonio.

2004   Late Archaic Period Hilltop Settlements in Northwestern Chihuahua, Mexico. In *Identity, Feasting, and the Archaeology of the Greater Southwest,* edited by B. J. Mills, pp. 276–294. University Press of Colorado, Boulder.

Hard, R. J., J. E. Zapata, B. K. Moses, and J. R. Roney

1999   Terrace Construction in Northern Chihuahua, Mexico: 1150 BC and Modern Experiments. *Journal of Field Archaeology* 26: 129–146.

Haury, E. W.

1962   The Greater American Southwest. In *Courses toward Urban Life*, edited by R. Braidwood and G. Willey, pp. 106–131. Viking Fund Publications in Anthropology 32. Wenner-Gren Foundation for Anthropological Research, New York.

Heerwagen, A.

1956   Mixed Prairie in New Mexico. In *Grasslands of the Great Plains*, edited by J. E. Waver and F. W. Albertson, pp. 284–300. Johnson Publishing, Lincoln, Neb.

Hill, J.

2001   Proto-Uto-Aztecan: A Community of Cultivators in Central Mexico. *American Anthropologist* 103:913–934.

Huckell, B. B.

1995   *Of Marshes and Maize: Preceramic Agricultural Settlements in the Cienega Valley, Southeastern Arizona.* Anthropological Papers of the University of Arizona No. 59. University of Arizona Press, Tucson.

1997   The Archaic Prehistory of the North American Southwest. *Journal of World Prehistory* 10:305–374.

Huckell, B. B., L. W. Huckell, and K. B. Benedict

2002   Maize Agriculture and the Rise of Mixed Farming-Foraging Economies in Southeastern Arizona during the Second Millennium. In *Traditions, Transitions, and Technologies: Themes in Southwestern Archaeology, Proceedings of the 2000 Southwest Symposium*, edited by S. Schlanger, pp. 137–159. University Press of Colorado, Boulder.

Huckell, B. B., L. W. Huckell, and S. K. Fish

1995   *Investigations at Milagro, a Late Preceramic Site in the Eastern Tucson Basin.* Technical Report 94(5). Center for Desert Archaeology, Tucson.

Johnson, A. E.

1960   The Trincheras Culture of Northern Sonora. *American Antiquity* 29:174–186.

Kaplan, H., and K. Hill

1985   Food Sharing among Ache Foragers: Tests of Explanatory Hypotheses. *Current Anthropology* 26:223–245.

1992   The Evolutionary Ecology of Food Acquisition. In *Evolutionary Ecology and Human Behavior*, edited by E. A. Smith and B. Winterhalder, pp. 167–202. Aldine de Gruyter, New York.

Krider, R. Reed

1998   Paleoclimatic Significance of Late Quaternary Lacustrine and Alluvial Stratigraphy, Animas Valley, New Mexico. *Quaternary Research* 50:283–289.

Legler, R. P.

1970   Habitat Preference of the Desert Cottontail with Additional Notes on the Black-tailed Jackrabbit. Master's thesis, New Mexico State University, Las Cruces.

Lehmer, D. J.

1948   *The Jornada Branch of the Mogollon.* University of Arizona Bulletin, Social Science Bulletin 17, vol. 19, no. 2.

Mabry, J. B.

2002   The Role of Irrigation in the Transition to Agriculture and Sedentism in the Southwest. In *Traditions, Transitions, and Technologies: Themes in Southwestern Archaeology, Proceedings of the 2000 Southwest Symposium,* edited by S. Schlanger, pp. 178–199. University Press of Colorado, Boulder.

2003   Diversity in Early Southwestern Farming Systems and Optimization Models of Transitions to Agriculture. In *Subsistence and Resource Use Strategies in Early Agricultural Communities in Southern Arizona,* edited by M. W. Diehl. Anthropological Paper No. 34. Center for Desert Archaeology, Tucson. (Draft.)

Mabry, J. B. (editor)

1998   *Archaeological Investigations of Early Village Sites in the Middle Santa Cruz Valley. Part II: Analysis and Synthesis.* Anthropological Papers No. 19. Center for Desert Archaeology, Tucson.

Mabry, J. B., D. L. Swartz, H. Wöcherl, J. J. Clark, G. H. Archer, and M. W. Lindeman

1997   *Archaeological Investigations of Early Village Sites in the Middle Santa Cruz Valley: Description of the Santa Cruz Bend, Square Hearth, Stone Pipe, and Canal Sites.* Anthropological Papers No. 18. Center for Desert Archaeology, Tucson.

MacNeish, Richard S. (editor)

1993   *Preliminary Investigations of the Archaic in the Region of Las Cruces, New Mexico.* Historic and Natural Resources Report No. 9. Cultural Resources Management Branch, Directorate of Environment, Fort Bliss, Tex.

Martin, P. S., J. B. Rinaldo, E. Bluhm, H. C. Cutler, and R. Grange, Jr.

1952   *Mogollon Cultural Continuity and Change: The Stratigraphic*

Analysis of Tularosa and Cordova Caves. Fieldiana, vol. 40. Field Museum of Natural History, Chicago.

Matson, R. G.

1991 *The Origins of Southwestern Agriculture.* University of Arizona Press, Tucson.

Mauldin, R. P.

1993 The Relationship between Ground Stone and Agricultural Intensification in Western New Mexico. *Kiva* 58:317–330.

1995 Groping for the Past: Investigating Archaeological Patterns across Space and Time in the Southern Southwestern United States. Ph.D. dissertation, Department of Anthropology, University of New Mexico, Albuquerque.

1997 Patterns of Climate and Production in the Past and Present Jornada. In *Proceedings of the Ninth Jornada-Mogollon Conference,* edited by R. P. Mauldin, J. D. Leach, and S. Ruth, pp. 11–28. Publications in Archaeology No. 12. Centro de Investigaciones Arqueologicas, El Paso, Tex.

McGuire, R. H., and J. McNiff

1990 Cerros de Trincheras and the Cultural Landscape of Northern Sonora Mexico. Paper presented at the 55th Annual Meeting of the Society for American Archaeology, Las Vegas.

McGuire, R. H., and M. E. Villalpando

1993 Proyecto reconocimiento arqueológico en el Valle del Altar. Report to Instituto Nacional de Antropología e Historia, Mexico City.

McGuire, R. H., M. E. Villalpando C., V. D. Vargas, and E. Gallaga M.

1999 Cerro de Trincheras and the Casas Grandes World. In *The Casas Grandes World,* edited by C. F. Schaafsma and C. L. Riley, pp. 134–146. University of Utah Press, Salt Lake City.

Mehringer, P. J., P. S. Martin, and C. V. Haynes, Jr.

1967 Murray Springs, a Mid-Postglacial Pollen Record from Southern Arizona. *American Journal of Science* 265:786–797.

Metcalfe, S. E., A. Bimpson, A. J. Courtice, S. L. O'Hara, and D. M. Taylor

1997 Climate Change at the Monsoon/Westerly Boundary in Northern Mexico. *Journal of Paleoliminology* 17:155–171.

Minnis, P. E.

1992 Earliest Plant Cultivation in the Desert Borderlands of North America. In *The Origins of Agriculture: An International Perspective,* edited by C. W. Cowan and P. J. Watson, pp. 121–142. Smithsonian Institution Press, Washington and London.

Moerman, D.

2001   Native American Ethnobotany Database: Foods, Drugs, Dyes, Fibers of Native North American Peoples. University of Michigan, Dearborn. http://www.umd.umich.edu/cgi-bin/herb/.

Nordt, Lee

2003   Late Quaternary Fluvial Landscape Evolution in Desert Grasslands of Northern Chihuahua, Mexico. *Geological Society of American Bulletin* 115:596–606.

O'Donovan, M.

2002   *New Perspectives of Site Function and Scale of Cerro de Trincheras, Sonora, Mexico: The 1991 Surface Survey.* Arizona State Museum Archaeological Series No. 195. University of Arizona Press, Tucson.

O'Laughlin, T. C.

1980   *The Keystone Dam Site and Other Archaic and Formative Sites in Northwest El Paso, Texas.* Publications in Anthropology No. 8. University of Texas at El Paso, El Paso.

Ortega-Ramírez, J.

1995a   Correlación estratigráfica de los depósitos cuaternarios de la Laguna de Babícora, Chihuahua, México. *Geofísica Internacional* 34:117–129.

1995b   Los paleoambientes holocénicos de la Laguna de Babícora, Chihuahua, México. *Geofísica Internacional* 34:107–116.

Ortega-Ramírez, J. R., A. Valiente-Banuet, J. Urrutia-Fucugauchi,
         C. A. Martera-Gutiérrez, and G. Alvarado-Valdez

1998   Paleoclimatic Changes during the Late Pleistocene-Holocene in Laguna Babícora, near the Chihuahuan Desert, México. *Canadian Journal of Earth Science* 35:1168–1179.

Polyak, V. J., and Y. Asmerom

2001   Late Holocene Climate and Cultural Changes in the Southwestern United States. *Science* 294:148–151.

Rhode, D.

1995   Estimating Agricultural Carrying Capacity in the Zuni Region, West-Central New Mexico: A Water Allocation Model. In *Soil, Water, Biology, and Belief in Prehistoric and Traditional Southwestern Agriculture*, edited by H. W. Toll, pp. 85–101. Special Publication 2. New Mexico Archaeological Council, Albuquerque.

Roney, J. R., and R. J. Hard

2000   *Una investigación arqueológica de los Sitios Cerros con Trincheras del Arcáico Tardío en Chihuahua, México: Las investigaciones de campo de 1999*. Special Report No. 26-S. Center for Archaeological Research, University of Texas at San Antonio.

2002   Early Agriculture in Northwestern Chihuahua. In *Traditions, Transitions, and Technologies: Themes in Southwestern Archaeology, Proceedings of the 2000 Southwest Symposium*, edited by S. Schlanger, pp. 160–177. University Press of Colorado, Boulder.

2004   A Review of Cerros de Trincheras in Northwestern Chihuahua. In *Surveying the Archaeology of Northwest Mexico*, edited by G. E. Newell and E. Gallaga, pp. 127–147. University of Utah Press, Salt Lake City.

Roth, B. J., and B. B. Huckell

1992   Cortaro Points and the Archaic of Southern Arizona. *Kiva* 57: 353–370.

Sauer, C., and D. Brand

1931   Prehistoric Settlements of Sonora with Special Reference to Cerros de Trincheras. In *University of California Publications in Geography* 5:67–148. University of California Press, Berkeley.

Schmidt, K., and J. Nisengard

1999   1998 Investigations: A Report on the Faunal Remains for Cerro Juanaqueña, Cerro Los Torres, and Cerro Vidal, Chihuahua, Mexico. Unpublished manuscript on file at the Center for Archaeological Research, San Antonio.

2000   Recent Faunal Analysis from Cerros de Trincheras Sites in Northwestern Chihuahua. Paper presented at the 65th Annual Meeting of the Society of American Archaeology, Philadelphia.

Shaw, R. H.

1988   Climate Requirement. In *Corn and Corn Improvement*, edited by G. F. Sprague and J. W. Dudley, pp. 609–638. 3rd ed. Agronomy No. 18. American Society of Agronomy, Madison, Wis.

Shuster, R. A., and R. A. Bye, Jr.

1984   Part II: Preliminary Results from the Dolores Archaeological Program Gardens. In *Dolores Archaeological Program: Synthetic Report 1978–1981*, pp. 94–99. U.S. Department of the Interior, Bureau of Reclamation, Engineering and Research Center, Denver.

Simms, S. R.

1986   Acquisition Cost and Nutritional Data on Great Basin Resources. *Journal of California and Great Basin Anthropology* 8 (2):117–126.

1987   *Behavioral Ecology and Hunter-Gatherer Foraging: An Example from the Great Basin*. BAR International Series 381. British Archaeological Reports, Oxford, England.

Smiley, F.

1994   The Agricultural Transition in the Northern Southwest: Patterns in the Current Chronometric Data. *Kiva* 60:165–189.

Smith, B. D.

1998   *The Emergence of Agriculture.* 2nd ed. Scientific American Library, New York.

Smith, G. D., and M. McFaul

1997   Paleoenvironmental and Geoarchaeologic Implications of Late Quaternary Sediments and Paleosols: North-Central to Southwestern San Juan Basin, New Mexico. *Geomorphology* 21: 107–138.

Stacy, V. K. P.

1974   Cerros de Trincheras in the Arizona Papaquería. Ph.D. dissertation, Department of Anthropology, University of Arizona, Tucson.

Turner, E. S., and T. R. Hester

1995   *A Field Guide to Stone Artifacts of Texas Indians.* 2nd ed. Gulf Publishing, Houston.

Turpin, S. A.

1991   Time Out of Mind: The Radiocarbon Chronology of the Lower Pecos River Region. In *Papers on Lower Pecos Prehistory,* vol. 8, edited by S. A. Turpin, pp. 1–49. Studies in Archeology 8. Texas Archeological Research Laboratory, University of Texas at Austin.

Urrutia-Fucugauchi, J., J. Ortega-Ramírez, and R. Cruz-Gatica

1997   Rock-Magnetic Study of Late Pleistocene–Holocene Sediments from the Babícora Lacustrine Basin, Chihuahua, Northern Mexico. *Geofísica Internacional* 36:77–86.

Van Auken, O. W.

2000   Shrub Invasions of North American Semiarid Grasslands. *Annual Review of Ecological Systems* 31:197–215.

Van Devender, T. R.

1990   Late Quaternary Vegetation and Climate of the Chihuahuan Desert, United States and Mexico. In *Packrat Middens: The Last 40,000 Years of Biotic Change,* edited by J. L. Betancourt, T. R. Van Devender, and P. S. Martin, pp. 104–133. University of Arizona Press, Tucson.

1995   Desert Grassland History: Changing Climates, Evolution, Biogeography, and Community Dynamics. In *The Desert Grassland,* edited by M. P. McClaran and T. R. Van Devender, pp. 68–99. University of Arizona Press, Tucson.

Van Devender, T. R., and R. D. Worthington

1977   The Herpetofauna of Howell's Ridge Cave and the Paleoecology of the Northwestern Chihuahuan Desert. In *Transactions of the Symposium on the Biological Resources of the Chihuahuan Desert Region: United States and Mexico*, edited by R. H. Wauer and D. H. Riskind, pp. 85–106. No. 3, National Park Service Transactions and Proceedings Series. U.S. Department of the Interior, Washington, D.C.

Ward, G. K., and S. R. Wilson

1978   Procedures for Comparing and Combining Radiocarbon Age Determinations: A Critique. *Archaeometry* 20:19–31.

Waters, M. R.

1989   Late Quaternary Lacustrine History and Paleoclimatic Significance of Pluvial Lake Cochise, Southeastern Arizona. *Quaternary Research* 32:1–11.

Waters, M. R., and C. V. Haynes

2001   Late Quaternary Arroyo Formation and Climate Change in the American Southwest. *Geology* 29:399–402.

Whalen, M. E.

1994   Moving Out of the Archaic on the Edge of the Southwest. *American Antiquity* 59:606–621.

Wilcox, D. R.

1979   Warfare Implications of Dry-Laid Masonry Walls on Tumamoc Hill. *Kiva* 45:15–38.

Wilkens, D. E., and D. R. Currey

1999   Radiocarbon Chronology and b^{13}C Analysis of Mid- to Late-Holocene Aeolian Environments, Guadalupe Mountains National Park, Texas, USA. *Holocene* 9:363–371.

Wills, W. H.

1988   Early Agriculture and Sedentism in the American Southwest: Evidence and Interpretations. *Journal of World Prehistory* 2: 445–488.

Winterhalder, B.

1986   Diet Choice, Risk, and Food Sharing in a Stochastic Environment. *Journal of Anthropological Archaeology* 5:369–392.

Winterhalder, B., and C. Goland

1997   An Evolutionary Ecology Perspective in Diet Choice, Risk, and

Plant Domestication. In *People, Plants, and Landscapes: Studies in Paleobotany,* edited by K. J. Gremillion, pp. 123–259. University of Alabama Press, Tuscaloosa.

York, J. C., and W. A. Dick-Peddie

1969   Vegetation Changes in Southern New Mexico during the Past Hundred Years. In *Arid Lands in Perspective,* edited by W. G. McGinnies and B. J. Goldman, pp. 157–199. University of Arizona Press, Tucson.

Zavala, B. G.

1998   Building Trincheras: An Analysis of Architectural Features at Cerro de Trincheras. Master's thesis, Department of Anthropology, State University of New York at Binghamton.

Zeanah, D. W., J. A. Carter, D. P. Dugas, R. G. Elston, and J. E. Hammett

1995   *An Optimal Foraging Model of Hunter-Gatherer Land Use in the Carson Desert.* Intermountain Research, Silver City, Nev.

CHAPTER 7

Late Archaic Stone Tool Technology across the Borderlands

BRADLEY J. VIERRA

Introduction

The Late Archaic (ca. 3000–1500 BP) along the U.S./Mexican Borderlands is characterized by a diverse set of agricultural and foraging economic strategies. Current research indicates that areas of the Sonoran and Chihuahuan Deserts contain evidence for an early dependence on agriculture with sedentism, vs. foragers who repeatedly reoccupied specific site locations in the Tamaulipas region of South Texas. This varied archaeological record provides an excellent opportunity to evaluate current arguments concerned with explaining technological variation. This chapter presents the preliminary results of the analyses of chipped stone artifacts from the Late Archaic *trincheras* site of Cerro Juanaqueña, Chihuahua, Mexico, and contrasts this information with other sites along the Borderlands. It discusses the possible effects of subsistence, mobility, and raw material availability on Late Archaic stone tool technology.

Late Archaic Stone Tool Technology

Recent research on stone tool technology has emphasized residential mobility as a possible explanation for technological variation. This perspective often assumes that mobility limits the size and number of tools that a group can efficiently carry with it (Carr 1994; Ebert 1979; Kuhn 1994; Shott 1986). For example, William Parry and Robert Kelly (1987) suggest that bifaces are portable tools that can also act as cores, which is important for mobile groups with varying access to lithic materials, whereas a simple flake technology is sufficient for sedentary groups with access to locally available materials. Another important aspect of bifacial technologies is the ability to increase tool use-life through resharpening (Kelly 1988).

The effect of lithic material availability on stone tool technology is another possible explanation for technological variation. These arguments are often framed in respect to curated vs. expedient components of lithic technology (*sensu* Binford 1977, 1979). That is, a cost-benefit analysis of procurement/production costs as compared to maintenance/replacement costs provides the following two predictions: (1) a greater emphasis on the curated component of the technology in lithic resource poor areas and (2) a greater emphasis on the expedient aspect of the technology in lithic resource–rich areas (Andrefsky 1994; Bamforth 1986).

Other studies of stone tool technology have emphasized the importance of time constraints, energy efficiency, and risk reduction in explaining technological variation and long-term changes in technology (Jeske 1992; Nelson 1992; Torrence 1983, 1989; Vierra 1995). With the shift to agricultural-based economies the conflicting demands of subsistence pursuits, labor, technology, and social activities need to be balanced (Jeske 1992). This process has a *residual effect* on the stone tool technology, when increasing amounts of energy are diverted into other aspects of technology and labor organization. More specifically, there is a deemphasis of the stone tool technology per se and an increased emphasis on corporate labor group structure and that aspect of technology associated with agricultural intensification. This includes milling equipment, ceramics, storage facilities, architecture, and agricultural features. We need to remember that increasing "sedentism" actually reflects the increasing use of logistical mobility and changes in labor organization.

Like that of many other Southwestern lithic researchers, my own past work has focused on understanding the organizational relationship between the use of biface and flake components of chipped stone tool technology. Much of this work has centered on the Colorado Plateau and northwestern New Mexico. Here my research has illustrated the link between changes in stone tool technology and an increasing dependence on agriculture from Late Archaic to Pueblo III times. This trend is characterized by (1) the long-term replacement of bifacial knives with simple flake tools, (2) a shift from the use of higher-quality materials like cherts and chalcedonies for biface production to lower-quality materials like silicified wood and basalt for expedient flake production, (3) an increase in the variety of lithic materials being worked, and (4) the increased use of marginally retouched and unretouched flakes. These patterns correspond with increasing mano grinding surface area and the ubiquity of maize in flotation samples through time. These changes in chipped stone and ground stone technology witnessed a distinctive shift between Basketmaker III and Pueblo I times, presumably reflecting the intensification of an agricultural economy by circa AD 700 (Vierra 1993a, 1993b, 1994c, 1995, 1996).

Similar long-term patterns have been reported for the Chihuahuan Desert of southern New Mexico. For example, several researchers have documented changes in raw material selection between Archaic and Formative times, but the exact nature and timing of these technological changes are poorly understood (Carmichael 1986; O'Laughlin 1980:170; Vierra et al. 1998; Whalen 1980). Nonetheless, most researchers would agree that the shift to an economy more heavily dependent on maize agriculture probably did not occur until quite late, for example, with the presence of plaza pueblos during the El Paso phase circa AD 1250 (Hard et al. 1996).

Lithic studies in the Sonoran Desert of southern Arizona have also documented similar changes between Archaic and Hohokam lithic assemblages (Bostwick and Shackley 1987). Recent studies of Late Archaic villages situated in alluvial valleys have identified the presence of structures, storage features, middens, and burials associated with early agriculture at circa 1000 BC (Huckell 1990, 1995; Mabry 1998, this volume). Sliva (1998:343) describes the Late Archaic flaked stone assemblage at the Santa Cruz Bend village site as an "expedient technology expected for sedentary or semi-sedentary populations."

Finally, the Late Archaic archaeological record of South Texas has been characterized as representing generalized foragers. These hunter-gatherers were residentially mobile, with seasonal mobility being conditioned by the abundance and distribution of plant resources. Food tended to be consumed on a daily basis, with little or no dependence on storage and no evidence of agriculture. Middens and cemeteries have been documented, but they presumably reflect the repeated reuse of specific resource patches and not sedentism. The chipped stone technology is often characterized as emphasizing the bifacial component, with heat-treatment commonly being used to increase tool-use life in lithic resource poor areas (Black 1989; Hester 1980, 1981, 1995, this volume; Hester and Collins 1974; Taylor and Highley 1995; Vierra 1998).

Given this disparity in the timing of an increasing dependence on agriculture and early village formation across the Borderlands, how does the chipped stone assemblage at Cerro Juanaqueña compare with these varying regional patterns? This chapter addresses three basic issues concerning the archaeological implications of residential site stability and labor organization. If Cerro Juanaqueña represents an early village site that is reliant on agriculture, then I would expect the chipped stone assemblage to (1) be dominated by the reduction and use of locally available materials, (2) reflect the full range of core reduction and tool production/maintenance activities, and (3) be characterized by an increased emphasis on the production and use of expedient flake tools.

The discussion begins with a review of the chipped stone assemblage from Cerro Juanaqueña, including information on material selection, core reduction, and tool production/maintenance. Then the site is discussed from a regional perspective. I identify the raw material procurement range for the site and contrast the chipped stone assemblage with a regional baseline of sites that reflect varying degrees of agricultural dependence and residential mobility but similar raw material availability.

The Cerro Juanaqueña Chipped Stone Assemblage

Preliminary work by Hard and Roney (this volume) at the Late Archaic *cerros de trincheras* site of Cerro Juanaqueña has documented the presence of maize agriculture circa 1250 BC at a site with over 400 terrace features (Hard and Roney 1998; Hard et al. 1999; Roney and Hard 2000). The surface of the site is littered with Late Archaic dart points and heavily worn basin-shaped metates. The labor investment in the construction of these features implies a degree of residential stability and labor organization beyond that of simple foragers. Although there is currently only limited evidence for the presence of structures at the site, these excavations have yielded a variety of floral remains, faunal remains, and chipped stone debris indicative of domestic refuse. Plant remains include domesticated varieties of both maize and amaranth.

In all 12,763 pieces of debitage, 29 cores, 9 cobble unifaces, 2 split pebbles, 7 manuports, a hammerstone, and 105 retouched tools have been analyzed from the 1997–1999 field seasons (Table 7.1). This sample was derived from eighty-six units that were excavated in sixteen separate terrace and rock-ring features across the site. The terraces included in this sample are 97, 126, 163, 175, 273, 287, 290, 297, 387, and 413, and the rock-rings are 1A, 28, 234, 239, 250, and 286. Figure 7.1 illustrates the distribution of these features across the site. The initial two field seasons focused on the excavation of test pits that were dug to a depth of 1.2 m. In contrast, the 1999 field season emphasized horizontal stripping to a maximum depth of 80 cm. For example, about 50% of the chipped stone artifacts recovered during the test excavations were present in the upper two levels. This contrasts with about 70% during the horizontal excavations. Table 7.2 presents the results of the analysis of chipped stone artifacts from these two excavation strategies. A chi-square analysis of the contingency table indicates that there is a significant difference in the distribution of artifacts by excavation method (chi-sq = 31.4, $df = 2$, $p < 0.001$). Adjusted residuals were therefore calculated in order to determine which of the contingency table cells were contributing to the significant chi-square value. Values greater than 1.96 or −1.96 are significant at the .05 level. It appears that relatively more pieces of debitage were recovered from the horizontal excavations vs. more cores and retouched tools from the test pits than expected. Much of this is due to

Table 7.1. Chipped stone artifact type by material type

Artifact type		Basalt	Rhyolite	Andesite	Obsidian	Chalcedony	Chert	Quartzite	Quartz	Quartz crystal	Total
						Material Type					
Cores	Cores	0	16	0	1	8	4	0	0	0	29
	Cobble uniface	0	8	0	0	0	1	0	0	0	9
	Split pebble	0	0	0	2	0	0	0	0	0	2
Debitage	Debris	10	440	0	4	78	104	0	2	1	739
	Core flake	93	2229	2	40	774	526	1	1	0	3666
	Biface flake	0	142	0	13	199	42	0	0	0	396
	Und. frag.	2	228	0	16	205	67	0	0	0	518
	Microdeb.	20	2837	0	147	3867	515	0	0	0	7386
	Other deb.	1	27	1	3	12	14	0	0	0	58
Retouched Tools	Retouched piece	0	9	0	0	5	4	0	0	0	18
	Notch	0	7	0	1	4	1	0	0	0	13
	Denticulate	0	3	0	0	0	0	0	0	0	3
	Biface	0	15	0	2	17	6	0	0	0	40
	Projectile point	0	10	0	1	4	6	0	0	0	21
	Uniface	0	4	0	0	1	0	0	0	0	5
	Drill	0	1	0	0	0	1	0	0	0	2
	Perforator	0	2	0	0	0	0	0	0	0	2
	Cruciform	0	0	0	0	1	0	0	0	0	1
Other artifacts	Hammerstone	0	1	0	0	0	0	0	0	0	1
	Manuports	0	5	0	2	0	0	0	0	0	7
Total		126	5984	3	232	5275	1291	1	3	1	12916

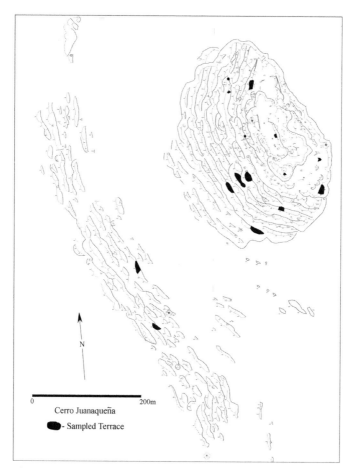

Figure 7.1. Cerro Juanaqueña site map

Table 7.2. Artifact type by excavation season

Artifact Type	1997–1998	1999	Total
Cores	19	10	29
	5.0	−5.0	
Debitage	3171	9592	12763
	−4.5	**4.5**	
Retouched Tools	37	68	105
	2.4	−2.4	
Total	3227	9670	12897

    Note: Top value in cell represents artifact count and bottom value represents adjusted residuals. Significant ($p < 0.05$) positive values are shown in boldface.

    Chi-square = 31.4, $df = 2$, $p < 0.001$

increased amounts of microdebitage recovered during the horizontal stripping. That is, microdebitage composes 20–50% vs. 40–70% of the debitage from the test pits and horizontal excavations, respectively. Overall, both excavation strategies provide a representative sample of the site's chipped stone assemblage. However, relatively few cores were recovered from these excavations.

Material Selection

Analysis of the debitage assemblage indicates that it is dominated by rhyolite (46%), with less chalcedony (41%), chert (10%), obsidian (2%), and other materials. The cores and retouched tools appear to represent the same variation in material type as that exhibited by the debitage. However, the sample size is small for the cores. Nonetheless, the analysis of a contingency table of core vs. biface flake by material type reveals some significant differences (Table 7.3; chi-sq = 191.9, df = 4, p < 0.001). An evaluation of the adjusted residuals indicates that there are relatively more rhyolite and chert core flakes vs. chalcedony and obsidian biface flakes than expected. In addition, significantly more core flakes are made on medium- and coarse-grain materials vs. fine-grain materials for biface flakes (Table 7.4; chi-sq = 215.8, df = 2, p < 0.001). It therefore appears that higher-quality materials were being selected for the production of bifaces with longer use-lives, vs. lower-quality materials for simple expedient flake tools.

The majority of the raw materials that were being worked at the site were available from local river gravel sources. That is, 97% of the cortex on the rhyolites, chalcedony, chert, and basalt debitage is water-worn (i.e., stream-rolled) cortex. The Río Casas Grandes is located on the valley floor below Cerro Juanaqueña. An infield analysis was conducted of these gravels, including the analysis of seven 1 by 1 m surface units for a total sample of 248 cobbles. Of these cobbles, 89% are rhyolite (n = 220), with a little basalt (n = 18; 7.3%) and chalcedony (n = 9; 3.6%). Although no cherts were identified in these samples,

Table 7.3. Core and biface flake by material type

Flake Type	Material Type				
	Rhyolite	Obsidian	Chalcedony	Chert	Other
Core Flake	2229	40	774	526	97
	9.6	−3.7	−12.9	**2.0**	**3.3**
Biface Flake	142	13	199	42	0
	−9.6	**3.7**	**12.9**	−2.0	−3.3

Note: Top value in cell represents artifact count and bottom value represents adjusted residuals. Significant (p < 0.05) positive values are shown in boldface.
  Chi-square = 191.9, df = 4, p < 0.001

Table 7.4. Core and biface flake by material grain type

Flake Type	Material Grain Type		
	Fine	Medium	Coarse
Core Flake	886	2279	501
	−14.0	**7.5**	**7.7**
Biface Flake	226	169	1
	14.0	−7.5	−7.7

Note: Top value in cell represents artifact count and bottom value represents adjusted residuals. Significant ($p < 0.05$) positive values are shown in boldface.
Chi-square = 215.8, df = 2, $p < 0.001$

they have been observed in nearby limestone outcrops and surface lag gravels. This indicates that the site occupants were preferentially selecting for both chalcedony and cherts from the local sources.

Local materials dominate the debitage, with obsidians representing only about 2% of the assemblage. In addition, one core, two split pebbles, four retouched tools, and two manuports are also made of obsidian. The manuports simply consist of unmodified pebbles. An X-ray fluorescence analysis was conducted on 52 pieces of debitage, 20 retouched tools, a core, and 7 pebble manuports at the site. This includes both excavated materials and surface-collected items. Six separate regional obsidian sources were identified: Unknown A (n = 36; 45%), Lago Fredrico (n = 18; 23%), Antelope Wells (n = 11; 14%) Sierra Fresnal (n = 10; 13%), Los Jagueyes (n = 3; 4%) and Unknown B (n = 2; 3%) (Shackley 1998, 1999).

Thirty-one of these artifacts were recovered from subsurface contexts at the site and forty-nine from surface contexts. Although the sample size is too small to conduct a statistical test of a contingency, Figure 7.2 illustrates some obvious differences. The majority of the excavated samples were identified as being from the Unknown A source (n = 22; 71%), with some from Lago Fredrico (n = 4), Sierra Fresnal (n = 3), Los Jagueyes (n = 1), and Unknown B (n = 1). In contrast, the surface artifacts are more evenly distributed among the five sources: Unknown A (n = 14), Lago Fredrico (n = 14), Antelope Wells (n = 11), Sierra Fresnal (n = 7), Los Jagueyes (n = 2), and Unknown B (n = 1). The more distant Antelope Wells source is only represented in the surface assemblage. Four surface-collected arrow points are made of Antelope Wells, Lago Fredrico, and Los Jagueyes materials, which may indicate that some of these surface artifacts were introduced to the site by later visitors and not by the original Late Archaic occupants.

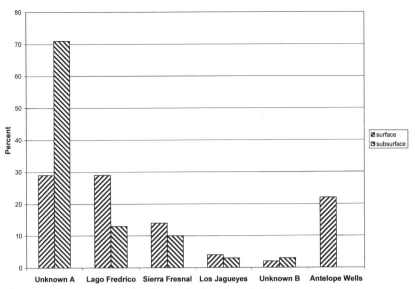

Figure 7.2. A comparison of surface and subsurface obsidian types

Lithic Reduction

Given the few cores represented in the sample, the evidence for core reduction activities is primarily represented by the debitage. Nonetheless, at least five separate reduction techniques were used at the site: split cobble, cobble uniface, large flake blank, split pebble, and bipolar. It appears that the site occupants were bringing river cobbles and obsidian pebbles to the site for reduction, with four rhyolite cobbles and two obsidian pebble manuports being present. Once on the site they either split the cobbles and used the fresh surface as a striking platform for single-faced cores or simply removed flakes from unprepared cortical platforms (i.e., cobble unifaces). In a few cases, large flakes were used as cores, and small obsidian pebbles were split and reduced using a multidirectional technique. Finally, a single chalcedony bipolar core remnant is represented. The cores are fully reduced, with eleven being expended, ten being core fragments, and six being classified as still usable. A single core was rejected due to hinging, and one was reused as a hammerstone. In addition, nine cobble unifaces are represented in the assemblage, four being exhausted, three being still usable, one being a fragment, and one exhibiting extensive stepping.

The debitage mostly consists of microdebitage (i.e., 10 mm or less in size; 57.8%) and core flakes (28.7%), with some angular debris (5.7%), undetermined flake fragments (4.0%), biface flakes (3.1%), and other debitage. They indi-

Table 7.5. Material type by platform type

Material Type	Platform Type		
	Cortical	Single-Faceted	Multifaceted
Rhyolite	785	668	116
	14.0	−10.7	−5.0
Obsidian	4	17	10
	−3.0	0.4	**4.3**
Chalcedony	123	401	125
	−12.2	**6.3**	**9.5**
Chert	102	233	0
	−3.5	**7.3**	−6.4

Note: Top value in cell represents artifact count and bottom value represents adjusted residuals. Significant ($p < 0.05$) positive values are shown in boldface.

Chi-square = 304.3, $df = 6$, $p < 0.001$

cate that a range of core reduction and tool production/maintenance activities occurred at the site. A study of the whole flakes present indicates that 46.2% are cortical core flakes ($n = 621$), 44.7% are noncortical core flakes ($n = 600$), and 9.0% are biface flakes ($n = 122$), representing all segments of the reduction process. Information on debitage platform type corresponds with the data on core reduction technique. That is, most of the platforms are single-faceted ($n = 1,368$; 50%), with fewer cortical ($n = 1,021$; 37%) and multifaceted ($n = 293$; 11%), and a few crushed/collapsed ($n = 58$; 2%) and battered ($n = 6$; 0.2%) platforms. The large amount of cortex and the presence of cortical and single-faceted platforms indicate that both cobble unifaces and prepared platform cores were reduced at the site. A chi-square analysis of the platform by material type contingency table with adjusted residuals demonstrates that there are significantly more rhyolite cortical platforms, chert single-faceted platforms, and chalcedony single- and multifaceted platforms (chi-sq = 304.3, $df = 6$, $p < 0.001$; Table 7.5).

Overall, the analyses indicate that different reduction trajectories may be represented among the material types. That is, cobble unifaces may primarily have been used for simple flakes, prepared chert cores for flakes and tool blanks (e.g., marginally retouched tools), and prepared chalcedony cores for tool blanks (e.g., bifacial tools). The small obsidian sample seems to reflect reduction of prepared cores for flakes and tool blanks, but nodule size would presumably be a limiting factor. For example, only 9 of the 140 projectile points analyzed from excavation and surface collections across the entire site are made of obsidian. At least 3 (and possibly 6) of these points are arrow and not dart points (also see Carmichael 1986:99).

The retouched tools are dominated by two groups of artifacts, the bifaces and projectile points, and to a lesser degree by the retouched pieces and notches. Informal tools like the retouched pieces, notches, and denticulates tend to be made on large thick flake blanks. They exhibit steep unidirectionally retouched edges that were often produced using a hard hammer percussion technique with steep angles of ca. 70 degrees. Most bifaces and projectile points (87%) appear to have been broken during manufacturing and use activities. For example, a single-early stage biface was made on a large flake blank, and several biface fragments exhibit perverse manufacturing breaks. Several large triangular bifaces appear to represent point preforms. In contrast, some projectile points exhibit impact fractures or base fragments with hafting polish. A sample of 140 projectile points from excavations and surface collections across the site indicates that several forms are represented. Most of these are stemmed ($n = 47$), corner-notched ($n = 44$), or side-notched ($n = 34$) types, with a few triangular ($n = 5$), contracting ($n = 2$), basal-notched ($n = 1$), and undetermined ($n = 7$) point forms. Figure 7.3 illustrates some of the variation exhibited by these point types.

Several other retouched tool types are represented at the site. Two perforators were manufactured by unidirectionally retouching the distal end of a flake to form a point. The two drills are bidirectionally retouched flakes with diamond-shaped cross sections and heavily worn and polished ends. The ends are blunt, with some evidence of resharpening. Four unifaces exhibit invasive retouch but, like the retouched pieces, have unidirectionally retouched edges with angles of about 70 degrees. A single cruciform was also recovered.

Summary

Earlier in this chapter, I have proposed several expectations for the chipped stone assemblage from Cerro Juanaqueña if the site represents an early village reliant on agriculture. The first prediction was that the assemblage should be dominated by the reduction and use of locally available materials. This seems to be true. Most of these materials were obtained from the gravels of the Rio Casas Grandes. It is, however, unclear as to whether the Unknown obsidian types were procured from nearby or from a more distant source. Most of the obsidian exhibits nodule (i.e., naturally weathered) and not waterworn cortex, which indicates that they may have been obtained from primary and not secondary sources. Most of the obsidian sources in northern and central Chihuahua, however, are at least 10 million years old and have been subjected to long-term erosion and secondary deposition (Shackley, personal communication, 2003). Nonetheless, obsidian only represents about 2% of the assemblage.

Second, the assemblage should reflect the full range of core reduction and

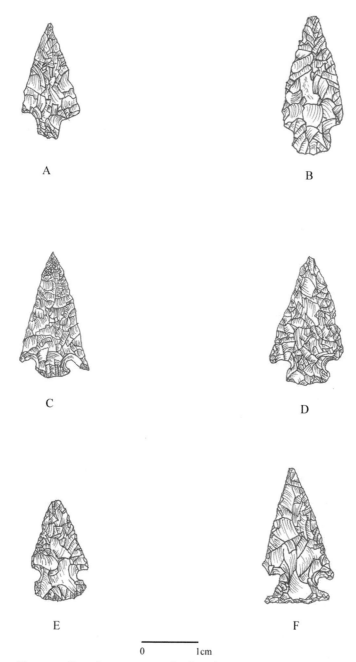

A

B

C

D

E

F

0   1cm

Figure 7.3. Cerro Juanaqueña projectile points

tool production/maintenance activities. This also seems to be true. Cobbles were obtained from the river gravels and then brought to the site and reduced, using several different techniques. The paucity of cores in the assemblage, however, could indicate that they were being discarded along the periphery or off the terraces. The debitage reflects that all segments of the reduction process are represented. Indeed, there is abundant microdebitage, indicating that reduction activities occurred on the terraces, although some of these tiny items might have also washed onto these features from up-slope contexts.

Third, the chipped stone assemblage should be characterized by an increased emphasis on the production and use of expedient flake tools. This does not seem to be true. There is a mixture of formal and informal tools. That is, bifaces and projectile points dominate the retouched tool assemblage, with fewer retouched pieces and notches. Most of the formal tools are broken, having been discarded due to manufacture and use-breakage. In addition, other domestic tools are represented at the site, including perforators, drills, unifaces, and a cruciform.

How does the chipped stone assemblage at Cerro Juanaqueña compare to other regional studies of Late Archaic stone tool technology?

A Regional Perspective

Obsidian Procurement

Let us begin by placing the site within the context of regional procurement patterns. Figure 7.4 illustrates a series of Archaic catchment areas linking upland with lowland resource areas through mostly X-ray fluorescence sourced obsidian artifacts and their source locations (Vierra 1994a, 1994b). These catchments include the Jemez Mountains, Chuska Mountains, Coconino Plateau, and Mogollon Highlands. On the Colorado Plateau this appears to include an area of about 8,500 sq km, vs. a much larger area of 38,000 sq km for the southern Basin and Range. This provides empirical support for the contention in Wills (1988:57) that Archaic foraging ranges on the plateau would be smaller due to shorter distances between resource patches, vs. the resource homogeneity exhibited across the Basin and Range, which would induce greater residential mobility.

Nonetheless, some of these southern groups may have been moving long distances in order to integrate upland resource areas into their annual rounds. Several studies, however, have identified evidence of increasing territoriality and a subsequent decrease in regional mobility by Late Archaic times (e.g., Roth 2000; Shackley 1990; Vierra 1994a, 1994b). M. R. Miller and Steve Shackley's (1998) study of obsidian from the Hueco Bolson near El Paso, Texas, indicates

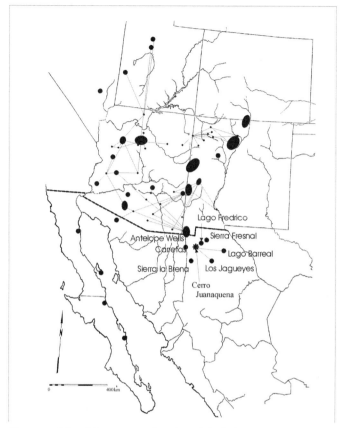

Figure 7.4. Material sources and projected Archaic procurement
ranges (base map adapted from Cameron and Sappington 1984;
Nelson and Holmes 1979; Shackley 1990; Vierra 1994a)

that these materials were solely derived from local Rio Grande gravels. There
was no evidence of obsidian having been obtained from sources in the Mogollon Highlands to the west or in Chihuahua to the south.

As previously discussed, only 2% of the debitage assemblage at Cerro
Juanaqueña is composed of obsidian, with four separate obsidian sources having been identified in the excavated sample. An unknown source dominates
this collection, with materials also having been derived from Lago Fredrico,
Sierra Fresnal, and Los Jagueyes. These sources reflect a 31,000-sq-km procurement region within northern Chihuahua that is primarily oriented to the
east of Cerro Juanaqueña. Some of these obsidians, however, could have been
obtained from secondary sources located closer to the site. The Antelope Wells,
Carretas, and Sierra La Brena sources located to the north, west, and southwest

of the site are absent from the excavated sample. Nineteen of twenty obsidian flakes identified with cortex during the analysis exhibit nodule cortex, indicating a primary and not secondary source for these materials. Only a single flake exhibited water-worn cortex that would have been derived from secondary sources. The absence of Antelope Wells obsidian at Cerro Juanaqueña underscores the lack of contact to the west, since this obsidian does occur in Late Archaic contexts from both southern Arizona and Sonora, Mexico (Mabry, this volume; and Carpenter et al., this volume).

Chipped Stone Technology

Given the lack of Archaic research in northern Chihuahua, comparisons are made here between the chipped stone assemblage at Cerro Juanaqueña and nine other sites that represent a variety of types located in settings with local gravel sources (Figure 7.5). Together they represent a quarry, two Ceramic

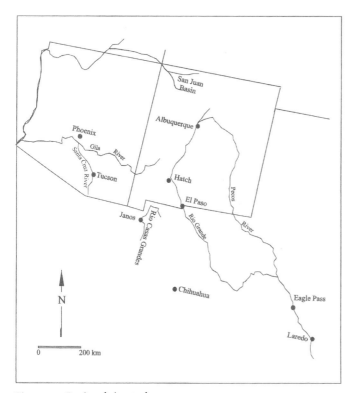

Figure 7.5. Regional site study area

period habitation sites, Late Archaic habitation, and temporary campsites. This includes a set of Late Archaic sites with structures located along the Rio Grande at El Paso (Keystone Dam site; O'Laughlin 1980) and the Santa Cruz River at Tucson (Santa Cruz River Bend site; Sliva 1998, personal communication, 1999). Also included are two temporary Late Archaic campsites that are situated along the Rio Grande near Hatch (LA 37450; Doleman 1997; Vierra n.d.), and Eagle Pass (41MV120; Vierra 1998). All of these sites are found in riverine settings with local gravel material sources. Rhyolite, chert, and silicified wood are the dominant materials at LA 37450, rhyolite at the Keystone Dam site, chert at 41MV120, and metamorphic, igneous, and chert materials at the Santa Cruz River Bend site.

To increase the baseline of comparison, both Late Archaic winter habitation sites and summer campsites in the San Juan Basin of northwest New Mexico were included (Burgett et al. 1994; Hogan et al. 1983; Kerley and Hogan 1983; Redd et al. 1994; Vierra 1994c). Chert derived from local lag gravels was mostly reduced at these sites. In addition, a quarry site near Hatch (LA 37451; Doleman 1997), a twelfth-century pithouse site, and a fourteenth-century Pueblo site located near Albuquerque were also included to document the full range of lithic reduction activities potentially represented in these riverine settings (Sullivan and Akins 1994; Vierra 1997). Rhyolite is the dominant material at the quarry site and chert at the Ceramic period sites along the Rio Grande valley near Albuquerque. Overall, chert is the most common material reduced on all these sites, with a medium-grained rhyolite (or welded tuff) similar to chert being reduced at the Hatch, El Paso, and Cerro Juanaqueña sites. The Santa Cruz River Bend site has the most distinctive lithic assemblage, with metamorphic and igneous rock materials. Each of the assemblages is considered here in terms of the varying degrees to which core reduction and tool production/maintenance activities are represented, comparing debitage type, core and retouched tool type, presence of cortex, and flake platform type.

Debitage

Debitage is an excellent indicator of the range in lithic reduction activities that were occurring on the site (Shott 1994). This analysis focuses on three specific debitage types: core flakes, biface flakes, and angular debris. Core flakes and angular debris are generally by-products of core reduction activities, vs. biface flakes of bifacial core or tool production/maintenance (Hayden and Hutchings 1989; Prentiss and Romansky 1989; Tomka 1989). Figure 7.6 shows that core flakes dominate most assemblages, with fewer angular debris and biface flakes. The quarry and Ceramic period assemblages contain the lowest proportion of

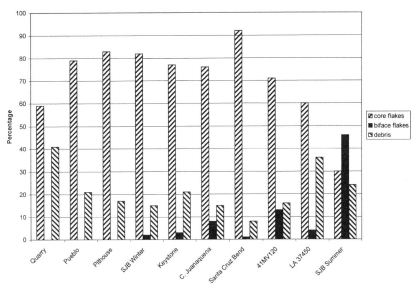

Figure 7.6. Intersite comparison of debitage types

biface flakes (0.0–0.3%), the Archaic habitation sites the median percentage (0.6–8.2%), and the Archaic campsites the highest percentage (4.5–46.5%). Cerro Juanaqueña contains the highest percentage of biface flakes (8.2%) among the Archaic habitation sites, and the Santa Cruz Bend site the lowest percentage (0.6%).

A chi-square analysis of Table 7.6 indicates that there is a significant difference in the distribution of these types across the sites (chi-sq = 8743.7, df = 18, $p < 0.001$). An inspection of the adjusted residuals indicates relatively more angular debris in the quarry and pueblo assemblages, more core flakes in the Ceramic period and Archaic habitation assemblages, and more biface flakes in two of the three Archaic campsites than expected. The campsites at LA 37450 and in the San Juan Basin contain significantly more angular debris that mainly appears to be the by-product of reducing tabular pieces of silicified wood.

This analysis, however, has one limitation: it is difficult to find comparative chipped stone artifact samples that were recovered using a single screen mesh size. In this case, four of the ten sites were excavated using 1/4-inch mesh (i.e., the pueblo, pithouse, Keystone Dam, and Santa Cruz Bend sites) vs. the remaining six sites, for which 1/8-inch mesh was used. This could reduce the recovery rate for smaller biface flakes at these sites. In the case of the Santa Cruz Bend site, the dominance of core flakes over both biface flakes and angu-

Table 7.6. Debitage type by site

| | Debitage Type | | | |
Site	Core Flake	Biface Flake	Debris	Total
Quarry	211	0	149	360
	−5.5	−6.5	**11.7**	
Pueblo	1953	1	531	2485
	8.0	−17.8	**4.8**	
Pithouse	2161	9	446	2616
	13.1	−17.8	−1.2	
SJB Habitation	410	12	77	499
	5.2	−5.9	−1.4	
Keystone Dam	310	11	83	404
	2.3	−5.1	1.4	
Cerro Juanaqueña	3666	396	739	4801
	7.9	−5.5	−4.9	
Santa Cruz Bend	5762	39	482	6283
	40.2	−29.1	−24.1	
41MV120	2145	388	474	3007
	−0.4	**4.7**	−3.2	
LA 37450	1499	122	891	2502
	−13.7	−10.3	**24.3**	
SJB Campsites	1187	1847	941	3975
	−63.4	**80.4**	**10.3**	

Note: Top value in cell represents artifact count and bottom value represents adjusted residuals. Significant ($p < 0.05$) positive values are shown in boldface.

Chi-square = 8743.7, df = 18, $p < 0.001$

lar debris may in part be the result of a sampling bias—that is, the excavation mostly of structures and extramural features where tools were primarily used and discarded (vs. outside activity areas where core reduction and tool production/maintenance were more likely to occur).

Cores, Bifaces, and Retouched Flake Tools

How does a comparison of cores, bifaces, and retouched flake tools compare with the preceding debitage analysis? The biface category is composed of both bifacial knives and projectile points, whereas the retouched flake category consists of retouched pieces, notches, and denticulates. Figure 7.7 indicates that we again see a general increase in the number of bifaces from the quarry and pueblo sites (5.3–9.2%) to the pithouse and Archaic habitation sites (16–49%) to the Archaic campsites (43–59%). The sample for the Keystone Dam site is too small for any reliable interpretation.

A chi-square analysis of Table 7.7 also indicates that there is a significant difference in the distribution of cores and tool types across the sites

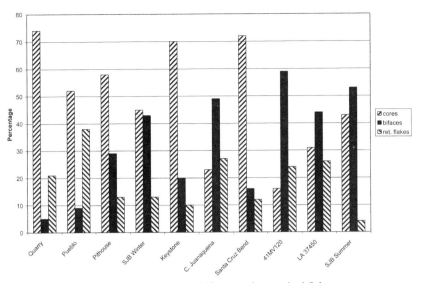

Figure 7.7. Intersite comparison of cores, bifaces, and retouched flakes

Table 7.7. Artifact type by site

| Site | Artifact Type | | | |
	Cores	Bifaces	Retouched Flakes	Total
Quarry	42	3	12	57
	3.6	−4.5	0.8	
Pueblo	34	6	25	65
	0.3	−4.2	**4.8**	
Pithouse	62	31	14	107
	1.6	−0.8	−1.1	
SJB Habitation	18	17	5	40
	−0.7	1.4	−0.8	
Keystone Dam	7	2	1	10
	1.2	−0.9	−0.6	
Cerro Juanaqueña	29	61	34	124
	−6.4	**4.2**	**3.3**	
Santa Cruz Bend	207	46	35	288
	8.6	−7.1	−2.6	
41MV120	13	47	19	79
	−6.3	**5.3**	1.7	
LA 37450	19	27	16	62
	−3.2	1.9	1.9	
SJB Campsites	65	80	6	151
	−2.0	**5.8**	−4.6	

Note: Top value in cell represents artifact count and bottom value represents adjusted residuals. Significant ($p < 0.05$) positive values are shown in boldface.

Chi-square = 229.2, $df = 18$, $p < 0.001$

(chi-sq = 229.2, df = 18, $p < 0.001$). An evaluation of the adjusted residuals indicates that the quarry and pueblo sites contain relatively more cores and retouched flakes, and the Archaic campsites more bifaces. Nonetheless, Cerro Juanaqueña does contain significantly more bifaces and retouched flakes vs. the Santa Cruz Bend site, which contains relatively more cores. The paucity of cores at Cerro Juanaqueña and 41MV120 is probably due to two different factors. At Cerro Juanaqueña they appear to have discarded cores along the periphery or outside the terraces (and therefore outside the excavation units), whereas the paucity of cores at 41MV120 appears to reflect gearing-up activities, with cores (and bifacial tools) being removed from the site for use during continued annual movements. Finally, it should be noted that this analysis does not consider the importance of unifaces at the Santa Cruz Bend site, where they actually outnumber bifaces.

Cortex

Local gravels were a source of raw material for all the sites, so the presence of cortex is a good indication of the degree of core reduction and tool production/maintenance occurring at these locations. Figure 7.8 shows a general decline in the presence of cortex from quarry and pueblo sites (52–71%) to pit-

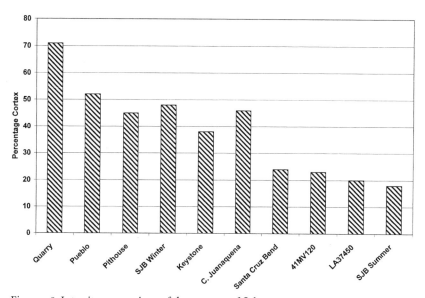

Figure 7.8. Intersite comparison of the amount of flake cortex present

Table 7.8. Cortex by site

Site	Cortex		Total
	Absent	Present	
Quarry	48	118	166
	−12.2	**12.2**	
Pueblo	514	558	1072
	−17.5	**17.5**	
Pithouse	1204	981	2185
	−18.0	**18.0**	
SJB Habitation	103	97	200
	−6.2	**6.2**	
Keystone Dam	199	122	321
	−3.7	**3.7**	
Cerro Juanaqueña	736	637	1373
	−15.2	**15.2**	
Santa Cruz Bend	1532	645	2177
	−1.1	1.1	
41MV120	725	213	938
	4.1	−4.1	
LA 37450	640	159	799
	5.6	−5.6	
SJB Campsites	6890	1524	8414
	29.5	−29.5	

Note: Top value in cell represents artifact count and bottom value represents adjusted residuals. Significant ($p < 0.05$) positive values are shown in boldface.

Chi-square = 1483.7, $df = 9$, $p < 0.001$

house and Archaic habitation sites (24–48%) to Archaic campsites (18–22%). This pattern also reflects an emphasis on the initial stages of core reduction at the quarry and pueblo sites vs. the production/maintenance of bifaces at the Archaic campsites, in part reflecting a gearing-up tactic at lowland raw material sources.

A chi-square analysis of Table 7.8 indicates that there is a significant difference in the distribution of cortex by site (chi-sq = 1483.7, $df = 9$, $p < 0.001$). A review of the adjusted residuals indicates that there is relatively more cortex present at the quarry, Ceramic period, and Archaic habitation sites, vs. a lack of cortex at the Archaic campsites. The one exception is the Santa Cruz Bend site, which exhibits no significant difference but does have a higher proportion of noncortical debitage than the other Archaic habitation sites. This may also represent a sampling bias toward late-stage core reduction for tool use. As Sliva points out, larger chipped stone artifacts were typically recovered from use or storage contexts and smaller items from secondary refuse (Sliva 1998:354).

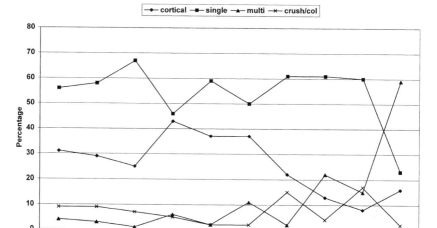

Figure 7.9. Intersite comparison of flake platform type

Platform Type

A final comparison involves platform type. These types are classified as cortical, single-faceted, multifaceted, and crushed/collapsed. Figure 7.9 illustrates that most flakes exhibit single-faceted platforms across all the sites. There is, however, a general decrease in the proportion of cortical platforms from quarry to Archaic campsites and an increase in multifaceted platforms on these campsites. The exceptions to this pattern are the peaks in cortical platform represented at the San Juan Basin, Keystone Dam, and Cerro Juanaqueña habitation sites. These peaks presumably reflect the increased reduction of cobble unifaces at these sites.

A chi-square analysis of Table 7.9 indicates that there is a significant difference in the distribution of platform types across the sites (chi-sq = 3436.3, $df = 27$, $p < 0.001$). The adjusted residuals reveal that Cerro Juanaqueña exhibits relatively more cortical and multifaceted platforms, reflecting a mix of both core reduction and tool production/maintenance activities. In contrast, there are significantly more crushed/collapsed platforms at the Santa Cruz Bend site and LA 37450. This is presumably related to the hard hammer reduction of igneous materials at the Santa Cruz Bend site (Sliva, personal communication, 2000), whereas crushed/collapsed platforms occur on all materials at LA 37450 (i.e., rhyolite, chert, and silicified wood).

Table 7.9. Platform type by site

| Site | Platform Type | | | | |
	Cortical	Single-Faceted	Multifaceted	Collapsed/ Crushed	Total
Quarry	60	106	7	17	190
	2.5	−0.5	−2.8	0.0	
Pueblo	423	843	42	135	1443
	5.1	0.7	−9.2	0.6	
Pithouse	420	1139	14	121	1694
	1.0	**8.6**	−13.1	−2.7	
SJB Habitation	156	169	21	18	364
	8.6	−4.3	−2.6	−2.7	
Keystone Dam	86	138	6	4	234
	4.7	0.4	−3.7	−3.9	
Cerro Juanaqueña	1021	1368	293	58	2740
	18.3	−8.9	**2.0**	−13.9	
Santa Cruz Bend	906	2607	104	638	4255
	−4.6	**5.8**	−19.0	**16.5**	
41MV120	223	1138	411	80	1852
	−12.7	**3.6**	**19.4**	−7.4	
LA 37450	109	801	201	224	1335
	−14.1	1.9	**6.9**	**10.6**	
SJB Campsites	90	125	322	12	549
	−4.2	−16.8	**36.5**	−5.6	

Note: Top value in cell represents artifact count and bottom value represents adjusted residuals. Significant ($p < 0.05$) positive values are shown in boldface.

Chi-square = 3436.3, df = 27, $p < 0.001$

Summary

This regional comparison reveals three general lithic assemblage groups: (1) the quarry and the pueblo site with an emphasis on core reduction activities, (2) the pithouse and Late Archaic habitation sites with a mix of core reduction and biface production/maintenance, and (3) the Late Archaic campsites with an increased emphasis on biface production/maintenance. The chipped stone assemblage at Cerro Juanaqueña, however, reflects a greater emphasis on the production/maintenance of bifaces than that reported for the Late Archaic village at the Santa Cruz Bend site. It would appear that other factors besides economics, including site sampling methods and raw material type, are also affecting interassemblage variation.

Technology and Labor Organization

This study indicates that the chipped stone assemblage from Cerro Juanaqueña is similar to other Late Archaic habitation sites but contrasts with an emphasis on the production/maintenance of bifacial tools at Late Archaic summer camp-sites and an emphasis on core reduction at later Ceramic period sites. Solely based on the chipped stone assemblage, the artifacts from Cerro Juanaqueña seem to represent a technology oriented toward a mixed foraging and agricultural economy. But is this an accurate reflection of the site?

As Lewis Binford (1980:13) pointed out, technology consists not solely of tools but also of labor. Indeed, technological organization is a direct reflection of corporate labor group structure and economic organization. As previously noted, we cannot study the chipped stone component of a site in isolation from the other technological components to get a full and accurate picture of the past. These other components include heavy-duty tools, milling equipment, ceramics, storage facilities, architecture, and agricultural features.

Marsha Ogilvie's dissertation (2000, this volume) is important in understanding this point. Her biological research identified differences in femur bone structure for Southwestern foragers vs. agriculturalists. Her study of the Tucson Basin Late Archaic populations, however, revealed an important pattern: the males resembled foragers, vs. the females, who resembled agriculturalists. This implies that important changes in labor organization were occurring during the Late Archaic. Would we not also expect these changes to be reflected in the technology being employed by men vs. women (e.g., see Crown 2000)? If so, then my study of the chipped stone technology at Cerro Juanaqueña may be providing a biased view of the site.

Anyone walking over the Cerro Juanaqueña is immediately impressed by two things: the large number of terraces and the presence of numerous basin-shaped metates that have extremely deep grinding basins. Both of these aspects of technology would seem to suggest a high degree of residential stability. The depths of these metate-grinding surfaces are similar to those exhibited by Southwestern Ceramic period trough metates, with a mean depth of 8 cm ($s = 3.9$, $n = 44$) (Hard and Roney, this volume). Comparisons of mano grinding surface length (mean = 116 mm, $s = 2.7$, $n = 48$) with those of Late Archaic and Pueblo manos from northwestern New Mexico indicate that they are situated between Basketmaker III and Pueblo I manos in size (Figure 7.10) (Vierra 1993a). I have suggested elsewhere that the Pueblo I period is characterized by a heavy dependence on maize agriculture (Vierra 1996). Therefore, the Cerro Juanaqueña manos also reflect a diet becoming more reliant on domesticated plants (e.g., maize and amaranth). I suggest that these differences between chipped and ground stone assemblages would seem to imply that the division of labor represented at the Tucson Basin sites is also represented at Cerro Juanaqueña.

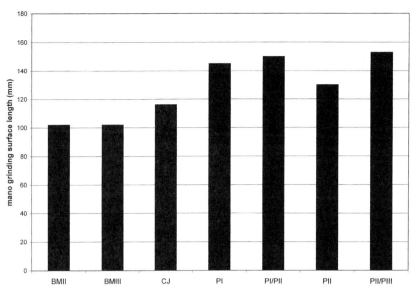

Figure 7.10. Comparison of mano grinding surface length for Cerro Juanaqueña and a sequence from Late Archaic (Basketmaker II) through Ceramic periods in northwestern New Mexico

Conclusion

This chapter presents some of the preliminary results of the analyses of chipped stone artifacts from the Late Archaic *cerros de trincheras* site of Cerro Juanaqueña in relation to material selection, core reduction, and tool production/maintenance activities. This information is contrasted with data from other sites located along the Borderlands and from sites situated in similar settings with access to gravel raw materials sources.

The chipped stone assemblage at Cerro Juanaqueña is dominated by the use of rhyolite and chalcedony materials that were locally available from river gravels. Nonlocal materials are represented by a small amount of obsidian. The full range of core reduction and tool production/maintenance activities is present. However, different reduction trajectories are represented among the material types. The abundance of microdebitage indicates that these activities were occurring on the terraces, although the paucity of cores would seem to reflect that these items were being discarded along the periphery or off the terraces. The assemblage contains a mix of formal and informal tools: that is, mostly bifaces and projectile points, with fewer retouched pieces and notches. These bifacial tools reflect both manufacturing and use-breakage. Several domestic tool types are also present, including perforators, drills, unifaces, and a cruciform.

Regional comparisons indicate that the Cerro Juanaqueña chipped stone assemblage resembles those described for Late Archaic habitation sites, consisting of a mix of core reduction and tool production/maintenance activities. This contrasts with a greater emphasis on biface production/maintenance at the Late Archaic campsites, however, and an emphasis on core reduction at the quarry and pueblo sites. The assemblages at these campsites may in part reflect a gearing-up tactic at lowland raw material sources, whereas the pueblo site reflects an economy more heavily dependent on maize agriculture. In summary, the Cerro Juanaqueña assemblage seems to represent a chipped stone technology oriented toward a mixed foraging and agricultural economy. Differences between chipped and ground stone assemblages may reflect important changes in sexual division of labor.

REFERENCES CITED

Andrefsky, W., Jr.
1994   Raw-Material Availability and the Organization of Technology. *American Antiquity* 59:21–34.
Bamforth, D.
1986   Technological Efficiency and Tool Curation. *American Antiquity* 51:38–50.
Binford, L. R.
1977   Forty-seven Trips. In *Stone Tools as Cultural Markers,* edited by R. Wright, pp. 24–36. Australian Institute of Aboriginal Studies, Canberra, Australia.
1979   Organization and Formation Processes: Looking at Curated Technologies. *Journal of Anthropological Research* 35:255–273.
1980   Willow Smoke and Dogs' Tails: Hunter-Gatherer Settlement Systems and Archaeological Site Formation. *American Antiquity* 45:4–20.
Black, S. L.
1989   South Texas Plains. In *From the Gulf to the Rio Grande: Human Adaptation in Central, South, and Lower Pecos Texas,* edited by T. Hester, S. Black, D. Steele, B. Olive, A. Fox, K. Reinhard, and L. Bennett, pp. 39–62. Research Series No. 33. Arkansas Archaeological Survey, Fayetteville.
Bostwick, T., and M. S. Shackley
1987   Settlement Strategies and Lithic Technology: An Examination

of Variability in Hunter-Gatherer and Agriculturalist Chipped Stone Assemblages in the Sonoran Desert. Paper presented at the 1987 Hohokam Symposium, Arizona State University, Tempe.

Burgett, G. R., L. T. Neff, and M. A. Sale

1994   Site 442-3. In *Excavation and Interpretation of Aceramic and Archaic Sites,* vol. 14, pp. 177–198. Office of Contract Archeology, University of New Mexico, Albuquerque.

Cameron, C. M., and R. L. Sappington

1984   Obsidian Procurement at Chaco Canyon: A.D. 500–1200. In *Recent Research on Chaco Prehistory,* edited by W. J. Judge and J. Schelberg, pp. 153–172. Reports of the Chaco Center No. 8. National Park Service, Albuquerque.

Carmichael, D. L.

1986   *Archaeological Survey in the Southern Tularosa Basin of New Mexico.* Publications in Anthropology No. 10. El Paso Centennial Museum, University of Texas, El Paso.

Carr, P. J. (editor)

1994   *The Organization of North American Prehistoric Chipped Stone Tool Technologies.* Archaeological Series 7. International Monographs in Prehistory, Ann Arbor, Mich.

Crown, P. L.

1995   Gendered Tasks, Power, and Prestige in the Prehispanic American Southwest. In *Women and Men in the Prehispanic Southwest: Labor, Power, and Prestige,* edited by P. L. Crown, pp. 3–42. School of American Research Press, Santa Fe.

2000   Women's Role in Changing Cuisine. In *Women and Men in the Prehispanic Southwest,* edited by P. Crown, pp. 221–266. School of American Research, Santa Fe.

Doleman, W. H.

1997   *Prehistoric Occupations near the Lower Placitas Arroyo: Excavations along State Road 26 West of Hatch, New Mexico.* Office of Contract Archeology, University of New Mexico, Albuquerque.

Ebert, J. I.

1979   An Ethnoarchaeological Approach to Reassessing the Meaning of Variability in Stone Tool Assemblages. In *Ethnoarchaeology: Implications of Ethnography for Archaeology,* edited by C. Kramer, pp. 59–74. Columbia University Press, New York.

Hard, R. J., R. P. Mauldin, and G. R. Raymond

1996   Mano Size, Stable Carbon Isotope Ratios, and Macrobotanical Remains as Multiple Lines of Evidence of Maize Dependence in the American Southwest. *Journal of Archaeological Method and Theory* 3:253–318.

Hard, R. J., and J. R. Roney

1998 A Massive Terraced Village Complex in Chihuahua, Mexico, 3000 Years Before the Present. *Science* 279:1661–1664.

Hard, R. J., J. E. Zapata, B. K. Moses, and J. R. Roney

1999 Terrace Construction in Northern Chihuahua, Mexico: 1150 B.C. and Modern Experiments. *Journal of Field Archaeology* 26:129–146.

Hayden, B., and W. K. Hutchings

1989 Whither the Billet Flake? In *Experiments in Lithic Technology*, edited by D. Amick and R. Mauldin, pp. 235–258. BAR International Series No. 528. British Archaeological Reports, Oxford, England.

Hester, T. R.

1980 *Digging into South Texas Prehistory.* Corona, San Antonio.

1981 Tradition and Diversity among the Prehistoric Hunters and Gatherers of Southern Texas. *Plains Anthropologist* 26:119–128.

1995 The Prehistory of South Texas. *Bulletin of the Texas Archeological Society* 66:427–459.

Hester, T. R., and M. B. Collins

1974 Evidence of Heat Treating of Southern Texas Projectile Points. *Bulletin of the Texas Archeological Society* 45:119–224.

Hogan, P., J. Elyea, and P. Eschman

1983 Intensive Lithic Analysis. In *Economy and Interaction along the Lower Chaco River,* edited by P. Hogan and J. Winter, pp. 275–286. Office of Contract Archeology, University of New Mexico, Albuquerque.

Huckell, B. B.

1990 Late Preceramic Farmer-Foragers in Southeastern Arizona: A Cultural and Ecological Consideration of the Spread of Agriculture into the Arid Southwestern United States. Ph.D. dissertation, Department of Arid Lands Resource Sciences, University of Arizona, Tucson. UMI Microfilms, Ann Arbor.

1995 *Of Marshes and Maize: Preceramic Agricultural Settlements in the Cienega Valley, Southeastern Arizona.* Anthropological Papers of the University of Arizona No. 59. University of Arizona Press, Tucson.

Hunter-Anderson, R. L.

1986 *Prehistoric Adaptation in the American Southwest.* Cambridge University Press, Cambridge.

Jeske, R. J.

    1992   Energetic Efficiency and Lithic Technology: An Upper Mississippian Example. *American Antiquity* 57(3):467–481.

Kelly, R. L.

    1988   Three Sides of a Biface. *American Antiquity* 53:717–734.

Kerley, J., and P. Hogan

    1983   Preliminary Debitage Analysis. In *Economy and Interaction along the Lower Chaco River,* edited by P. Hogan and J. Winter, pp. 255–262. Office of Contract Archeology, University of New Mexico, Albuquerque.

Kuhn, S. L.

    1994   A Formal Approach to the Design and Assembly of Mobile Toolkits. *American Antiquity* 59:426–442.

Mabry, J. (editor)

    1998   *Archaeological Investigations of Early Village Sites in the Middle Santa Cruz Valley (Parts I and II).* Anthropological Papers No. 19. Center for Desert Archaeology, Tucson.

Miller, M. R., and M. S. Shackley

    1998   New Interpretations of Obsidian Procurement and Movement in the Jornada Mogollon Region of West Texas, Southern New Mexico and Northern Chihuahua. Paper presented in the symposium Recent Advances in Geochemical Compositional Analysis and Sourcing in Texas, Annual Meetings of the Texas Archaeological Society, Waco.

Nelson, F. W., and R. D. Holmes

    1979   *Trace Element Analysis of Obsidian Sources and Artifacts from Western Utah.* Antiquities Section Selected Papers No. 15. Utah State Historical Society, Salt Lake City.

Nelson, M. C.

    1992   Technological Strategies Responsive to Subsistence Stress: Analysis of Prehistoric Southwestern Hunting Weaponry. Paper presented at the 57th Annual Meetings of the Society for American Archaeology, Pittsburgh.

Ogilvie, M. D.

    2000   A Biological Reconstruction of Mobility Patterns at the Foraging to Farming Transition in the American Southwest. Ph.D. dissertation, University of New Mexico.

O'Laughlin, T. C.

    1980   *The Keystone Dam Site and Other Archaic and Formative Sties in Northwest El Paso, Texas.* Publications in Anthropology No. 8. El Paso Centennial Museum, University of Texas, El Paso.

Parry, W. J., and R. L. Kelly

1987   Expedient Core Technology and Sedentism. In *The Organization of Core Technology*, edited by J. K. Johnson and C. A. Morrow, pp. 285–304. Westview Press, Boulder, Colo.

Prentiss, W. C., and E. J. Romansky

1989   Experimental Evaluation of Sullivan and Rozen's Debitage Typology. In *Experiments in Lithic Technology*, edited by D. Amick and R. Mauldin, pp. 89–100. BAR International Series No. 528. British Archaeological Reports, Oxford, England.

Redd, I. L., K. D. Wellman, and G. R. Burgett

1994   Site 423–158 (LA 88526). In *Excavation and Interpretation of Aceramic and Archaic Sites*, vol. 14, pp. 125–156. Office of Contract Archeology, University of New Mexico, Albuquerque.

Roney, J. R., and R. J. Hard

2000   Early Agriculture in Northwestern Chihuahua. Paper presented at the Southwest Symposium "At the Millennium: Change and Challenge in the Greater Southwest," Santa Fe.

Roth, B. J.

2000   Obsidian Source Characterization and Hunter-Gatherer Mobility: An Example from the Tucson Basin. *Journal of Archaeological Science* (27):305–314.

Shackley, M. S.

1990   Early Hunter-Gatherer Procurement Ranges in the Southwest: Evidence from Obsidian Geochemistry and Lithic Technology. Ph.D. dissertation, Department of Anthropology, Arizona State University. University Microfilms, Ann Arbor.

1998   Source Provenance of Archaeological Obsidian from Cerro Juanaqueña, Cerro Vidal, and Cerro Los Torres, Northwestern Chihuahua. Report prepared for Robert Hard. Archaeological XRF Laboratory, University of California, Berkeley.

1999   Source Provenance of Archaeological Obsidian from the 1999 Season at Cerro Juanaqueña and Cerro El Canelo, Northwestern Chihuahua. Report prepared for Robert Hard. Archaeological XRF Laboratory, University of California, Berkeley.

Shott, M. J.

1986   Technological Organization and Settlement Mobility. *Journal of Anthropological Research* 42(1):15–52.

1994   Size and Form in the Analysis of Flake Debris: Review and Recent Approaches. *Journal of Archaeological Method and Theory* 1:69–110.

Sliva, R. J.

1998   Flaked Stone Artifacts. In *Archaeological Investigations of Early Village Sites in the Middle Santa Cruz Valley (Part I)*, edited by J. Mabry, pp. 299–356. Anthropological Papers No. 19. Center for Desert Archaeology, Tucson.

Sullivan, R., and N. Akins

1994   *Archaeological Excavations at LA 15260: The Coors Road Site, Bernalillo County, New Mexico.* Notes No. 147. Office of Archaeological Studies, Santa Fe.

Taylor, A. J., and C. L. Highley

1995   *Archaeological Investigations at the Loma Sandia Site (41LK28): A Prehistoric Cemetery in Live Oak County, Texas.* Vols. 1 and 2. Studies in Archeology 20. Texas Archeological Research Laboratory, Austin.

Tomka, S. A.

1989   Differentiating Lithic Reduction Techniques. In *Experiments in Lithic Technology,* edited by D. Amick and R. Mauldin, pp. 137–162. BAR International Series No. 528. British Archaeological Reports, Oxford, England.

Torrence, R.

1983   Time Budgeting and Hunter-Gatherer Technology. In *Hunter-Gatherer Economy in Prehistory: A European Perspective,* edited by G. Bailey, pp. 11–22. Cambridge University Press, Cambridge.

Torrence, R. (editor)

1989   *Time, Energy and Stone Tools.* Cambridge University Press, Cambridge.

Vierra, B. J.

1993a   Explaining Long-Term Changes in Lithic Procurement and Reduction Strategies. In *Across the Colorado Plateau: Anthropological Studies for the Transwestern Pipeline Expansion Project: Architectural Studies, Lithic Analyses and Ancillary Studies,* vol. 17, pp. 139–381. Office of Contract Archaeology and Maxwell Museum of Anthropology, Albuquerque.

1993b   Technological Variation and Subsistence Strategies: Explaining Changes in Stone Tool Technology. Paper presented at the Fifth Occasional Anasazi Symposium, Farmington.

1994a   Archaic Hunter-Gatherer Mobility Strategies in the American Southwest. In *Excavations and Interpretations of Aceramic and Archaic Sites,* vol. 14, pp. 385–398. Office of Contract Archeology, University of New Mexico, Albuquerque.

1994b   Archaic Hunter-Gatherer Mobility Strategies in Northwestern New Mexico. In *Archaic Hunter-Gatherer Archaeology in the American Southwest,* edited by B. J. Vierra, pp. 121–154. Contributions in Anthropology Vol. 13. Eastern New Mexico University, Portales.

1994c   A Study of Basketmaker II Lithic Technology. In *Excavations and Interpretations of Aceramic and Archaic Sites,* vol. 14, pp. 413–424. Office of Contract Archeology, University of New Mexico, Albuquerque.

1995   *Subsistence and Stone Tool Technology: An Old World Perspective.* Anthropological Research Papers No. 47. Department of Anthropology, Arizona State University, Tempe.

1996   Late Archaic Settlement, Subsistence and Technology: An Evaluation of Continuity vs. Replacement Arguments for the Origins of Agriculture in the Northern Southwest. Paper presented at the Conference on the Archaic Prehistory of the North American Southwest, Albuquerque.

1997   Lithic Analyses. In *Excavations at Valencia Pueblo (LA 953) and a Nearby Hispanic Settlement (LA 67321),* edited by K. Brown and B. Vierra, pp. 277–322. Office of Contract Archeology, University of New Mexico, Albuquerque.

1998   *41MV120: A Stratified Late Archaic Site in Maverick County, Texas.* Archaeological Survey Report No. 251. Center for Archaeological Research, University of Texas, San Antonio.

n.d.   Data on file with author.

Vierra, B. J., P. Lukowski, G. Smith, S. Sitton, B. Boeke, V. Provencio, M. Sechrist, A. Sullivan, J. Johnson, S. Wilcox, and M. Yduarte

1998   *Assessment of 431 Archaeological Sites in Dona Ana Range Firing Groups C, D, G, H, I, and J, Fort Bliss, Texas, and New Mexico.* TRC/Mariah Associates, El Paso.

Whalen, M. E.

1980   *Special Studies in the Archaeology of the Hueco Bolson.* Publications in Anthropology No. 9. El Paso Centennial Museum, University of Texas, El Paso.

Wills, W. H.

1988   *Early Prehistoric Agriculture in the American Southwest.* School of American Research Press, Santa Fe.

1995   Archaic Foraging and the Beginnings of Food Production in the American Southwest. In *Last Hunters, First Farmers,* edited by T. Price and A. Gebauer, pp. 215–242. School of American Research Press, Santa Fe.

CHAPTER 8

Late Archaic Foragers of Eastern Trans-Pecos Texas and the Big Bend

ROBERT J. MALLOUF

Introduction

Late Archaic sites (ca. 3000–1300 BP) are ubiquitous across the Big Bend and eastern Trans-Pecos region of far West Texas and are found in virtually all environmental settings—from low-lying Chihuahuan Desert basins to the tops of tree-clad mountain peaks. Available data suggest the onset of mesic conditions in the early Late Archaic (ca. 3000–2200 BP). Attendant to wetter conditions was the expansion of diverse material cultures, rich in perishable items, and a subsistence regime based on hunting and broad spectrum gathering. The region appears to have experienced significant population increases during the period 3000–2500 BP. While maize and possible other cultigens are suspected of occurring in regional Late Archaic deposits, such finds have typically been poorly documented and constitute a questionable database from which to postulate distributions, densities, or significance. Both experimentation with cultigens and greatly increased reliance on the use of rock ovens for the processing of desert succulents near the end of the Late Archaic and during the early Late Prehistoric (ca. 1300–900 BP) may be a reflection of economic stresses resulting from a reentrenchment of more xeric climatic conditions. Taken as a whole, the data suggest that transitional Late Archaic populations had knowledge of but made only cursory or experimental use of cultigens.

In their classic work *Method and Theory in American Archaeology* Gordon Willey and Philip Phillips (1958:126) declared the Trans-Pecos "Big Bend culture" to be a "bridge between the Archaic cultures of the East and the Desert [Archaic] cultures in the Southwest." Regrettably, the long Archaic sequence in the eastern Trans-Pecos region, unlike some other areas of the Borderlands, has received very little substantive archaeological attention since Willey and Phillip's rather vague revelation of almost a half-century ago. Compounding the inadequacies of the scientific database has been a high rate of attrition by

Figure 8.1. A desert basin environment on the upper reach of Terlingua Creek in the Big Bend

looting of critical rockshelter and cave deposits—our richest sources of information on the Archaic and its subperiods.

This chapter is intended to provide a synopsis of our current understanding of the Late Archaic while explicating some of the problems faced by modern researchers as we attempt to bring the eastern Trans-Pecos and the Big Bend back into the mainstream of archaeological methodology and theory. Contemporary issues related to the introduction of cultigens in the region are addressed as far as extant data permit, but we must await the findings of future controlled investigations to clarify the chronology and mechanisms of introduction as well as the overall significance of cultigens in the lifeways of Late Archaic peoples.

The Big Bend and eastern Trans-Pecos region of Texas comprises roughly 30,000 sq m of the northern Chihuahuan Desert, extending from the New Mexico state boundary on the north to the Rio Grande on the south and from approximately the Pecos River on the east to the vicinity of Hudspeth County on the west. This vast region is a mosaic of tree-clad mountains interspersed with broad, dry, desert basins, deep canyon systems, igneous and limestone plateaus and outliers, high grasslands, erosionally dissected badlands, and a host of other landforms. The Rio Grande and Pecos River are the largest and virtually only perennial streams in the region, but numerous springs are also present—most commonly along geologic contacts in foothill areas of the mountain ranges. The lower elevations (Figure 8.1) are characterized by common plant assemblages of the Chihuahuan Desert, with creosote (*Larrea tridentata*) dominating the basins, and rich assortments of desert succulents such as sotol (*Dasylirion* sp.), lechuguilla (*Agave lechuguilla*), prickly pear (*Opuntia* sp.) and yucca (*Yucca* sp.), along with ocotillo (*Fouquieria splendens*), bear grass (*Nolina* sp.), mesquite (*Prosopis glandulosa*), catclaw (*Mimosa biuncifera*), buckeye (*Ungnadia speciosa*), and many other species (Figure 8.2), found in the foothill zones (Powell 1988; Wauer 1980). The higher elevations (Figure 8.3) typically are dominated by oak (*Quercus* sp.), juniper (*Juniperus* sp.), and piñon pine (*Pinus cembroides*) assemblages, with a variety of grasses present in upland plateau areas such as the Marfa Plain. Rich assortments of riparian vegetation that snake along the major drainages and their more prominent intermittent tributaries often stand in stark contrast to the immediately surrounding treeless terrain (Figure 8.4). These and a multitude of other plant species provided abundant sources of food and fiber for Late Archaic populations.

Modern faunal assemblages are typical of the northern Chihuahuan Desert and Basin and Range physiographic province as well, including such large mammals as mule deer (*Odocoileus hemionus*) and white-tailed deer (*Odocoileus virginianus*), pronghorn antelope (*Antilocapra americana*), black bear (*Ursus americanus*), mountain lion (*Felis concolor*), and a host of smaller mammals, amphibians, and reptiles (Davis and Schmidly 1994; Dixon 1987; Raun 1965). Other large mammals once native to the eastern Trans-Pecos but no longer

Figure 8.2. Buttrill Spring in the foothills zone of the Rosillos Mountains

Figure 8.3. High-elevation oak-juniper-pine assemblage in the Davis Mountains (Mount Livermore in the background)

present (unless reintroduced recently) include the grizzly bear (*Ursus arctos*), gray wolf (*Canis lupus*), bison (*Bos bison;* see below), elk (*Cervus elaphus*), and possibly mountain sheep (*Ovis canadensis*), all of which may have been preyed upon by Late Archaic hunters and gatherers.

Paleoenvironmental research in palynology (e.g., Bryant 1974; Bryant and Shafer 1977; Hall 1985), packrat midden and macrofossil studies (e.g., Dering 1979; Van Devender 1990, 1995; Van Devender and Spaulding 1979; Wells 1966, 1977), geomorphology (e.g., Ely 1997; Patton and Dibble 1982), and other disciplines implies an overall regional drying trend punctuated by brief mesic interludes during the Holocene that resulted in gradual upward displacement of pine-juniper woodlands with an attendant spread of desert succulents. Based on a recent study of calcic soils in the Tularosa and Hueco basins of the El Paso district, B. J. Buck and H. C. Monger (1999) postulate a significant period of increased effective moisture across the northern Chihuahuan Desert from about 4000 to 2200 BP. An earlier palynological study conducted by V. M. Bryant and R. G. Holloway (1985) in the Lower Pecos River region narrows the chronological parameters of this notable climatic event to about 3000 to 2500 BP, a 500-year interval that corresponds to the early Late Archaic in the eastern Trans-Pecos and Big Bend (see also Dering, this volume; and Mallouf 1981). This increased moisture regime is undoubtedly linked to movements of bison and bison hunters into the Trans-Pecos from the north and east during the Late Archaic and may in part account for postulated human demographic changes that appear to be reflected in the regional archaeological record. Sources of potable water in arroyo systems and perennial springs were probably much more abundant in the Late Archaic than at present, making hospitable vast areas of the intermontane basins that today, because of overgrazing and lowered water tables, seem inhospitable in the extreme.

Rockshelters (Figure 8.5), well-elevated terraces, dune systems, and other landforms suitable for human habitation abound in the Trans-Pecos and were occupied on a regular basis by Late Archaic populations. Major primary sources of siliceous stone used by Late Archaic populations for tool-making are particularly abundant across the southern half of the region, including hornfels (Figure 8.6) and rhyolites in the area of Big Bend National Park,

Figure 8.4. Well-elevated grasslands of the Marfa Plain

Figure 8.5. Large rockshelters in volcanic tuff above Cañon Colorado on the Rio Grande

Figure 8.6. A hornfels tool-stone source in the Chisos Mountains

limestone cherts in the western Stockton Plateau, chalcedony and opalite of the Frenchman Hills/Marfa Plain, various felsites and chalcedonies of the Lobo Valley/Van Horn area, and indurated tuff and agates of the Davis Mountains. Sources of knappable rhyolites and trachytes, as well as basalts, sandstones, and limestones for the production of ground-stone implements, are ubiquitous across the Trans-Pecos and were used by the region's inhabitants through time.

The increased effective moisture regime of the early Late Archaic, in combination with a plethora of desirable biotic resources, numerous sources of high-quality siliceous tool stone, and an excellent range of landforms and raw materials for habitation, offered a natural setting of maximum potential for hunter-gatherer–based economies.

Problems with the Regional Database

It would be grossly misleading to address the subject of Late Archaic archaeological resources and lifeways in the Trans-Pecos without first explicating the major problems that exist with our database. A generalized characterization of the problem is relatively simple, in the sense that it is directly attributable to a paucity of substantive controlled excavations in Archaic deposits during the past half-century. Most of the large-scale scientific excavation conducted in Archaic deposits of the Trans-Pecos actually occurred prior to 1940 and included work by such well-known researchers as J. Charles Kelley, Joe Ben Wheat, T. N. Campbell, Donald J. Lehmer, Edwin F. Coffin, M. R. Harrington, Victor J. Smith, A. T. Jackson, Frank M. Setzler, and others, with much of this work being focused in the southern (or Big Bend) section of the Trans-Pecos. With the notable exception of some areas in the southern Guadalupe Mountains and Salt Flats, the central and northern half of the Trans-Pecos, including the Davis Mountains, Rustler Hills, Delaware Mountains, Apache Mountains, and Sierra Diablo, remains largely unexplored archaeologically to this day. And of the pre-1940 work, only that of Kelley, Campbell, and Lehmer (1940) and a handful of others provides the kind of excavation detail that is of real value to contemporary researchers.

As noted earlier, this poor state of affairs is exacerbated by the fact that literally hundreds—and probably thousands—of rockshelters across the region have been damaged and/or completely destroyed by untold numbers of artifact collectors. The region's few museums are replete with undocumented and poorly provenienced collections placed by well-meaning collectors and landowners. Scattered among these collections are many unique and exciting perishable artifacts as well as varied biotic and skeletal remains that cannot be related in time or space.

In contrast, there has been a great deal of archaeological survey conducted in the Trans-Pecos; but most of it has been concentrated in the extreme north (Guadalupe Mountains area) and extreme south (Big Bend National Park and Big Bend Ranch State Park area) of the region. Much of the survey work has been conducted by professional and avocational archaeologists since 1960, and we must of necessity draw heavily from this work in our interpretations. In a nutshell, because of the largely surficial nature of the usable database, we are severely restricted at this time in drawing meaningful conclusions concerning Late Archaic lifeways in the region. We hope to improve this rather bleak situation in the near future through planned excavations in known Archaic-age deposits.

Defining Late Archaic Components in the Trans-Pecos Region

Based primarily upon chronological and typological interpolations from more intensively studied regions to the east and north and upon presence-absence criteria of ceramics and related indicators of agriculture, the temporal range of the Late Archaic period can be characterized as falling roughly between 3000 and 1300 BP. This dating varies somewhat depending upon criteria used by the investigator and the subarea in question. In the southern (or Big Bend) section the beginning of the Late Archaic is correlated roughly with the advent of the significant paleoclimatic event that led to more mesic conditions (discussed above) and a transition from use of contracting-stem (such as Langtry, Arenosa, and Almagre) to side-notched, corner-notched, expanding, and parallel-stemmed dart points (such as Shumla, Charcos, and Palmillas).

The end of the Late Archaic corresponds to the inferred replacement of the atlatl by the bow and arrow. As yet unpublished chronometric data from the Davis Mountains (Tall Rockshelter) and Glass Mountains (Homer Mills Site) indicate that the atlatl and Paisano dart points (Figure 8.7) were still in use in the central Trans-Pecos as late as 900 BP (AD 1100). These same data indicate a possible temporal overlap of Late Archaic Paisano dart points with Late Prehistoric Livermore arrow points between 1300 and 900 BP and are strongly suggestive of technological and cultural continuity from the late Archaic into the Late Prehistoric period. This dating of the terminal Archaic contrasts strongly with that of the western Trans-Pecos (or El Paso district), where the advent of agricultural practices and attendant ceramic complexes are used as criteria for termination of the Archaic much earlier—around 1900 BP (e.g., O'Laughlin 1980). This discordance in the archaeological record is a reflection of the fact that

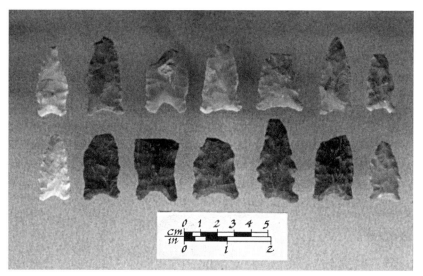

Figure 8.7. Specimens of Paisano dart points from the Glass Mountains, Homer Mills Collection. These dart points were still in use in the central Trans-Pecos as late as 900 BP.

lifeways in most of the eastern Trans-Pecos—where a basically Archaic socio-economic regimen persisted throughout the Late Prehistoric and into the early Historic periods—followed a markedly different evolutionary path than those of regions to the west. Viewed strictly from the standpoint of material assemblages, interregional cultural ties appear to have been stronger to the east and north than to the west throughout the Late Archaic in the eastern Trans-Pecos. Cultural influences emanating from areas south in Chihuahua and Coahuila, while present, remain very poorly understood at this time.

The Late Archaic archaeological construct has roots in early cultural constructs such as the Chisos focus (southern and eastern Trans-Pecos) of Kelley, Campbell, and Lehmer (1940) and the Hueco phase (northern and western Trans-Pecos) of E. B. Sayles (1935). Hueco and Chisos phase peoples were early characterized as hunter-gatherers living in rockshelters and open camps who practiced a form of incipient gardening to supplement their wild food staples and who had some knowledge of ceramics (Kelley, Campbell, and Lehmer 1940). Lehmer (1958:131) went on to suggest that agriculture "appeared first in the Hueco Phase of the El Paso district" and "spread to the southeastern Trans-Pecos with the arrival of the Chisos Focus during the period of the post-Calamity erosion." With time, these early normative constructs have generally fallen into disuse or have been modified and/or replaced by the term "Late Archaic," which is more a temporal than a cultural construct.

As in many areas of Texas and the Greater Southwest, Archaic components in the Trans-Pecos have been identified primarily on the presence of certain dart-point styles and the absence of ceramics. Potential weaknesses involved with this approach immediately become apparent when one considers that the paucity of excavation data for the region implies an attendant scarcity of contextual radiocarbon assays for point types in the region as well. As a result, most chronological assignments for dart-point types in the Trans-Pecos must be interpolated from better-studied adjoining regions to the east, such as West-Central Texas and the Lower Pecos River—thus constituting a somewhat risky premise for regional chronology-building. A number of dart-point styles (discussed below), however, based upon known associations and some chronometric parameters, can be assigned to the Late Archaic with a measure of confidence.

A few cultural feature types are also tentatively assigned Late Archaic affinities, but combinations of material attributes are commonly needed to make confident temporal assignments. This is in part because, at least within the Trans-Pecos, later prehistoric peoples (post–1300 BP) commonly scavenged and curated points and other stone implements from the surfaces of Late Archaic and earlier sites and often incorporated such specimens (sometimes in modified form) into their own tool kits, where they also were subject to discard. The common occurrence of arrow-and-dart point mixtures on the surfaces of Trans-Pecos sites that otherwise have the look of single-component camps may in part be related to this phenomenon. In some instances scavenged and subsequently discarded or lost dart points might form the only temporally diagnostic residue in what are in reality Late Prehistoric components—thus leading to inaccurate temporal placement of sites. The hard evidence for tool scavenging in the Trans-Pecos comes primarily from burials, so it is clear that some modes of prehistoric "collecting" had ritualistic as well as more practical underpinnings. Clearly, our past reliance on the long-lived, conventional survey formula "dart points + debitage + scattered burned rock—ceramics = Archaic" needs to be reevaluated carefully in the Trans-Pecos, and this simplistic concept is in need of similar scrutiny in adjoining regions as well.

Having noted some qualifiers, we can now turn to a brief overview of the material culture of Late Archaic peoples. As indicated earlier, Late Archaic dart-point styles in the Trans-Pecos are typically of side-notched, corner-notched, expanding, and parallel-stem configurations and include such common Texas types as Shumla, Paisano, Frio, Charcos (probably a Shumla variant), Conejo, Ensor, Ellis, Figueroa, Lange, Marcos, Montell, and Palmillas. A number of southern New Mexico styles, such as San Pedro, Hueco, and Carlsbad, as well as a few point styles more typical of northern Chihuahua and Coahuila in

Figure 8.8. Circular bedrock mortars in upper reach of Terlingua Creek

Mexico, such as Jora and Gobernadora (possibly Middle to Late Archaic), also occur with variable frequency, depending on the subarea in question.

Other common lithic tool forms include a variety of unifacial scrapers, a wide range of relatively crude bifacial and unifacial expediency tools (such as might be used in plant gathering and processing), bifacial drills (often fashioned from dart points) and knives, crude gouge-like implements, occasional corner-tang knives, hammerstones, tubular pipes, and abrading stones (Figure 8.8). Ground-stone implements such as circular to oval manos, slab and bedrock metates, circular to oval bedrock mortars (Figure 8.8), and elongated pestles seem to be quite common in Late Archaic components, although tight associations are typically lacking. Additional tool and ornament forms currently known or inferred to occur in Late Archaic deposits include bone awls and rasps, various forms of basketry, woven matting and bags, cradle boards, fiber sandals, compressed grass "bedding," atlatls and attendant weights, rabbit sticks (Figure 8.9), agave knives, a wide variety of cordage of both plant fiber and human hair, digging sticks, cactus spine needles, possible snares and tumpline baskets, bone-shell-and-seed beads, and possibly kaolinite pendants and beads, marine and freshwater shell pendants, and shell and stone gorgets.

The most common feature types encountered in Late Archaic components are a variety of circular-to-oval stone hearths of both pavement and open ring styles, typically 1.00 to 1.50+ m in diameter. Other feature types include rock-

Figure 8.9. A combination rabbit stick and shaft straightener, possibly of Late Archaic affinity, from Sunny Glen Canyon

lined storage pits, flexed burials with burial furniture, and occasional caches (e.g., Mallouf n.d.; Wulfkuhle 1988) of dart points and dart point preforms. Annular (ring) middens found throughout the Trans-Pecos and Big Bend are generally believed attributable to the end of the Late Archaic, continuing into the Late Prehistoric period (e.g., Greer 1968; see also Wiseman 1999). Domed burned rock middens, while generally having a distribution related to West-Central and Central Texas (e.g., Prewitt 1994), do occur in localized econiches of the southern Trans-Pecos region as well (Mallouf n.d.; see also Turpin 1996), and evidence of their probable use during the latter half of the Late Archaic is slowly coming to light.

Late Archaic Settlement Systems

Although there are significant subareas for which we have few or no data, numerous archaeological surveys carried out in the Big Bend and Trans-Pecos during the past thirty years have generated a workable, if preliminary, database for settlement system analyses.

The most obvious data trend in the Trans-Pecos is related to site densities: Late Archaic sites, based on surface evidence, appear to greatly outnumber earlier and later sites in the region. With few exceptions, evidence of presumed Late Archaic occupation can be found in or on most suitable landforms and in most econiches in the region—from the floors of the hottest, driest basins to the tops of tree-clad mountain peaks. In terms of sheer site density, the foothill zones of the region's mountain ranges, with their rich assortment of flora and fauna and prolific sources of knappable stone and springs, were favored for habitation. Late Archaic sites are also common, however, along what are now dry basin arroyo systems, around landform anomalies (such as isolated and

free-standing bedrock outcrops) in the basins, on ridge and mesa tops, in saddles and on slope catsteps (small, level step-like areas that occur on steep talus
slopes), in rockshelters in the faces of sheer bluffs, in boulder falls and high
elevation meadows, and in naturally sheltered niches on the tops of mountains
and pinnacles often at great distances from water sources (both then and now).
Clearly, many of these sites represent special activities, such as plant collecting,
tool stone procurement, and, at least in the case of some mountain top sites,
possibly ritualistic behavior.

Campsites containing the stratigraphically deepest (sometimes exceeding
5 m) and/or thickest Archaic deposits most often occur adjacent to springs in
the foothill environments, in large rockshelters, and along deeply incised basin
arroyo systems. When available, landforms suitable for camping immediately
at or close to springs were invariably occupied. In the absence of springs, water-
retaining *tinajas* (natural basins in bedrock) were often the focus of settlement
(e.g., Turpin 1996). Although often spatially restricted by the physical size of
the available landform, such open campsites—even when quite small in
horizontal extent—frequently contain thick Archaic midden deposits characterized by dense, carbon-laden soils, an abundance of burned rock, some
preserved faunal material, high densities of debitage and knapped tools, and
numerous ground-stone implements, including manos, metates, and bedrock
mortars (e.g., Mallouf and Wulfkuhle 1989). Minor test excavations carried out
at a number of such sites in the Big Bend unfortunately suggest a rather high
propensity for temporally mixed deposits due to bioturbation and colluvial
dynamics. Long-term efforts to document private collections from selected
foothill sites invariably reveal high densities of Late Archaic dart points (Mallouf n.d.). A similar pattern is noted among private collections in far northeastern Chihuahua (Mallouf 1999). As might be expected, the preservation of
perishable artifacts and plant macrofossils, as well as pollen, in open foothill
campsites is highly variable but tends to be poor.

Bluff and boulder fall rockshelters, and to a lesser extent caves and sinkholes,
are found throughout much of the eastern Trans-Pecos—most commonly in
volcanic tuff and limestone deposits. Sometimes reaching 250 m in length and
50 m in width (drip line to back wall; e.g., Coffin 1932), rockshelters served as
preferred habitat for Late Archaic as well as some earlier and later populations
and frequently contain substantial Late Archaic deposits (Figure 8.10). Impressive bluff rockshelters in the deep canyons of the Rio Grande such as Mariscal,
Boquillas, and the Lower Canyons frequently are accessible only from the river,
a testimony to the tenacity and adaptability of their occupants. In the igneous
Davis Mountains of the central Trans-Pecos occupied rockshelters are found
along both mainstem canyons and their rugged tributaries, sometimes at very

Figure 8.10. Mapping and testing a rockshelter with a Late Archaic component in Sunny Glen Canyon

high elevations in the upper reaches of the canyon systems. And in the Guadalupe Mountains to the north, both early and recent excavations indicate a strong Late Archaic presence in limestone rockshelters (e.g., Mera 1938; Roney 1985). As noted earlier, most regional excavations in rockshelters were carried out between 1920 and 1950; while much of that work is of limited scientific value today, the early findings do serve to demonstrate the excellent interpretive potentials of regional shelter deposits. Nonetheless, although some stratigraphic and chronometric data are presently available from rockshelters, they are extremely limited in scope and appear quite inadequate when compared to an intensively studied region such as the Lower Pecos River to the east (e.g., Turpin 1991).

Basin arroyo systems and their tributaries were also focal points of Late Archaic occupation, but the character of these components along arroyos can be quite different from that of foothill/spring and rockshelter sites. In the lowest desert basins of the Big Bend, such as along the Terlingua and Tornillo drainage systems, open campsites of the Late Archaic commonly occur both on the ground surface and in deeply buried contexts where they are exposed in arroyo walls (Figure 8.11). The buried deposits in this setting tend to consist of thin, sometimes stratified midden soils containing scatters of burned rock, debitage and tools, and hearths. Rough, broken terrain forming the valley walls of the low basin drainages often yields evidence of small, activity-specific sites—probably related to plant collecting/processing—that are suspected to be primarily Archaic in age.

The plant communities can become much more diversified as one moves into higher elevations along the middle and upper reaches of arroyo systems,

Figure 8.11. A deeply buried Late Archaic component at the base of an alluvial bluff near Hen Egg Mountain

and the character of arroyo sites may change dramatically, depending upon the environmental setting encountered. An excellent example of this transition is found along the middle to upper reaches of Gilliland Draw, the largest drainage system in the Glass Mountains (Mallouf n.d.) of the Big Bend. Moving up this drainage from the creosote-dominated basin into the foothills, one enters a limestone-ringed canyon with an impressive diversity of plant life, including dense assortments of desert succulents such as sotol, yucca, and lechuguilla mixed with grasses, oak, juniper, algarita, and many other woody species. Attendant to this rather dramatic change in vegetation patterns is a change in the character of arroyo sites—from the large scattered hearthfields of the basin to much smaller campsites accompanied by domed burned rock middens now believed to be of transitional Late Archaic into Late Prehistoric age (ca. 1300 to 800 BP). Similar, if sometimes less dramatic, examples of changes in site character attendant to elevational and biotic transitions abound in the Big Bend and in more northerly areas as well.

Interestingly, while substantial buried Archaic deposits are thought to occur in terraces along the mainstem Pecos River, this pattern of occupation is not necessarily repeated along the Rio Grande in the Big Bend. The deeper and more substantial Archaic deposits tend to be located away from the mainstem Rio Grande, possibly due to the dynamic and unpredictable nature of that river prehistorically or due to extensive lateral cutting by the river that has removed much of the evidence. Numerous large and small rockshelters in well-elevated bluffs overlooking the Rio Grande, however, do contain substantial Archaic deposits (e.g., Mallouf and Tunnell 1977; Tunnell and Mallouf 1975).

In addition to rockshelters and open campsites there are a wide range of special activity sites in the eastern Trans-Pecos and Big Bend that can, with some confidence, be attributed to Late Archaic populations. Tool stone sources such as Burro Mesa and a host of extensive hornfels outcrops in and around Big Bend National Park (Mallouf 1985) and chalcedony sources in the Frenchman Hills of the Marfa Plain (Mallouf n.d.) attracted people through time; innumerable knapping stations and short-term camps—many inferred to be of Late Archaic affiliation—are found on and in the near vicinity of such outcrops. Numerous chalcedony, felsite, and chert sources near Michigan Draw and in other areas of the Plateau district of Van Horn were frequented by Late Archaic peoples who established camps along the nearby arroyos. As noted by J. A. Hedrick (1988), Late Archaic dart points make up the lion's share of temporally diagnostic artifacts recovered in the Plateau district of the central Trans-Pecos. Although caching behavior is poorly understood at present, Late Archaic point preform caches found inside habitation sites near Sunny Glen Canyon (Wulfkuhle 1988) and Elephant Mountain (Mallouf n.d.) in the Big

Figure 8.12. Evidence suggests that mountain-top ritualism, so prevalent in the Late Prehistoric period, may have roots in earlier Late Archaic populations

Bend have relevance in understanding the importance of toolstone sources within the broader spectrum of Late Archaic settlement systems.

Late Archaic populations commonly occupied and reoccupied basin/foothill campsites and bluff/boulderfall rockshelters, but they also expanded into ecological niches for the most part ignored by earlier inhabitants. These include basin anomalies such as restricted but highly visible outcropping bedrock (often exhibiting bedrock mortars) and/or isolated dune formations in otherwise homogeneous basin environments, slope catsteps, and the tops of mountain peaks (Mallouf 1985; Mallouf and Wulfkuhle 1989). A good example of a basin anomaly site occurs near the Rosillos Mountains in the Big Bend, where hearths, middens, and dart points are eroding out of a buried stratum in an isolated dune system that has yielded a corrected date of 1,990 ± 80 b.p. (Mallouf, Cloud, and Mandel n.d.).

Archaic components that have middens with scattered burned rock are found in protected niches on the tops of mountains as well and are sometimes suggestive of ritual activities (Figure 8.12). Mountain-top sites are typically at long distances from water and other needed resources. It is possible that mountain-top ritualism and mortuary practices that are so prevalent in the following Late Prehistoric period of the Trans-Pecos have roots in Late Archaic or even earlier times (Mallouf 1985). Rock art, including both petroglyph and pictograph sites, is also found throughout the region and in virtually all environmental settings, but rock art panels or motifs specific to the Late Archaic cannot, as a rule, be assigned with confidence. A possible exception are petroglyphs in the form of Late Archaic Shumla dart points found at a site in the Lower Canyons of the Rio Grande (e.g., Mallouf and Tunnell 1977) and in some areas to the west. On some rock art panels, the Shumla forms appear to transform or evolve into anthropomorphic shaman motifs.

Mortuary data are generally sketchy for the Late Archaic, although there are numerous verbal accounts of dart points having been found with burials in rockshelters, high-elevated crevasses, and cairns by relic collectors. A bone collagen date of 2870 ± 560 b.p. exists for a flexed, talus-slope burial professionally excavated in the Big Bend, placing it in the early Late Archaic period (Biesaart n.d.). A second professionally investigated burial in the Big Bend, also flexed, is from a midden deposit beneath a collapsed overhang and dates between 3490 ± 80 and 1830 ± 70 b.p. The age of this burial was determined by bracketing the feature between charcoal dates from overlying and underlying midden strata (Huebner and Powell n.d.). It can therefore be stated with some confidence that Late Archaic populations buried their dead under boulder niches on talus slopes and in rockshelters. Most other burial data from the Trans-Pecos pertain to post-Archaic and early Historic remains.

Since the early 1980s (in conjunction with research being carried out primarily at Late Prehistoric sites in the Big Bend) I have made a point of locating and examining buried cultural deposits that are exposed in arroyo cuts. The primary objective of this work has been to continue building the database begun in the late 1930s (by Kelley, Campbell, and Lehmer 1940; and Albritton and Bryan 1939) concerning the recognition of archaeological-geological relationships in the area and to obtain associated bulk carbon and charcoal samples from such buried deposits for radiocarbon assay. Of considerable interest is the fact that the majority of recovered dates thus far, from deposits immediately below the ground surface to depths of over 6 m, often fall in the range of ca. 2500 to 1300 BP, in the latter half of the Late Archaic. This same period saw a reentrenchment of xeric climatic conditions attended by minor shifts in subsistence patterns, an expansion of dart-point styles, and greater diversification of material culture.

Settlement data, when combined with other lines of evidence emanating from survey, subsurface testing, documentation of private collections, typological considerations, and frequencies of specimen and feature occurrence, provide a rather strong case for a notable increase in population during the Late Archaic in the Big Bend as well as for the development of a highly diversified subsistence base.

Late Archaic Subsistence Practices

Paleoenvironmental studies generally concur that by 3000 BP, with the advent of the Late Archaic, biotic communities were at least similar to those we see today. Prevailing mesic conditions between 3000 and roughly 2200 BP probably served to enrich the densities and diversity of available biotic resources, including the enhancement of available grassland environments. During this time bison may have moved into the eastern Trans-Pecos in unprecedented numbers, followed by bison hunters from the High Plains and West-Central Texas. This would at least in part account for rather strong eastern and northern influences recognizable in the Late Archaic archeological record. It should be noted, however, that Late Archaic bison kill sites like those commonly found in the Plains (e.g., Tunnell and Hughes 1955) have yet to be discovered in the region—even in subareas with highly suitable bison habitat, such as the Toyah basin and the elevated grasslands of the Marfa Plain.

Although some general patterns of subsistence can be postulated for Late Archaic foragers and collectors in the Trans-Pecos, for reasons discussed earlier we unfortunately lack scientifically derived information from our major sources of subsistence data—regional rockshelters. It is virtually impossible confidently to assign most museum collections of perishable biotic materials recovered during large-scale rockshelter excavations prior to 1940 to Late Archaic origins. Based upon investigations carried out at a variety of open sites (e.g., Cloud 1998; Hines, Tomka, and Kibler 1994; Mallouf n.d.), minor subsurface testing of a few rockshelters (Hamilton n.d.; Mallouf 1998, n.d) and reevaluation of some preexisting rockshelter assemblages (e.g., Hamilton n.d.; Holloway 1985; Ward 1992; Wulfkuhle 1988) over the past thirty years, we can infer with confidence that Late Archaic populations were hunting a wide variety of animals, including deer and rabbits, and collecting when available wild plants such as agave, prickly pear, sotol, yucca, and many other species. Actual documented and dated associations within the region are few and far between, however, necessitating some interpolations from regions to the east and north (e.g., Katz and Katz 1985; Marmaduke 1978; Shafer 1986; Williams-Dean 1978).

Viewed as a whole, the subsistence lifeway of regional Late Archaic populations can generally be portrayed as one of residential mobility determined by resource availability. The degree of mobility required—whether high, moderate, or low—may have been tempered by the fact that some major plant foods, such as sotol and lechuguilla, were available year-round and in large quantities in foothill zones throughout much of the region. Whether or not desert succulents actually constituted a food staple in the region during the Late Archaic is still open to interpretation, however, in part because burned rock middens do not appear to be a common feature of early Late Archaic assemblages. During the later transitional Archaic, as the climate became drier, plant-processing features such as annular middens came into more general use in the region, but they typically occur in incipient rather than maturated form.

Interestingly, this pattern is particularly obvious in subareas of the region that are dominated by volcanics, such as the western Big Bend and Davis Mountains areas. Even in limestone-dominated environments such as the Glass Mountains (discussed earlier) where maximum plant diversity and densities occur, transitional Archaic domed rock middens, while visually obvious, tend to be much smaller on average than those of West-Central and Central Texas. This fact, coupled with very high densities of dart points and other hunting-related tools commonly found in Late Archaic components, would seem to argue for a subsistence pattern that made use of but never emphasized the processing of desert succulents as a staple food source. Instead, subsistence practices were focused on hunting and the collecting of a broad spectrum of plant supplements. The common occurrence of ground-stone implements in Late Archaic assemblages does not, in and of itself, argue against such an interpretation, as they would be needed in the preparation of a wide range of wild foodstuffs.

If hunting and broad spectrum collecting, rather than focused plant processing and baking, was indeed the dominant subsistence mode, then a high degree of mobility is implied throughout the Late Archaic. Foothill environments, where water and toolstone sources are most plentiful and biotic resources tend to be most diverse and concentrated, would logically represent preferred habitat for such foragers, as is attested by the regional archaeological record.

While substantive evidence for the use of cultigens such as maize during the Late Archaic period is lacking, certain trends offer grounds for speculation. Existing museum collections (mainly pre-1940 excavations) that can be related to specific sites and that have a predominance of Late Archaic material infrequently contain a few corncobs. Examined private collections from rockshelters (Mallouf n.d.), however, tend to reflect a stronger possible correlation of corncobs with Late Prehistoric assemblages containing Toyah arrow points (ca. 800 to 400 BP). Recent testing by the Texas Archeological Society of a large rockshelter in the Marfa Plain that contains extensive Archaic and Late Prehistoric deposits yielded a corncob in a matrix of vegetal matting from a definite Late Prehistoric, rather than Late Archaic, context. Three other corncobs and a corn kernel (Figure 8.13) have also been recovered at this shelter, but all are from disturbed contexts (Corbin and Beene n.d.; Mallouf n.d.).

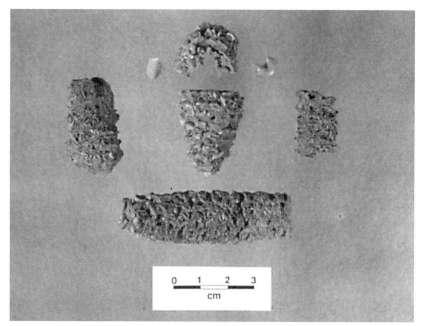

Figure 8.13. Examples of corncobs and kernels from rockshelters in the Marfa Plain (*top and middle rows*) and the Guadalupe Mountains (*bottom row*)

In sum, examples of indirect and/or unsubstantiated evidence for at least a cursory use of cultigens during the Late Archaic and Late Prehistoric abound from the southern Trans-Pecos. If cultigens were indeed known to Late Archaic populations, it seems probable that their introduction occurred during the latter half of the Late Archaic, sometime during the period 2500 to 1300 BP, a time that corresponds to the reentrenchment of xeric conditions. The mechanism of introduction was likely through western trade routes that also yielded such desirable items as marine shell. Clearly, the use of cultigens was cursory at best, possibly serving only as a dietary supplement, and may have been restricted to occasional, relatively haphazard and experimental plantings in suitable soils near springs or along segments of larger drainages such as Terlingua and Alamito Creeks in the Big Bend. Experimentation with cultigens in the transitional Late Archaic, along with the use of annular and domed rock middens, may have been a direct outgrowth of economic stresses resulting from increasingly dry climatic conditions. This pressing research issue is only one of many issues that reinforce our need for substantive, carefully controlled excavations in regional rockshelters.

Summary and Conclusions

The highly diversified terrain combined with a plethora of natural resources in the eastern Trans-Pecos region provided a maximum environment for broad-spectrum foragers of the long Archaic period. Paleoenvironmental data indicate that the first half of the Late Archaic (ca. 3000 to 2200 BP) witnessed an increased moisture regime that likely enhanced the resource base for hunters and gatherers and may have influenced a postulated human population increase that peaked from about 2500 to 1300 BP. Attendant to population growth was a notable diversification of material culture and expansion of settlement into previously ignored econiches, such as dissected pediment remnants, ridges and saddles, catsteps on steep colluvial slopes, and the tops of mountain peaks. The use of mountain-tops during the Late Archaic may signal the beginnings of a ritual lifeway of increasing complexity that became more pronounced during the succeeding Late Prehistoric period. Adaptive adjustments—related especially to subsistence practices—came into play with the slow reentrenchment of xeric conditions after 2200 BP and probably extended throughout the remainder of the Late Archaic to as late as 900 BP, as the bow and arrow supplanted the atlatl as the principal weapon of choice. The proliferation of annular and domed burned rock ovens for the processing of desert succulents during the terminal Late Archaic may reflect an adaptive response to long-term aridity, with attendant changes in plant communities.

The presence of cultigens—primarily maize—in early undocumented and/or poorly documented Late Archaic and Late Prehistoric assemblages of the eastern Trans-Pecos has long posed an interpretive issue for archaeologists. The question of whether or not Late Archaic foragers were also conducting some form of subsistence farming is still with us, and the paucity of controlled scientific excavations in Late Archaic rockshelter deposits during the past half-century (as well as very recent limited testing in regional rockshelters) has done little to clarify the situation. Taken as a whole, the data suggest that Late Archaic populations had knowledge of cultigens and might on occasion have experimented with them around springs and other water sources. Such experimentation might have taken on increased significance during the terminal Late Archaic, when long-term xeric conditions were also serving as a catalyst for more intensified use of rock ovens in processing desert succulents. The evolution from experimentation to the seasonal growing of supplemental foodstuffs during the succeeding Late Prehistoric period might seem a logical step.

As indicated above, frequency of maize increases in succeeding Late Prehistoric assemblages—particularly in those containing Toyah arrow points (ca. 800 to 400 BP). It should be noted, however, that the presence by 800 BP of farmers along the Rio Grande in the Big Bend (the La Junta phase), whether through indigenous development (Mallouf 1999) or through colonization by Jornada Mogollon peoples from the west (Kelley, Campbell, and Lehmer 1940), did little to impact or change the basically Archaic lifeways of foraging peoples across most of the eastern Trans-Pecos region.

The cultural importance of the eastern Trans-Pecos region rests in its transitional role not only between east and west (as suggested by Willey and Phillips in 1958) but also between Plains and Desert cultures to the north and south. Contrary to Lehmer's (1958:131) characterization of the Trans-Pecos as a culturally "marginal area," this archaeologically poorly known region can best be viewed as a culturally dynamic arena in which human adaptations within a changing environment were tested and fine-tuned and in which innovations were accepted or rejected as deemed appropriate for survival.

ACKNOWLEDGMENTS

I would like to thank the following individuals who are helping to facilitate research into the prehistory of the Trans-Pecos region: John Fort III; Betty MacGuire; Charles Lykes; Charles Burr; Homer Mills; Jim, Jane, and Hester Ann White; Harry (Hat) and Pam Turmer; Kathleen Olsen; Harold Courson; John Poindexter; Al Micallef; Bill Hubbard; Ruth Russell; James Olson; Bonnie Korbell; John and Mary Ann Luedecke; James King; Monroe Elms; David Williams; Jim Dacus; and Gary Dunshee. Thanks also for assistance from Rebecca Hart and Kelly García of the Center for Big Bend Studies and Brad Vierra, volume editor.

REFERENCES CITED

Albritton, C. C., Jr., and K. Bryan
    1939   Quaternary Stratigraphy of the Davis Mountains, Trans-Pecos, Texas. *Bulletin of the Geological Society of America* 50:1423–1474.

Biesaart, L. A.
    n.d.   Black Willow Burial. Notes on file, Center for Big Bend Studies, Sul Ross State University, Alpine, Tex.

Bryant, V. M., Jr.
    1974   Late Quaternary Pollen Records from the East-Central Periphery of the Chihuahuan Desert. In *Transactions of the Symposium on the Biological Resources of the Chihuahuan Desert Region,* edited by R. H. Wauer and D. H. Riskind, pp. 3–21. Series 3. National Park Service Transactions and Proceedings, Chihuahuan Desert Research Institute, Alpine, Tex.

Bryant, V. M., Jr., and R. G. Holloway

    1985   A Late Quaternary Paleoenvironmental Record of Texas: An Overview of the Pollen Evidence. In *Pollen Records of Late Quaternary North American Sediments,* edited by V. M. Bryant, Jr., and R. G. Holloway, pp. 39–70. American Association of Stratigraphic Palynologists, Dallas.

Bryant, V. M., Jr., and H. J. Shafer

    1977   The Late Quaternary Paleoenvironment of Texas: A Model for the Archeologist. *Bulletin of the Texas Archeological Society* 48:1–25.

Buck, B. J., and H. C. Monger

    1999   Stable Isotopes and Soil-Geomorphology as Indicators of Holocene Climate Change, Northern Chihuahuan Desert. *Journal of Arid Environments* 43:357–373.

Cloud, W. A.

    1998   City of Alpine East Trunk Sewer Line Project, Brewster County, Texas. Unpublished manuscript, Center for Big Bend Studies, Sul Ross State University, Alpine, Tex.

Coffin, E. F.

    1932   *Archaeological Exploration of a Rock Shelter in Brewster County, Texas.* Museum of the American Indian, Indian Notes and Monographs 48. Heye Foundation, New York.

Corbin, J., and D. Beene

    n.d.   San Esteban Rockshelter. Notes on file, Center for Big Bend Studies, Sul Ross State University, Alpine, Tex.

Davis, W. B., and D. J. Schmidly

    1994   *The Mammals of Texas.* Texas Parks and Wildlife Press, Austin.

Dering, J. P.

    1979   Pollen and Plant Macrofossil Vegetation Record Recovered from Hinds Cave, Val Verde County, Texas. Master's thesis, Department of Biology, Texas A&M University, College Station.

Dixon, J. R.

    1987   *Amphibians and Reptiles of Texas.* Texas A&M University Press, College Station.

Ely, L. L.

    1997   Response of Extreme Floods in the Southwestern United States to Climatic Variations in the Late Holocene. *Geomorphology* 19:175–201.

Greer, J. W.

    1968   Notes on Excavated Ring Midden Sites, 1963–1968. *Bulletin of the Texas Archeological Society* 38:39–43.

Hall, S. A.

1985   Quaternary Pollen Analysis and Vegetational History of the Southwest. In *Pollen Records of the Late Quaternary North American Sediments,* edited by V. M. Bryant, Jr., and R. G. Holloway, pp. 95–124. American Association of Stratigraphic Palynologists Foundation, Dallas.

Hamilton, D. L.

n.d.   Prehistory of the Rustler Hills: Granado Cave (41CU8). Unpublished manuscript on file, Department of Anthropology, Texas A&M University, College Station.

Hedrick, J. A.

1988   A Preliminary Report on Archeological Resources in Southern Culberson County in the Vicinity of Van Horn, Texas. *Bulletin of the Texas Archeological Society* 59:129–156.

Hines, M. H., S. A. Tomka, and K. W. Kibler

1994   *Data Recovery Excavations at the Wind Canyon Site, 41HZ119, Hudspeth. County, Texas.* Prewitt and Associates Reports of Investigations 99. Prewitt and Associates, Austin.

Holloway, R. G.

1985   Diet and Medicinal Plant Usage of a Late Archaic Population from Culberson County, Texas. *Bulletin of the Texas Archeological Society* 54:319–329.

Huebner, J., and J. Powell

n.d.   Comanche Springs Burial. Notes on file, Texas Archeological Research Laboratory, University of Texas, Austin.

Katz, S. R., and P. Katz

1985   *The Prehistory of the Carlsbad Basin, Southeastern New Mexico: Technical Report of Prehistoric Archeological Investigations in the Brantley Project Locality.* Bureau of Reclamation, Amarillo.

Kelley, J. C., T. N. Campbell, and D. J. Lehmer

1940   *The Association of Archaeological Materials with Geological Deposits in the Big Bend Region of Texas.* West Texas Historical and Scientific Society Publication 10. Sul Ross State Teachers College, Alpine, Tex.

Lehmer, D. J.

1958   A Review of Trans-Pecos Texas Archeology. *Bulletin of the Texas Archeological Society* 29:109–144.

Mallouf, R. J.

1981   Observations concerning Environmental and Cultural Interactions during the Terminal Pleistocene and Early Holocene in the

Big Bend of Texas and Adjoining Regions. *Bulletin of the Texas Archeological Society* 52:121–146.

1985 A Synthesis of Eastern Trans-Pecos Prehistory. Master's thesis, Department of Anthropology, University of Texas, Austin.

1998 Archeological Investigations at Goat Cave, Jeff Davis County, Texas. *Journal of Big Bend Studies* 10:37–61.

1999 Comments on the Prehistory of Far Northeastern Chihuahua, the La Junta District, and the Cielo Complex. *Journal of Big Bend Studies* 11:49–92.

n.d. Notes on file. Center for Big Bend Studies, Sul Ross State University, Alpine, Tex.

Mallouf, R. J., W. A. Cloud, and R. D. Mandel

n.d. Notes on file. Center for Big Bend Studies, Sul Ross State University, Alpine, Tex.

Mallouf, R. J., and C. Tunnell

1977 *An Archeological Reconnaissance in the Lower Canyons of the Rio Grande.* Office of the State Archeologist Survey Report 22. Texas Historical Commission, Austin.

Mallouf, R. J., and V. A. Wulfkuhle

1989 An Archeological Reconnaissance in the Rosillos Mountains. *Journal of Big Bend Studies* 1:1–24.

Marmaduke, W. S.

1978 Prehistoric Culture in Trans-Pecos Texas: An Ecological Explanation. Ph.D. dissertation, Department of Anthropology, University of Texas, Austin.

Mera, H. P.

1938 *Reconnaissance and Excavation in Southeastern New Mexico.* Memoirs of the American Anthropological Association 51. American Anthropological Association, Menasha, Wis.

O'Laughlin, T. C.

1980 *The Keystone Dam Site and Other Archaic and Formative Sites in Northwest El Paso, Texas.* El Paso Centennial Museum Publications in Anthropology 8. University of Texas, El Paso.

Patton, P., and D. S. Dibble

1982 Archeologic and Geomorphic Evidence for the Paleohydrologic Record of the Pecos River in West Texas. *American Journal of Science* 282:97–121.

Powell, M. A.

1988 *Trees and Shrubs of Trans-Pecos Texas.* Big Bend Natural History Association. Big Bend National Park, Tex.

Prewitt, E. R.

1994   Burned Rock Middens: A Summary of Previous Investigations and Interpretations. In *The Burned Rock Middens of Texas: An Archeological Symposium,* pp. 25–32. Texas Archeological Research Laboratory Studies in Archeology 13. University of Texas, Austin.

Raun, G. R.

1965   *A Guide to Texas Snakes.* Texas Memorial Museum Notes 9. University of Texas, Austin.

Roney, J. R.

1985   Prehistory of the Guadalupe Mountains. Master's thesis, Department of Anthropology, Eastern New Mexico University, Portales.

Sayles, E. B.

1935   *An Archaeological Survey of Texas.* Medallion Papers 17. Gila Pueblo, Globe, Ariz.

Shafer, H. J.

1986   *Ancient Texans: Rock Art and Lifeways along the Lower Pecos.* Texas Monthly Press, Austin.

Tunnell, C. D., and J. T. Hughes

1955   *An Archaic Bison Kill in the Texas Panhandle.* Panhandle-Plains Historical Review 28. Canyon, Tex.

Tunnell, C., and R. J. Mallouf

1975   *Cultural Resources in the Canyons of the Rio Grande.* Office of the State Archeologist Special Report 17. Texas Historical Commission, Austin.

Turpin, S. A.

1991   Time Out of Mind: The Radiocarbon Chronology of the Lower Pecos Region. In *Papers on Lower Pecos Prehistory,* pp. 1–50. Texas Archeological Research Laboratory Studies in Archeology 8. University of Texas, Austin.

1996   West of the Pecos: Prehistoric Adaptations in the Transition to the Eastern Trans-Pecos Region. *Journal of Big Bend Studies* 8:1–14.

Van Devender, T. R.

1990   Late Quaternary Vegetation and Climate of the Chihuahuan Desert, United States and Mexico. In *Packrat Middens: The Last 40,000 Years of Biotic Change,* edited by J. L. Betancourt, T. R. Van Devender, and P. S. Martin, pp. 104–113. University of Arizona Press, Tucson.

1995   Desert Grassland History: Changing Climates, Evolution, Biogeography, and Community Dynamics. In *The Desert Grassland,* edited by M. P. McClaran and T. R. Van Devender, pp. 68–99. University of Arizona Press, Tucson.

Van Devender, T. R., and W. G. Spaulding

1979   Development of Vegetation and Climate in the Southwestern United States. *Science* 204:701–710.

Ward, C. G.

1992   Shelby Brooks Cave: The Archeology of a Dry Cave in the Texas Trans-Pecos. Master's thesis, Department of Anthropology, University of Texas, Austin.

Wauer, R. H.

1980   *Naturalist's Big Bend: An Introduction to the Trees, Shrubs, Wildflowers, Cacti, Mammals, Birds, Reptiles and Amphibians, Fish, and Insects.* Texas A&M University Press, College Station.

Wells, P. V.

1966   Late Pleistocene Vegetation and Degree of Pluvial Climatic Change in the Chihuahuan Desert. *Science* 153:970–974.

1977   Post-Glacial Origin of the Present Chihuahuan Desert Less Than 11,500 Years Ago. In *Transactions of the Symposium on the Biological Resources of the Chihuahuan Desert Region*, edited by R. H. Wauer and D. H. Riskind, pp. 67–83. National Park Service Transactions and Proceedings Series 3. Chihuahuan Desert Research Institute, Alpine, Tex.

Willey, G. R., and P. Phillips

1958   *Method and Theory in American Archaeology.* University of Chicago Press, Chicago.

Williams-Dean, G.

1978   Ethnobotany and Cultural Ecology of Prehistoric Man in Southwest Texas. Ph.D. dissertation, Department of Biology, Texas A&M University, College Station.

Wiseman, R. N.

1999   The Dating of Annular Middens from Surface Artifacts: A Problem from the Northern Trans-Pecos Region in New Mexico. *Journal of Big Bend Studies* 11:37–48.

Wulfkuhle, V. A.

1988   The 1933 Excavation of Meriwether Rockshelter C (41BS809) in Brewster County, Texas. In *The Third Symposium on Resources of the Chihuahuan Desert Region*, pp. 117–132. Chihuahuan Desert Research Institute, Alpine, Tex.

CHAPTER 9

Ecological Factors Affecting the Late Archaic Economy of the Lower Pecos River Region

PHIL DERING

Introduction

This chapter evaluates the economy and environment of the Lower Pecos River region of Southwest Texas and Coahuila, Mexico, in order to explore the reasons why farming was never adopted in the region. First, the bio-physical environment and Archaic period economy of the region are described. Then the environment and economy are compared to areas in the Southwest where farming was adopted during the Late Archaic. These comparisons show that the Lower Pecos environment and subsistence strategies were not favorable for a transition to farming.

The Lower Pecos Environment

The Lower Pecos River region is located at the southern edge of the Edwards Plateau on the Rio Grande, encompassing the Pecos and Devils Rivers and their canyon tributaries (Turpin 1995; Figure 9.1). The regional vegetation is a shrub–short grass savanna (McMahan et al. 1984). Deep and narrow canyons sustain several trees, including oak, littleleaf walnut, mesquite, and native pecan. On the adjacent uplands the xeric vegetation includes desert hackberry, Texas persimmon, various acacias, yucca, prickly pear, lechuguilla (a small agave), and sotol.

The Lower Pecos area is a semidesert with an average growing season of 300 days, occasionally interrupted by killing frosts. The average rainfall of 40 cm peaks in the spring and fall, with a summer drought. Except for northeastern Brazil, this region exhibits greater interannual rainfall variability than any other semiarid savanna in the world (Norwine 1995:140).

The paleoenviroment of the region has been determined by pollen, geomorphological, and macrobotanical studies (Bryant and Holloway 1985; Dering 1979; Patton and Dibble 1982). Throughout the Holocene the region expe-

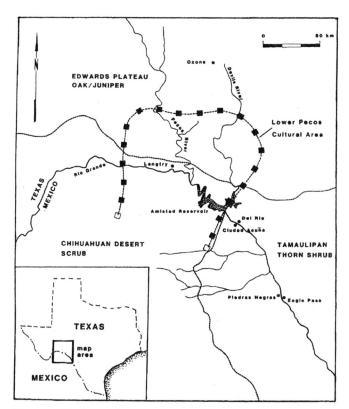

Figure 9.1. The Lower Pecos region

rienced a gradual reduction in effective moisture punctuated by at least two events. The first was a very dry period beginning around 6800 BP, marked by intense erosion and decreasing arboreal pollen frequencies. The second event, a mesic interval, occurred during the Late Archaic between 3000 and 2500 BP. It was represented by elevated levels of arboreal and grass pollen and by the incursion of bison herds into the region. After 2500 BP reduction in effective precipitation continued throughout the rest of the Archaic period (Bryant and Holloway 1985).

Assessing the Lower Pecos Archaic Economy: Diet-Breadth Studies

The following discussion assesses archaeological evidence, experimental studies, and ecological data within the framework of the diet-breadth model. Two fundamental assumptions drawn from behavioral ecology are made. First, I assume that foragers optimized organization of resource procurement, as reflected in their diet. Accordingly, the archaeological record should show that the Lower Pecos foragers considered both costs and benefits within a particular environmental context when deciding to obtain a certain resource (Kelly 1995:53–54). Second, I assume that the diet-breadth model can serve as an explanatory device in conjunction with archaeological data. The diet-breadth model predicts whether a resource will be taken when a forager encounters it. Resource acquisition is divided into search costs (the time required to find a resource) and handling costs (the time needed to collect and process it for consumption). Resources are ranked according to their post-encounter return rate, expressed as the amount of energy acquired per unit of time. As foragers encounter high-ranked resources, low-ranked resources are dropped from the diet even if they are abundant. As high-ranked resources become rarer, diet breadth (number of resources taken) expands (Diehl 1997; Kelly 1995:78).

Analyses of plant remains and coprolites document a broad-spectrum diet during the Archaic period that included plant resources, large and small game, and riverine resources (Brown 1991; Dering 1999; Sobolik 1996). Much of the diet was based on the xerophytic plants prepared in earth ovens—lechuguilla, sotol, and prickly pear (Bryant 1974; Huebner 1991; Sobolik 1996). Earth ovens occur in the archaeological record from 6000 BP through the Protohistoric period (Brown 1991).

Earth-Oven Experiments and the Archaeological Record

Because earth-oven resources are so prominent in the archaeological record, earth-oven studies are necessary to assess the paleoeconomy of the region. Recent experiments have measured the time required to prepare these plant resources, the amounts of wood, rock, and plant material required to construct ovens, and the yield of edible food calories from the primary plant resources lechuguilla and sotol, which must be cooked at high temperatures for forty-eight hours. Oven yields, material inputs, and time estimates are presented in Figure 9.2. Return rates were calculated according to the time invested in plant gathering (or pursuit time) and processing, referred to as handling cost, usually expressed as energy return per unit of time expended (kcal/hr; Table 9.1).

Assuming an average requirement of 1,500 kcal/day for each person in the group (Leslie et al. 1984:157), an oven loaded with lechuguilla yields 5.1 person-days of calories, enough for a small family-sized group for one or two days but insufficient for the accumulation of surplus. Also, the fuel requirements of earth ovens are substantial, and the standing deadwood in any given area would be stripped very quickly.

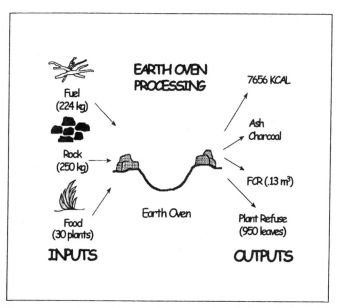

Figure 9.2. Earth-oven inputs and outputs. Note the large fuel wood input for relatively low caloric return. The high volume of waste increases the archaeological visibility of earth-oven activities.

Table 9.1. Return-rate calculations for lechuguilla and sotol prepared in earth ovens ($n = 5$)

	Lechuguilla	Sotol
Handling time in hours-range (average)	9.9–11.4	10.9–11.4
	(10.7)	(11.1)
Oven yield, processed dry weight	1.8–3.4	1.5–2.1
in kg-range (average)	(2.6)	(1.6)
Energy/unit in kcal/kg	3190	3290
Return rate in kcal/hr–range (average)	631–790	418–628
	(730)	(486)

Earth-oven data establish return rates for lechuguilla and sotol that can be compared to other plant and animal resources worldwide (Figure 9.3). Both lechuguilla and sotol return rates are comparable to those of lower-ranked resources such as grass seed and many root foods. Earth-oven processing of low-ranked plant resources probably is consistent with a broad-spectrum, low-return diet.

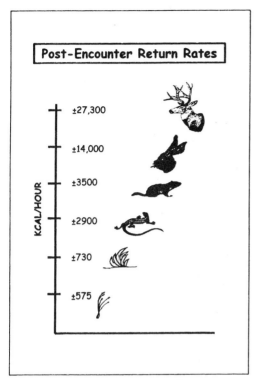

Post-Encounter Return Rates

KCAL/HOUR

±27,300

±14,000

±3500

±2900

±730

±575

Figure 9.3. Return rates of resource classes compared. Note that *Agave lechuguilla* prepared in earth ovens is rated just above grass seed but well below other resources such as small reptiles and mammals (Dering n.d.).

Mobility and Subsistence Strategies

Mobility in the Lower Pecos region was not determined by water but rather by the rapid depletion of local food resources. Use of low-ranked earth-oven resources indicates that high-ranked resources were often depleted in the canyon areas. The low caloric yield of earth ovens means that logistical trips to distant lechuguilla or sotol patches would not have been profitable. Earth-oven use would have severely taxed local fuel and lechuguilla/sotol resources. As return rates of local resources declined, hunter-gatherers reached a point of diminishing returns and moved their residence (Kelly 1992).

Rainfall can be remarkably localized in the region, especially in drought years (Norwine 1995), forcing hunter-gatherers to map onto continually changing distributions of regional resources (Binford 1980). Both subsistence organization and territorial boundaries would have been adjusted to correspond with seasonal or annual changes in the physical or social environment (Hitchcock and Bartram 1998:33; Simms 1987:89; Thomas 1983:21). Depending on conditions in a given year or even a given decade, a specific area would be visited in different seasons or utilized for different activities (cf. Binford 1982). For example, rockshelter sites contain flower and fruit fragments representing every season of the year (Alexander 1974; Irving 1966; Williams-Dean 1978), which were previously thought to indicate extended residence.

Discussion and Conclusions

How do environmental conditions of the Lower Pecos River region compare to the Southwestern deserts where farming was adopted? Stone and Bostwick (1996) note three primary environmental conditions that favored the adoption of farming in the southern Southwest. First, landforms offer a suitable farming situation with a reliable water supply. The Basin and Range Province contains streams with relatively broad terraces and alluvial fans, which provide suitable soils and opportunities for water control. By contrast, the Lower Pecos region has narrow streams entrenched in canyons that are susceptible to unpredictable catastrophic floods.

Regions favorable for the transition to farming should also house diverse resources within a short distance, enabling access to a variety of seasonal resources (Figure 9.4). Due to extreme changes in elevation, many areas of the Basin and Range Province encompass several biotic zones within relatively short distances. By contrast, the Lower Pecos is a dissected plateau with relatively little diversity. The Burro Mountains of Coahuila (130 km to the southwest) may have provided this diversity, but the archaeology is poorly known and the area is subject to unpredictable rainfall.

Finally, predictable rainfall with proper timing for the growing season favors plant production. Rainfall in southern Arizona peaks in the summer, ideal for growing the tropical cultigens maize, squash, and beans. By contrast, the Lower Pecos region has rainfall peaks in spring and fall, with a pronounced summer drought and extreme annual variation.

The foraging economy of the Lower Pecos differs in some key respects from the economy of the foragers of the southern Southwest. While both were dependent on plants, especially desert succulents and mesquite, the Lower Pecos lacked diversity in seasonal availability of local resources. Rather than follow seasonal resources up mountain massifs as practiced in the Basin and

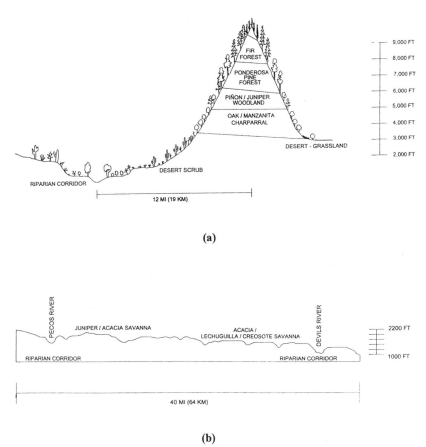

(a)

(b)

Figure 9.4. Cross sections of (a) a typical basin in the Basin and Range Province of southern Arizona and (b) the Lower Pecos region, a dissected plateau (after Emory 1857; Lowe 1964)

Range Province, Lower Pecos inhabitants had to travel extremely long distances to find comparable diversity. Low productivity in the region dictated high residential mobility throughout the Archaic period. Unpredictable rainfall distribution suggests that foragers followed relatively unpredictable pockets of diversity across the landscape. Similar variation in season rounds has been demonstrated in the Kalahari Desert (Hitchcock and Bartram 1998).

Botanical data have documented a reduction in diet-breadth at Late Archaic farming sites in the Tucson Basin (Diehl 1997). Similarly, a reduction in diet breadth in the Lower Pecos may have occurred during a brief period of climatic amelioration around 2500 BP, but it was manifested by a switch to bison hunt-

Table 9.2. Seed/fruit resources with highest densities in Area A (Early Archaic) and Area F (Late Archaic) samples

Plant Resources	Part	Density (seeds/liter)	
		Area A (Early Archaic)[1]	Area F (Late Archaic)[2]
Prickly pear, nopal	Seed	87.2	109.4
Littleleaf walnut	Nut	26.6	39.0
Drummond wild onion	Bulb fragments	17.4	12.7
Desert hackberry	Nutlet	6.1	12.5
Honey mesquite	Pod, seed, endocarp	8.8	6.7
Blackbrush acacia	Seed	7.9	11.1
Persimmon	Seed	5.3	7.1
Lechuguilla	Stem, leaf base, quids	4.3	3.2
Dropseed grass	Seed	3.6	17.1
Sotol	Seed	2.8	3.2
Sotol	Stem, leaf base	2.0	23.6
Texas cupgrass	Seed	2.5	9.0
Prickly pear, nopal	Pad fragments	0.3	6.9
Seed/fruit densities, all taxa/resource types		176.8	248.8

[1] Area A Samples: n = 15 samples, 1.5 liters each, total 22.5 L.
[2] Area F Samples: n = 15 samples, 1.5 liters each, total 22.5 L.

ing rather than to cultigens. Botanical and faunal studies in the Lower Pecos indicated that diet breadth remained broad for most of the Archaic period, a condition consistent with a low-return rate diet in a marginal environment (Lord 1984; Sobolik 1993, 1996; Table 9.2).

The Lower Pecos region lacked the environmental and economic conditions favorable for adoption of agriculture when compared to the southern Southwest. The lack of environmental diversity, unsuitable soils and landforms, and unpredictable rainfall distribution were factors unfavorable to farming. These same factors encouraged subsistence strategies organized around small, residentially mobile groups that followed irregular seasonal rounds as they mapped onto changing resource density.

REFERENCES CITED

Alexander, R. K.
1974   The Archeology of Conejo Shelter, A Study of Cultural Stability at an Archaic Rockshelter in Southwestern Texas. Ph.D. dissertation, Department of Anthropology, University of Texas, Austin.

Binford, L. R.

1980   Willow Smoke and Dogs' Tails: Hunter-Gatherer Settlement Systems and Archaeological Site Formation. *American Antiquity* 45(1):4–20.

1982   The Archaeology of Place. *Journal of Anthropological Archaeology* 1(1):5–31.

Brown, K. M.

1991   Prehistoric Economics at Baker Cave: A Plan for Research. In *Papers on Lower Pecos Prehistory*, edited by S. A. Turpin, pp. 87–140. Studies in Archaeology 8. Texas Archeological Research Laboratory, University of Texas, Austin.

Bryant, V. M., Jr.

1974   Prehistoric Diet in Southwest Texas. *American Antiquity* 39:407–420.

Bryant, V. M., Jr., and R. G. Holloway

1985   A Late Quaternary Paleoenvironmental Record of Texas: An Overview of the Pollen Evidence. In *Pollen Records of Late Quaternary North American Sediments*, edited by V. M. Bryant and R. G. Holloway, pp. 39–70. American Association of Stratigraphic Palynologists, Dallas.

Dering, J. P.

1979   Pollen and Plant Macrofossil Vegetation Record at Hinds Cave, Val Verde County, Texas. Master's thesis, Department of Biology, Texas A&M University, College Station.

1997   Macrobotanical Remains: Appendix D. In *Hot Rock Cooking on the Greater Edwards Plateau: Four Burned Rock Midden Sites in West Central Texas*, edited by S. L. Black, L. W. Ellis, D. G. Creel, and G. T. Goode, pp. 571–600. Studies in Archeology 22. Texas Archeological Research Laboratory, University of Texas, Austin.

1998   *Archaeological Context and Land Use in the Western Rio Grande Plains*. Technical Report 1. Center for Ecological Archaeology, Texas A&M University, College Station.

1999   Earth-Oven Plant Processing in Archaic Period Economies: An Example from a Semi-Arid Savannah in South-Central North America. *American Antiquity* 64:659–674.

Diehl, M.

1997   Rational Behavior, the Adoption of Agriculture, and the Organization of Subsistence during the Late Archaic Period in the Greater Tucson Basin. In *Rediscovering Darwin: Evolutionary*

Theory and Archeological Explanation, edited by C. M. Barton and G. A. Clark, pp. 251–265. Archaeological Papers of the American Anthropological Association No. 7. American Anthropological Association, Washington, D.C.

Emory, W. H.

1857   *Report on the United States and Mexican Boundary Survey under the Direction of the Secretary of the Interior.* A. O. Nicholson, Washington, D.C.

Hitchcock, R. K., and L. E. Bartram

1998   Social Boundaries, Technical Systems, and the Use of Space and Technology in the Kalahari. In *The Archaeology of Social Boundaries,* edited by M. T. Stark, pp. 12–49. Smithsonian Institution Press, Washington, D.C.

Huebner, J.

1991   Cactus for Dinner, Again!: An Isotopic Analysis of Late Archaic Diet in the Lower Pecos Region of Texas. In *Papers on Lower Pecos Prehistory,* edited by S. Turpin, pp. 175–190. Studies in Archeology 8. Texas Archeological Research Laboratory, University of Texas, Austin.

Irving, R. S.

1966   The Preliminary Analysis of Plant Remains from Six Amistad Reservoir Sites. In *A Preliminary Study of the Paleoecology of the Amistad Reservoir Area,* edited by D. A. Story and V. M. Bryant, Jr., pp. 61–90. University of Texas, Austin.

Kelly, R. L.

1992   Mobility/Sedentism: Concepts, Archaeological Measures, and Effects. *Annual Review of Anthropology* 21:43–66.

1995   *The Foraging Spectrum: Diversity in Hunter-Gatherer Lifeways.* Smithsonian Institution Press, Washington, D.C.

Labadie, J. H.

1994   *Amistad National Recreation Area: Cultural Resources Study.* National Park Service, United States Department of the Interior, Southwest Regional Office, Santa Fe.

Leslie, P. W., J. R. Blindon, and P. T. Baker

1984   Caloric Requirements of Human Populations: A Model. *Human Ecology* 12:137–163.

Lord, K. J.

1984   The Zooarchaeology of Hinds Cave (41VV456). Ph.D. dissertation, Department of Anthropology, University of Texas, Austin.

Lowe, C. H.

1964 *Arizona's Natural Environment.* University of Arizona Press, Tucson.

McMahan, C. A., R. G. Frye, and K. L. Brown

1984 *The Vegetation Types of Texas, Including Cropland.* Texas Parks and Wildlife Department, Austin.

Norwine, J.

1995 The Regional Climate of South Texas: Patterns and Trends. In *The Impact of Global Warming on Texas,* edited by J. Norwine, J. R. Giardino, G. R. North, and J. Valdes, pp. 138–155. Geo Books, Texas A&M University, College Station.

Patton, P., and D. S. Dibble

1982 Archeologic and Geomorphic Evidence for the Paleohydrologic Record of the Pecos River in West Texas. *American Journal of Science* 282:97–121.

Shafer, H. J.

1981 The Adaptive Technology of the Prehistoric Inhabitants of Southwest Texas. *Plains Anthropologist* 26(92):129–138.

1988 The Prehistoric Legacy of the Lower Pecos Region of Texas. *Bulletin of the Texas Archeological Society* 59:23–52.

Simms, S.

1987 *Behavioral Ecology and Hunter-Gatherer Foraging: An Example from the Great Basin.* BAR International Series 381. British Archaeological Reports, Oxford, England.

Sobolik, K. D.

1993 Direct Evidence for the Importance of Small Animals to Prehistoric Diets: A Review of Coprolite Studies. *North American Archaeologist* 14(3):227–244.

1996 Nutritional Constraints and Mobility Patterns of Hunter-Gatherers in the Northern Chihuahuan Desert. In *Case Studies in Environmental Archaeology,* edited by E. J. Reitz, L. A. Newsom, and S. J. Scudder, pp. 195–214. Plenum Press, New York.

Stone, C., and T. Bostwick

1996 Environmental Contexts and Archaeological Correlates: The Transition to Farming in Three Regions of the Arizona Desert. In *Early Formative Adaptations in the Southern Southwest,* edited by B. J. Roth, pp. 17–26. Monographs in World Archaeology No. 25. Prehistory Press, Madison, Wis.

Thomas, D. H.

1983   *The Archaeology of Monitor Valley: Gatecliff Shelter.* Anthropological Papers of the American Museum of Natural History 59: Part 1. American Museum of Natural History, New York.

Turpin, S. A.

1995   The Lower Pecos River Region of Texas and Northern New Mexico. *Bulletin of the Texas Archaeological Society* 66:541–560.

Williams-Dean, G.

1978   Ethnobotany and Cultural Ecology of Prehistoric Man in Southwest Texas. Ph.D. dissertation, Department of Biology, Texas A&M University, College Station.

CHAPTER 10

An Overview of the Late
Archaic in Southern Texas

THOMAS R. HESTER

Introduction

This chapter examines some of the data that have emerged in recent years, illuminating various aspects of prehistoric cultural patterns during the latter part of the Archaic in southern Texas (Figure 10.1). The region under consideration is known as the Rio Grande Plain, south of the Edwards Plateau and between the Guadalupe River and the Rio Grande. The South Texas coastal strip, with its own distinctive archaeological record, is not included (see Ricklis 1995).

The South Texas area is usually referred to as the Rio Grande Plain; it is semiarid, with a mosaic of local environments that range from abundant in resources to very meager (Hester 1981) and a modern-day vegetation pattern that is characterized as the "Brush Country." The mesquite, thorny brush, and prickly pear that dominate the landscape today can be traced back to at least the middle Holocene; despite the exaltations of early European settlers over the abundant grasslands, there is increasing evidence that a mixed brush-grassland savanna has been in place throughout much of the region for several millennia. To be sure, European settlement has led to the spread of thorn brush, the diminution of water resources, and the elimination of certain animal species (notably bison, pronghorn antelope, black bear, and wolf).

The time frame for the discussion in this chapter utilizes the chronology outlined in Grant Hall et al. (1986). The Late Archaic dates roughly from 400 BC to AD 600, and the designation has been used to encompass cultural phenomena that have been variously described as "Late," "Transitional," or "Terminal" Archaic. Regardless of the terminology, the archeological record is distinctive and is truncated around AD 600–700 by the introduction of the bow and arrow, pottery (by AD 900), and some distinctive shifts in subsistence and settlement that are part of the Late Prehistoric, as outlined in Hester (1995).

Extensive surveys (as at Choke Canyon and Chaparrosa Ranch), several

Figure 10.1. General locations of sites and locales mentioned in the text: 1. Choke Canyon area (41LK59, 67, 201); 2. Chaparrosa Ranch (41ZV10); 3. Smith Creek site (41DW270); 4. 41MV120; 5. 41ME34; 6. Lino site (41WB437); 7. Shrew site (41WN73); 8. Falcon Reservoir; 9. Karnes County cemeteries (Silo and Haiduk sites); 10. Olmos Basin site (41BX1); 11. 41LK201

excavations (41LK201, 41ZV10, 41MV120, 4lWB437), and the discovery and salvage of burials and cemeteries have brought the latter part of the Archaic into sharper focus. In the northern portion of South Texas, the diagnostic dart-point types include Marcos, Montell, Shumla, Ensor, Frio, and Fairland. There appears to be a clear internal temporal break, with Montell, Marcos, and Castroville (Figure 10.2) occurring earlier (the Late Archaic), followed by small side-notched dart points known as Ensor, Frio, and Fairland (the Transitional Archaic; Figure 10.2). The putative "Shumla" points (Figure 10.2; discussed later in this chapter) are best not cross-dated with a similar point style with that name, in the Late Archaic of the Lower Pecos, because the coastal plain examples are probably not related. Indeed, they reflect a very distinctive technology, in which most, if not all, of these specimens are made on heat-treated local cherts (as initially documented by Hester and Collins 1974).

The great numbers of Transitional Archaic points at sites and in private collections in southern Texas are especially notable (cf. Hester and Whatley 1997; Woerner and Highley 1982). This may reflect a bias in terms of the erosion of upper or late sediments at sites. However, it may also suggest either increased populations or much-intensified hunting activities in the region.

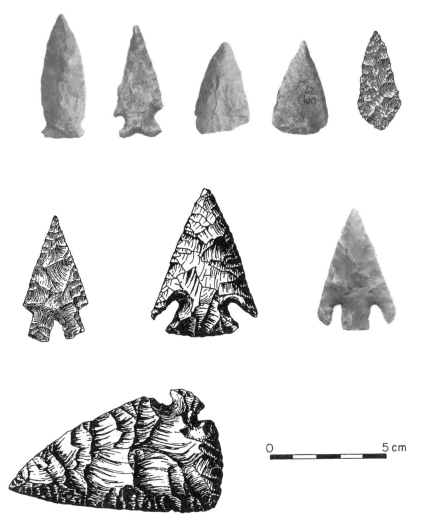

Figure 10.2. Some diagnostic points of the Late and Transitional Archaic in southern Texas. *Top row, left to right:* Ensor, Frio, Matamoros, Catan, Desmuke; *middle row:* Montell, Marcos, "Shumla"-like; *bottom row:* corner-tang biface (the Marcos point and corner-tang biface are from the Haiduk site). (Drawings by Kathy Roemer and Richard McReynolds)

These diagnostics help to identify the Late Archaic and Transitional Archaic in the northern part of the region; but when one moves to the south, in the Laredo area, stemmed points drop out significantly (although not altogether), and the Late Archaic and Transitional Archaic are characterized by small triangular and convex-based dart points (Matamoros, Catan, Desmuke; Figure 10.2). There have been few excavations of any size in this region, and the only contextual or comparative data of substance are available from the excavations at the Lino site (Quigg et al. 2000) as well as from collection documentations, surveys, and burial salvage (Bettis 1997; Boyd et al. 1997:418).

Life in the South Texas Late Archaic

In the fieldwork in the Choke Canyon reservoir basin (Figure 10.1), forty-four sites yielded diagnostics of the Late and Transitional Archaic, including Ensor, Frio, Ellis, Fairland, and Marcos points. Sites had extensive deposits of fire-cracked rock, both hearths and earth ovens (these continue from the latter part of the Middle Archaic); and grinding implements (manos, metates) are commonly found. These implements may reflect further intensification of the exploitation of mesquite and acacia beans (as well as other plant resources) after these species spread during the Middle Archaic. At site 41LK67, however, Kenneth M. Brown et al. (1982:15) excavated a large accumulation of fire-cracked rock (55 kg), with considerable quantities of mussel shell; they note that "the cooking of mussels may have been at least one of the functions" (this was Feature 8, radiocarbon-dated at 400 BC). Hall (1981) reported the use of similar rock features in roasting mussels from 41LK59 at Choke Canyon.

Additionally, excavations in a Late Archaic component at site 41LK201 (Highley 1986) yielded an Ensor point and a Late Archaic "gouge" (adze) form, along with sandstone hearths and considerable fauna. One of the hearths, Feature 5 (Figure 10.3), radiocarbon-dated at 480 BC, contained wood from mesquite and acacia and had in association fragments of metates, an abrading stone, and a grooved sandstone weight. The fauna includes mostly small game and fish, as well as whitetail deer. Important items include catfish, freshwater drum, turtle, rabbits, rats, mice, squirrels, and tortoises. As at 41LK67, freshwater mussels, along with *Rabdotus* land snails, were also abundant. Among the small fauna was the pine vole, no longer in the region. While the fauna and the wood species suggest an environment very similar to that in the area today, the presence of the pine vole warrants closer review of local conditions.

Thus the Choke Canyon Late Archaic subsistence and vegetation data suggest exploitation of small animals, especially turtles, fish, and rodents, supplemented by deer. *Rabdotus* snails and mussel shells are common, reflecting their collection as food sources, cooked in rock features. Hall et al. (1982) also note that among the Late Archaic subsistence items at site 41LK59 one of the mussel species is so small (25 mm in maximum length) that the only efficient way to have harvested them would have been with a scoop or dredging device of some

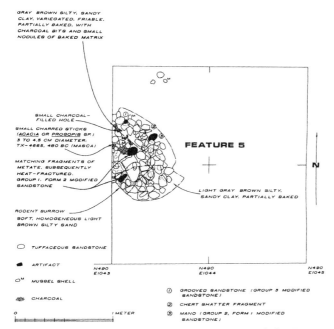

GRAY BROWN SILTY, SANDY
CLAY, VARIEGATED, FRIABLE,
PARTIALLY BAKED, WITH
CHARCOAL BITS AND SMALL
NODULES OF BAKED MATRIX

SMALL CHARCOAL-
FILLED HOLE

SMALL CHARRED STICKS
(ACACIA OR PROSOPIS SP.)
3 TO 4.5 CM DIAMETER;
TX-4665, 480 BC (MASCA)

FEATURE 5

MATCHING FRAGMENTS OF
METATE, SUBSEQUENTLY
HEAT-FRACTURED,
GROUP I, FORM 2 MODIFIED
SANDSTONE

LIGHT GRAY BROWN SILTY,
SANDY CLAY, PARTIALLY BAKED

RODENT BURROW
SOFT, HOMOGENEOUS LIGHT
BROWN SILTY SAND

○ TUFFACEOUS SANDSTONE

● ARTIFACT   N490   N490   N490
                            E1043   E1044   E1045
○ᴹ MUSSEL SHELL

🔲 CHARCOAL   ① GROOVED SANDSTONE (GROUP 3 MODIFIED
                                       SANDSTONE)
0   1 METER   ② CHERT SHATTER FRAGMENT
                                ③ MANO (GROUP 2, FORM 1 MODIFIED
                                   SANDSTONE)

Figure 10.3. Late Archaic hearth: Feature 5, 41LK201, Choke Canyon Project (from Highley 1986)

sort. In terms of settlement, the Late Archaic (and Transitional Archaic) campsites at Choke Canyon, and elsewhere in the interior of South Texas, are almost
always located adjacent to present stream channels or adjacent sloughs.

Recent excavations by the Texas Archeological Research Laboratory under
the auspices of the Texas Department of Transportation have been carried out
at the Smith Creek site, 41DW270, located about 120 km north-northeast of
Choke Canyon (Figure 10.1; Hudler et al. 2002). Of interest here is an Ensor
component within Stratum V in the upper part of the site. The stratum averages 30 cm in thickness and is extensively disturbed on both the east and west
ends of the block excavation in which it was exposed. This component includes
eight fire-cracked rock features (clusters of sandstone and chert cobbles), some
of which provided faunal and botanical data. Only one radiocarbon date comes
from the zone; it is seemingly too late, at AD 1025–1225, and is likely intrusive
from a Late Prehistoric occupation (with Scallorn arrow points) above it.

The rock features are hearths or baking facilities with (in addition to faunal remains) associated snails and mussel shells, along with wood charcoal
from hickory, hackberry, and unidentified hardwoods, all still part of the local

riparian forest today. The operative word in characterizing the dietary preferences of the Ensor component peoples is "turtle"—several different aquatic species from the adjacent creek. There are also fish (sunfish, catfish, alligator gar), snakes, frogs, lizards, rats, rabbits, birds, domestic dog, deer, pronghorn antelope, and a single bison. While the excellent preservation provides us with a more detailed faunal list than from other Late and Transitional Archaic sites in South Texas, the emphasis is clearly still on small game (especially turtles, fish, rodents, and reptiles). There is an indication here of greater availability of deer and pronghorn, and at least one bison.

Late Archaic components in the more arid reaches of South Texas, between the Nueces and the Rio Grande, have provided very little information. At site 41ZV10 (Figure 10.1), which I excavated in 1975 (Hester 1978), the upper deposits contained vertically separated Late Prehistoric and Late Archaic occupations. The mixed Late/Transitional Archaic occupation, at a depth of 30–35 cm, was marked by numerous fire-cracked rock features, but with little preservation of charcoal or associated cultural materials despite the use of block excavation to look for such associations. Indicative of the vertical mixing in the upper and lower deposits was the presence of such diagnostics in the upper deposits as Ensor (Transitional Archaic), Zavala (Late Prehistoric), and a single Montell point (Late Archaic). Deeper in the sediments were Late Archaic diagnostics such as Marcos and Shumla-like points. A single radiocarbon date of AD 1150 came from ZV10, most closely "associated" with the Shumla-like points, and is almost certainly much too late. While the chronological framework of the Late Archaic is hardly bolstered by the ZV10 data, the faunal record is informative. It includes whitetail deer, pronghorn antelope, turtles, snakes, fish, rabbits, mice, and *Rabdotus* snails. Mussel shell is present but not common, as the adjacent creek bed probably did not support significant mussel populations.

Vierra (1998) has published site 41MV120 (Figure 10.1), just 55 km to the southwest. As at ZV10, the lithic assemblage was meager. While Vierra has the same Shumla-like points, Marcos and Montell points, and also Ensor points, his excavated sequence is a bit different from mine. With all due respect to Vierra, I do not put any more credence in his sequence than I do in the one I came up with at ZV10. That site was badly disturbed by vertisol cracks and rodent burrowing, and MV120 had rodent burrows to a depth of 1 m. Further evidence of disturbance at MV120 is the mixing of Middle Archaic Marshall and Langtry points, which (whatever label is put on one of these periods) are not temporally associated with the Late Archaic types that I just noted. This is easily testable by looking at the sequences 120 km to the northeast of MV120 on the edge of the Edwards Plateau (e.g., Mueggenborg 1994).

No identifiable fauna came from MV120, though mussel shells and *Rabdotus* snails were present. There were also very few features, but charcoal from one was identified as mesquite from thin-sectioning. Vierra (1998:226, 227, 232) and his colleagues suggest that MV120 components represent "warm-season" occupations, based on mussel shell analysis, and also infer a "short-term" occupation, with the assemblage being "geared towards the production of cores, bifaces and projectile points for use during annual rounds."

At site 41ME34, on the northern Rio Grande Plain about 30 km south of the Balcones Escarpment (Figure 10.1), Late and Transitional Archaic occupations were excavated in separate areas of the site (Hester 1987). Along the banks of a small tributary to Live Oak Creek, deposits up to 1.45 m in depth yielded a sequence of Early Archaic, Middle Archaic, Late Archaic, and Late Prehistoric materials. The Transitional Archaic occupations were missing, however, but were found about 20 m from the creek and characterized by numerous Frio points. Unfortunately, organic preservation was extremely poor in this area, and no data can be added regarding either faunal remains or plant species identification from wood charcoal.

The Lino site in Webb County (Figure 10.1; 41WB437) has been excavated by J. Michael Quigg et al. (2000) and is interpreted as a stratified Late Archaic campsite. The radiocarbon dates, however, range from what the Choke Canyon sequence would place in the "middle" of the Late Archaic (ca. 2000 BP) to Middle Archaic times (ca. 3400 BP). Occupation 1 at 2000 BP represents Late Archaic activities, with triangular dart points (Tortugas, Matamoros) and Nueces tools, a lunate, beveled-bit form (a second early-stage Nueces tool is misclassified as a Clear Fork tool). Occupation 1 is certainly important in beginning to define the variation with the Late Archaic in the Laredo area (especially given the problem with the ages of triangular points noted above). However, the Transitional Archaic (with Frio and similar small, stemmed points, as well as Matamoros and Catan) is not present. We know that these stemmed diagnostics occur in the area, based on local surveys, the study of a large collection from the Laredo area (by Bettis 1997), and a surface site near Freer, Texas, 100 km northeast of Laredo (David Calame, Sr., personal communication, 2000), with Frio points as well as specimens of the Matamoros and Desmuke types.

Occupation 2 is stratigraphically below Occupation 1 and is estimated to date at 2300 BP but yielded no diagnostics. Occupation 3 is deeper and estimated at 2700 BP. With this date, the parameters of the Late Archaic as defined at Choke Canyon begin to be stretched. Indeed, this is evident in the diagnostics, which include large triangular points (Tortugas) as well as a rounded base point and a small triangular point (Matamoros?; reworked Tortugas?). Taking the broad view, within the context of south Texas chronology, I would place Occupation 3 in the late part of the Middle Archaic (cf. Taylor and Highley 1995). Occupations 4 and 5, and possibly 6, extend further back into the Middle Archaic, with Occupation 4 dominated by Tortugas points, a possible Abasolo, and fragments of large thin bifaces. Occupation 5 has round-based points (called Refugio by Quigg et al. 2000), a Langtry-like point, and a rhomboidal "gouge" form. Despite the title of the Lino site report, Quigg et al. (2000) acknowledge the Late/Middle Archaic nature of this sequence. Though the authors seem to despair at the difficulty of interpreting South Texas chronology based on the nature of diagnostic artifacts (e.g., triangular points), I would argue that the Lino site excavations have greatly added to the definition of the South Texas Middle and Late Archaic.

To return to the issue of the Late Archaic, after this digression into regional culture history, the Lino site has produced valuable information from Occupation 1 relating to Late Archaic campsite activities. Found 20–40 cm below the surface, it was the best preserved, densest occupation excavated at the site, with twelve features in the 53 sq m that were exposed: a rock-filled basin, two concentrations of mussel shell, and nine burned rock clusters. In addition to the lithic diagnostics noted above, other material culture included a sandstone grooved abrader (Turner and Hester 1999), very similar to one found at 41ZV10, and a small mussel-shell pendant.

Although no faunal remains (except for mussel shells and *Rabdotus* snails) were preserved in the Late Archaic, and earlier, occupations, the investigators made an intensive effort to recover evidence on diet and environment from the analysis of lipids, the extraction of organics from fifty-three burned rocks and five ground-stone tools (for both stable isotope and lipid studies), and the identification of wood species from charcoal thin-sections. Gas chromatography was used in the analysis of the fatty acids in the lipid samples. Based on an extensive suite of comparative data from comparable analyses of modern plant and animal resources, Quigg et al. (2000:240ff.) suggest the presence of seeds (including Texas ebony), mesquite beans, prickly pear fruit/seeds, and fruit of the tasajillo plant. Lipid results also pointed to the likely presence of white-tail deer. Microwear analyses failed to reveal any traces of use wear that were specific to tasks or species. Overall, for the Late Archaic, the Lino site appears to represent multifamily, short-term occupations utilizing plant and animal resources that are present in the area today.

It is somewhat curious that Quigg et al. (2000:241) go to some length to discount the use of large prairie snails (*Rabdotus*) as foodstuffs. They chose as an archaeological citation of dense snail-shell occurrence and the propensity of Texas archaeologists to accept these as food items the La Jita site (Hester

1971), which is not in "south Texas" (as they assert), but rather in the Edwards Plateau, nearly 400 km to the north! Indeed, they ignore all of the evidence, both archaeological and ethnohistorical (e.g., Campbell 1983), from South and Lower Pecos Texas, which clearly demonstrates that *Rabdotus* snails were collected as a food source (a thoughtful review of this controversy is provided by Brown 2002, who concludes that these snails were indeed procured for food).

Trade, Exchange, and Symbolism

Another facet of the Late and Transitional Archaic lifeways that is coming to light in South Texas involves trade. Large, thin bifaces manufactured in Central Texas were traded into the region beginning at least in Middle Archaic times and continued into the Historic era, as reported by Alvar Núñez Cabeza de Vaca in the 1530s (Hester 1999). Such specimens have been found with isolated Late Archaic burials (as at the Shrew site in Wilson County; Labadie 1988) as well as in caches of bifaces made of Central Texas chert that occur both in mortuary and nonmortuary contexts (cf. Miller 1993).

On the Tamaulipas side of Falcon Lake (Figure 10.1), a burial excavated at the Toyah-1 site (Boyd et al. 1997:418) had mortuary offerings that include a cache of fifty to fifty-two large bifaces. All but one was triangular. One, however, is a distinctive stemmed biface characteristic of the Central Texas Late Archaic (Figure 10.4; Hester 1995:442; Hester and Green 1972). Under ultraviolet fluorescence conducted at the Texas Archeological Research Laboratory by Michael B. Collins, this biface and several triangular ones in the mortuary cache had a distinctive orange fluorescence clearly indicative of Edwards Plateau chert.

At the Silo site Transitional Archaic cemetery (Figure 10.1), discussed more fully below, subtriangular cache-style bifaces were placed with one burial (Lovata 1997). The symbolic nature of lithics in the Late Archaic is clearly seen at the Silo site in the presence of large, corner-tanged bifaces (Turner and Hester 1999). This occurrence is mirrored by massive corner-tang bifaces found at the Ernest Witte site (Hall 1981) in Southeast Texas, of Late Archaic date. Hall (1981) has written extensively on the mortuary offerings of the Ernest Witte site, which included a variety of exotic stone as well as many marine shell ornaments. He hypothesized an import/export system that evolved along with expanding populations from Middle into Late Archaic times, but which diminished around AD 200.

Interestingly, the acquisition of obsidian (from sources in New Mexico, Idaho, and Wyoming) that is so well represented in Central and South Texas in the Late Prehistoric does not appear in South Texas during the Late Archaic.

0 ▬▬▬▬▬ 5
centimeters

Figure 10.4. Stemmed biface from Falcon Reservoir. This specimen,
typical of the Central Texas Late Archaic, was found in a cache of triangular bifaces.

Death in the Late Archaic

Several cemeteries, as well as a number of isolated burials, are dated to the
South Texas Late Archaic. Particularly informative are two cemeteries on the
San Antonio River drainage in Karnes County. One is the Haiduk site (Fig-
ure 10.1), excavated by the landowner some years ago, but with the skeletal
remains and associated artifacts preserved and published (Mitchell et al. 1984).
The remains of an adult male and an adult female were found with more than

fifty mortuary offerings. These included corner-tang bifaces, Marcos points, triangular bifaces, and other Late Archaic artifacts (Figure 10.2). More recently, an isolated burial in the same area that was scientifically excavated had a Transitional Archaic Fairland point in the chest area (Huebner et al. 1996). Stable isotope analysis of this burial indicates a diet weighted toward C_4/CAM plants, such as prickly pear cactus. There is little indication of the use of riverine resources. While this is only a single example, the suggested dietary pattern is in contrast with the emphasis on aquatic/riverine resources seen at Choke Canyon and at DW270. Nonetheless, it is informative in that it helps to identify plants that may have been intensively utilized, evidence for which is lacking from excavated campsites.

Near these two sites is the Silo Site (Figure 10.1; 41KA102: Lovata 1997). Human remains had been exposed by the erosion of a wall of an old silage trench, and salvage efforts led to the recovery of twenty-five individuals in an area of 4.5 m³. We do not know what percentage of the entire cemetery population may be represented. All of the recovered diagnostics can be assigned to the Transitional Archaic (including Ensor and Fairland points; Figure 10.5). Of those burials excavated, twelve were juveniles (less than twenty years old), and thirteen were adults (older than twenty). Of the adults, seven were conclusively sexed as males, and one as a female. The cemetery was a locale that had seen repeated use, perhaps over many generations; a large number of the burials had been cut through for later interments, often creating commingled masses of skeletal elements.

Most of the burials were flexed, however, with one hand on the pelvis, and the other on the face. There was one double burial of an adult male (twenty-five to thirty-five years old), and a juvenile (gender unknown, five to six years old). One child (four to seven years old) was extended dorsally. And one body (an adult female, twenty-five to thirty-five years old) was buried face down in an extended position. Associated with the double burial were two very large corner-tang bifaces (Figure 10.6) and a large biface (Figure 10.7, placed with the juvenile); three additional specimens of this style were found with the burial of an adult male (Figure 10.8).

The Silo and Haiduk sites in Karnes County further reinforce the chronological break between Late Archaic (Marcos) and Transitional Archaic (Ensor and similar types). Whatever the shift in dart-point styles may have meant, the importance of the corner-tang biface as a symbolic artifact to be included with certain burials encompasses the entire latter part of the Archaic.

On the northern edge of the Rio Grande Plain, and immediately below the Balcones Escarpment, the Olmos Dam site (41BX1; Figure 10.1) excavations by Paul D. Lukowski (1988) revealed a portion of a Transitional Archaic cemetery

0   5 cm

Figure 10.5. Artifacts from the Silo Site, 41KA102. The top row includes two Ensor points; and the middle row includes a Marcos fragment and a Fairland. The Marcos was a surface find, but this type occurs with Late Archaic burials at the Haiduk site upstream. (Photograph courtesy of Troy Lovata)

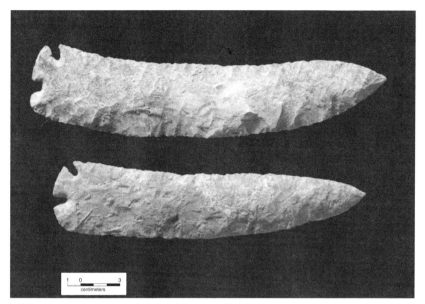

Figure 10.6. Two corner-tang bifaces from the Silo Site, found with a double burial at the site. Scale is 30 cm long. (Photograph courtesy of Troy Lovata)

Figure 10.7. Three large bifaces from the Silo Site. Scale is 30 cm long. (Photograph courtesy of Troy Lovata)

Figure 10.8. Three corner-tang bifaces from a burial at the Silo Site. Scale is 30 cm long.

dating between 2000 and 3000 BP. The only associated lithic was a small side-notched dart point, perhaps of the Godley form, which Hall (1981) also links to the last part of the Archaic. The most distinctive grave inclusions were conch-shell pendants, large antler racks of whitetail deer, and long bone awls or hair-pins. Eleven individuals were excavated: seven adults, a young juvenile, and three infants. The single dart point noted above penetrated the right parietal of Burial 5, a young adult male, causing his death; he also suffered from periostitis, the only such pathology found in the sample.

An interesting facet of the Olmos Dam mortuary pattern is the use of white-tail deer antler racks. This trait is also seen in the late Middle Archaic cemetery at Loma Sandia and perhaps, like the corner-tang bifaces, reflects a certain degree of continuity in mortuary offerings in the late part of the Archaic.

Closing Observations

The existing data on the South Texas Archaic appear to reflect local variation in diet, although this is biased by generally poor preservation in the Nueces–Rio Grande corridor. Still, the emphasis was on small game, especially turtles, fish, and rodents. Clearly, large game animals (such as deer, antelope, and the occasional bison) were hunted, but their importance is hard to measure with the limited faunal sample from Late and Transitional Archaic sites. Mussels were an important food source at sites adjacent to streams with significant mussel populations (e.g., the Frio River in the Choke Canyon area); and in some areas *Rabdotus* snails were aggressively collected as a food supplement. We do not yet have enough sizable, well-studied faunal samples from regional sites to deal with seasonality issues in a meaningful way. Poor preservation of archaeobotanical remains hampers our ability to evaluate nonmeat components of diet, although the stable isotope studies by J. A. Huebner et al. (1996) and especially the isotopic and lipid analysis done for the Lino site (Quigg et al. 2000, using organics extracted from burned rocks) hold great potential. To date, archaeobotanical research has focused on thin-sectioning of wood charcoal. At both Choke Canyon and Lino there appears to be little, if any, difference from the mesquite/prickly pear/brushlands associations typical of the region today.

Cemeteries indicate the use of specific locales for burials over considerable periods, and the grave goods may eventually provide some insight into the role of certain goods as symbolic (the corner-tang bifaces), as reflective of trade relationships (the large triangular bifaces), and as indicators of status or wealth. These cemeteries represent a measure of continuity from the Middle Archaic through the Transitional Archaic, perhaps 1,000 years, in which symbolic lithics, trade contacts, and the evolution of status or prestige were all important. Though the use of the concept of "territory" is loaded with ambiguities, it is likely that the cemeteries are reflecting the territorial patterns of South Texas groups. Kelly (1995) suggests that "territory" represents an area that is defended. This may well be the case, as death from dart-point wounds is represented at some of the known cemeteries (Archaic through Late Prehistoric in South and Southeast Texas; see Patterson 2000).

Yet another indication of violence is an apparently isolated Transitional Archaic burial from site 41LK21 in the lower Nueces River drainage. Three

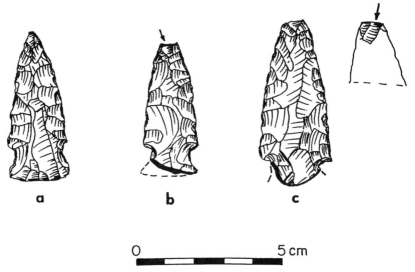

0   5 cm

Figure 10.9. Projectile points from a burial at 41LK21.

Ensor points, two with impact flutes, were found in the chest area of the individual (Figure 10.9; Hester 1989). New research into the ethnohistoric record (Maria Wade, personal communication, 2000) of Central and Southwest Texas provides examples of the awareness of territorial boundaries that were not to be crossed.

REFERENCES CITED

Bettis, A. C., Jr.
    1997   Chipped Stone Artifacts from the Killam Ranch, Webb County, Texas. *Texas Archeological Research Laboratory Research Notes* 5(2):3–23. Texas Archeological Research Laboratory, University of Texas at Austin.
Boyd, J. B., D. E. Wilson, T. R. Hester, and T. K. Perttula
    1997   Southern Island, A Prehistoric Cemetery Site in the Falcon Reservoir, Tamaulipas, Mexico. *Bulletin of the Texas Archeological Society* 68:387–425.
Brown, K. M.
    2002   Appendix F: Snails from the Quarter-Inch and Eighth-Inch Screens. In *The Smith Creek Bridge Site (41DW270), A Terrace*

Site in DeWitt County, Texas, by K. Hudler, K. Prilliman, and T. Gustavson, pp. 411–475. Studies in Archeology 35, Texas Archeological Research Laboratory, University of Texas at Austin, and Archeology Studies Program Report 17, Environmental Affairs Division, Texas Department of Transportation.

Brown, K. M., D. R. Potter, G. D. Hall, and S. L. Black

1982   *Excavation at 41LK67, a Prehistoric Site in the Choke Canyon Reservoir, South Texas.* Choke Canyon Series 7. Center for Archaeological Research, University of Texas at San Antonio.

Campbell, T. N.

1983   The Coahuiltecans and Their Neighbors. In *Handbook of North American Indians,* vol. 10, pp. 343–358. Smithsonian Institution, Washington, D.C.

Hall, G. D.

1981   *Allens Creek: A Study in the Cultural Prehistory of the Lower Brazos River Valley, Texas.* Research Report 61. Texas Archeological Survey, University of Texas at Austin.

Hall, G. D., S. L. Black, and C. Graves

1982   *Archaeological Investigations at Choke Canyon Reservoir, South Texas: The Phase I Findings.* Choke Canyon Series 5. Center for Archaeological Research, University of Texas at San Antonio.

Hall, G. D., T. R. Hester, and S. L. Black

1986   *The Prehistoric Sites at Choke Canyon Reservoir, Southern Texas: Results of Phase II Archaeological Investigations.* Choke Canyon Series 10. Center for Archaeological Research, University of Texas at San Antonio.

Hester, T. R.

1971   Archeological Investigations at the La Jita Site, Uvalde County, Texas. *Bulletin of the Texas Archeological Society* 41:51–148.

1978   A Summary of the 1975 Archaeological Investigations at Chaparrosa Ranch, Southern Texas. In *Background to the Archaeology of Chaparrosa Ranch, Southern Texas,* edited by T. R. Hester, pp. 40–46. Special Report 6. Center for Archaeological Research, University of Texas at San Antonio.

1981   Tradition and Diversity among the Prehistoric Hunters and Gatherers of Southern Texas. *Plains Anthropologist* 26(92):119–128.

1987   Archaeological Excavations at Site 41ME34, Medina County, Texas. *La Tierra* 14(4):3–5.

1989   A Late Archaic Burial from the Lower Nueces River Drainage, Live Oak County, Texas. *La Tierra* 16(2):2–3.

1995   The Prehistory of South Texas. *Bulletin of the Texas Archeological Society* 66:427–459.

1999   Artifacts, Archaeology and Cabeza de Vaca in Southern Texas and Northeastern Mexico. *Bulletin of the Texas Archeological Society* 70:17–28.

Hester, T. R., and M. B. Collins

1974   Evidence for Heat Treating of Southern Texas Projectile Points. *Bulletin of the Texas Archeological Society* 45:219–224.

Hester, T. R., and L. M. Green

1972   Functional Analysis of Large Bifaces from San Saba County, Texas. *Texas Journal of Science* 24(3):343–350.

Hester, T. R., and C. M. Whatley

1997   Archaeological Materials from the Middle Rio Grande, Southern Texas and Coahuila. *La Tierra* 24(2):3–12.

Highley, C. L.

1986   *Archaeological Investigations at 41LK201, Choke Canyon Reservoir, Southern Texas.* Choke Canyon Series 11. Center for Archaeological Research, University of Texas at San Antonio.

Hudler, D., K. Prilliman, and T. Gustavson

2002   *The Smith Creek Bridge Site (41DW270): A Terrace Site in DeWitt County, Texas.* Studies in Archeology 35, Texas Archeological Research Laboratory, University of Texas at Austin, and Archeology Studies Program Report 17, Environmental Affairs Division, Texas Department of Transportation, Austin.

Huebner, J. A., R. Blackburn, C. K. Chandler, J. L. Mitchell, and E. H. Schmiedlin

1996   Human Burial Recovery from 41KA89, Karnes County, Texas. *La Tierra* 23(1):16–20.

Kelly, Robert L.

1995   *The Foraging Spectrum: Diversity in Hunter-Gatherer Lifeways.* Smithsonian Press, Washington, D.C.

Labadie, Joseph H.

1988   *Archaeological Excavations at the Shrew Site 4lWN73, Wilson County, Southern Texas.* Contract Reports in Archaeology 2. Highway Design Division, Texas State Department of Highways and Public Transportation, Austin.

Lovata, T. R.

1997   Archaeological Investigations at the Silo Site (41KA102), a Prehistoric Cemetery in Karnes County, Texas. Master's thesis, Department of Anthropology, University of Texas at Austin.

Lukowski, P. D.

1988   *Archaeological Investigations at 41 BX 1, Bexar County, Texas.* Archaeological Survey Report 135. Center for Archaeological Research, University of Texas at San Antonio.

Miller, K. A.

1993   A Study of Prehistoric Biface Caches from Texas. Master's thesis, Department of Anthropology, University of Texas at Austin.

Mitchell, J. L., C. K. Chandler, and T. C. Kelly

1984   The Rudy Haiduk Site (41KA23): A Late Archaic Burial in Karnes County, Texas. *La Tierra* 11(2):12–39.

Mueggenborg, H. E.

1994   Excavations at the Blue Hole Site, Uvalde County, Texas, 1990. *Bulletin of the Texas Archeological Society* 62 (for 1991):1–74.

Patterson, L. W.

2000   Late Archaic Mortuary Tradition of Southeast Texas. *La Tierra* 27(2):28–44.

Quigg, J. M., C. Lintz, G. Smith, and S. Wilcox

2000   *The Lino Site: A Stratified Late Archaic Campsite in a Terrace of the San Idelfonzo Creek, Webb County, Southern Texas.* Technical Report 23757, TRC Mariah Associates, Inc., and Archeological Studies Report 20, Environmental Affairs Division. Texas Department of Transportation, Austin.

Ricklis, R. A.

1995   Prehistoric Occupation of the Central and Lower Texas Coast: A Regional Overview. *Bulletin of the Texas Archeological Society* 66:265–300.

Taylor, A. J., and C. L. Highley

1995   *Archeological Investigations at the Loma Sandia Site (41LK28): A Prehistoric Cemetery and Campsite in Live Oak County, Texas.* Vols. 1 and 2. Studies in Archeology 20. Texas Archeological Research Laboratory, University of Texas at Austin.

Turner, E. S., and T. R. Hester

1999   *A Field Guide to Stone Artifacts of Texas Indians.* Field Guide Series. Gulf Publishing, Houston.

Vierra, B. J.

1998   *41MV120: A Stratified Late Archaic Site in Maverick County, Texas.* Archaeological Survey Report 251, Center for Archaeological Research, University of Texas at San Antonio, and Archeology Studies Program Report 7. Texas Department of Transportation, Austin.

Woerner, M. C., and L. Highley

1982   The Bromley F. Cooper Collection of Pre-Archaic and Archaic Dart Points from McMullen County. *La Tierra* 10(1):3–28.

CHAPTER 11

Many Perspectives But a Consistent Pattern: Comments on Contributions

R. G. MATSON

Introduction

How and why agriculture arrived in some places and not in others has come to be an important question in the archaeology of the greater Southwest. The contributions in this volume address a range of adaptations from certain early agricultural communities to others where agriculture was only of marginal importance and even where agriculture was absent. The "Borderlands" is now the geographical locus for the investigation of this question. Bruce Smith, the other discussant, looks at the chapters in the larger context of agricultural origins in general.

The understanding of the coming of agriculture in the Southwest has changed dramatically in the last fifteen years. Perhaps most dramatic has been the redating of Tehuacán maize to no older than 4,700 radiocarbon years ago, rather than the 7,000 that had been accepted for thirty years (Long et al. 1989). Very recently two cobs have been dated from Guilá Naquitz that extend the age of maize to 5,400 years ago (Benz 2001; Piperno and Flannery 2001). When this shrinking of the age of maize is combined with the 1984 discovery of the agriculture-based Milagro San Pedro site by the Huckells (Huckell 1990; Huckell and Huckell 1984) dating to 2,900 radiocarbon years ago, the time between the earliest dated domesticated maize in Mexico and the first clear agricultural settlements in the United States Southwest is dramatically condensed, from circa 5,000 years (7000 BP maize in Mexico, 2000 BP Basketmaker II in the Southwest) to no more than 2,400 years (5400–3000 BP).

Smith's (1997) recent redating of ancient maize from Tamaulipas to no more than 3,930 radiocarbon years also supports a relatively recent age for the development of maize. Further, these earliest forms of maize are unlikely foundations for agriculturally dependent economies. The earliest dates for agricultural villages in Mexico are no more than 3,400 radiocarbon years ago—and some say no more than 3,200 years. Maize was likely not in widespread use as a cereal grain until shortly before then, when more productive varieties were developed. As the chapters by Hard and Roney and by Carpenter et al. indicate, extensive use of maize in the southern portions of the greater Southwest occurred very soon after this.

Another change in our understanding of early use of maize in the Southwest has been in its dietary significance. This development occurred well north of the Borderlands, on the Colorado Plateau, home of the Anasazi. Not that long ago many archaeologists believed that maize was not a critical part of the Anasazi subsistence pattern until relatively late, maybe even as recently as AD 1000 (Plog 1979). Even today one can read accounts that appear to support this view (Cordell 1997). Although some have long argued that certain Basketmaker II variants were agriculturally based (Eddy 1972), according to all current main lines of investigation (settlement pattern, coprolite analysis, midden analysis, and isotope analyses) the major Basketmaker II variants were approximately as dependent on maize agriculture as their later Pueblo descendants were (Androy 2003; Chisholm and Matson 1994; Martin 1999; Martin et al. 1991; Matson 1991, 1999; Matson and Chisholm 1991). These reports include the variants found at Black Mesa, Cedar Mesa, the Kanab area, and Navajo Reservoir as well as canyon dwellers in the Cedar Mesa area. On the Colorado Plateau by at least 2,000 years ago, the early users of maize were not modified hunters and gatherers but committed and dependent maize agriculturalists.

The situation in the Basin and Range Province to the south is not quite as certain, but most of the evidence is in accord with very early maize dependence. Huckell's (1990) dissertation presents evidence for extensive maize use in the "Milagro" phenomenon, 2,900 radiocarbon years ago, although (unlike on the Plateau) isotopic and coprolite support for this is not available. The contributions by Hard and Roney and by Carpenter et al. should be read carefully to see what evidence they present on this issue. There is no doubt, however, that the slightly later archaeological material reported by Mabry is agriculturally based, and this is still earlier than the Basketmaker evidence. Often, though, investigations do not distinguish between the presence of maize and evidence for dependence on it, which—particularly if the hypothesis of early use as a source of sugar (discussed below) turns out to be true—are two different things.

In contrast with the view twenty years ago, in both the Plateau and Basin and Range Provinces we now recognize a preceramic period with extensive use of maize. W. D. Lipe (1999:133) has called this the PPN (Pre-Pottery Neolithic), a term that emphasizes both the preceramic and agricultural aspects of this stage (technically, this should be the PPF, Pre-Pottery Formative). Given the compression of the period between the first known use of maize and agricultural villages in the Southwest, the likelihood of agriculture's "evolving in situ from indigenous hunters and gatherers" (Matson 1991:34) in the Southwest becomes less probable, and some sort of faster transfer between Mexico and the Southwest becomes more likely. The Borderlands is the area in which this should be investigated.

Agricultural villages could have expanded into all unoccupied niches where corn could be grown under the central Mexican regime of planting after the first monsoon rain in the summer (Matson 1991:207–216). Given the general accepted derivation of maize from Río Balsas teosinte, we can see this expansion occurring in all directions (Iltis 2000). As maize agriculture radiated north to the lowland Basin and Range Province, the main change in growing maize was from direct rainfall dry-farming (hereafter called "rainfall farming") and planting after the first monsoon rains to planting after the first flood, as not enough rain falls in the lowland Basin and Range for rainfall farming (Matson 1991:209–212). The location of the earliest agricultural villages in the Basin and Range Province is in good floodwater-farming environments (despite Cordell 1997:140 to the contrary). According to current dates, this spread from the Río Balsas region to the land under the Mogollon rim took less than 500 years— and may have happened in 200 years or less.

Christy Turner (1993) has presented evidence that this expansion included population movements, that is, migrations from deep in Mexico. His data are dental measurements that show that Western Basketmakers have many similarities with populations from central Mexico, which are not shared by Eastern Basketmakers or later Anasazi. The logic of a rapid spread of agriculture from central Mexico to the Southwest is buttressed by this evidence of biological affinity, best explained by migration(s) of the maize agriculturalists themselves.

This migration hypothesis is more than plausible, even compelling, according to current evidence (Matson 1991, 2003). This evidence, however, may well be radically revised at any time. The recent redating of maize is from collections thirty-five to fifty years old, and new investigations may discover older maize in Mexico. This would not necessarily result in significant change, as it is the varieties of maize that could be the basis of subsistence whose age is important, and this appears to be relatively securely dated.

There are intriguing hints that teosinte was originally domesticated not as a cereal but as a source of sugar (Iltis 2000:30; Smalley and Blake 2003). The recently dated Guilá Naquitz maize can be seen as supporting this new idea. Benz (2001) points out that these cobs do not appear to be different than the later (4700 BP) San Marcos Cave examples. This is hard to understand if the cobs were under intense selection pressures but would be reasonable if the stalks were valued for their sugar content and the cobs only used for reproduction. This idea might explain some recent dates in the Southwest that appear to be earlier than any agricultural villages in the New World (Mabry, this volume). In any event, maize that could reasonably be the basis of a sedentary agricultural lifeway appears to date only a little more than 3,000 radiocarbon years ago, far after these early small cob forms (less than 5 cm long) appear.

Earlier agricultural villages in Mesoamerica than currently recognized may exist. Because most early Formative villages are recognized by ceramics, the possibility of an earlier undiscovered "PPF" stage exists. As the amazing concentration of early PPF sites in Tucson only came to light after 1984, the equivalent PPF preceramic stage may well exist in Mexico. I understand, however, that the PPF is found in west Mexico (where it dates slightly later than the earliest Formative villages in central Mexico), so this possibility is probably on the way to resolution.

Even if agriculture came to the United States Southwest via a migration of maize farmers, the previously indigenous inhabitants would be exposed to, and possibly adopt, agriculture. I would expect the PPF would consist of a mosaic (Matson 2003) of migrants, indigenous Archaic people becoming agriculturalists, and other local indigenous populations remaining hunters and gatherers, although possibly picking up some attributes from the agriculturalists. Why some groups became agriculturalists and others did not is intriguing. Is it simply environmental, and agriculture was practiced where possible (as implied by Doleman, this volume)? Did the increased population density gained with successful agriculture trump everything else—including the almost certain greater instability because of crop failures that accompanied maize agriculture?

Given the possibility of a migrant group entering the space of other groups, one might expect large-scale conflict. Defensive sites, rock-art iconography, and human remains all testify that this is true for Basketmaker II (Farmer 1997; Hurst and Turner 1993; Matson 1994; Matson and Cole 1992, 2002). It is not certain, however, that this conflict is between the Western (migrants?) and Eastern (indigenous?) Basketmakers (Matson 1991, 1999, 2003). One might expect this pattern also to be found in the Basin and Range farther south, and this might explain the existence of early "Trincheras" defensive sites as reported by Hard and Roney in this volume.

This is the current understanding of the context for the advent of agriculture in the greater Southwest. Although most of this new understanding is based on research undertaken away from the Borderlands—either on the Colorado Plateau or deep within Mexico—it is clear that the resolution of this new set of questions will be dependent on Borderlands research (and, secondarily, research farther south). This new set of questions is the prism through which I review these chapters (discussed in the order of chapters in the original manuscript), looking at the PPF where it is, and where it is not, and why it is where it is.

The Carpenter et al. chapter includes an extensive review of Late Archaic and Early Agricultural sites in Sonora, Mexico. I found this review the most comprehensive available for this area, and it will be an important reference for some time. The heart of the chapter is the summary discussion of the La Playa site, which I was lucky to visit with John Carpenter in 1992 in a trip organized by Paul Fish. The extent of the site, the amount of fire-cracked rock, and the roasting pits are amazing. I find the evidence that the roasting pits (*hornos*) may have been used for a variety of foods but mainly for maize troubling. Do we know of any other situation with numerous roasting features that were used most frequently for maize?

The large number of burials is a unique feature. It would be very interesting to discover the reliance on C4 plants and to do a detailed morphological analysis comparing these remains with others in the Southwest and in Mexico in order to see if the patterns reported by Turner (1993) hold up with this new data set. The extensive shell industry reported raises the issue of the destination of the shell products. Arthur Vokes (personal communication, 2001) reports that a different method was used in producing *Glycymeris* bracelets at La Playa than was used later but that this is not discernible in the final product, which makes the identification of the destination of these bracelets difficult. The tentative identifications of source minerals (argillite and obsidian) with locations to the north in the U.S. Southwest indicate close connections at this time.

Carpenter et al. also suggest that the initial entrance of maize into the Southwest may have been in association with the Cortaro point and a reentry into the Sonoran Desert (after the Altithermal) by the "Proto-Sonoran-Uto-Aztecan" speakers. This is an interesting idea, but much remains to be done before this idea can be considered likely. Carpenter et al. suggest a "mixed" hunting and gathering and agricultural adaptation at La Playa, so an earlier adaptation would not rely on maize for a staple. Perhaps such an adaptation did occur, but with maize as a source of sugar, as suggested earlier. Certainly the early (circa 4,000-year-old) forms of maize currently known would not have been a good subsistence staple. Furthermore, the Hopi (Miller 1983) are traditionally considered to be most closely related to the northern Uto-Aztecan speakers; if they are partially descendants of San Pedro people (via the Western Basketmakers and the Kayenta Anasazi), as appears likely, then the San Pedro includes Northern Uto-Aztecan speakers as well as Southern Uto-Aztecan speakers. Hill (2001), though, has presented a fairly radical alternative revision of the Uto-Aztecan languages that would be more consistent with this scenario. I raise these points to demonstrate that other alternatives would also fit the observations made and that the situation was probably much more complicated than we can discern today.

Two points were missing in this chapter that I expected to see discussed: first, the very obvious aggrading nature of Río Boquillas and thus the presence of floodwater agriculture at the La Playa site and, second, the relationship between La Playa and the neighboring Trincheras type site. The La Playa site is clearly on a aggrading plain and thus fits the pattern seen elsewhere of the borderland PPF sites around Tucson and as reported in northern Chihuahua. This fits the pattern I predicted in 1985 (Matson 1991), prior to my knowledge of the Milagro site. The Trincheras site is nearby and, I expect, would have begun at the same period as the La Playa site, based on the work in Chihuahua and the dating of the Tumamoc Hill Trincheras site in Tucson (Fish et al. 1986; Wilcox 1978) (not that I thought of this on that visit in 1992). Do the authors have some reason to dismiss this idea for the Trincheras type-site? If so, it would be nice to know.

Carpenter et al.'s chapter summarizes the current understanding of this very large and important PPF site and explains how the authors view its archaeological context. The apparent close connection with more northern sites is surprising but may be the result of this stage being better known to the north than elsewhere in Sonora.

Jonathan Mabry takes us on a rapid tour of the new information on the PPF that has appeared in the last few years from Tucson, buttressed by a very thorough literature review of both the recent archaeological and paleoenvironmental research. This work reinforces several ideas put forward by Bruce Huckell (1984, 1990): namely, that the San Pedro phase includes both agricultural villages and nonagricultural sites; that the San Pedro was followed by a closely related Cienega phase, which is now being subdivided; and that the Cochise tradition should be reconceptualized as being part of the general Southwestern Archaic.

Mabry points out that the distinctions presented by Doleman (this volume) in discussing the environmental differences between southeastern Arizona and southwestern New Mexico also apply within southeastern Arizona and may explain some of the archaeological variability that exists there. He also argues for a clear separation between the San Pedro phase and the earlier Archaic and a possible connection between the introduction of farming and Uto-Aztecan speakers. This general position is not too different from the arguments presented in the chapter by Carpenter et al., but Mabry sees farming and Uto-Aztecan speakers arriving prior to the San Pedro phase, perhaps with the Cortaro point. In a previous version of this chapter, he argued for the correlation with the San Pedro phase, a position not too different from that presented in the chapter by Carpenter et al. (this volume), although it did differ in details. I suspect it is too soon to be able to decide which of these various pictures is to be preferred. Certainly this contribution has different assumptions from those in some other chapters, where migrations appear to be ruled out on some unknown grounds.

Mabry describes three new traits for the San Pedro phase: (1) irrigation ditches from the Santa Cruz River and either drainage ditches or ditches diverting floodwaters to fields from higher grounds; (2) the likely presence of cotton, and (3) a limited ceramic technology. The presence of irrigation ditches is as early as any other noted in the Americas. The Tucson finds are reinforced by similar ditches reported by Jonathan Damp (2001) at Zuni, with similar dates. These findings indicate that ditch irrigation likely arrived as part of the PPF adaptation. One might expect that ditches would be first used in the Basin and Range Province, as farming was dependent on floodwater farming in contrast to the rainfall farming standard in central Mexico. The Zuni example lacks clear archaeological settlement associations but also is in a "floodwater" farming setting. The lack of significant difference in time between central Mexico and the Southwest for a number of "advanced" agricultural characteristics is certainly a surprise.

The size of the Cienega phase villages is astounding, as is the presence of "large, communal-ceremonial structures" (Mabry, this volume). It is possible that this level of aggregation did not occur again in the Southwest for more than 1,000 years! The relatively modest nature of the domestic structures may indicate many occupations rather than a few large ones, giving a more modest picture of the size and duration of the settlements.

Mabry reports the possible presence of a domesticated bean dated to 1200 BC (calendrically corrected). Bruce Smith (2001) has recently reviewed the evidence for this domesticate and reports that the earliest known bean in Mexico is dated to 250 BC. I will read his comment on this find with interest. One probably needs several examples, or at least a very good one that can be examined by a number of investigators, to accept that the age of this domesticate has increased by a thousand years. Mabry also discusses how the introduction of agriculture likely was dependent on a favorable hydraulic regime, something also previously argued by Huckell (1990) and indicated by several other contributions to this volume.

Mabry reviews the evidence for what he describes as "the long, unnamed interval of incipient agriculture that preceded the San Pedro phase." This includes several direct radiocarbon dates on maize in the middle Santa Cruz Valley, a cluster of pits at the Las Capas site, the Sweetwater Locus of the Los Pozos site, which included pit structures and pits, and a maize date from McEuen

Cave reported by Huckell et al. (1999). I question the use of the word "agri-culture" to describe this material; use of domesticated plants, yes, but a seden-tary way of life based on domesticated plants remains to be demonstrated. The reports from Las Capas and the Sweetwater Locus have yet to be published, and from Mabry's summary only the Sweetwater Locus has the potential to have the sort of information to determine "agriculture" or "PPF." Remembering that maize has a long history—3,000 years—from the earliest dates in Mexico to the first well-established use as the foundation of "agricultural villages," it should not be surprising that we have dates for maize that precede the PPF in the Southwest, particularly if the "Sweetness" hypothesis is correct. The reported dates for the Sweetwater Locus (3300 and 3200 b.p.) are coeval with the first established Formative villages in Mexico—not an impossible situation, but an unlikely one, if this Southwestern site is the result of dependence on maize.

It is perplexing to try to understand how the Tucson PPF sites were missed when the freeways were built in the 1960s, or even why it took until the late 1980s for them to be discovered. That these amazing sites were not known in what may be the area with the largest concentration of archaeologists in the Americas makes me leery of assuming that something similar, but earlier, is not present (but as yet undiscovered) in Mexico or elsewhere in Mesoamerica or in other parts of the Southwest.

William Doleman takes it as his task to explain why sites demonstrating a "reliance" on maize agriculture occur by 1000 BC in southeastern Arizona but not until AD 500–600 in southern New Mexico highlands and AD 1000–1100 in the lowlands. Basically he looks to see if there are geographical or environ-mental factors that may explain this difference. He examines a number of ways of measuring the similarities and differences between the two areas.

First he looks at the average number of plant communities ("biomes") per unit distance in a cross section in the valleys. He finds twice as many per 100 km in southeastern Arizona as in New Mexico, indicating more diversity per unit area in the west. I find it difficult to evaluate his precipitation table; most values appear to be similar to me, except for the rainfall reliability, which is defined as the minimum rain that would fall in 95 of 100 years. Finally, he compares biotic richness (focusing on number of species) in the two areas. It is no surprise that the Sonoran Desert is more diverse than the Chihuahuan Desert. Finally, there is some evidence that there is less variability, both climatically and in terms of plant productivity, in the west than in the east.

The combination of all these factors indicates more diversity, more predict-ability, and different environments that are closer at hand in the west. Doleman argues that the Arizona Archaic peoples would have less large-scale residential mobility and therefore have fewer scheduling conflicts in adopting agriculture than those in New Mexico.

Although this is a logically consistent argument, it assumes that the averages are the important measure and that agriculture originates in the Southwest through adoption by indigenous hunters and gatherers, both highly questionable. For instance, I find it difficult not to see the Mimbres valley as an ideal place for early floodwater agriculture. The average value is assumed to indicate that significant locations (or exceptions) like that do not occur. More to the point, the early Cerro Juanaqueña Trincheras site is located out in the Chihuahuan Desert, with all the disadvantages cited by Doleman—albeit with a nice aggrading floodplain and flooding river adjacent to it—and is currently the oldest known PPF site in the Southwest. And there is certainly enough evidence for a migration from the south, so that it also merits discussion.

Hard and Roney report on their excavations at Cerro Juanaqueña, the earliest Southwestern farming community yet discovered, and what the results there indicate about the introduction of farming to the extreme southeastern part of the Southwest. Significant new features include the dating of other Trincheras sites as well as good evidence for agricultural dependency and for long-duration occupation of Cerro Juanaqueña.

Two other Trincheras sites along the Río Casas Grandes are found to date to the same period as Cerro Juanaqueña, which now appears to begin just over 3,000 radiocarbon years ago, approximately 100 years earlier than the dates from the earliest villages around Tucson. A third Trincheras site, Cerro Vidal, has two dates of a little more than 2,000 years ago but no older. As Cerro Juanaqueña also has some dates of this order, the authors suggest that this pinpoints another episode of Trincheras activity. There are also dates (Fish et al. 1986) of Trincheras sites in Arizona of this order that may indicate that most, or even all, Trincheras sites were originally built during the PPF. David Wilcox (1978) found that the Tumamoc Hill site in Tucson would have been an effective defensive structure in the atlatl age, supporting such an inference.

Excavations of rock ring structures on the terraces at Cerro Juanaqueña indicate that they are likely poorly preserved houses, with a variety of stone tools. This inference is in accord with the abundant ground stone found at this site. Two large storage pits were also excavated, indicating extensive food storage, and at least one contained maize.

The faunal remains show that jackrabbits and cottontails are the most common animals, a pattern that continues over much of the Southwest during agricultural times (Brand 1995). Although many different kinds of remains were found in the flotation analyses, maize was the most common, indicating that it was a dietary staple, a conclusion in agreement with a wide variety of information now available from this remarkable site.

Also present is a possible domesticated amaranth, the first yet found in the Southwest. It would be very interesting to see if amaranth shows up in early agricultural villages in Mexico. Along with these domesticates, many wild plants are also present, showing that collecting was still an important activity.

Hard and Roney conclude that Cerro Juanaqueña was probably occupied for nine months of the year, most likely by a group of 200 individuals for about 200 years. Thus this site, located adjacent to an aggrading floodplain of a river, in an ideal floodwater farming location, is not only the earliest farming community noted in the Southwest but probably a large sedentary one, where defense was an important consideration. I know of no one who predicted such a community, indicating that the past is indeed independent of archaeologists and their wishes.

After reviewing these findings, Hard and Roney discuss different alternatives for the arrival of agriculture in the Southwest and develop an optimal foraging theory model focusing on the return per hour for farming, following Barlow (1997). This is all well and good, but likely beside the point. The important economic factor is population density, even if caloric returns per hour are the same or even lower. (A good summary comparing foraging and agricultural returns is found in *Environment, Subsistence, and System* by Roy Ellen [1982:133].) The extraordinary population at Cerro Juanaqueña is almost impossible to see from a hunting and gathering economy even in resource-rich areas. Similarly, I (Matson 2003) have calculated that the Basketmaker II on Cedar Mesa had approximately eighteen times the population density of the mainly hunting and gathering Walapai in similar environments. The different times for the development of agriculture in the Southwest discussed by Hard and Roney are more apt to be the results of developments allowing more areas to be agricultural rather than different rates of return. Hard and Roney do discuss this as well.

Hard and Roney also review paleoecological evidence that the first occupation of Cerro Juanaqueña corresponds to a moist period. Huckell (1990) found something similar; the San Pedro Cochise appeared to co-occur with a period of stream aggradation, which is necessary for main stem floodwater farming (as opposed to *ak chin* style), a finding also supported in the chapter by Mabry.

Mallouf's chapter introduces us to the problems in understanding the Late Archaic—defined as 3000–1000 BP—of the Trans-Pecos/Big Bend region. Despite a long history of archaeological research and extensive recent survey there are few modern excavations of the quality needed to resolve the issues that are central to this volume. Interestingly enough, palynological work suggests an increased effective moisture period of circa 3000–2500 BP, close to the time of introduction of agriculture elsewhere. The eastern portions of this area probably were always inhabited by hunters and gatherers, while the people to the west, around El Paso, apparently became dependent on agriculture by about 1900 BP with the introduction of the Hueco phase, according to Mallouf. The Hueco phase, though, is dated by others as beginning significantly earlier (MacNeish 1993).

The Late Archaic is associated with a plethora of dart-point styles, most of them found only in Texas, although San Pedro points are present too. Large hearths, slab-lined storage pits, and burned rock middens also occur, indicating relatively large-scale resource processing and storage.

The settlement pattern data show a concentration in the intermediate elevations, with the largest middens adjacent to springs. Mallouf reports a complicated pattern with many environmental foci as well as one showing a population increase in the Late Archaic. The Late Archaic subsistence pattern is inferred "with confidence" to include hunting a wide variety of animals and collecting agave, prickly pear, sotol, and yucca. Well-documented and dated assemblages are rare, because of the historic excavations and large-scale potting of rock-shelter sites. It would be interesting to see how the complicated settlement pattern matches with the inferred subsistence use. Mallouf points out that the burned rock middens only become common toward the end of the Late Archaic, indicating that agave and sotol were not important in the first part of this period. Dering's chapter points to an explanation of this late occurrence; these plants actually do not produce a high return and thus would be added to the subsistence effort only after higher-return procurement systems had been exploited. Mallouf indicates that before the exploitation of sotol and agave there was a greater emphasis on hunting and a greater residential mobility.

Mallouf's review of cultigen use in the Late Archaic indicates that (although early excavations and private collections from rockshelters appear to show maize in some of these collections) recent, more controlled excavations find that the maize is from the succeeding late prehistoric period. There is no convincing evidence for large-scale use or local planting, and such material as may be present may have been obtained via trade from the west. If maize was used, it was only toward the end of the Late Archaic.

Why was maize not used? No compelling reason is given. One wonders if some obvious environmental or climate factor might appear if a study like Doleman's was carried out. Not having personal familiarity with this area, I have no suggestions to make. The fact that maize was used in the last 1,000 years indicates that growing maize is possible, at least in some situations with certain technologies. Certainly, a general trend to a more intensified subsistence pattern with a growing focus on resources that take extensive processing and are storable is evident, a trend one might expect to be compatible with an agricultural way of life. The next chapter examines the economics of the intensified use of agave and similar resources.

Dering looks at the economy and environment of the Late Archaic around the confluence of the Pecos River and the Rio Grande, which overlaps with part of the area described by Mallouf. This region is relatively flat but incised by deep canyons. Dering reports that the rainfall peaks in spring and fall, with a strong summer drought. It also occurs in extremely variable annual amounts, which together with the annual pattern may explain the lack of agriculture in this region. The analysis of plant remains and coprolites shows a long-standing reliance on agave, sotol, and prickly pear, with the first two processed in earth ovens. Dering's very interesting yield experiments with sotol and agave (lechuguilla) demonstrate that, despite the high archaeological visibility, the gross yield and caloric yield per hour are minor, with a typical oven yielding only about two days of food for a family, far below many other resource estimates. Because few calories are present it does not make sense to move the resource far for processing, which means both the plant resource and the wood needed for roasting would rapidly be depleted in areas where both are present.

Dering uses this information to reinterpret the archaeology of the region as one where the hunter-gatherers would be forced to "map onto continually changing distributions of regional resources." Thus rockshelters showing evidence of use during all seasons of the year do not mean long duration residence over a number of seasons but instead reuse over a long period at varying seasons. Accordingly, we have a very mobile pattern in response to sparse and unpredictable resources (Dyson-Hudson and Smith 1978; Matson 1985).

Dering contrasts this environment with that of the southern Basin and Range, pointing out (as did Doleman) the greater diversity of environments in the southern Basin and Range and how the difference in timing and reliability of precipitation would affect agriculture. His conclusions appear to be well founded and plausible; thus we have a reasonable explanation for the lack of agriculture in the Lower Pecos region.

One change in the Late Archaic that Dering does not discuss is the increased use of sotol and dropseed grass. I predict that this change is also one increasing diet breadth and a move to less productive resources.

Dropseed grass (*Sporobolus* sp.) is abundant in Early Archaic coprolites on the Colorado Plateau (Hogan 1980; Van Ness 1986). Is its early use on the Colorado Plateau indicative of the paucity of resources there? If so, this means that evolutionary pressures create different adaptive stages in neighboring areas. Or does early plateau dropseed use just reflect a greater productivity of this resource in that environment?

Hester's chapter is concerned with the area farthest south and east, the Rio Grande Plain, up to the coastal strip. He discusses the thousand years between approximately 500 BC and AD 500. This period appears to be represented by a variety of dart points not clearly similar to any others in the Borderlands.

It is interesting that the informative investigations are from sites in riparian environments with mussels, snails, fish, frogs, and turtles—hardly resources discussed in other chapters—along with mammals. The other material remains, particularly ground stone tools, appear to be those expected for the "Archaic." It is assumed that in more arid areas the usual resources (mesquite beans, prickly pear fruit, etc.) are exploited. Hester reviews an interesting and promising attempt by Quigg et al. (2000) to look at lipids extraction from burned rocks and ground stone to support such inferences.

In general, this material appears to be only distantly related to events elsewhere, in terms of either artifacts or subsistence patterns. The Borderlands, as defined in the introduction to this commentary, do not extend to this region. (As defined in the volume introduction, though, they do.) It would be interesting to discover why, because it is not far from Tamaulipas, with its evidence of earlier use of domesticated plants. I suspect that the precipitation is not sufficient to grow maize by rainfall agriculture and that floodwater farming is not easy without a high level of technology. Clearly, the PPF is not present here.

Chapter 4 gives us a very different perspective on the adoption of maize agriculture. Ogilvie compares three populations on the basis of the "gracilization" of femora and amount of mobility based on other information. The three skeletal populations consist of Big Bend Late Archaic, Tucson PPF, and Pueblo IV Pottery Mound (central New Mexico) samples. The idea is that the cortical thickness and cross-sectional shape of the femur is directly related to the mobility of the individual. Ogilvie presents evidence that this relationship is supported in a number of other studies. Hunters and gatherers are expected to be the most mobile and therefore have the most robust femora; and sedentary maize agriculturalists, the least. She predicts that the three populations will show measurements that reflect this trend. Her expectation is that the Tucson PPF would be "transitional" in cortical thickness. This derives from her understanding that the Tucson PPF economy was a mixed hunting and gathering subsistence system, according to Huckell and Mabry. This last assumption is somewhat surprising, given that Brian Chisholm and R. G. Matson (1994),

S. L. Martin (1999), Matson (1991), and Matson and Chisholm (1991) (and Huckell 1990) present evidence showing that the PPF is consistent with a dependent agricultural adaptation.

Although the expected trend is found, Olgivie's analysis also shows a very interesting detailed picture. In the Big Bend Archaic samples males and females show very similar values; but in the PPF male femora are fully as robust as in the Big Bend population, although the females are similar to the Pottery Mound females! In the Pottery Mound sample the male values fall between the Big Bend and PPF females, and the females are the least robust of any sample, although apparently not significantly different from the PPF females at these sample sizes.

One can conclude from this that the effect of maize agriculture altered first female mobility and then male mobility. These findings support other evidence that the PPF is not "transitional" but rather a variety of maize dependency. It also substantiates the idea that the females were the main agriculturalists, while the males were the long-distance foragers. Julian Steward (1937, 1955) would have liked this, and the late James Hill (1970) would have as well. Is this the earliest evidence for the Southwestern matrilocality? This chapter is a very interesting and provocative study—provocative in the interpretation and because the sample sizes are still relatively modest (only seven PPF females).

Vierra's chapter looks at the lithic assemblage found at Cerro Juanaqueña, but in a very broad context of assemblages from northern New Mexico, the Colorado Plateau Archaic and Pueblo, and Archaic Texas. I read this chapter always thinking about the Cedar Mesa Basketmaker II (Keller 1982; Matson 1981, 1991, 1994; Matson and Lipe 1975; Matson et al. 1988, n.d.; Nelson 1994) and comparisons I have made at different levels with other Basketmaker II, San Pedro, and PPF Mogollon assemblages (Matson 1991).

Vierra notes that a full range of lithic reduction techniques are found at Cerro Juanaqueña, in accord with David Pokotylo's (1978) expectation for base-camps and as has been found to hold for a variety of Archaic (Magne 1985) and Anasazi contexts (Matson 1981). This finding is consistent with other evidence, such as the terraces and worn ground stone implements, indicating a long residential duration at this site. Although most of the raw material is from local river gravels, the identified obsidian sources of the excavated material indicate access to areas to the south and east and not the well-known sources to the north, in the southern Colorado Plateau. This is consistent with the idea that the inhabitants of this early agricultural site have their origins and connections in those areas and not with the Southwestern Archaic people in the Southern Mogollon Highlands, that is, consistent with a migration from farther south (and east?) in Mexico. Interestingly enough, later projectile point types (surface collected) do show the more northern connections, strengthening this interpretation.

I was struck by the biface to core ratio being essentially the same as that of the Cedar Mesa Basketmaker II. There the ratio ranges from 1.70 in Basketmaker II to 0.83 in Pueblo III (Nelson 1994:284). The general shift from more bifaces to less bifaces and more expedient tools occurs within the Anasazi on Cedar Mesa (Matson 1981; Matson et al. n.d.; Nelson 1994). I mistrust, though, taking some of these comparisons at face value. There are significant differences in some of these variables between Cedar Mesa and Black Mesa Basketmaker II (Christenson 1987; Matson 1981; Matson et al. n.d.), with no more than 100 years and 40 km of separation (the two mesas are visible from each other). In this case, it is the extensive use of "baked siltstone" at Black Mesa that accounts for many of the differences.

In contrast to Vierra's summary statement about the Cerro Juanaqueña lithic assemblage being "oriented toward a mixed foraging and agricultural economy," the features he cites, as far as I can tell, are present in the Basketmaker II, which is definitely agricultural (Brand 1995; Chisholm and Matson 1994; Martin 1999; Matson 1991, 1994; Matson and Chisholm 1991), as Hard and Roney (this volume) also indicate for Cerro Juanaqueña. I suspect that two factors make lithic technology not very sensitive to this issue. First, the differences between Archaic (and PPF) and later Pueblo lithic technologies are apt to have to do more with the transition from atlatls to bow and arrows than with anything else. Specifically, one needs large cores of high-quality material to make large atlatl points, and making large bifaces produces a strong signal in many aspects of lithic analysis. Second, chipped stone technology is not apt to be sensitive to the amount of agriculture, because it is not an important component of that activity and because the traditional tasks associated with sensitive parts of lithic technology—hunting and butchering—coexist along with agriculture, as suggested by Olgivie's research. Elsewhere Vierra (2001) has presented an interpretation that is complementary to the one I am offering here. Be that as it may, detailed, careful work like that presented by Vierra will enable us to discover these relationships.

The contributions in this volume demonstrate the great progress we have made in understanding the origins of the Southwest culture area. Now, more than ever, it appears to be a complex development, mainly dependent not on a single process but on a complex series of events, as shown by the variety of approaches used by the various investigators and the resulting contributions. In some areas we appear to have continuity with indigenous Archaic populations and a gradual process of resource intensification, which may or may not end up with agriculture at some later time. In other cases large, complex,

Neolithic/Formative villages appear as out of nowhere, indicative of migration of agricultural people from elsewhere. Situations that are in between and indeterminate also exist. We need a broad range of contributions, looking at this period from many perspectives, to unravel this complicated pattern. Almost none of these contributions could have been written twenty years ago.

REFERENCES CITED

Androy, Jerry
    2003   Agriculture and Mobility during the Basketmaker II Period: The Coprolite Evidence. Master's thesis, Department of Anthropology, Northern Arizona University, Flagstaff.

Barlow, K. R.
    1997   Foragers That Farm: A Behavioral Ecology Approach to the Economics of Corn Farming for the Fremont Case. Ph.D. dissertation, Department of Anthropology, University of Utah, Salt Lake City. UMI Dissertation Services, Ann Arbor.

Benz, B.
    2001   Archaeological Evidence of Teosinte Domestication from Guilá Naquitz, Oaxaca. *Proceedings of the National Academy of Sciences* 98:2104–2106.

Brand, M.
    1995   Prehistoric Anasazi Diet: A Synthesis of Archaeological Evidence. Master's thesis, Department of Anthropology and Sociology, University of British Columbia, Vancouver.

Chisholm, B., and R. G. Matson
    1994   Carbon and Nitrogen Isotopic Evidence on Basketmaker II Diet at Cedar Mesa, Utah. *Kiva* 60:239–256.

Christenson, A.
    1987   Projectile Points: Eight Millennia of Projectile Change on the Colorado Plateau. In *Prehistoric Stone Technology on Northern Black Mesa, Arizona,* edited by W. J. Parry and A. Christenson, pp. 143–198. Center for Archaeological Investigations Research Paper 12. Southern Illinois University at Carbondale, Carbondale.

Cordell, L. S.
    1997   *Archaeology of the Southwest.* 2nd ed. Academic Press, San Diego.

Damp, J.
    2001   The Origins of Zuni as Seen from Zuni. Paper presented at the Zuni/Mogollon Seminar, Museum of Northern Arizona, Flagstaff.

Dyson-Hudson, R., and E. Smith
1978   Human Territoriality: An Ecological Reassessment. *American Anthropologist* 80:21–41.

Eddy, F. W.
1972   Culture Ecology and the Prehistory of the Navajo Reservoir District. *Southwestern Lore* 38(1 and 2):1–75.

Ellen, R.
1982   *Environment, Subsistence, and System: The Ecology of Small Scale Social Formations.* Cambridge University Press, Cambridge.

Farmer, J. D.
1997   Iconographic Evidence of Basketmaker Warfare and Human Sacrifice: A Contextual Approach to Early Anasazi Art. *Kiva* 62:391–420.

Fish, P., S. Fish, A. Long, and C. Miksicek
1986   Early Corn Remains from Tumamoc Hill, Southern Arizona. *American Antiquity* 51:563–572.

Hill, James
1970   *Broken K Pueblo: Prehistoric Social Organization in the American Southwest.* Anthropological Papers of the University of Arizona No. 18. University of Arizona Press, Tucson.

Hill, Jane
2001   Proto-Uto-Aztecan: A Community of Cultivators in Central Mexico? *American Anthropologist* 103(4):913–934.

Hogan, P. F.
1980   The Analysis of Human Coprolites from Cowboy Cave, Appendix IX. In *Cowboy Cave,* by J. D. Jennings, pp. 201–211. Anthropological Papers No. 103. University of Utah Press, Salt Lake City.

Huckell, B. B.
1984   *The Archaic Occupation of the Rosemont Area, Northern Santa Rita Mountains, Southeastern Arizona.* Archaeological Series No. 147. Vol. 1. Cultural Resource Management Division, Arizona State Museum, Tucson.

1990   Late Preceramic Farmer-Foragers in Southeastern Arizona: A Cultural and Ecological Consideration of the Spread of Agriculture in the Arid Southwestern United States. Ph.D. dissertation, Department of Arid Lands Resource Sciences, University of Arizona, Tucson.

Huckell, B. B., and L. W. Huckell
1984   Excavations at Milagro, a Late Archaic Site in the Eastern Tucson Basin. Report on file, Arizona State Museum, Tucson.

Huckell, B. B., L. W. Huckell, and S. K. Fish

1995   *Investigations at Milagro, a Late Preceramic Site in the Eastern Tucson Basin.* Technical Report 94(5). Center for Desert Archaeology, Tucson, Arizona.

Huckell, B. B., L. W. Huckell, and M. S. Shackley

1999   McEuen Cave. *Archaeology Southwest* 13(1):12.

Hurst, W. B., and C. Turner II

1993   Rediscovering the "Great Discovery": Wetherill's First Cave and Its Record of Basketmaker Violence. In *Anasazi Basketmaker: Papers from the 1990 Wetherill-Grand Gulch Symposium,* edited by V. M. Atkins, pp. 143–191. Cultural Resource Series No. 24. Bureau of Land Management, Salt Lake City, Utah.

Iltis, H.

2000   Homeotic Sexual Translocations and the Origin of Maize (*Zea mays,* Poaceae): A New Look at an Old Problem. *Economic Botany* 54:7–42.

Keller, D. R.

1982   Lithic Source Identifications through Macroscopic Analysis: An Example from Cedar Mesa, Southeastern Utah. *Kiva* 47(3):163–169.

Lipe, W. D.

1999   Basketmaker II (1000 B.C.–A.D. 500). In *Colorado Prehistory: A Context for the Southern Colorado River Basin,* edited by W. D. Lipe, M. Varien, and R. H. Wilhausen, pp. 132–165. Colorado Council of Professional Archaeologists, Denver.

Long, A., B. F. Benz, D. J. Donahue, A. J. T. Jull, and L. J. Toolin

1989   First Direct AMS Dates on Early Maize from Tehuacán, Mexico. *Radiocarbon* 31:1035–1040.

MacNeish, Richard S. (editor)

1993   *Preliminary Investigations of the Archaic in the Region of Las Cruces, New Mexico.* Historic and Natural Resources Report No. 9. Cultural Resources Management Branch, Directorate of Environment, Fort Bliss, Tex.

Magne, M.

1985   *Lithics and Livelihood: Stone Tool Technologies of Central and Southern British Columbia.* National Museum of Man Mercury Series, Paper No. 133. Archaeological Survey of Canada, Ottawa.

Martin, D. L., A. H. Goodman, G. J. Armelagos, and A. L. Magennis

1991   *Black Mesa Anasazi Health: Reconstructing Life from Patterns of*

Death and Disease. Center for Archaeological Investigations, Occasional Paper No. 14. Southern Illinois University, Carbondale.

Martin, S. L.

1999   Virgin Anasazi Diet as Demonstrated through the Analysis of Stable Carbon and Nitrogen Isotopes. *Kiva* 64:495–514.

Matson, R. G.

1981   Site Function and Lithic Reduction Analysis at Cedar Mesa, Utah. Paper presented at the 46th Annual Meeting of the Society for American Archaeology, San Diego.

1985   The Relationship between Sedentism and Status: Inequalities among Hunters and Gatherers. In *Status, Structure, and Stratification: Current Archaeological Reconstructions,* edited by M. Hanna and B. Kooyman, pp. 233–241. Proceedings of the 13th Annual Chacmool Conference, Calgary, Alberta.

1991   *Origins of Southwestern Agriculture.* University of Arizona Press, Tucson.

1994   Anomalous Basketmaker II Sites on Cedar Mesa: Not So Anomalous after All. *Kiva* 60:219–238.

1999   The Spread of Maize to the Colorado Plateau. *Archaeology Southwest* 13(1):10–11.

2003   The Spread of Maize Agriculture in the U.S. Southwest. In *Examining the Farming/Language Dispersal Hypothesis,* edited by P. Bellwood and C. Renfrew, pp. 341–356. McDonald Institute for Archaeological Research, University of Cambridge.

Matson, R. G., and B. Chisholm

1991   Basketmaker II Subsistence: Carbon Isotopes and Other Dietary Indicators from Cedar Mesa, Utah. *American Antiquity* 56:444–459.

Matson, R. G., and S. Cole

1992   Ethnicity and Conflict among the Basketmaker II of the United States Southwest. Paper presented at the 25th Annual Chacmool Conference, Calgary, Alberta.

2002   Ethnicity and Conflict among the Basketmaker II of the United States Southwest. In *The Archaeology of Contact: Processes and Consequences,* edited by K. Lesick, B. Kulle, C. Cluney, and M. Peuramaki-Brown, pp. 206–217. Archaeological Association of the University of Calgary, Calgary.

Matson, R. G., and W. D. Lipe

1975   Regional Sampling: A Case Study of Cedar Mesa, Utah. In *Sam-*

pling in Archaeology, edited by J. Mueller, pp. 124–143. University of Arizona Press, Tucson.

Matson, R. G., W. D. Lipe, and W. Haase

1988   Adaptational Continuities and Occupational Discontinuities: The Cedar Mesa Anasazi. *Journal of Field Archaeology* 15:245–264.

n.d.   Human Adaptation on Cedar Mesa, Southeastern Utah. Manuscript in possession of the senior author, Laboratory of Archaeology, University of British Columbia.

Miller, W.

1983   Uto-Aztecan Languages. In *Handbook of North American Indians,* vol. 10, *Southwest,* edited by A. Ortiz, pp. 113–124. Smithsonian Institution, Washington, D.C.

Nelson, R.

1994   Basketmaker II Lithic Technology and Mobility Patterns on Cedar Mesa, Southeastern Utah. *Kiva* 60:277–288.

Piperno, D. R., and K. V. Flannery

2001   The Earliest Archaeological Maize (*Zea mays* L.) from Highland Mexico: New Accelerator Mass Spectrometry Dates and Their Implications. *Proceedings of the National Academy of Sciences* 98:2101–2103.

Plog, F. T.

1979   Prehistory: Western Anasazi. In *Handbook of North American Indians,* vol. 9, *Southwest,* edited by A. Ortiz, pp. 108–130. Smithsonian Institution, Washington, D.C.

Pokotylo, D.

1978   Lithic Technology and Settlement Pattern in Upper Hat Creek Valley, B.C. Ph.D. dissertation, Department of Anthropology and Sociology, University of British Columbia, Vancouver.

Quigg, J. M., C. Lintz, G. Smith, and S. Wilcox

2000   *The Lino Site: A Stratified Late Archaic Campsite in a Terrace of the San Idelfonzo Creek, Webb County, Southern Texas.* Technical Report 23757, TRC Mariah Associates, Inc., and Archeological Studies Report 20, Environmental Affairs Division. Texas Department of Transportation, Austin.

Smalley, John, and Michael Blake

2003   Sweet Beginnings. *Current Anthropology* 44(5):675–703.

Smith, B. D.

1997   Reconsidering the Ocampo Caves and the Era of Incipient Cultivation of Mesoamerica. *Latin American Antiquity* 9:342–383.

2001   Documenting Plant Domestication: The Consilience of Biological and Archaeological Approaches. *Proceedings of the National Academy of Sciences* 98:1324–1326.

Steward, J.

1937   Ecological Aspects of Southwestern Society. *Anthropos* 32:87–104.

1955   *The Theory of Culture Change: The Methodology of Multilineal Evolution.* University of Illinois Press, Urbana.

Turner, C. G., II

1993   Southwest Indian Teeth. *National Geographic Research and Exploration* 9(1):32–53.

Van Ness, M.

1986   Desha Complex Macrobotanical Fecal Remains: An Archaic Diet in the American Southwest. Master's thesis, Department of Anthropology, Northern Arizona University, Flagstaff.

Vierra, B. J.

2001   Mobility, Labor, and Technology: A Re-evaluation of Late Archaic Village Formation along the Borderlands. Paper presented at the 66th Annual Meetings of the Society for American Archaeology, New Orleans.

Wilcox, D.

1978   Warfare Implications of Dry-Laid Masonry Walls on Tumamoc Hill. *Kiva* 45:15–38.

CHAPTER 12

Documenting the Transition to Food Production along the Borderlands

BRUCE D. SMITH

Introduction

The chapters in this volume offer a range of new approaches and insights regarding the transition to food production economies along the Borderlands of northwestern Mexico and the southwestern United States. The authors of these chapters also clearly grapple, in interesting ways, with many of the same general challenges and difficulties faced by researchers attempting to unravel similarly complex transitions to food production witnessed in other world areas.

The transition from a hunting and gathering way of life to agriculture marks a major turning point in human history and has long been recognized as a central topic of inquiry in archaeology. Simplistic short answer approaches to resolving the how and why aspects of this "Neolithic Revolution" continue to be popular, as exemplified by Brian Hayden's proposal that the initial domestication of plants and animals worldwide can be universally explained in terms of occurring within contexts of competitive feasting (Hayden 1990, 1995). In reality, the transition from hunting and gathering to agriculture defies such simple universal "explanations," as it consists of a number of complex and intellectually engaging regionally scaled sets of spatially and temporally discrete historical-developmental trajectories of transformation. In some regions of the world this developmental transition involved the initial domestication of wild species of plants and animals; in other regions, like the Borderlands of northeastern Mexico and the Southwestern United States, it began with the arrival of already domesticated species.

Between 10,000 and 5,000 years ago, human societies in more than a half-dozen regions of the world independently domesticated a variety of different species of plants and animals (Bar-Yosef 1998; Price and Gebauer 1995; Smith 1998). As these domesticates were subsequently carried outward from their "primary" centers of domestication, farther and farther afield from the homeland of their wild progenitor populations, they fueled the transition from a hunting and gathering way of life to some form of food-production economy along an ever-expanding frontier, forming a time-transgressive zone between food procurement and food production. This major evolutionary trajectory in human history—the addition of domesticates to human diets and the shift to food production (and often eventually to agriculture)—thus did not occur in just a few places. Rather it has taken place, over time, across much of the earth's land surface. As a result, research on the transition from foraging to farming is not the exclusive purview of those scholars working in the already identified independent primary centers of initial domestication. Rather it represents a complex and challenging general area of inquiry open to researchers in many world areas, including the Borderlands, which witnessed "the Southwest's 'Neolithic' transition" (Mabry, this volume).

In each of the "primary" centers of domestication, for example, the initial transformation of wild plants and animals into managed, controlled resources did not rapidly result in the development of agricultural economies. Rather there were clearly long periods along these various regional developmental trajectories during which domesticates were part of the economic base but were not yet majority contributors to human nutritional budgets. In fact, in each of these primary centers there is a broad conceptual and developmental territory that separates hunting and gathering on one side from agriculture on the other. This "middle ground" is occupied by a rich variety of low-level food-producing societies (Smith 2001).

There is also, very clearly, no single and straight developmental pathway across this middle ground, no single evolutionary track leading to agriculture. There was a range of different historical-processual paths available to emerging food-production societies. Some of these developmental pathways led to full agricultural economies, while others did not. This vast middle ground of low-level food production that stretches between hunting-gathering and agriculture is not, then, purely a transitional puparial plane of existence, inhabited by societies on their way from one steady-state adaptation to another. As they were added to existing food capturing and collecting economies, domesticates of different kinds (in different combinations, in different regions of the world) enabled low-level food-producing societies to expand, enrich, and reshape their already successful and stable long-term solutions to surviving in quite varied regional and subregional contexts of both cultural and natural constraints and opportunities. The archaeological record for a number of world areas, including the Borderlands zone considered in this volume, shows that such low-level food production "solutions" endured and flourished for thousands of years before the emergence of any full agricultural economies.

The Borderlands: A Close to Laboratory Controlled Setting for Studying the Transition to Food Production

Areas such as the Borderlands, which were outside of a primary center of initial domestication, often provide the most promising opportunities to study and compare the full range of different developmental pathways taken early on by low-level food-production societies. For example, it is often a much more straightforward matter to identify and date the first appearance of an introduced domesticate in the archaeological record of such "nonprimary" regions than it is to document its earlier initial creation out of wild progenitor populations. With introduced domesticates, it is not necessary to address the often complex and murky "lead-up" context of initial human creation of a domesticate—the period of experimentation, manipulation, cultivation, and happenstance that precedes such transformations (e.g., Colledge 1998). Introduced domesticates are by this point also often morphologically quite distinct from their wild ancestor and not infrequently have been carried (or herded) out beyond the geographical range of their progenitor populations into regions where there are few if any local "look-alikes" to complicate recognizing them in the archaeological record. Such introduced domesticates, of course, are also often fully formed in another sense—they are the finished product of a process of deliberate human selection and represent significantly enhanced potential energy-source additions for societies auditioning them for inclusion into their local economies.

Until recently the Borderlands also seemed to represent a promising "limited variables laboratory" of sorts in which to study the transition to food production. Interest centered on a single introduced food crop—maize, which appeared to have arrived at about 1500 BC and to have spread quite rapidly across a wide range of different cultural and environmental subareas. More recently, however, the temporal separation of evidence for when maize first arrived in different subareas has expanded substantially (Mabry, this volume), suggesting that the early history of the initial arrival and diffusion of the crop plant throughout the region was more variable and drawn out than previously thought. Additional complexity is provided by the other crop plants introduced into the Southwest, which until now have not been as frequently documented or drawn as much attention as maize (Mabry, this volume). Squash (*Cucurbita pepo*) has been recovered in the same contexts as maize in a few sites, indicating that while it was certainly present in the Southwest by 1500 BC its date of arrival and its relative dietary importance in different subareas are far from clear. Similarly, Gayle Fritz et al. (2000) recently identified a domesticated thin-testa amaranth at Cerro Juanaqueña, which she considers to have been introduced from Mexico by about 1250 BC rather than domesticated locally. Finally, the common bean (*Phaseolus vulgaris*), long considered to be a late arrival in the Southwest, has recently been proposed as possibly being present in the region by at least ca. 1200 BC (rather than 200 BC) (Mabry, this volume), indicating that it may have been present in the early mix of other crop plants arriving from Mexico—amaranth, squash, and maize.

The recent documentation of amaranth, a small-seeded annual, as one of the early arrivals from Mexico is interesting in that it is similar in many respects to a number of the indigenous Southwestern wild plant foods which have been considered likely candidates for independent local domestication (e.g., *Chenopodium*, little barley, etc.; Adams 1987). The question of whether any local food plants were domesticated prior to the arrival of any Mexican crops, thereby preadapting some Southwestern societies to the easy accommodation of additional cultigens, still remains an open and interesting possibility. Mabry (this volume) mentions the parallel long-standing idea that intensive collecting of wild foods preadapted some Borderlands groups for adoption of cultigens arriving from the south.

This general issue of how easily Mexican domesticates were adopted into existing economies, and how quickly and how completely they became important dietary components along the Borderlands, is approached in the chapters of this volume from four overlapping and complementary perspectives: (1) what are the characteristics and habitat requirements of the introduced domesticates; (2) how well did the different environmental settings of the Borderlands meet those requirements; (3) how easily could the introduced domesticates be folded into the existing hunting and gathering economies of human societies in the region; and (4) how can one best measure the relative dietary contribution of the introduced domesticates to early food-production economies? Doleman (this volume) articulates the overlapping nature of these perspectives clearly under the general conceptual heading of "congruence": "The issue of successful incorporation of cultigens into hunter-gatherer subsistence thus becomes a question of congruence of hunter-gatherer ecology and the organization of mobility, the spatial ecology of natural biotic systems, and the restrictive demands of agriculture."

Profiling Introduced Domesticates

The four crop plants so far identified as being early introductions into the Borderlands from farther south in Mexico—maize, pepo squash, the common bean, and amaranth—are, I think, generally similar in terms of their basic requirements for successful sustained cultivation. Certainly it would be worthwhile for someone to take a closer look at possible differences between these crop plants in this regard. Of the four, maize appears to have had the most stringent moisture requirements through the growing season and is the most closely considered crop in this volume.

It is worth noting that the attribute profiles of these introduced domesticates (individually and in combination) defined and dictated to a considerable extent the outer parameters, the optimum potential for change in the Late Archaic societies of the Borderlands. When compared to Europe, another well-documented region of the world where the transition to food production was fueled by introduced rather than indigenous domesticates, the Mexican crop complex introduced into the Borderlands can be seen to have provided a relatively narrow range of possibilities for the expansion and augmentation of existing hunting and gathering economies across a range of diverse environmental settings.

The most obvious absence and limitation in the complex of domesticates introduced into the Borderlands was the absence of a livestock protein source. While the common bean would eventually take center stage as a critically important source of protein across many parts of the Pre-Columbian Americas, the continued widespread reliance on wild as opposed to domesticated animal species for protein in the New World certainly served to shape and constrain subsequent trajectories of cultural development.

Consider the range of alternative pathways of cultural development that would have opened up if Borderland groups, like circum-Mediterranean societies, had enjoyed the full range of Near Eastern livestock species (i.e., goat, sheep, cattle, pig) to draw from in selectively shaping and supplementing their economies in ways that could be sustained over the long term. With high biotic potential, high tolerance for close confinement, and an omnivorous diet, pigs (*Sus scrofa*), for example, could have been a significant plug-in addition to the "sedentary" river valley maize farming societies of regions like the Tucson Basin. Pigs could have substantially reduced reliance on wild animals as protein sources and the need for associated seasonal hunting trips, thereby enabling higher occupancy of permanent year-round river valley settlements. They could also have supported substantial subsistence independence at the household level, as was the case over thousands of years in the Near East (Zeder 1998). Interestingly, while strengthening the long-term trend of household-scale subsistence independence along the Borderlands, pigs, because of their large "package size" (efficient use of their meat during a brief window of opportunity before spoilage), also would have shaped multiple household bonds of integration. Cattle too, with their added draft-animal benefits for transport and field plot preparation, could have substantially changed the course of cultural development in the Americas.

But for the eastern end of the arc of the Borderlands, it is the caprines—sheep and goats—that would have provided the most interesting potential expansion of possibilities in the development of food-production economies. In dramatic contrast with the crop plants introduced from Mexico into the Borderlands—which were not a good match, not a viable set of additions, for the economies of societies of what is today South Texas (Hester, Dering, and Mallouf, this volume)—sheep, and particularly goats, could perhaps have fit comfortably into the environments and extant economies of the area. An interesting comparison is provided in this respect by the initial transition to food production in southern Spain, where seasonally mobile hunter-gatherer societies in low-rainfall dispersed-resource environments, when presented with the entire Near Eastern spectrum of domesticated plants and animals to choose from, initially selected only caprines, particularly goats, to add into and successfully supplement their foraging and hunting economies. When viewed, then, both within a context of comparison to the different transitions to food production that occurred across Europe and in terms of the types of domesticates that were available, the hunting and gathering societies of South Texas can be seen not so much as failing to make the transition to food production as never having been presented with a worthwhile domesticate to integrate into their way of life. As Mallouf (this volume) states: the Late Archaic landscapes "offered a natural setting of maximum potential for hunter-gatherer–based economies," and "innovations were accepted or rejected as deemed appropriate for survival."

Research on the transition to food production in a number of regions of Europe (Price 2000) also serves to underscore the growing recognition that across the arch of the Borderlands quite different selective solutions to achieve the best integration of domesticates into existing economies developed in different environmental and cultural contexts that were often situated in close spatial proximity to each other. The solutions as to how best to take advantage of available domesticates appear to have varied substantially over relatively short distances. The transition to food production in the Borderlands and the greater Southwest was not a lock-step uniform process and in recent years has been broken down into a number of quite locale-specific developmental puzzles—variations on a common theme. It is not surprising, as a result, that most of the contributors to this volume very appropriately approach the characterization of the adoption of domesticates in particular regions of the Borderlands in a relative context of comparison with other (often nearby) areas.

Research on the transition to food production in Europe also provides another interesting general comparison to the Borderlands: it shows that, just as alternative patterns of selective adoption and reliance on domesticates can vary quite substantially among a number of adjacent environmental and cultural areas, so too can the delivery systems for new domesticates also exhibit considerable variability within small geographical areas. In both northern Greece and central Italy (Smith 1998), for example, large early settlements (seemingly clear examples of colonization by societies based on food-production economies) have been documented in proximity to other indigenous groups which either selectively adopted only a few of the available Near Eastern domesticates or maintained hunting and gathering economies. The best European example of transition to food production through colonization is of course the LBK (Linear Band Keramic) cultures of the northern European plain. The relatively standardized material culture assemblages, economies, and long-house settlements of LBK societies were targeted at tightly defined soil and river valley settings and were scattered across a broad area from northern France eastward into Russia.

While obviously quite different in many respects, these LBK settlements share some interesting general abstract similarities with Cerro Juanaqueña and other Late Archaic *cerros de trincheras* settlements of the Borderlands (Hard and Roney, this volume). Like LBK settlements, the Late Archaic *cerros de trincheras* of the Borderlands appear to be distinctly different in a number of respects from other contemporary settlements in adjacent areas. As has been documented for LBK, Hard and Roney link the placement of the *trincheras* settlements on the landscape to river valley settings having particular geomorphological features and resource zones. Parallel in a fashion to well-documented long-house communities, Cerro Juanaqueña and other *trincheras* sites of the Río Casas Grandes share a quite distinctive pattern of hillside terrace residential architecture on a relatively large scale, along with more mutedly distinctive floral, faunal, and material cultural assemblages. All of these general similarities to LBK combine to suggest that perhaps Cerro Juanaqueña and other related sites reflect an expansion into this area of the Borderlands by societies with an already established food-production economy.

If these Late Archaic colonists of the Casas Grandes are at all similar to LBK societies in one final respect, however, identifying the area to the south where they originated and tracing the pathways and sequencing of their expansion may prove to be challenging. LBK societies appear to have systematically expanded westward across the loess soil bands of the northern European plain, sequentially occupying frontier zones of preferred soils and woodland habitats. This LBK "wave" of expansion, however, also very clearly often involved "island hopping" across sometimes substantial intervening landscapes that did not meet their exacting environmental requirements for colonization. Backtracking to the progenitor populations of the Río Casas Grandes *trincheras* sites thus could well involve looking fairly far afield for source areas that satisfy the guidelines that Ray Thompson and others established for identifying "site unit intrusion" a half-century ago (Thompson 1958).

A similar "source area identification" challenge faces researchers in Sonora, where evidence of extensive (possibly Late Archaic) canal networks and an apparent discontinuity in the archaeological record lends support to the possibility that, following the Altithermal climatic downturn, the Sonoran Desert was repopulated by "maize-bearing" Uto-Aztecan–speaking peoples, moving into the region from the south (Carpenter et al., this volume; see also Huckell 1995; Mabry, this volume). Carpenter and his co-investigators further argue that the initial adoption of domesticates along the Borderlands should be viewed in a much larger context, as the leading edge of a time-transgressive radiation of low-level food-production economies north out of Mexico, and that the well-watered alluvial plains in extreme southern Sonora and Sinaloa are the logical areas in which to search for earlier evidence of this expansion. Mabry (this volume), in contrast, points out the absence of evidence of irrigation technology south of the Sonoran Desert and suggests that canal systems could have been developed locally after the arrival of crop plants in the region.

Clearly, then, in areas as diverse as the northern European plain, the coastal zones of the Mediterranean, and the southwestern Borderlands—indeed throughout much of the world—the initial appearance of domesticates and the transition to food production is not a simple and uniform formulaic process with a single end point but rather a richly complex dialectical drama acted out at the local level. In each of these local historical dramas, the stage is set in large measure by the environment. The relative abundance and distribution of wild resources and the extent to which they satisfy the requirements of potential outside dietary additions can be seen to dictate in large measure the nature and the relative importance of the roles potentially open to newly introduced domesticates.

Environmental and Cultural Variation and the Adoption of Domesticates across the Borderlands

Environmental characterization is a major theme throughout the chapters of this volume, particularly in regard to establishing how well different regions along the arc of the Borderlands were capable of supporting the sustained cultivation of introduced crop plants. These often detailed environmental analyses focus on the identification and quantification of variables relevant to successful crop production.

Environmental assessments in five of the chapters are framed within a comparative approach—how well does a particular area compare with another in terms of its climate, landscape, biotic communities, soils, and water in being capable of supporting crop cultivation? These comparisons are all made along a generally west to east–trending axis and match up western areas that were more suited to growing introduced crop plants with the less promising areas of the eastern half of the Borderlands arc. Hard and Roney offer the tightest spatial pairing in their river valley habitat-scale comparison of the fluorescence of Late Archaic food-production economies along the Río Casas Grandes valley in northern Chihuahua with the parallel absence of any such contemporary transformation in the Rio Grande valley of south-central New Mexico, only 30–200 km to the northeast. In a more spatially separated pairing, Doleman provides a quite detailed and insightful larger-scale comparison between the Chihuahuan Desert region of southern New Mexico (which includes the Rio Grande Valley region discussed by Hard and Roney) and the Sonoran Desert region of southeastern Arizona. Dering and Ogilvie, in turn, both draw comparisons between this Sonoran Desert zone and the Pecos River region of Southwest Texas. Vierra compares lithic assemblages and adaptations of the Río Casas Grandes region with a number of different locales to the north and to the east. Like Ogilvie, he compares hunter-gatherer, early food-production, and later Pueblo period "agricultural" societies. In the noncomparative chapters, Mabry considers Late Archaic societies in southeastern Arizona, while Carpenter, Sánchez, and Villalpando synthesize what is known regarding the western end of the Borderlands in Sonora, Mexico. At the eastern end of the arc, Mallouf and Hester both discuss environmental settings which were unaccommodating to crop-plant cultivation.

Given the generally semiarid environments of the Borderlands, it is no great surprise that water is the most important variable in terms of the relative potential of different locales for crop cultivation. Particularly obvious in this regard are the amount and seasonal distribution of rainfall and its variability from year to year. Citing the work of Stone and Bostwick (1996), Dering, for example, outlines why the lower Pecos, given its precipitation patterns, was not favorable for a transition to farming. Not only does the region receive less rain per year on the average than do regions farther west, but the rain is also scattered seasonally in the spring and fall, separated by a pronounced summer growing season drought. Dering also points out that the lower Pecos experiences greater interannual rainfall variability than any other semiarid savanna in the wild.

Farther west along the arc of the Borderlands, Doleman notes that average annual rainfall in the northern Chihuahuan Desert zone of southern New Mexico, at 9.5 inches, is lower than the 13.3 inches that fall on average in the Sonoran Desert zone of southern Arizona. Rainfall is also far more reliable and more predictable from year to year in the Sonoran Desert zone and is properly timed for the growing season (Dering, this volume). Similarly, Hard and Roney note that the Jornada Region of southern New Mexico receives half the summer rainfall that the Río Casas Grandes locale of Cerro Juanaqueña receives and is vulnerable to serious flooding. As a number of authors mention, however, reliance on rainfall alone—dry farming—should still be generally considered a fairly risky enterprise along the Borderlands even in those regions that enjoy the best-timed, most reliable from year to year, and highest rates of precipitation. As a result, when dependent upon direct moisture falling on the fields, introduced crop plants played only a minor role, if any, throughout most of the western arc of the Borderlands until AD 200–700: "Low-investment plant and harvest farming strategies appear to have been ubiquitous across the Southwest during the Late Archaic period. In most places, however, these small fields were not very productive and yielded only a minor part of the diet" (Hard and Roney, this volume).

So although rainfall was certainly a factor in permitting low-level cultivation along the Borderlands, other environmental elements were also present in those few areas of Sonora and Chihuahua, Mexico, and southeastern Arizona where crop cultivation became a more productive undertaking. Chief among these other prerequisites was the availability of water during the growing season from sources other than direct rainfall. Interestingly, in the Trans-Pecos and Big Bend regions of Texas, which received the lowest and least reliable levels of rainfall, it was quite likely such sources of water other than direct rainfall that allowed even the most limited experiments with cultivation: "Clearly, the use of cultigens was cursory at best, possibly serving only as a dietary supplement, and may have been restricted to occasional, relatively haphazard and experimental plantings in suitable soils near springs or along segments of larger drainages" (Mallouf, this volume).

In areas farther west along the arc of the Borderlands, Carpenter et al., Dering, Doleman, Hard and Roney, Mabry, and a number of earlier authors (e.g., Huckell 1995; Stone and Bostwick 1996) identify the sources of additional growing-season water, which, when present, allowed more productive and more predictable cultivation of domesticated crop plants beyond that possible through direct rainfall. These include overbank sheet flooding, taking advantage of high floodplain water tables, runoff seepage from uplands rainfall as well as surface runoff from growing season showers, more labor-intensive water management (i.e., *ak chin* check dams and redirection of uplands runoff), and river valley main channel feeder and drainage canals. The topography of stream valleys and patterns of floodwater dispersal can play a central role in the relative success of river valley cultivation. Dering, for example, points out that stream valleys in the lower Pecos are very often entrenched in canyons and are susceptible to unpredictable and catastrophic floods. In a similar vein, Mallouf (this volume) mentions the dynamic and unpredictable nature of the Rio Grande in southwestern Texas and New Mexico.

In stark contrast and only a hundred kilometers south, in Chihuahua, Hard and Roney (this volume) describe the 2-km-wide floodplain just below the settlement of Cerro Juanaqueña, formed by the convergence of the Río San Pedro and Río Casas Grandes, which allowed a rapid deceleration of floodwater, as being ideal for overbank sheet flooding of cultivated fields. Similarly, Mabry (this volume) notes that settlements in the Tucson Basin region of southeast Arizona were situated in stream valley settings that benefited both from overbank flooding and from surface runoff from growing season showers. Hard and Roney (this volume), too, consider the potential contribution of surface and seepage runoff at Cerro Juanaqueña as well as the potential use of a still active spring as a water source and the possible planting of deep tap root varieties of crops that could reach down to the water table. They also consider the possibility (as yet undocumented) that, given the evidence for other substantial building projects, the occupants of Cerro Juanaqueña may have constructed irrigation canals. Carpenter et al. (this volume) identify canal systems at the La Playa site on the Río Boquillas in Sonora that date between 1200 to 600 BC; and clear evidence of substantial canal construction has been documented by Mabry and others in the Tucson Basin of southeastern Arizona.

Along with more reliable sources of water for cultivation, the other main variable recognized as a prerequisite for more than a minor reliance on crop plants was the easy accessibility of a full and evenly balanced range of regional biotic resource zones within a one- or two-day walk of river valley settlements. In his detailed comparison of the environmental structure of two regions of the Borderlands with generally similar Basin and Range physiography, Doleman (this volume) shows that "the southeastern Arizona environment is twice as fine-grained as that of southern New Mexico, with the various economically important biomes being more closely packed and more evenly represented areally . . . In essence, everything a seasonal forager could ask for was much closer to hand in southeastern Arizona." As a result of this tighter geographic packing of biomes, river valley cultivators did not have to go as far to acquire wild resources even in years of low crop yields (Doleman, this volume). As Wills and Huckell (1994) and Stone and Bostwick (1996) conclude (along with Doleman, Mabry, and Hard and Roney in this volume), it is not all that difficult to identify essential environmental ingredients that enabled hunter-gatherer societies of some parts of the Borderlands to successfully and productively add cultivation of introduced crop plants as a major new component to established patterns of seasonal utilization of wild plant and animal communities of diverse resource zones. A river valley setting was necessary, with annual rainfall levels within the catchment sufficient to provide reliable perennial stream flow. Although of little interest to earlier hunter-gatherer societies with stable if seasonally occupied settlements along such alluvial corridors, a river valley's capacity for supplementing direct precipitation with other water (and nutrient) delivery systems was of critical importance in defining its relative potential for significant crop plant cultivation (e.g., nondestructive overbank sheet flooding, surface runoff and seepage from catchment basin growing-season showers, water tables within tap-root reach, and topography amenable to canal construction).

Up out of the floodplain corridors, the environmental attributes that were essential in supporting emerging food-production societies were those that had similarly enabled relatively sedentary and stable precursor hunting and gathering societies to maintain long-term communities in the same river valley settings. These included fine-grained or closely packed resource zones with reliable, predictable, and high-level carrying capacity for human harvesters (e.g., wild animal species with high biotic potential, capable of recovering from sustained annual predation) and wild plant species that invest considerable energy into reproductive propagules rather than vegetative growth. In those areas with this general set of river valley and upland attributes, crop cultivation could easily be added as a welcome supplement to preexisting seasonal rounds of exploitation of wild plants and animals without creating any scheduling conflicts (Wills and Huckell 1989).

The contributors to this volume, as well as other scholars interested in the nature and context of the initial adoption of introduced domesticates along the arc of the Borderlands, clearly have made considerable progress in recent years in unraveling the complex developmental puzzle of why societies made a more rapid and more substantial transition to food production in some Borderland areas and not in others. In terms of being able to characterize and accurately establish the relative dietary contribution that crop plants actually made to the economies of the Late Archaic societies in the Borderlands, however, the contributors to this book have faced the same challenges that are faced by scholars working on the transition to food production in other regions of the world.

Characterizing the Economic Importance of Crop Plants to Late Archaic Societies of the Borderlands

Hunting and gathering and agriculture have often been considered as two steady economic states, two general categories of adaptational solutions. This dualistic epistemology carries with it the assumption that any transition from hunting and gathering to agriculture must be rapid. It is becoming increasingly evident, however, that there is a vast conceptual and developmental middle ground between hunting and gathering and agriculture (Smith 2001). Past societies exhibited a wide range of stable long-term economic solutions in which domesticates played a minor but important dietary role. If some sort of reasonable, commonsense (if somewhat subjective) boundary is established for agriculture—say a 40, 50, or 60% annual caloric input from domesticates—then many of these fast societies would fall in the middle ground somewhere between hunting and gathering and agriculture.

Because many such societies endured and evolved for thousands of years along the Borderlands as well as in other world regions without developing an "agricultural" level of dietary reliance on domesticates, they deserve to be recognized and acknowledged as stable long-term economic solutions in and of themselves, rather than simply being labeled as on their way to agriculture with modifiers such as "early," "initial," or "incipient" (e.g., "incipient agriculture").

Very little has yet been worked out, however, regarding either what terminology is appropriate for classifying and characterizing these societies of the middle ground or what kinds of archaeological evidence can be employed for pattern recognition of their natural groupings. Like researchers working on "middle ground" or "low-level food production" societies (Smith 2001), the authors in this volume struggle with these problems of poorly defined terminology, pattern recognition, and the identification of archaeological criteria for measuring crop plant importance.

In their comparative analyses, both Vierra and Ogilvie employ hunting and gathering societies at the eastern end of the Borderlands and later "full-blown" agriculturalists to bracket the "middle ground" societies of the region. Ogilvie documents a clear trend of reduced mobility in females (as reflected in increased femoral gracilization) from hunter-gatherers across the "middle ground" to later Pueblo "agricultural" societies and identifies femoral shape indices as good general markers of the dietary importance of crop plants (Ogilvie, this volume).

Similarly, Vierra (this volume) documents a "middle ground" lithic assemblage at the Cerro Juanaqueña site as representing a mixed foraging and agricultural economy that falls between those that he describes for hunter-gatherer sites in the region and later Pueblo sites. He concludes, for example, that the large number of heavily worn basin-shaped metates at the site indicates "a degree of residential stability and labor organization beyond that of simple foragers." At the same time, the chipped stone assemblage exhibited more evidence of biface production and retouch than would be found in Pueblo assemblages, along with less indication of expediency flake production.

Hard and Roney (this volume) likewise found the manos at Cerro Juanaqueña to be somewhat larger than typical Archaic forms and small compared to those of later Pueblo sites. They concluded that because "mano size is related to agricultural dependence," the manos at Cerro Juanaqueña reflected a middle range of agricultural use—between most Puebloan occupations and dominantly hunter-gatherer adaptations (also see Vierra, this volume). Hard and Roney also identified a number of other archaeological indices of the relatively dietary contribution of crop plants, including maize ubiquity indices for features (60%) and flotation samples (40%) as well as a range of indicators of at least long-term seasonal (spring-summer-fall) sedentism (e.g., substantial household trash, significant planning and labor investment in terrace construction, substantial evidence of food processing and storage). They conclude that while maize was a dietary staple, occupants of the site relied on a mixed diet of maize, domesticated amaranth, and a range of wild taxa.

In his consideration of Tucson Basin sites in southeastern Arizona, Doleman (this volume) lists similar archaeological indicators of the relative dietary importance of maize: "With multiple habitation structures, abundant storage features and cultigen remains, and even irrigation canals, these sites indicate *reliance* on agriculture, not just casual use of cultivated food." Mabry (this volume) cites similar criteria and offers a similar characterization for southeastern Arizona societies: "the abundance of maize remains, storage pits and roasting pits containing maize remains, and grinding tools with maize residues reflect the importance of maize production at early agricultural sites in this region . . . The flotation samples and faunal assemblages . . . , however, indicate a wider variety of exploited wild plants and animals than is represented at later Hohokam sites."

Finally, Carpenter et al. (this volume) characterize the Late Archaic inhabitants of the La Playa site as having "a mixed foraging and farming strategy with intensive maize cultivation combined with an equally extensive utilization of wild plants and animals." They note: "Maize undoubtedly provided a critical storable food source for the winter and early spring months. Yet, even in light of intensification strategies and radically altered settlement patterns, it may have contributed a relatively small percentage of the total calories consumed. Both the low incidence of caries and the ground stone assemblage lend support to this inference."

All of the authors in this volume who address this general issue concur in characterizing those Late Archaic societies of the Borderlands that added domesticates to their economies as falling somewhere in the vast and still largely unexplored conceptual middle ground between hunter-gatherers and subsequent "true" agriculturalists. In the absence of any well-developed consensus terminology for the "middle ground," however, it is not surprising that the volume contributors (like everyone else) struggle with further characterization and categorization of these "in between" societies of the Borderlands. Often this terminological gap is filled by drawing on the established labels for societies on either side of the "middle ground."

Researchers interested in hunter-gatherers may label "middle ground" societies as "affluent" or "complex" hunter-gatherers, while those scholars interested in agricultural societies may view them in terms of agriculture. Doleman (this volume), for example, articulates the potential range of variation in the role of domesticates for societies of the "middle ground" as "the degree of dependence on agriculture, ranging from [casual] use of cultigens to supplement the hunter-gatherer diet to full reliance on cultigens for primary nutrition." His use of the term "agriculture," however, reflects one of the most prevalent terminological problems in discussing and describing societies and economies of the "middle ground"—equating the presence of domesticates with the existence of agricultural economies. The "agriculture" label is often then softened or modified to indicate a category of agriculture that is less than and on its way to "fully committed," "full blown," "fully developed," or "settled" agriculture. I have suggested (Smith 2001) that the use of such watered-down agricultural terminology (e.g., "incipient Southwest farmers," "incipient agriculture," "early agricultural systems," "early agriculture," "early agricultural production") could easily be replaced with the neutral label "low-level food production." If societies of the "middle ground" were freed of the terminological hegemony of agriculture on the one side and hunting-gathering on the other and simply labeled "low-level food-production societies," they would come into clearer focus as a sprawling, heterogeneous, and distinct category of stable, flexible, long-term steady-state economic adaptation.

Moving beyond these terminological difficulties, it is clear that the contributors to this volume, as well as a number of other scholars working in northwestern Mexico and the Southwest, are making remarkable progress in developing accurate and illuminating profiles of the initial low-level food-production economies of the region—their technology, settlements, seasonal rounds, subsistence systems, and specific niches within the diverse environmental settings of the Borderlands. They are charting the "middle ground"—not just for the Borderlands, but in general. They take a careful case-study, regional-scale comparative approach, combined with the expanded recognition and investigation of multiple markers of relative reliance on domesticates (e.g., caries rates, femoral robusticity, mano size, cultigen ubiquity indices, corporate labor investments in terraces and canals, biface and expediency flake tool ratios, river valley settlement placement, resource catchment richness indices). When combined with parallel efforts in Europe (Price 2000) and elsewhere, their approach provides a clear indication of the long-term research promise of the "middle ground."

REFERENCES CITED

Adams, K.
    1987   Barley (*Hordeum*) as a Possible Domesticate in the Prehistoric American Southwest. In *Specialized Studies in the Economy, Environment, and Culture of La Ciudad, Part III*, edited by J. Kisselburg, G. Rice, and B. Shears, pp. 203–237. Anthropological Field Studies 20. Arizona State University, Tempe.
Bar-Yosef, O. (editor)
    1998   The Transition to Agriculture in the Old World. *The Review of Archaeology* 19.
Colledge, S.
    1998   Identifying Pre-Domestication Cultivation Using Multivariate Analysis. In *The Origins of Agriculture and Crop Domestication*, edited by A. Damania, J. Valkoun, G. Willcox, and C. Qualset, pp. 121–131. ICARDA (International Center for Agricultural Research in the Dry Areas), Aleppo, Syria.
Fritz, G., K. Adams, and J. Roney
    2000   Evidence for Cultivation of *Amaranthus* 3,000 Years Ago at Cerro Juanaqueña, Chihuahua. Paper presented at the 22nd Annual Meeting of the Society of Ethnobiology, Oaxaca, Mexico.
Hayden, B.
    1990   Nimrods, Piscators, Pluckers, and Planters: The Emergence of Food Production. *Journal of Anthropological Archaeology* 9: 31–69.

1995   A New Overview of Domestication. In *Last Hunters—First Farmers*, edited by D. Price and A. Gebauer, pp. 273–300. School of American Research Press, Santa Fe.

Huckell, B. B.

1995   *Of Marshes and Maize: Preceramic Agricultural Settlements in the Cienega Valley, Southeastern Arizona.* Anthropological Papers of the University of Arizona No. 59. University of Arizona Press, Tucson.

Price, D. (editor)

2000   *Europe's First Farmers.* Cambridge University Press, Cambridge.

Price, D., and A. Gebauer (editors)

1995   *Last Hunters—First Farmers.* School of American Research Press, Santa Fe.

Smith, B.

1998   *The Emergence of Agriculture.* Paperback ed. W. H. Freeman, New York.

2001   Low Level Food Production. *Journal of Archaeological Research* 9:1–43.

Stone, C., and T. Bostwick

1996   Environmental Contexts and Archaeological Correlates: The Transition to Farming in Three Regions of the Arizona Desert. In *Early Formative Adaptations in the Southern Southwest,* edited by B. J. Roth, pp. 17–26. Monographs in World Archaeology 25. Prehistory Press, Madison, Wis.

Thompson, R. (editor)

1958   *Migrations in New World Culture History.* University of Arizona Social Science Bulletin 27 (vol. 29, no. 2). University of Arizona Press, Tucson.

Wills, W. H., and B. B. Huckell

1989   Economic Implications of Changing Land-Use Patterns in the Late Archaic. In *Themes in Southwest Prehistory,* edited by G. J. Gumerman, pp. 33–52. School of American Research Press, Santa Fe.

Zeder, M.

1998   Pigs and Emergent Complexity in the Ancient Near East. In *Ancestors for the Pigs,* edited by S. Nelson, pp. 109–122. MASCA Research Papers in Science and Archaeology. University Museum, Philadelphia.

CONTRIBUTORS

John P. Carpenter
Departamento de Antropología
Universidad de las Américas–Puebla
Ex-Hacienda Santa Catarina Mártir
Cholula, Puebla 72820
Mexico
email: chichimecatl@hotmail.com

Phil Dering
Shumla Archeobotanical Services
P.O. Box 944 (US Postal Service
    Address)
110 Alpine St. (Physical Address)
Comstock, TX 78837
email: pdering@msn.com

William H. Doleman
Archaeological Records Management
    Section (ARMS)
New Mexico Historic Preservation
    Division
Department of Cultural Affairs
228 East Palace Ave., Room 320
Santa Fe, NM 87501
email: bdoleman@arms.state.nm.us

Robert J. Hard
University of Texas at San Antonio

Department of Anthropology
rhard@lonestar.utsa.edu

Thomas R. Hester
University of Texas at Austin
Department of Anthropology
Prc#5 Texas Arch Research Lab
Austin, TX 78712-1100
email: t.r.hester@mail.utexas.edu

Jonathan B. Mabry
Desert Archaeology, Inc.
3975 N. Tucson Blvd.
Tucson, AZ 85716
jmabry@desert.com

Robert J. Mallouf
Center for Big Bend Studies
Box C-71
Sul Ross State University
Alpine, TX 79832
email: mallouf@sulross.edu

R. G. Matson
University of British Columbia
Department of Anthropology and
    Sociology
6303 NW Marine Drive

Vancouver, BC, Canada V6T 1Z1
email: mesa@interchange.ubc.ca

Marsha D. Ogilvie
Department of Anthropology
University of New Mexico
Albuquerque, NM 87131
email: mogilvie@unm.edu

John R. Roney
Bureau of Land Management
435 Montano Rd, N.E.
Albuquerque, NM 87107
john_roney@blm.gov

Guadalupe Sánchez
Department of Anthropology
University of Arizona
Tucson, AZ 85721
email: guadalupe_sanchez_
    miranda@hotmail.com

Bruce D. Smith
Smithsonian Institution
Department of Anthropology MRC
112
Museum of Natural History
Washington, DC 20560-0001
email: Smith.Bruce@nmnh.si.edu

Bradley J. Vierra
Ecology Group
ENV-ECO, MS M887
Los Alamos National Laboratory
Los Alamos, NM 87545
email: bvierra@lanl.gov

María Elisa Villalpando C.
Sección de Arqueología
Centro INAH–Sonora
Hermosillo, Sonora
Mexico
email: laelisa@rtn.uson.mx

INDEX

Numbers in bold indicate illustrations.

Agave, and other CAM-rich plants, 89,
  289, 290
Agriculture (*see also* Transition)
  arrival of, in southeastern Arizona, as a
    set of systems, 55
  and Central Mexican planting regime,
    281
  earliest dates for (*see* Maize, early dates
    for)
  eastern boundary of, in the American
    Southwest, 3
  explanations for incorporation of and
    reliance on, 116, 117
  incorporation of, in various regional/
    elevational settings, 113
  indigenous development of, involving
    native Southwestern crops, 62,
    300, 303
  and (limited) likelihood of in situ
    development, 280, 281, 287
Ak chin farming, 167, 169, 288
Altar Valley (SON), 17
Amaranth, domesticated, presence of, 4,
  54, 62, 152, 288, 303, 313
Amargosa phase
  as ancestral to the Piman-speaking
    Pinacateños, 17
  of lower Colorado River Valley, 48
  points, 16

Antelope drives, 95
Antelope Wells obsidian source, 30, 201
Antler racks, used as grave goods in
  South Texas burials, 272, 273
Archaic, concept of; termination of
  (*see* Transition)
Argillite, red, source of, in Tucson Basin,
  30, 283
Armijo points, **52**
  associated with maize, 62
Arroyo site (AZ), Chiricahua stage pit
  structure at, 61
"Atrisco Focus," 48
Avra Valley, 43, 46

Baboquivari Mountains, 42
Basecamps, seasonal, for upland hunting
  and gathering, 59
Basketmaker II, on Colorado Plateau
  and dependence on maize, 280, 288
  lithic assemblages from, 293
  and resemblance to San Pedro Stage,
    48
  western vs. eastern, 281
Bat Cave (NM)
  continuity of deposits in, 62
  early maize dates from, 48, 54
Bedrock mortars, **229**
Bifaces, use of, in caches and as grave
  goods, in South Texas, 267, **268**, 269,
  270–272

Bifacial technologies
  advantages of: portability, increased
    tool life, 187
  decrease in use of, following agricul-
    tural transition, 188
"Big Bend culture," 219
Big Bend region (TX), lack of large-scale
  excavations in, 5, 219, 225, 240, 288
"Big Houses" (communal structures),
  57
Bison hunting, 5, 7, 46, 237, 253, 254, 273
Bison (modern), 45, 47, 248, 264
Bone remodeling, in response to habitual
  physical activities, 85, 116
Boquillas Valley (SON), 33
Borderlands, defined, 1, 2
Bow and arrow
  earliest dates for, 41
  introduction of, in South Texas, 259
  transition from atlatl to, 226, 240, 293
Brownsville Complex, xiv
Burials (see also Cemeteries)
  at La Playa site, 26, 27, 32, 283
  in South Texas, 260, 267

Carbon 4- and CAM-rich plants, 89,
  269
Carrying-capacity models, as explanation
  for increasing reliance on cultigens,
  117
Cemeteries, presence of
  in Cienega phase sites, 61
  at La Playa site, 4, 19
  in South Texas, 6, 260, 267–269, 272,
    273
  in Tucson Basin, 4
Ceramics
  appearance of, not reflecting change in
    subsistence, 114, 115
  earliest dates for, 41, 57
  introduction of, in South Texas, 259
  trade in, xiv
Cerro el Canelo (CHI), 148–151

Cerro Juanaqueña (CHI), 4, 6, 56, 57,
  141–174, 287, 288
  earliest date from, 161
  evidence of site planning at, 144, 145
  lithic assemblage from, 6, 190–199,
    202–209, 292, 293
  presence of possible domesticated
    amaranth in, 4, 54, 152, 190, 303
  probable connection with area to
    south and east, 292, 306
Cerro los Torres (CHI), 148–151
Cerro Trincheras, evidence of shell ornament production at, 27
Cerro Vidal (CHI), 149–151, 287
Chapalote (see also Maize, early races
  of), 32
Chaparrosa Ranch (TX), 259, 260
Cheno-am abundance
  in Hohokam features, 25
  in La Playa site hornos, 25
  in Tucson Basin sites, 25
"Chihuahua" tradition, 115
Chihuahuan terrace hilltop communities
  (see Cerro Juanaqueña; Cerro Trin-
  cheras; Cerro Vidal; Trinchera sites)
Chiricahua points, 22, 46, 61, 62
Chiricahua stage, 48, 54
  type site, 61
Chisos focus, 227
Choke Canyon (TX), 259, 260, 262, 263
Cienega Creek site, early maize in, 48, 54
Cienega phase
  definition of, 51, 114, 284
  new technologies and organization
    evident in, 57, 61
Cienega points, 24, 28, 29, 52
Cienega Valley, geomorphology of, 45
Clearwater site (AZ)
  association of maize with Armijo
    points at, 62
  earliest ceramic dates from, 57
  early maize dates from, 53
  presence of Cheno-ams in, 25

Climate change, 1
  at beginning of Late Holocene, 13, 21,
    41, 44–46, 161, 173, 219, 307
  as factor in increasing reliance on
    cultigens, 117
  in south-central New Mexico, 117
  in southeastern Arizona, 44, 117
Clovis points, 17
Cochise Archaic tradition, 13, 17, 114
  definition of, 47–49, 284
  southern extent of, 16, 18
Coffee Camp site (AZ), 58
"Collector" (logistical mobility) pattern,
  in the Tucson Basin, 59
Colorado Plateau, early cultivation of
  maize on, 280
Comca'ac (Seri) sites, 16, 29
  trade with, 29
Common bean (*Phaseolus vulgaris*)
  as important source of protein, 304
  from Las Capas, 54, 285, 303
  at Pottery Mound, 94
Communal-ceremonial structures (*see
  also* "Big Houses"), 4, 58, 61, 64, 285
Corporate organization, development of,
  during San Pedro phase, 61
Cortaro points/bifaces, 22, 31, **52**, 62,
  283
Cortical bone, thickness of, as indicator
  of physical activity levels, 85, **86,** 291
Costello-King site (AZ), 55
Cotton (*Gossypium* sp.)
  at Pottery Mound, 94
  presence of, at San Pedro phase
    sites, 63
  from Valley Farm site, 54
Cremation
  in Cienega phase southeastern Arizona
    sites, 57
  at La Playa site, 19
Crop complexes
  Mexican, 4, 55
  native Southwestern, 62, 303, 304

Crop failure, as source of increased instability after transition to agriculture,
  282
Cultigens, degree of dependence on, 5, 6,
  32, 113, 117, 118, 151, 153, 155, 167, 170,
  172, 239, 280, 286, 287, 301, 303, 309,
  312–315
Cultivation systems (*see* Farming)
Cutoff distance, between daily foraging
  and overnight logistical trips, 119

Dalton/Meserve points, 17
Defensive sites, as evidence of
  conflict, 282
  population packing, 173
Dentition, as indicator of diet, 27, 91
Desert Branch of the Hohokam, 33
Diet, as indicated by Carbon 4 and
  Crassulacean Acid Metabolism
  (CAM) analyses, 89
Diet breadth model, use of
  to assess Lower Pecos Archaic
    economy, 248–249, 290
  to compare foraging vs. farming, 7, 117
  to explain transition to agriculture,
    154–156, 164, 172
Division of labor (*see* Sexual division of
  labor)
Dog burials, at La Playa site, 19, 27
Domesticated
  animals, lack of, 304, 305
  plants (*see* Cultigens; Maize)
Doña Ana phase, level of agricultural
  dependence during, 114
Double Adobe IV site, early maize in, 48
Dropseed grass (*Sporobolus* sp.), use of,
  on Colorado Plateau, 290, 291
Dry farming, 47, 65, 167, 281, 309

Early Agricultural period
  definition of, 50, 51, 114
  earliest human remains from, 20
  origins of (*see also* Transition), 13

Earth ovens, 262
  fuel requirements of, 249, 290
  use of, to process xerophytic plants,
    249, 290
Economic Zonation Model, 92
Edwards Plateau chert, 267
El Paso phase, shift to dependence on
  agriculture during, 5, 114, 189
Empire points, **24, 52**
  recent recognition of, 23, 24
Ernest Witte site (TX), 267

Fairbank site (AZ), 46
Falcon Reservoir (TX), 260, 267, 268
Farming
  early dates for (see also Agriculture), 60
  types of (see also Labor investment),
    47, 167, 281, 309
Faunal remains, at La Playa site, 26
Femur (human), increasing gracilization
  of, through time, 85, **98,** 210, 291, 312
Fiber, extraction of, for subsistence and
  weaving, 90
Floodplain/floodwater farming, 7, 47, 65,
    167, 174, 281, 284, 285, 287, 288, 310
  requirements of, 122, 123, 168
Folsom points, 17
Forager (residential mobility) pattern, 60
Foraging radius, 120
Foraging range (see Procurement range)
Fresnal Shelter, evidence for
  ethnobotanic use of wild grasses/mes-
  quite in, 159, 170, 171

Geoglyphs (intaglios), 17, 32
Gila River, 42
Grave goods
  as indicative of symbolic use, of trade,
    and of status or wealth, 273
  at La Playa site, 26
  in South Texas burials and cemeteries,
    267–273
  in Trans-Pecos burials, 230

Ground stone
  as indicator of diet, 147, 188, 210, 238,
    266, 287, 313
  as site furniture, 153, 210
Guilá Naquitz (OAX)
  early maize from dates of, 4, 279
  similarity to maize from San Marcos
    Cave, 281
Gulf of Mexico coast, xiv
Gypsum points, 22

Haiduk site (TX), 260, 268, 270
Hematite, occurrence of, at La Playa site,
  30
Hillside terrace sites, early dates for, 56,
  149–151, 306
Hohokam and Mogollon cultures,
  common root of, 48
Hohokam features, presence of
  Cheno-ams in, 25
Hopi, as partial descendants of San Pedro
  people, 283
Hopi Blue Corn, taproot length of, 168
Hornos, at La Playa site, 4, **19,** 22, 25,
  283
Horseshoe Cave (TX), 90
Huastecan Late Postclassic, as source of
  exotics found in Brownsville Com-
  plex, xiv
Hueco Bolson assemblages, sources of
  obsidian in, 199, 200
"Hueco phase," 48, 115, 227, 289
Human remains, analysis of, to discern
  mobility patterns, 84–99, 291, 292
Hunter-gatherer ecology, theory of, 118
Hunter-gatherers, contemporaneous
  with agriculturalists, 59, 115, 116, 282,
  306
Hunting, as portrayed on Pottery Mound
  kiva murals, 95

Inheritance rules, development of, during
  San Pedro phase, 61

Irrigation canals
  development of, in northern Sonoran
    Desert, 56, 307
  earliest dates for, 41, 55, 56, 114
  as evidence of year-round occupation,
    64
  at La Playa site, 4, 25, 310
  at Las Capas, **56**
  possibility of, at Cerro Juanaqueña,
    169, 310
  in San Pedro phase sites, 61, 64, 285
  in Tucson Basin, 4, 169, 310, 313
  at Zuni, 285

Jade, trade in, xiv
Jornada Mogollon sites, level of agricul-
    tural dependence in, 114, 170–172

Keystone Dam site (TX), 114, 202–209

Labor investment
  in farming, levels of: plant-and-
    harvest, slash-and-burn, "typical"
    maize farming, 156–158, 172
  in hillside terraces, 57, 142, 143, 145, 313
Labor organization, effect of, on lithic
    technology, 209, 210
Labor scheduling (*see* Resource schedul-
    ing conflicts; Seasonality)
La Playa Plain ceramics, first identifica-
    tion of, 29
La Playa site (SON), 4, 13, 17, **19**, 283, 313
  archaeological description of, 18–30
  lack of evidence for domestic struc-
    tures at, 32
  relationship with neighboring Trinch-
    eras type site, 284
  skeletal analysis, of La Playa site buri-
    als, 26, 27
Las Capas site
  early canals at, 55
  early maize dates from, 53
  fired-clay figurines from, 57

probable common bean date from,
    54, 285
  tobacco from, 55
Late Archaic
  concept of, 2, 50, 114, 115, 259
  defining, for Trans-Pecos region,
    226–228
  population increase in, 5, 219, 236, 240,
    289
  subsistence strategies, 1, 2, 7, 187,
    236–239, 289
  villages, 1, 114, 285
Lechuguilla (*Agave lechuguilla*)
  and other CAM-rich plants, 89
  as part of Archaic diet, 5, 237, 249, 290
Lehner site (AZ), 46
Linear Band Keramik of northern
    Europe, and similarities to Trinch-
    eras settlements, 306
Lino site (TX), 260
Lithic material
  availability, effect of, on stone tool
    technology, 187
  types, in Trans-Pecos sites, 223–225,
    234, 235
  use, changes in, following transition to
    agriculture, 188, 189
Logistical strategy (*see* Mobility patterns)
Los Pozos, early maize dates from, 31, 53,
    285
Lower Pecos River region
  excavation of stratified rockshelters
    in, 5
  lack of evidence/suitable conditions
    for agriculture in, 247–254, 290

Maize
  arrival of, via diffusion or migration, 3,
    13, 63, 153, 239, 241, 281, 282, 287, 293,
    294, 301, 307
  dietary significance of (*see* Cultigens)
  early dates for, 2, 3, 4, 31, 48, 53, 91, 141,
    279, 285

Pantano site (AZ), early maize in, 48
"Peralta complex," 16, 18, 48
Petroglyphs, 17
Physiography
    of the Borderlands, 1
    as factor in village formation, 7
    of Sonora, 13–15
    of southeastern Arizona, 41–43
Picacho Dune Field, 45, 61
Piñon nuts, as high-return, storable
    resource, 95
Pinto points, 16, 18, 21, **22**, 30
Pithouse settlements (*see* Village
    formation)
Plainview points, 17
Plazas
    early dates for, 57
    possible presence of, in Cienega phase
        sites, 61
Pleistocene fauna, at La Playa site, 20
Population expansion, as factor in village
    formation, 7
Population packing
    as evidenced by defensive sites, 173
    as explanation for transition to agricul-
        ture, 117, 282, 288
Pottery Mound (NM)
    analysis of human remains from,
        93–95, 291, 292
    location of, 87
Pre-Pottery Neothilic (PPN) (a.k.a.
    Pre-Pottery Formative [PPF]), 280,
    282, 291, 292
Prickly pear (*Opuntia phaecantha*), 249,
    290
    and other CAM-rich plants, 89
Procurement range (territory), 121, 199,
    252
Productivity, biotic (*see also* Turnover
    rate), 128
Projectile points, identified
    in Big Bend/Trans-Pecos sites and
        private collections, 226, **227**, 228, 231

from Cerro Juanaqueña, 146, **198**
    in Sonoran sites, 16, 18, **22, 24**
    in southeastern Arizona Late Archaic/
        Early Agricultural sites, **52**
    in South Texas burials (cause of death;
        see also Grave goods), 269, 272–274
    in South Texas sites and private collec-
        tions, 260, **261, 270**
Property ownership, development of,
    during San Pedro phase, 61
Proto-Sonoran-Uto-Aztecan (PSUA)
    groups
    and early maize, 32, 283, 284
    heartland of, 31
    territorial extent of, 32, 33

Rainfall planting (*see* Dry farming)
Rainfall regime, 1
    effect of
        on species diversity, 59
        on suitability for agriculture, 308
    as factor in village formation, 7
Reproductive biology, constraints on
    male/female behavior imposed
    by, 84
Resource distribution, "patchiness," 59,
    60
Resource (extraction) scheduling
    conflicts, seasonal, 5, 132, 188
Resource return rates, 5, 7, 116, 120,
    155–159, 164–167, 249–251, 289
Resource structure, 116, 118, 164
    as factor in subsistence regime, 59, 60,
        119–122, 131, 252, 290
    as factor in village formation, 7
    measures of, 124–129
    spatial (*see* Resource distribution)
    stochastic (predictability), 60, 121, 122,
        124, 127
    temporal (*see* Seasonality)
Rincon Mountains, 43
Río Casas Grandes valley, *trinchera* sites
    in, 5, 141